Introducing SQL Server

Mike McQuillan

Apress®

Introducing SQL Server

ISBN-13 (pbk): 978-1-4842-1420-6

ISBN-13 (electronic): 978-1-4842-1419-0

Managing Director: Welmoed Spahr
Lead Editor: Jonathan Gennick
Technical Reviewer: Bradley Beard
Editorial Board: Steve Anglin, Mark Beckner, Gary Cornell, Louise Corrigan, Jim DeWolf, Jonathan Gennick, Robert Hutchinson, Michelle Lowman, James Markham, Susan McDermott, Matthew Moodie, Jeffrey Pepper, Douglas Pundick, Ben Renow-Clarke, Gwenan Spearing, Matt Wade, Steve Weiss
Coordinating Editor: Jill Balzano
Copy Editor: James Fraleigh
Compositor: SPi Global
Indexer: SPi Global
Artist: SPi Global
Cover Designer: Anna Ishchenko

Distributed to the book trade worldwide by Springer Science+Business Media New York, 233 Spring Street, 6th Floor, New York, NY 10013. Phone 1-800-SPRINGER, fax (201) 348-4505, e-mail orders-ny@springer-sbm.com, or visit www.springeronline.com. Apress Media, LLC is a California LLC and the sole member (owner) is Springer Science + Business Media Finance Inc (SSBM Finance Inc). SSBM Finance Inc is a Delaware corporation.

For information on translations, please e-mail rights@apress.com, or visit www.apress.com.

Apress and friends of ED books may be purchased in bulk for academic, corporate, or promotional use. eBook versions and licenses are also available for most titles. For more information, reference our Special Bulk Sales–eBook Licensing web page at www.apress.com/bulk-sales.

Any source code or other supplementary material referenced by the author in this text is available to readers at www.apress.com. For detailed information about how to locate your book's source code, go to www.apress.com/source-code/.

For Jo & Grace, thank you for supporting me.

Contents at a Glance

Contents

About the Author

Mike McQuillan is a software and database specialist who lives with his wife and daughter in the United Kingdom. Mike is a polyglot programmer who began messing around with computers in the 1980s, first with an Atari 800XL and then a Sinclair Spectrum. He took up databases in the 1990s, and quickly fell in love with SQL. He's been working with SQL Server since version 7, and is an SQL Server MCSA.

When he's not tinkering with computers, Mike and his family enjoy lengthy walks around Cheshire with the family pups, Dolly and Bertie (who keep his feet warm when he's writing).

About the Technical Reviewer

Bradley Beard is a software engineer with more than 15 years experience writing dynamic, interactive websites using ColdFusion and SQL Server. He graduated from Florida Institute of Technology in 2007 with a Master of Science in Computer Information Systems, and studied for his undergraduate degrees in CIS and Technology Management at Herzing University. In 2013, he earned the MCSA: SQL Server 2012 certification from Microsoft. His continual quest for learning has earned him shelves full of books at home and at work, most of which are about SQL Server, ColdFusion, or general web architectures or frameworks.

He lives in Palm Bay, Florida with his wife, Jessica, and children, Josh, Kaylee, Matthew, and Emma. He also apparently runs an animal shelter made up of his dogs, Lady and Bella, and cats, Spice, Simba, Mercury, and Dobby. In his free time, he enjoys fishing and spending time with his wife and kids.

Bradley is available for consultation and third-shift remote employment on ColdFusion and SQL Server by contacting bradley.beard@gmail.com.

Acknowledgments

Writing a book is a big undertaking, and I wouldn't have managed it without the support of my wonderful wife, Jo, and darling daughter, Grace. I love you both very much. I'd also like to thank my parents and the rest of my family and friends just for being around—life's been a pretty great ride so far and I'm sure it will only improve.

Bradley Beard deserves a mention for his excellent technical reviewing, and big thanks also go to Jonathan Gennick, Jill Balzano, and James Fraleigh at Apress for their hard work in ensuring this book made it to print.

Finally, a big thank-you to you, the reader, for taking the time to purchase and read this book. I hope you enjoy it as much as I enjoyed writing it.

CHAPTER 1

■ ■ ■

What Is SQL Server?

SQL Server is a relational database management system (RDBMS) developed by Microsoft. In order to find out exactly what that means, we need to ask three more questions:

- What is SQL?
- What is a server?
- What is an RDBMS?

To answer the first question, SQL is both a programming language and an acronym. It can be pronounced either "sequel" or literally with the letters *SQL*. It stands for Structured Query Language, and it is the language used to talk to databases. So from this, we can infer that SQL Server is actually a database server, which brings us to our second question: what exactly is a server?

A server is a computer that provides some kind of service (or multiple services). For example, a print server processes print requests, a web server hosts web sites, and a database server runs a database management system. This leads to the last question: what is an RDBMS?

An RDBMS is a collection of services that together support the storage and retrieval of relational data from some kind of file store. We'll take a look at the various servers provided by the SQL Server RDBMS a bit later in this chapter. But for now, I've answered our original question, and you have an idea of what SQL Server is.

In this chapter, we'll:

- take a quick SQL Server history tour,
- discover the services provided by SQL Server, and
- look at the types of databases used by SQL Server.

A Quick History of SQL Server

Not everybody likes history, so I'll keep this brief! In the 1980s, Oracle dominated the database market (to a certain extent, it still does). Late in that decade, Microsoft wanted to start competing with Oracle, so they built a database system together with another company, Sybase. This fared well enough to encourage Microsoft to continue development. In the mid-1990s, Microsoft and Sybase parted ways and Microsoft completely redeveloped SQL Server. The first major rewritten version was version 7.0, released in 1998. If you were to look at the internals of version 7.0 today you'd see a lot of similarities with the current version, SQL Server 2014.

Let's have a quick look at the versions released since version 7.0, along with core features added:

- **1998**: Version 7.0. A complete rewrite of the core database system. You are unlikely to see a version 7.0 system running today (although some do exist).

- **2000**: SQL Server 2000 released. Major performance improvements were included, along with basic XML support and an import/export tool called DTS (Data Transformation Services). Lots of systems still use SQL Server 2000 and higher today.

- **2005**: Major XML support is added to SQL Server 2005, along with the ability to run .NET code within the database.

- **2008**: SQL Server 2008 and 2008 R2 came along. The ability to store documents, pictures, videos, and other types of data directly in a structured manner was added, along with new ways to store dates and times.

- **2012**: You guessed it; the new version was called SQL Server 2012. This added greatly improved database availability features such as AlwaysOn and enhanced interaction with Windows Azure.

- **2014**: The version I am talking about, SQL Server 2014, was made available. One big new feature here was in-memory tables.

You don't need to exhaustively know the history of SQL Server, but having some knowledge of the past can inform the present. If you are planning to go into databases as a career, you may come across older versions of SQL Server. It can help to know what those versions can and can't do. Let's see what the current version of SQL Server—2014—can do.

SQL Server Services

A number of services make up SQL Server. Let's take a quick look at them:

- **Database Engine**: This is the core service, and most of the things we look at in this book will be using this service. It is responsible for all aspects of data management. If you want to add some data to a table, create a database, or pull some data from your databases, you'll be interacting with this service.

- **SQL Server Agent**: SQL Server's scheduling tool. You can use Agent to set jobs up to run at different times of the day, week, or month. Jobs are often created to run backups or other regular tasks.

- **SQL Server Browser**: If your SQL Server sits on a network, you probably have other machines connecting to it. Connecting remotely requires the SQL Server Browser service to be up and running. This allows other machines on the network to communicate with SQL Server. However, if SQL Server was installed with the default port and instance name configuration, then SQL Server Browser can be safely disabled. This service is disabled by default, so it must be enabled in order to be used.

- **SQL Server Full Text Search**: Let's say our database has a user record named "Mike McQuillan." I can use the SQL language to directly return this record—*but only if I specify the full name*. What if I don't know the full name? Assume all I know is "Mike." I can still find the record using the standard SQL Server LIKE operator. But it won't be a fast lookup.

Now imagine you were searching for "Mike" using something like Google or Bing. You'd just enter "find everybody called Mike" and voilà! The records would be returned. You can think of the Full Text Search as the Google/Bing part of SQL Server. It can be used to run complex searches on your database; it can even find words that sound similar or have similar meanings.

Again, we won't look at this service in this book, but remember it exists and it may save you one day!

Business Intelligence Services

SQL Server can be used as a complete Business Intelligence (BI) platform. This platform allows you to import data from databases and other systems, analyze it, and generate reports from that data. The aim of a BI system is to help your organization plan for the future.

The BI platform supplied by SQL Server is vast and won't be covered in this book. It consists of three services, which I introduce here so you have a brief idea of what they are and what they are for:

- **SQL Server Integration Services (SSIS)**: This is SQL Server's ETL service—Extract, Transform, and Load. In other words, this service can import data to or export data from your databases. It can actually import or export to pretty much anything that is machine readable. You can also make changes to the data (Transform) as it goes in or out of the system. SSIS is the answer to the deprecated DTS functionality in SQL Server 2000, since it allows for the creation of import/export utilities.

- **SQL Server Reporting Services (SSRS)**: Have you ever received a bank statement, or perhaps some kind of application form? The chances are these documents are based on reporting templates. Somebody somewhere has created a template of a report, which is then used to generate individual statements, forms, letters, and so on for individual customers. SSRS is the service SQL Server provides to allow you to create these templates.

- **SQL Server Analysis Services (SSAS)**: If your company wants to put some kind of reporting platform together, it could do a lot worse than SSAS. This huge component of SQL Server allows data to be grouped and structured in such a way that reporting becomes easy. You can use SQL Server Management Studio, Excel, .NET programs, or lots of other tools to interact with SSAS. It can perform analyses over time periods, individuals, items, and anything else you can think of. It also supports drilling down into your data via a process called *data mining*.

  Unfortunately, SSAS is just too big a topic to cover in a basics book, even at a simple level. Dedicated books for SSAS exist, and even some of those weighty tomes are far from comprehensive.

  There is a strong chance you'll never need to touch SSAS. But just be aware that it is there and give yourself an idea of what it can do; you never know when it may come in handy.

Editions of SQL Server

There are many different versions of SQL Server, each tailored for a specific need. Here's a quick rundown of what each edition is for:

- **Enterprise:** This is the highest version of SQL Server available. It includes every feature available but is extremely expensive.

- **Business Intelligence:** Aimed specifically at organizations using SQL Server as a BI platform.

- **Standard:** The version of SQL Server most commonly found in production environments. This provides solid data management and BI features, which is usually more than enough for most organizations. It lacks certain high-end features (e.g., in-memory tables) that are found in the Enterprise Edition.

- **Web:** Supports scaling options for SQL Servers supporting web sites.

- **Developer:** This is exactly the same as Enterprise Edition, but intended for developer use only. The rule here is you cannot use this version in production. If you are serious about developing in SQL Server, this is the version to go for. This is great if you are studying for SQL Server certification exams, for example. It's also inexpensive (around $60/£50).

- **Express:** The easiest way to try SQL Server. This is a free version, which has most of SQL Server's core features, but is limited in certain aspects (e.g., the maximum database size allowed is 4GB).

We'll be using SQL Server Express in this book, and we'll look at downloading and installing it in the next chapter.

All versions of SQL Server come as either 32-bit or 64-bit. The 64-bit versions can access more memory (if supported). Which version you want depends on your processor. If you are in doubt, open PC Info (Windows 8) or System in Control Panel (Windows 7). This will tell you whether your processor is 32-bit or 64-bit. The 32-bit version will run on 64-bit systems, so if you are still in doubt, download the 32-bit edition. Unless you have specific requirements, this decision won't hugely affect development machines.

SQL Server Tools and Utilities

SQL Server comes with a number of programs that can be used to manage various aspects of the system. There are also a bunch of utilities to help you perform all sorts of tasks:

- **SQL Server Management Studio (SSMS):** Learn to love this program—you'll use it pretty much every day. This is the standard interface that 99% of SQL Server DBAs use. SSMS allows you to manage multiple SQL Servers, write and run SQL scripts, and also manage other services such as SSIS and SSAS. This program is amazingly powerful and we'll use it throughout this book.

- **SQL Server Data Tools (SSDT):** If you've done any .NET programming, you've probably used Microsoft Visual Studio. This is a programming environment for .NET, much as SSMS provides a scripting environment for SQL Server. SSDT is based upon Visual Studio and allows you to create and edit SSIS, SSRS, and SSAS solutions.

- **SQL Server Configuration Manager:** Should you have to manage any of the services involved with SQL Server, you can use this utility. You can start and stop services, as well as manage network configuration.

- **SQL Server Profiler/Extended Events**: If you are having problems with particular queries, you can use one of these tools to analyze the query. They can also identify if locks are occurring within databases, among other things. It is important to note that SQL Server Profiler is being deprecated in a future version of SQL Server, so at some point it won't be around. Extended Events (built into SSMS) should be used instead. We'll look at both of these tools in Chapter 20**.**

- **SQLCMD**: SQLCMD—short for SQL Command—is a utility that allows users to execute queries and manage various aspects of the server from the command line. It can also be called from SSMS, as we'll see in future chapters.

- **SQL Server Import and Export Wizard**: If you need to run a fairly simple import to or export from a database, you can use this wizard. Alternatively, you can create your own routines using SSIS.

- **SQL Server Installation Center**: Think of this as an installation wizard on steroids. If you need to change any aspect of your SQL Server installation (e.g., add SSIS to a server), you'll use the Installation Center.

- **Reporting Services Configuration Manager**: Once SSRS is installed, you need to configure it. This handy little utility gives you the interface to do just that.

- **Database Engine Tuning Advisor**: If your database is slow, run this utility. It will give you some basic advice on indexes and foreign keys that are missing.

Many of these utilities can make your life easier; the Import And Export Wizard can be extremely useful. Find out what each one does, and then you'll have them in your back pocket should you ever need them. We'll use some of these tools and utilities throughout the book.

Time to Kick Off

I've given you a pretty good grounding in what SQL Server can provide. You now know what the various components of SQL Server are, and which utilities are available to use with SQL Server.

Now it's time to install SQL Server on our computers so we can actually do something with it. It's download time!

CHAPTER 2

Obtaining and Installing SQL Server

As you saw in Chapter 1, there are plenty of versions of SQL Server available. We're going to use SQL Server Express, which is completely free, as the basis of this book. Although much more limited than other versions, Express is still very powerful and includes all of the features we are going to look at during the course of the book.

Once we've downloaded Express, we'll walk through installing it. You'll see that installing SQL Server is a bit more involved than the normal installation process you might be used to!

Downloading SQL Server Express

Just as there are multiple editions of SQL Server, so are there multiple editions of SQL Server 2014 Express. Use this URL to access the download page.

www.microsoft.com/en-gb/download/details.aspx?id=42299

If this link doesn't work (Microsoft is always changing them around), use your favorite search engine to look for *sql server express 2014 download*. The first result returned should be the one you are after.

When you are taken to the download page shown in Figure 2-1, you'll see a list of download options. Go for Express Advanced ("ExpressAdv"), as this contains everything we need to work through the examples in this book.

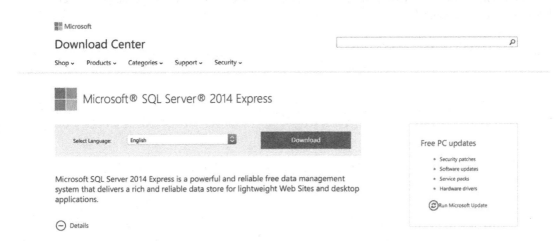

Figure 2-1. The SQL Server 2014 Express download page

Download the 32- or 64-bit version as appropriate. Once it has downloaded, double-click it to begin installation. The download is about 1.1GB, so it may take a while, depending on the speed of your Internet connection.

Now, you are probably used to installing programs where you click a **Next** button a few times and you're done. Things are even easier these days, as installing an application from an app store just involves clicking on an app and entering your password. Unfortunately, things are not so simple with SQL Server. There are a lot of things to configure before you can begin tinkering around with databases, so prepare to answer some questions.

We're installing the basic version, Express, but if you can install Express you'll be able to install any version. Let's take a quick look at what we are going to do:

- Allow the installer to extract files to our hard disk

- Choose to install a new stand-alone installation

- Follow the steps as guided by the installer

Before starting installation, you need to make sure SQL Server can be installed on your version of Windows. Versions of Windows supported are:

- Windows Server 2012

- Windows Server 2008

- Windows 8.1

- Windows 8

- Windows 7

Note that SQL Server Enterprise, Business Intelligence, and Web editions may only be installed on Windows Server 2012 or 2008.

Happy with your version of Windows? Cool, let's go!

Beginning Installation

Double-click the EXE file you downloaded and allow the installer to extract the files to the location requested (feel free to change this if you feel the need). After the extraction completes, you'll see the SQL Server Installation Center (Figure 2-2).

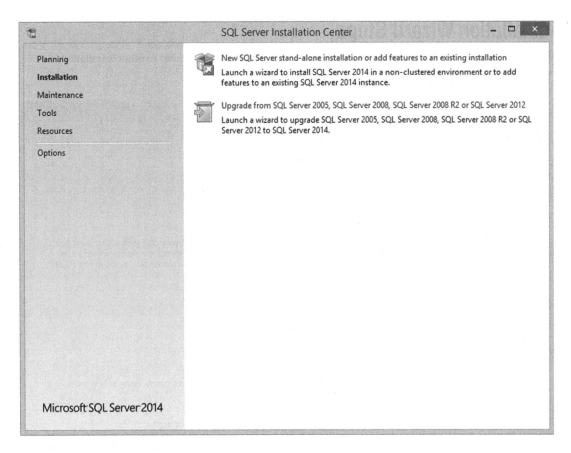

Figure 2-2. *SQL Server Installation Center*

This presents us with a few options. If you look to the left, you'll see we've actually started off at the second option, **Installation** (this is the default). Click **Planning,** which is worth a look. It gives you access to documentation telling you what SQL Server requires, and can also run a system check to ensure your machine can run SQL Server. There are plenty of other things there, too, so feel free to take a few minutes and have a play around.

All done? Hope you enjoyed yourself! Return to **Installation,** and choose **New SQL Server stand-alone installation or add features to an existing installation**. We are going to begin a clean installation of SQL Server. We are not upgrading from a previous version of SQL Server, so we can ignore the other option, but remember it is there should you ever need it. Likewise the other options presented on the left (**Maintenance, Tools, Resources, Options**)—you may never need them, but take a quick look so you know what they have to offer you.

Once you've clicked the **New SQL Server** option, the real installation wizard appears.

Installation Wizard Steps

You should now see the wizard in Figure 2-3, which probably looks pretty similar to other installation wizards you have seen.

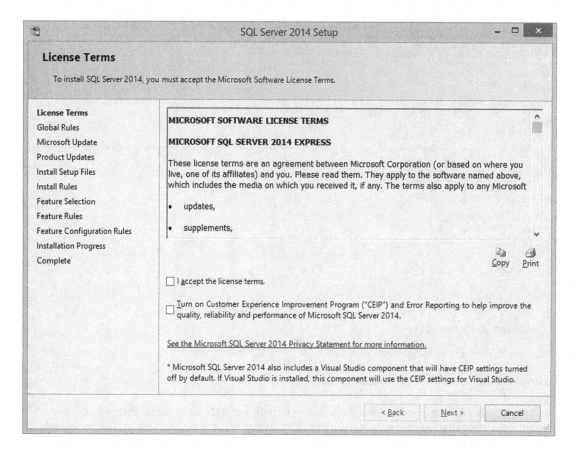

Figure 2-3. The license acceptance dialog

Take a look at all of the steps on the left! We need to configure a few things before SQL Server will be ready for use. Here is what we are going to do:

- The wizard will perform a couple of update checks to make sure we have the latest software. It may download some updates if required.

- We'll choose the features of SQL Server we want to install.

- We'll configure those features.

- SQL Server will install them.

- We'll be happy.

The first step on the road to happiness is to accept the license terms—you might even want to read them if you have a spare year. (Seriously, has *anybody* ever read a licensing agreement?!) You can also choose whether you want to send data to Microsoft to help them improve SQL Server.

Tick the license terms box, tick the Customer Experience Improvement Program box if you wish, and click **Next** to move on.

Updates and Features

Global Rules will install automatically, and then you'll be taken to the Microsoft Update page (Figure 2-4). The updates box is not checked by default, but it's a good idea to check for them, so I recommend checking the box before clicking **Next**.

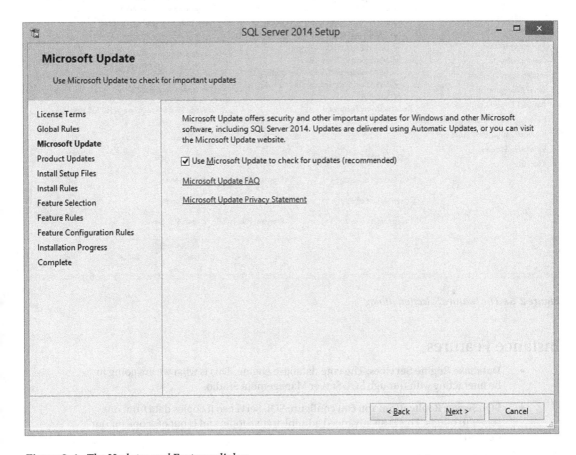

Figure 2-4. The Updates and Features dialog

Once you've done this, you'll probably be taken straight to the **Feature Selection** page. If you are not, let the update search complete/apply and then carry on.

Feature Selection is the most important page of the wizard. It is where you choose which pieces of SQL Server you want to install (you can see the checklist of options in Figure 2-5). I may as well tell you now that we are going to install everything (hence the reason for downloading the Express Advanced version), but here's a quick list of just exactly what those features are.

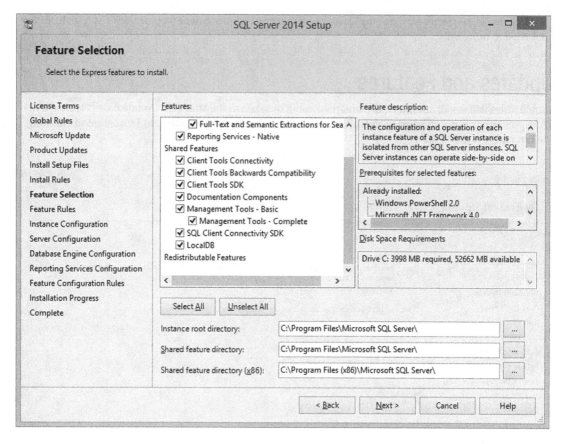

Figure 2-5. *The Feature Selection dialog*

Instance Features

- **Database Engine Services**: The core database engine. This is what we are going to be interacting with through SQL Server Management Studio.

- **SQL Server Replication**: You can configure SQL Server so it copies data from one server to others. This is an advanced administrative topic and is out of scope for our purposes.

- **Full-Text and Semantic Extractions for Search**: This is the full-text search feature I mentioned in Chapter 1. Again, this is an advanced topic so we won't look at it any further.

- **Reporting Services—Native**: These are the SQL Server Reporting Services (SSRS). SQL Server Express does not support SQL Server Integration Services (SSIS) or SQL Server Analysis Services (SSAS).

Shared Features

Most of these tools are required to allow you to communicate with your SQL Server. They can be used to manage other instances of SQL Server too (you'll find out what an instance is *very* soon).

- **Client Tools Connectivity**: Allows client machines to talk to SQL Server by installing a set of network libraries.

- **Client Tools Backward Compatibility**: Support for older client tools.

- **Client Tools SDK (Software Development Kit)**: Programming tools, which allow developers to write code to manage aspects of SQL Server.

- **Documentation Components**: Tools that allow you to view SQL Server help (formerly Books Online) via the Internet. You can also choose to download help to your computer (a good idea if you ask me!). Books Online can be accessed on the Web at https://technet.microsoft.com/en-us/library/ms130214.aspx.

- **Management Tools—Basic (and Complete)**: This is pretty much SQL Server Management Studio, although some other utilities like SQLCMD are also installed. The Complete option installs tools like SQL Server Profiler, and also adds support to SSMS for SSRS, SSAS, and SSIS.

- **SQL Client Connectivity SDK**: You need this if you intend to develop database applications.

- **Local DB**: A lightweight version of SQL Server, aimed at lower-powered devices like mobile phones and tablets.

Click the **Select All** button to add all items to the installation. Now note the three paths at the bottom of the wizard page:

- Instance root directory

- Shared feature directory

- Shared feature directory (x86)

I mentioned instances a moment ago. I'll explain properly in a moment, but for now, know that the **Instance root directory** is the directory in which all files for your database server instance will be placed.

A single server can host multiple instances of SQL Server, but they will share many features, such as SQL Server Management Studio. There is no point in installing a copy of SSMS per instance—this would just waste disk space—so the **Shared feature directory** stores files used across instances. Do you recall our brief conversation earlier about 32-bit and 64-bit versions of SQL Server? The presence of these two architectures is why we have two shared feature directories. The x86 version stores 32-bit files, and the other directory stores the 64-bit files. Some pieces of SQL Server are still 32-bit only, hence the need for the x86 version.

We now have to decide where these files should be placed. Most places I have worked keep the default C:\Program Files locations. Feel free to change this if you have a different disk structure. All I would say is ensure the databases you create are not put on the same drive as the SQL Server files—this will affect performance. Unfortunately, this is a situation I see on a regular basis.

I digress. If you have checked all the boxes and are happy with the installation directories, click **Next**. The installer will run a check, ensuring various prerequisites are present. I performed the installation on a clean server, so you can see from Figure 2-6 that I hit a problem with the .NET Framework 3.5.

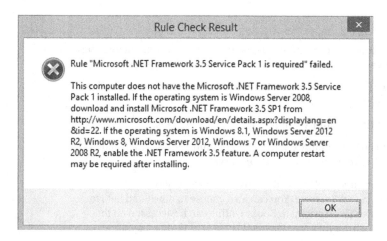

Figure 2-6. *The "Microsoft .NET Framework 3.5 Service Pack 1 is required" error*

The dialog shown in Figure 2-6 is displayed when you click the **Failed** message next to the appropriate item in the rule check list (not pictured). The dialog displayed after clicking a **Failed** message will explain how you can resolve the issues with that particular rule. Figure 2-6 shows that Microsoft has explained how to obtain and install the Microsoft .NET Framework 3.5 Service Pack 1 software, which will resolve the rule check failure.

I happen to be running Windows 8.1, so I followed the instructions for enabling .NET 3.5 (these instructions also apply to Windows 7 and 8). Open **Control Panel**, click **Programs**, and click **Turn Windows features on or off**. When the list of features appears (Figure 2-7), tick **.NET Framework 3.5 (includes .NET 2.0 and 3.0)**, then click **OK**. The selected features will install (you may be asked to download files from Windows Update).

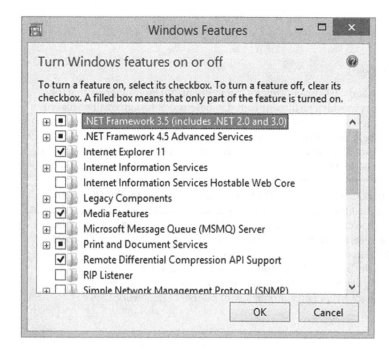

Figure 2-7. *Installing the .NET Framework 3.5*

Kick back for a moment if you are waiting for the file download and installation!

I didn't need to reboot when I did this, so hopefully you won't, either (Windows has really improved in this area). Return to the SQL Server installer, and click the button to **Re-run** the feature rule checks. This time all rules should pass and you'll be taken to the Instance Configuration page. Time to learn about instances. . . .

Database Instances

SQL Server now wants to know what type of instance you would like to create. The screen should look something like Figure 2-8.

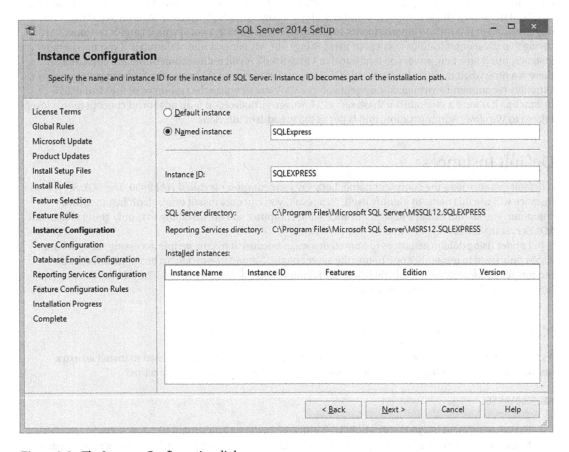

Figure 2-8. *The Instance Configuration dialog*

You can see there are two types of instances: Default and Named. But just what *is* an instance? An instance is a SQL Server installation that can house databases, SSAS, SSIS, and SSRS, as well as all of the other SQL Server instance components. Each instance has its own security. Assume we have two instances:

- Development
- Testing

15

Both of these instances can exist on the same computer. You may have full administration rights on Development, meaning you can do anything there—create databases, add users, and so on. Yet you may not have any access at all to Testing, meaning you cannot create databases on that instance—or even run a SELECT statement there.

You might be thinking, "Why do I need multiple instances? I'll just put all my databases on the same instance." Unfortunately, this doesn't give you any logical separation of concerns—it can often make sense to create an instance for a particular department or function. Instances also allow you to limit the number of databases each instance has to handle, as this can affect performance.

Say you have an instance with five databases on it. One particular database is used a lot, but the other four are used moderately. Users may complain that the applications accessing the moderately used databases are performing poorly; this is because the busy database is starving them of resources. At this point, it would be a good idea to move the busy database to its own instance, to reduce contention with the other databases.

I did mention a single computer can run multiple instances of SQL Server. I've rarely seen this implemented in production environments successfully. Note that I am *not* saying it cannot be done; I'm just saying that most organizations don't plan these things out. My general rule of thumb is if you need a new instance, put it on a new server (be it physical or virtualized). It will reduce contention and confusion. If there is a time when multiple instances of SQL Server need to run on the same physical computer or server, I strongly recommend a virtualization agent such as VMWare to utilize the resources of the virtualized instance as if it were a separate database server. However, virtualization is an advanced concept more closely related to Windows Administration, and is out of the breadth of this book.

Default Instances

A default instance uses the computer name. Let's say your computer is called HAL9000. The SQL Server instance will use this name to identify itself. As a result, you can only install one default instance on a computer. You should install a default instance if the computer you are installing to is only going to host one SQL Server instance.

I prefer using default instances to named instances because it means people accessing the database server only need to remember one name: the server name. Named instances can be useful but they do require people to remember two things: the server name and the instance name. They do have their place, however, as we'll see in the very next section.

Named Instances

As I just said, named instances need an extra name to identify them. Say you wanted to install an extra instance on the HAL9000 computer, called Aries. You would access this using the name:

HAL9000\ARIES

If you just typed in HAL9000 you would be connected to the default instance.

Named instances come into their own on development machines. You may be building software that needs to run on SQL Server 2005, 2008, 2012, and 2014. You can install a named instance of each of these on your development machine, giving each instance a unique name. Assuming my development machine is called HOLMES, I could have:

- HOLMES\SQL2005
- HOLMES\SQL2008
- HOLMES\SQL2012
- HOLMES\SQL2014

This kind of setup really aids development.

One last point: Each server can host up to 50 instances. I really hope I never come across a server with that many instances on it!

Clear on instances now? Cool! We'll continue with the installation.

The Instance Configuration Page

You'll note in Figure 2-8 that the SQL Server installer has selected a named instance by default. This is because we are installing SQL Server Express. Any other version of SQL Server will have a default instance selected when you hit this page.

It is conventional to install SQL Server Express as a named instance, called SQLEXPRESS. This is what the install defaults to and it is what most organizations use—in fact, I don't think I've ever seen SQL Express installed as a default instance. (This just goes to show that most people keep clicking **Next** during installation!)

We'll side with the majority and install as a named instance. Before we do, note the **Instance ID** text box in Figure 2-8. This is the internal ID SQL Server uses to identify the instance. It is good practice to keep it the same as the instance name—I can't think of a situation where you would want to change it. The Instance ID affects the name of the directory to which the instance files are installed.

If you change the value of the **Instance ID** text box, you'll see the end of the SQL Server directory and the Reporting Services directory values change to match it. We cannot modify these paths directly. The two paths at the middle of the screen show where the instance files will be installed. You'll see **MSSQL12** and **MSRS12** in these paths; this shows that we are using version 12 of SQL Server (this is Microsoft's internal version number; the public or marketing version is **2014**).

Make sure you have **Named instance** selected, and that **SQLEXPRESS** is present in both the **Named instance** and **Instance ID** textboxes. Then click **Next** to begin entering service account information.

Service Accounts

To be able to run correctly, SQL Server needs appropriate permissions. These permissions are obtained via a user account that is configured to run the SQL Server services. A service is a program like any other, except it has no user interface and is constantly running in the background. As an example, the SQL Server Database Engine runs as a service, and to work correctly it requires users to assign an account with appropriate permissions to it (Figure 2-9).

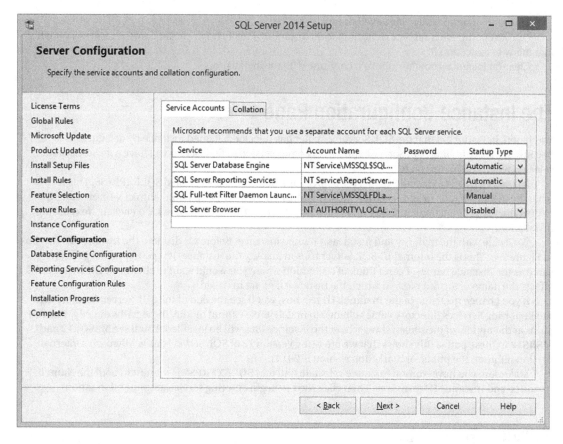

Figure 2-9. *Configuring service accounts dialog*

We can see four services in Figure 2-9:

- SQL Server Database Engine

- SQL Server Reporting Services

- SQL Full-text Filter Daemon Launcher

- SQL Server Browser

We were introduced to these services in Chapter 1 (the SQL Full-text service has a longer name on this screen, though). Strictly speaking, each service should be assigned a distinct user account. There are two reasons behind this:

- Each service has different permission requirements.

- Using the same account for all services will give an attacker access to all services should the account become compromised.

These are issues to consider if you are installing a nondevelopment instance. If you are installing a local instance on your own development machine, I wouldn't worry too much about configuring multiple accounts, unless you want some practice. If you are installing a production instance you should definitely use different accounts.

In the table listing the service accounts on this screen are four columns:

- Service

- Account Name

- Password

- Startup Type

Looking at the Startup Type first, you can see three values in the dropdown list: **Automatic**, **Manual**, and **Disabled**. **Automatic**means the service will start when Windows starts. **Manual** ensures the service won't start automatically but you can start it yourself should you wish, via the Services applet in the Control Panel. Finally, selecting **Disabled** makes the service unavailable for use; if you wish to use it you will have to enable it in the **Services** applet.

The Account Name and Password columns are self-explanatory; these are the account details the services will use. If this were an administration book I'd go into a lot more detail about these, but I'm mainly concentrating on development, so leave the default options selected.

Collation

On the same page is a Collation tab. Click this and you'll see a text box containing a value. Your Windows configuration will determine which value you see here. Figure 2-10 shows my Windows 8.1 machine's collation, Latin1_General_CI_AS. Windows 7 installations may see the value SQL_Latin1_General_CP1_CI_ AS instead.

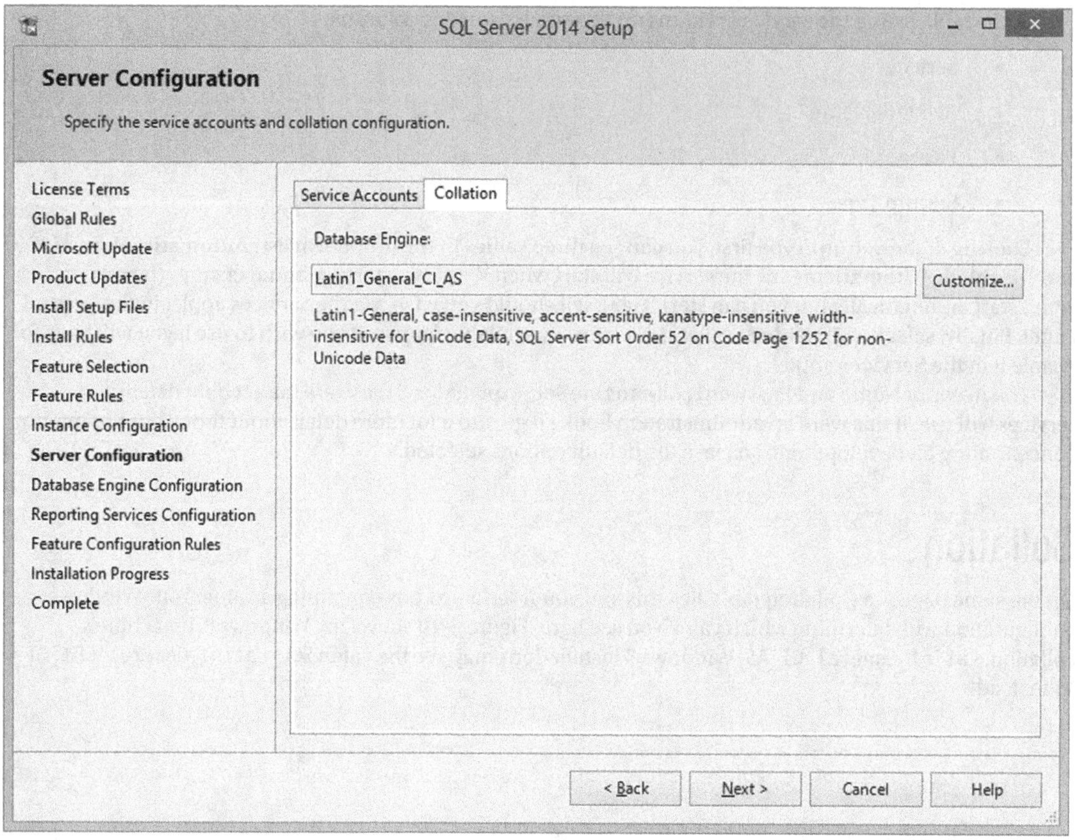

Figure 2-10. *Choosing a collation*

A collation tells SQL Server how it should consider the values used in the database. Latin1_General represents languages using common alphabets and rules for sorting and comparing characters, so immediately we are saying the language chosen for our database will follow certain well-established rules. Our language of choice in this instance will be US English, which complies with this definition of Latin1_General. *CI* stands for Case Insensitive, and this clause will ensure our queries will be treated the same no matter how values are specified. If CI is chosen, both of these queries will return the same result:

```
SELECT PupId, PupName, DateOfBirth FROM Pups WHERE PupName = 'Bertie';
```

```
SELECT PupId, PupName, DateOfBirth FROM Pups WHERE PupName = 'bertie';
```

If *CS* (Case Sensitive) was used, then only one of the above queries would return a result (assuming a record with the name Bertie exists).

The *AS* part is for Accent Sensitive, and it causes SQL Server to treat characters with accents as distinct characters—so *c* will not be the same as *ç*, for example. Usually you will keep the collation that the installer selects for you, unless you know you have specific requirements (e.g., you are going to be dealing with Japanese characters, in which case you'll need to specify Kana sensitivity).

Click the **Customize** button to view the collation options available to you (shown in Figure 2-11). If you feel the need to change your collation, go ahead. Just remember that while you can change a collation at the server level, database level, and even the column level, doing so is not a straightforward task for the uninitiated. This is one of those things it is better to do right first time.

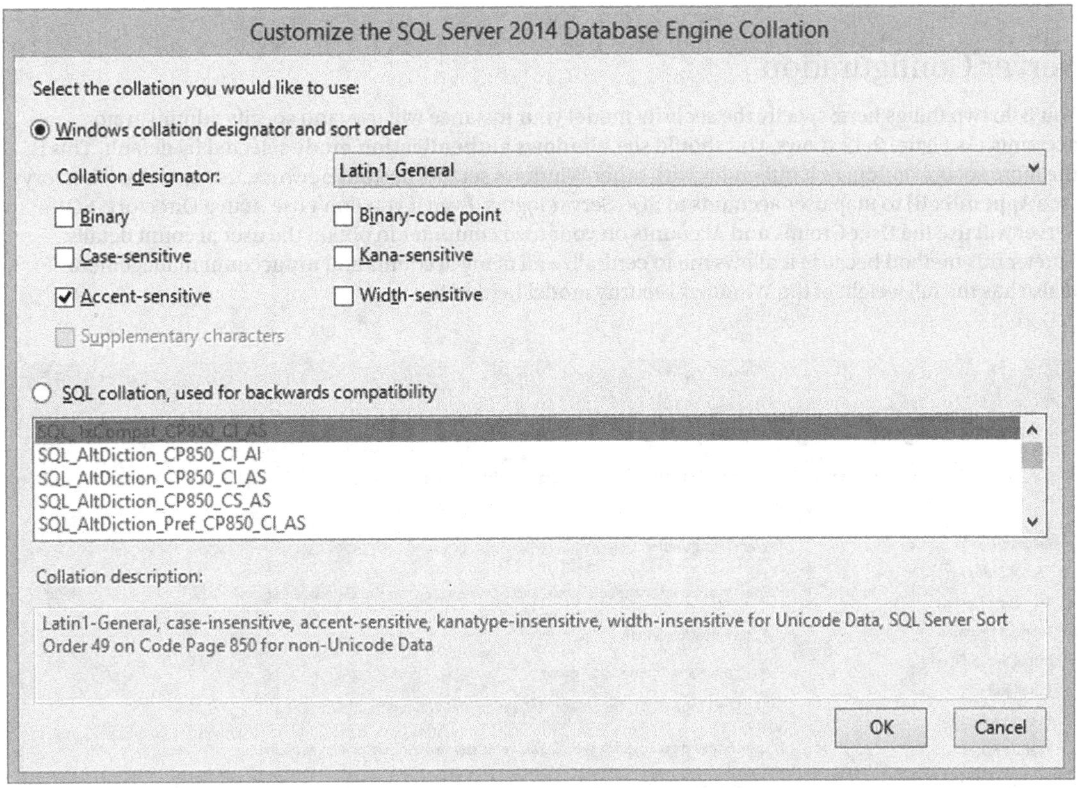

Figure 2-11. *Configuring the collation*

Also, if you have multiple servers and/or databases, make sure they all use the same collation, or you may find yourself having to use the COLLATE keyword in your queries. This isn't pleasant—you have been warned!

KEEPING COLLATIONS CONSISTENT

Unless you have specific needs regarding collation configuration, it is advisable to apply the required collation at the server level. If possible, use the same collation on all your servers. This will make any cross-server queries you need to write easier, and will also ensure the way SQL Server handles your data will be consistent from a collation point of view.

When you are happy with your selections, click **Next**. Still a little way to go yet. . . .

Database Engine Configuration

You can tell we are in the homestretch, as we now configure the individual pieces of SQL Server. First up is the main Database Engine, which is what we'll be engaging with once installation is complete. The following sections describe the four tabs on this screen.

Server Configuration

You'll do two things here: specify the security model your instance will use, and specify administrator accounts. As Figure 2-12 shows, you should see **Windows authentication mode** selected by default. This is the more secure option, as it integrates with other Windows servers on your network, using Active Directory (see **Appendix B**) to map user accounts to SQL Server logins. Even if you don't use Active Directory, SQL Server will use the User Groups and Accounts on your own computer to obtain the user account details. I prefer this method because it allows me to centralize all of my accounts and my account management. It also has the full weight of the Windows security model behind it.

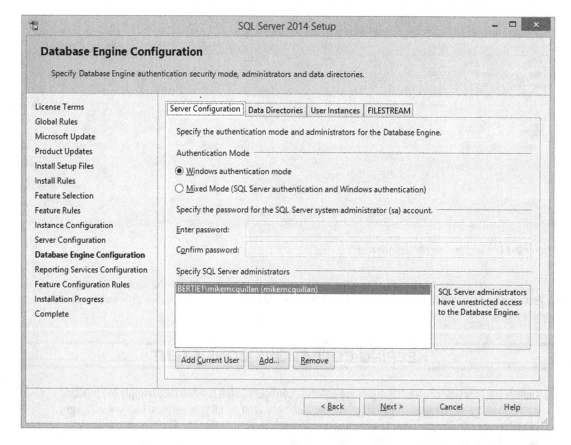

Figure 2-12. *The Server Configuration tab*

If you choose **Mixed Mode** you can still use Windows authentication, but you also will enable SQL Server authentication. This is SQL Server's own internal user account engine. There is a default account, **sa**, which originally came configured without a password (the installer will force you to specify one now). Lots of administrators never used to turn this account off—immediate security hole! Since **sa** is a system administration account, full access to the server can be gained via this account.

My issue with SQL Server authentication comes from connection strings. Connection strings are used by .NET and other applications to connect to SQL Server databases (a brief description can be found in **Appendix B**). You must specify a user account to connect to the SQL Server in the connection string. With Windows authentication, you don't need to provide any account details, but you have to specify the username and password if SQL Server authentication is used, which means those details can be seen (and used) by anybody who can access the configuration file containing the connection string (this pretty much includes all of your developers).

This is a Windows Authentication connection string:

```
Server=HOLMES\SQL2014;Database=WatsonDB;Trusted_Connection=True;
```

And here is a SQL Server Authentication version:

```
Server=HOLMES\2014;Database=WatsonDB;User Id=John.Watson;Password=Sherlock;
```

As you can see, the username and password are easily visible in the SQL Server Authentication version. Do yourself a favor and steer clear, unless you have a specific need (e.g., backward compatibility).

At the bottom of this screen, you can specify the administrator accounts. Accounts you add here will be configured as system administrators in SQL Server (I discuss the different levels of security available in Chapter 20). Your own user account should already be in this list. If it is not, click **Add Current User** to add yourself. You can add and remove other users using the buttons provided.

■ **Note**   System administrators (sysadmins) can perform any action on a SQL Server. The chapters in this book all presume you have sysadmin permission.

Data Directories

This is straightforward enough—it shows the paths where databases will be installed, as seen in Figure 2-13.

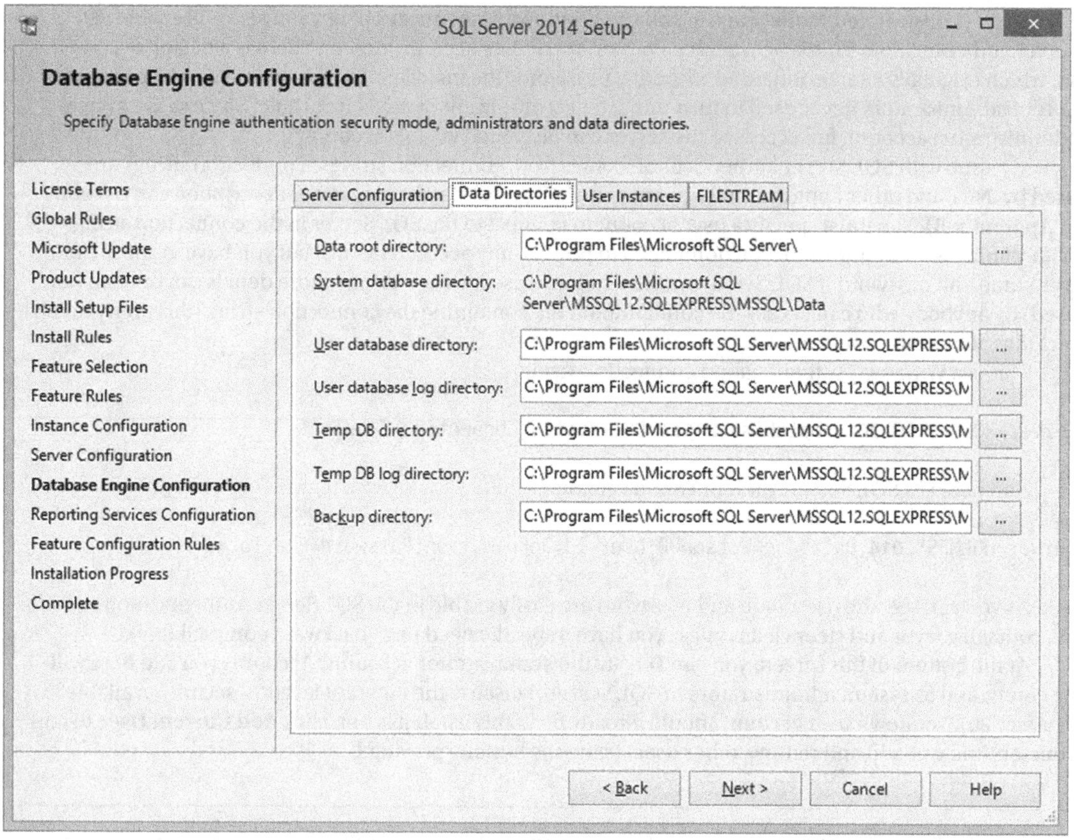

Figure 2-13. *The Data Directories tab*

Briefly, we have:

- **Data root directory**: The top-level directory, housing all other data folders.

- **System database directory**: For **master**, **msdb**, and so on (see Chapter 3). You cannot change this path.

- **User database directory**: The default directory where SQL Server will create your database files, if no alternative path is provided.

- **User database log directory**: As described, but for log files.

- **Temp DB directory**: The location where SQL Server will create the **TempDB** database.

- **Temp DB log directory**: As described, but for Temp DB's log file.

- **Backup directory**: The folder to which backups are saved, if no path is provided in the BACKUP DATABASE command.

We'll look at how databases are structured and what logs are used for in Chapter 3.

User Instances

As Figure 2-14 shows, this is turned on by default, and it allows users who do not have administrative rights to run their own separate instance of the SQL Server. This instance is generated from the parent instance. This feature should be used by developers who do not have local administrator permissions on their own machines (litmus test: if you can install apps on your machine, you are probably a local administrator). This is a surprisingly common configuration in many corporate environments, which is no doubt why Microsoft brought this feature into SQL Server Express.

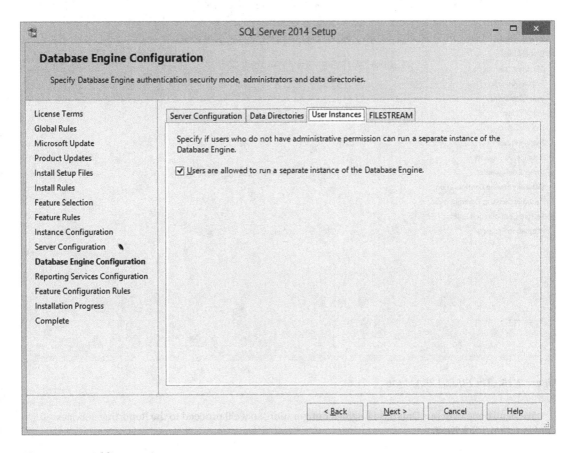

Figure 2-14. Adding user instance support

The user in question must have sysadmin permissions in SQL Server Express to use this feature.

FILESTREAM

This is way out of scope for this book, but I'll touch on it. Let's say you have a system that needs to store file attachments: documents, pictures, videos, and so forth. These cannot be easily stored in a typical SQL Server database. FILESTREAM creates a special folder on your computer or network to store these files. You then mark the appropriate columns for these files as FILESTREAM columns, and anything you insert or update into those columns will be saved in the special folder.

You can access content held in FILESTREAM just as you would any other SQL Server column. If you ever find yourself needing to store external files in a database, have a look at this feature—it may be just what you need. To turn this feature on, check the **Enable FILESTREAM** checkbox you can see in Figure 2-15.

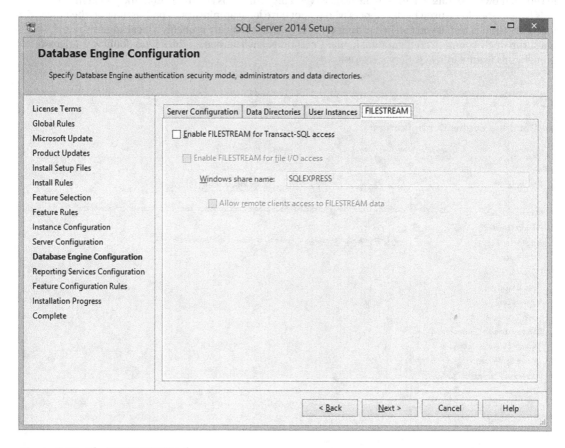

Figure 2-15. *The FILESTREAM tab*

We're all done with our Database Engine configuration, so we'll proceed to the Reporting Services Configuration. Click **Next**.

Reporting Services Configuration

Again, we won't spend too much time here as we won't be looking at Reporting Services in this book. There are two modes, of which the first, Native Mode, is commonly used (the other option integrates with Microsoft SharePoint and will only be enabled if you actually have SharePoint installed).

As Figure 2-16 shows, you can choose to **Install and configure**, which means the SSRS server will be ready to use once installation is complete (this is the default), or you can just **Install only**, which means you'll need to use the Reporting Services Configuration Manager to complete the installation.

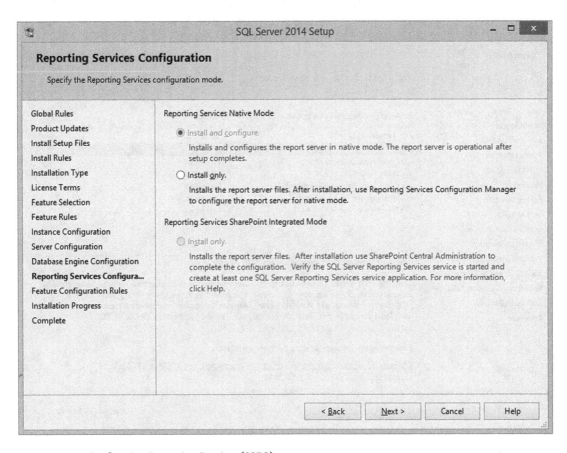

Figure 2-16. *Configuring Reporting Services (SSRS)*

Leave the defaults selected and click **Next** to move on. The end is in sight!

Installing

After clicking **Next,** SQL Server Express will finally(!) begin to install. Put your feet up or make a cup of tea while you wait. Be warned—this can take a while!

Once installation is finished, you'll see a nice confirmation message, just like the one in Figure 2-17.

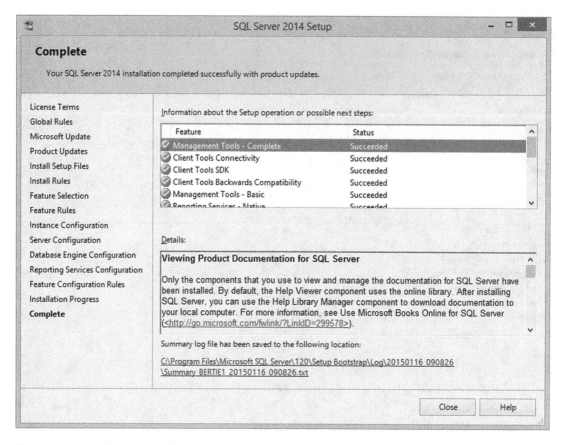

Figure 2-17. *Installation complete*

Click **Close** to close the installer. The SQL Server Installation Center will still be open, so you'll need to close that separately. All we need to do now is check that the SQL Server instance is ready to use.

Go to your Start Menu or Start Screen, and type *SQL Server 2014 Management Studio*. Once you've found it, click it to open. You'll be told user settings are being configured, and then you'll see something like Figure 2-18.

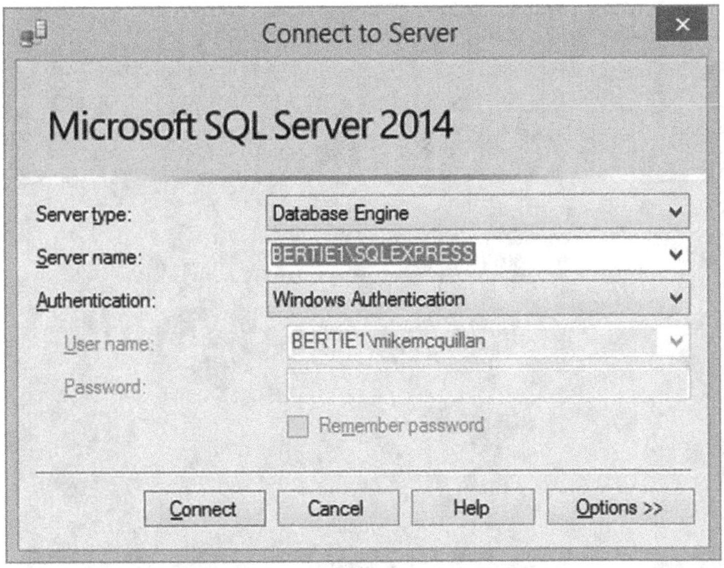

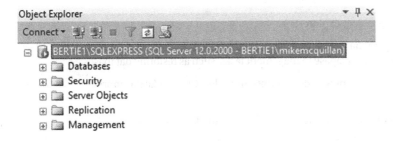

Figure 2-18. *The SQL Server login dialog*

This is the SQL Server Login screen. Click the **Connect** button and keep your eye on the Object Explorer on the left-hand side of the screen. You should see your server name appear with some items (such as Databases) below it, just like Figure 2-19.

Figure 2-19. *The server, as displayed in the Object Explorer*

Congratulations, you now have a working SQL Server!

A Very Quick SSMS Overview

Before we start looking at SQL Server for real, it is worth a glance at some SSMS basics. We'll be spending pretty much the rest of the book in this tool.

Figure 2-20 shows that there are two sections to SSMS: the Object Explorer on the left, and a large unused area on the right. Object Explorer lists all of the server and database objects you can manage through SSMS. It uses a tree node system, where you have a parent and clicking the + sign shows you the children. Children of a parent node may have children themselves. You can drag the edge of the Object Explorer to make it larger or smaller as desired. I often change it so it slides in and out of view, by clicking the little pin next to the X in the Object Explorer's title bar.

Figure 2-20. *A first view of SSMS*

There are five top-level items in Object Explorer:

- **Databases**: Lists all of your databases, including system databases. You can right-click this node to perform various database management tasks, such as restoring databases.

- **Security**: Supports management of user accounts and roles. Chapter 20 has more information about these.

- **Server Objects**: Shows server-wide objects, such as backup devices.

- **Replication**: Shows any replication jobs to which your SQL Server has subscribed (requested data from). We won't look at this; other versions of SQL Server have much stronger replication support.

- **Management**: Gives access to some management functions, like the ability to view your server logs.

The large empty area is used to display appropriate windows. You'll generally use it to write T-SQL queries. T-SQL, or Transact-SQL, is the dialect of the Structured Query Language developed by Microsoft and Sybase I originally referenced in Chapter 1. We'll see a lot more of T-SQL as the book progresses. Click **File ➤ New ➤ Query With Current Connection** (or just press Ctrl+N), and as Figure 2-21 demonstrates, a blank query window will appear, and most likely the Properties window will appear, too (press F4 on your keyboard if this doesn't appear on the right).

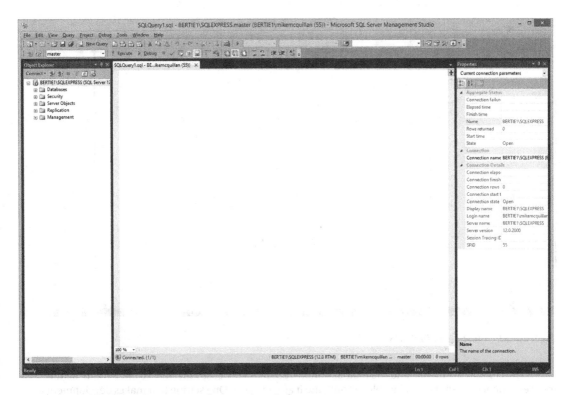

Figure 2-21. *SSMS showing query and properties windows*

I seldom use the Properties window, but that isn't to say it's no use. It lists various things about the connection you currently have to your SQL Server (you started a connection when you logged in). As you run queries, it will list the number of rows returned and the time it took to execute the query.

The main query window is where you will write your SQL code. If you type this statement in:

```
SELECT * FROM sys.databases;
```

you'll see a list of the databases available in the system. Figure 2-22 shows my list.

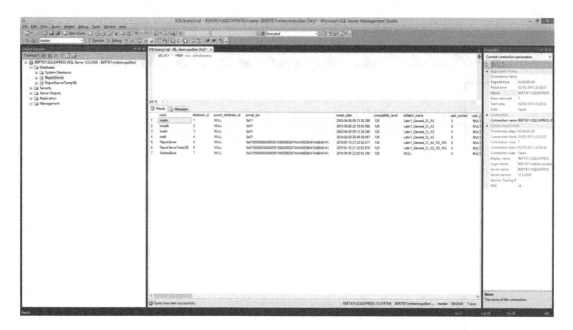

Figure 2-22. *A first query in SSMS*

Have a look at the menus and the toolbar options. SSMS is very customizable, so once you're a little more experienced with it you'll be able to configure it as you like it. One setting that makes development a little easier is to enable line numbers. This is done by navigating to **Tools ➤ Options ➤ Text Editor ➤ All Languages** and selecting **Line numbers**, then clicking **OK**. When an error occurs in a query, a line number is referenced. Enabling this feature makes it much easier to find the line causing the error.

Summary

We're done with the setup—now we're all ready to go and start developing. We'll kick off immediately in the next chapter by looking at how to create databases.

Let's go!

CHAPTER 3

■ ■ ■

Database Basics

In this chapter, we are going to look at databases: what they are, the types available to us, and how we manage them. We'll also take a look at some basic server settings, including security.

What Is a Database?

Think of a database as a container, with different compartments. Have you ever seen a neatly partitioned lunchbox? It might have a section for your sandwiches, a section for your salad, and a section for a tasty chocolate bar. Databases are very similar, except they don't have anything as tasty as a chocolate bar! Databases instead contain database objects. Some of the more common objects you will find in a database are the following:

- **Tables**: Used to store data.

- **Views**: An SQL statement that acts as a table. You'll learn about SQL statements throughout this book, and you'll actually write our first statement in this chapter (remember, SQL stands for Structured Query Language).

- **Stored procedures**: These execute code within your database and can be used to modify data in your tables. They have many other uses, too.

- **Functions**: A piece of code that performs a particular task, (e.g., returning the last day of a specified month).

There are lots of other types of objects, but in daily use you'll come across the items in this list on a constant basis.

Types of Databases

SQL Server uses two types of databases:

- **System databases**: These are databases that SQL Server requires to operate correctly. We'll take a look at these in a moment.

- **User databases**: These are created by users of SQL Server, and store any data required by those users or the organizations that own the servers. We'll be working with user databases for the majority of this book.

System Databases

There are five system databases.

- **Master**: This database stores all of the information needed for your SQL Server to function correctly. Logins and server configurations are two of the items stored here. If this database is unavailable your SQL Server will not start and you will not be able to log in to it.

- **MSDB**: We met the SQL Server Agent in **Chapter 1**, which acts as the scheduler for SQL Server. The **MSDB** database stores details about the jobs executed by the scheduler, along with job history. Backup details and history are also stored in this database. If something goes wrong with this database, your SQL Server will function, but certain aspects of it, such as scheduled jobs and backups, may fail (e.g., backups may complete, but won't be recorded).

- **Model**: The **Model** database is a template database, and every user database created starts as a copy of the Model database.

- **Resource**: This is the only database you cannot see via the Object Explorer in SQL Server Management Studio. It stores system objects, such as the **sys** tables (you'll see more of the **sys** tables as you work through the book).

- **TempDB**: You can think of this database as a scratchpad, accessed by all users of the SQL Server. Whenever you do something in SQL Server that requires a temporary object to be created, it will be created in this database. This database is deleted and recreated every time the server is restarted.

Note that if you have sysadmin permissions (more on permissions in Chapter 20), you can make changes in any of the preceding databases except for **Resource**. I cannot stress enough that you should never modify any of these databases, with the possible exception of **Model**. As I mentioned earlier, **Model** is used as a template for all user databases you create (more on this in just a moment). If your organization has certain standard tables (e.g., an Auditing table), it could be added to the **Model** database. Any new databases will then automatically contain this table.

■ **Caution**   **Model** is the exception to the rule: never modify a system database!

To see the system databases, open SSMS and log in as we did at the end of Chapter 2. Find the **Databases** node and expand it, then expand **System Databases**. As Figure 3-1 shows, you'll see all of the system databases there except for **Resource**.

Figure 3-1. *The system databases in Object Explorer*

The eagle-eyed among you may have noticed two ReportServer databases, sitting below System Databases. What are these? When I installed SQL Server in Chapter 2, I installed SSRS, too. SSRS uses these databases to store reports and data used during report generation. Interestingly, they exist as normal user databases, not system databases. You shouldn't modify anything in these databases if you are using SSRS, though. Doing so may break your SSRS installation.

User Databases

Now we come to the real start of our journey into SQL Server time and space. As a developer, you will spend most of your time creating objects within user databases. But you won't actually spend that much time creating them; after all, once a database is there, it's there! There are lots of options for creating databases but we'll stick to the simple path, and then afterward I'll give you a brief overview of the other things you can do.

There are a number of ways to create a SQL Server database (and as we continue through the book, you'll find there are multiple ways of doing just about anything). We'll take a look at two options:

- Creating a database through SQL Server Management Studio (SSMS)

- Creating a database using scripting

We'll also explore when we might use either of these options.

Creating a Database Using SSMS

At last! It's time to start using SQL Server. If you don't already have SSMS open and you have a Start Menu or a Start Screen, type in *SQL Server*—you should see **SQL Server 2014 Management Studio** in the list, depending upon the version of SQL Server you installed.

Open this up and you'll be presented with the login prompt shown in Figure 3-2.

Figure 3-2. The SQL Server login dialog

You'll see there are a few drop-down boxes within the login prompt. You should populate these as follows:

- **Server type**: Type *Database Engine*. You could also log in to SSIS, SSRS, and SSAS. Database Engine is the Relational Database Engine.

- **Server name**: The name you gave the server when you installed SQL Server (e.g., *BERTIE1*). If you installed the server as a default instance, you can just type *(local)* (including the parentheses) or a full stop/period here. If you installed the SQL Server as a named instance, as in Figure 3-2, you need to provide the full name of the instance, which is in the format `SERVER NAME\INSTANCE NAME`, (e.g., `BERTIE1\SQLEXPRESS`). For more information about default and named instances, refer to Chapter 2.

- **Authentication**: There are two types of authentication available; *Windows Authentication* and *SQL Server Authentication*. As I've said, my recommendation is to never use SQL Server Authentication, as you are opening up another potential route into your server. Windows Authentication integrates with your Windows server accounts. If your server runs as part of a larger network domain, any user account within the network's Active Directory can be granted access to SQL Server. This makes permissions easy to manage as you can allocate permissions to a group in Active Directory, and then just add users to that group as necessary. SQL Server Authentication uses individual usernames and passwords within SQL Server itself. So you would create a user account for yourself through SSMS and use that to log in (you can map logins to a SQL Server user account should you wish). If you followed the instructions in Chapter 2, you should only have configured Windows Authentication, so that is the one to choose.

If you did configure SQL Server Authentication and want to use a SQL Server account, the **User name** and **Password** boxes will become enabled. Enter the default user credentials:

- **User name: sa**

- **Password**: whatever you specified during installation

sa stands for System Administrator. This is a well-known account in SQL Server, and as a result could be used to compromise your server, as a hacker only needs to guess the password.

Once you are happy with everything, click **Connect** and you should be logged into SQL Server. If the login fails a prompt will appear; correct your login details and try again. Once login is successful the login prompt disappears and you will see your server name over on the left in the Object Explorer. You may learn to love the Object Explorer!

Click the + symbol next to your server name. A list of items will appear beneath it. The first item you can see is **Databases**. All available databases on the server are listed below this element. Click the + symbol next to **Databases**. An item called **System Databases** should appear underneath (other items may also appear; just ignore them).

Expand **System Databases** and you will see **master, model, msdb** and **tempdb** listed. Apart from being under the **System Databases** branch they don't actually look any different to user databases.

We're going to create our database in a folder called `c:\temp\sqlbasics`. If this folder doesn't exist on your computer, please create it before we proceed.

THE SQLBASICS FOLDER

As you work through the book I'll be asking you to save files you create in SQL Server Management Studio. These files, also known as scripts, will allow you to create and destroy the database we create together. The book will refer to a folder called c:\temp\sqlbasics. Feel free to use a different folder if you wish, but don't forget to save the files to it!

Right, let's create that database. Right-click the **Databases** node and a pop-up menu will appear as per Figure 3-3. Choose **New Database**.

Figure 3-3. *Creating a new database in SSMS*

A dialog will appear. The first thing we need to do is provide a database name. This may sound obvious, but database names are very important! The name should accurately describe the purpose of the database. I've seen many databases where the name of the database did not correlate to its purpose. This can make things difficult for developers and database administrators (DBAs), especially if they are new to the job. When you are creating objects or writing code, follow this maxim:

Always think about the next person.

The next person could be you! You need to be confident that you could come back to your code in a few months and pick it back up with minimal difficulty. We'll continue to reinforce this maxim throughout the book.

DBAS AND DEVELOPERS

Database Administrators—or DBAs for short—are the people tasked with ensuring SQL Server keeps on running. A DBA maintains SQL Server, fixes it when things are going wrong, and backs it up. A DBA is often responsible for testing and releasing your scripts, too.

A developer writes SQL code that is released onto SQL Server. Quite often, the same person will be a DBA and a developer (this has happened to me). Larger organizations will always have a team of DBAs dedicated to managing their SQL Server instances.

Back to database creation. We are going to create a simple address book database, which we'll build up throughout the rest of the book, so let's call our database **AddressBook**. Database names can include special characters, numbers, and even spaces. However, using these special characters and spaces is not a good idea. It leads to more typing and may cause issues with any systems that need some level of backward compatibility. As an example, look at these two queries (don't worry about what they do for the time being):

```
SELECT * FROM AddressBook.dbo.Contacts

SELECT * FROM [Address Book].dbo.Contacts
```

The second example uses the name **Address Book**, with a space. The existence of this space means we must wrap the name in square brackets. If we didn't do this, the query would not work.

In short, use simple and obvious names for your databases, and don't use any special characters—just capitalize each word in the name. This is known as CamelCase.

Type *AddressBook* into the **Database** name box. The next box allows you to specify the **Owner** of the database. This is set to *<default>*, which means the person creating the database is the owner. This translates to **dbo** within the database, of which more later. It is not particularly common to change the owner of a database, unless your organization has specific security requirements, so don't worry about this too much.

When you typed in the **Database** name, you may have noticed the **Database** files section underneath auto-populated (just like Figure 3-4). You should be looking at a table with columns for Logical Name, File Type, Filegroup, and so on. This table contains the files that make up our database.

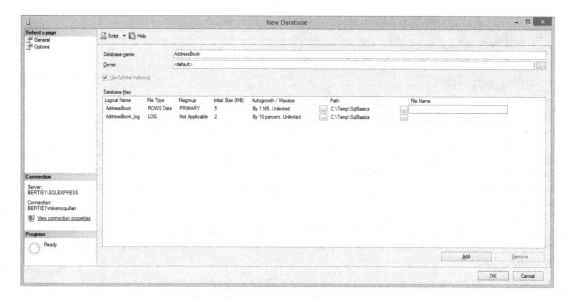

Figure 3-4. *The New Database dialog*

We'll take a quick look at what each of these columns is for:

- **Logical Name**: The name assigned to the file for user identification purposes. This name is used to restore the file, for example.

- **File Type**: There are a few file types, but mainly you'll deal with data files and log files. In the list you can see, one data file (ROWS Data) and one log file (LOG) are present.

- **Filegroup**: A filegroup can house multiple files, and is used to split up a database across disks. These are used for performance reasons. We'll touch on them shortly.

- **Initial Size (MB)**: How big the files should be when they are created. You need to figure this out by assessing how much data you expect the database to contain. Be aware that the file sizes you can see in Figure 3-4 may differ from the default file sizes assigned to your database files.

- **Autogrowth/Maxsize**: If the file reaches the initial size specified, SQL Server will use the values you specify here to autogrow the file, and also to limit the size of the file. You can set Maxsize to unlimited—more on this in the "Creating a Database Using T-SQL" section later in this chapter.

- **Path**: The folder where the database files will be created.

- **File Name**: The actual name of the physical file. This will be created automatically from the database name (it usually matches the logical name).

Click **OK** and after a couple of seconds the dialog will disappear (if you encounter an error, make sure you created the c:\temp\sqlbasics folder correctly). If you look under **Databases** in Object Explorer now, you'll see you have an **AddressBook** database!

Excellent, you have your first database. Let's see the files SQL Server created. Open Windows Explorer and go to c:\temp\sqlbasics. You should see two files (shown in Figure 3-5):

- AddressBook.mdf

- AddressBook_Log.ldf

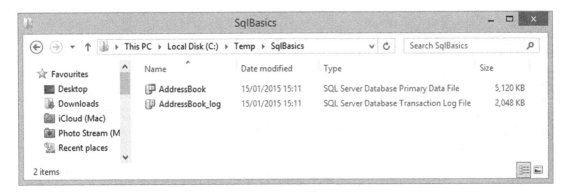

Figure 3-5. *The AddressBook database files*

It is highly likely that most of the databases you come across will use this simple structure. The MDF file is a Master Data File, and it is the file where SQL Server will store your data. The LDF file is a Log file that SQL Server uses to keep your database consistent (we will look at the log in Chapter 15).

There is a third type of file, the Secondary Data File (NDF). You need to create a filegroup if you want to use a secondary data file. You would use secondary data files when you want to maximize performance. You could put some of your tables in the Master Data File on Hard Disk 1, some files in a Secondary Data File on Hard Disk 2, and some files in another Secondary Data File on Hard Disk 3. This would maximize data reading and writing to/from the database as three hard disks could be used at the same time. You could also choose to back up or restore individual data files using their filegroups. This kind of configuration is not uncommon, but it is a bit more work to configure and manage. The performance gains are worth it if you have such a requirement.

If you are in doubt, always go with a simple database structure first. You can modify the structure in the future as your database grows.

Dropping a Database Using SSMS

Now that we've created our database, let's delete it!

Dropping a database using SSMS is scarily easy. Right-click the **AddressBook** database and click **Delete** in the pop-up menu that appears. A dialog appears, prompting you to confirm the deletion (Figure 3-6).

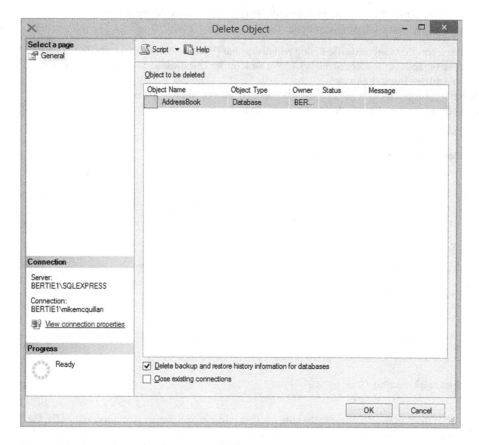

Figure 3-6. *Dropping a database using SSMS*

Note the two checkboxes at the bottom of the dialog shown in Figure 3-6:

- **Delete backup and restore history information for databases**: This will clear out the relevant history from the MSDB database. It is checked by default.

- **Close existing connections**: This is unchecked by default, and for good reason. If this box is unchecked and you attempt to drop the database, you will be prevented from doing so. You shouldn't use this option in production. However, quite often you will want to drop a development version of a database, and it is possible developers will be attached to the database. Checking this box in that scenario would be a valid use of this option.

You shouldn't need to change the defaults to drop the **AddressBook** database. Just click **OK** and the database should disappear from Object Explorer. If you browse to `c:\temp\sqlbasics`, you should find that the **AddressBook** MDF and LDF files have also disappeared.

Unless you had a backup, that database is now unrecoverable! So be really careful when dropping databases.

Okay, so now you know how to create (add) and drop (delete) databases using SSMS. However, SSMS is not always an option for us. What if you've been asked to build a database that can be deployed on different environments? You might have to create the database on a User Acceptance Testing environment, and then deploy it to a production environment. It is common to deploy to three or four environments before going into production. If you are using SSMS to manually create your databases and related objects, what are you going to do? Put a document together listing which buttons and boxes the deployment team needs to click and complete? Good luck with that!

No, you can't use SSMS for multi-environment deployments. For that, you need scripts. Scripts are the magic potions of the SQL Server world. You can manage just about anything from a script, and it can be executed in the blink of an eye on multiple servers.

Creating a Database Using T-SQL

In a moment, we'll create our first T-SQL script—to recreate our **AddressBook** database. Just before we do, it's worth understanding exactly what T-SQL is. SQL stands for Structured Query Language, and it is the standard language used to query databases—it is used by every major RDBMS (Relational DataBase Management System, a logical extension of a DBMS). It forms the basis of most RDBMS languages.

T-SQL is SQL Server's version of SQL. Oracle, a competing RDBMS, has a language called PL/SQL. You will find that many SQL statements you write for SQL Server will work in Oracle, and vice versa. But each RDBMS also implements many custom features, such as .NET integration in SQL Server and the FOR LOOP in Oracle.

On to the script. SSMS isn't just a tool used to manage databases; it is a fully fledged code editor, too. We'll use it for all of our scripting throughout the book. To create your first script, click the **File** menu, choose **New**, and click **Query with Current Connection** (alternatively, press Ctrl+N your keyboard or click the **New Query** button on the top menu).

An empty code window opens. What a world of possibilities in front of us!

Let's create a T-SQL script to create the database. As we are creating a database, this will be a Data Definition Language (DDL) script. There are two types of SQL statements. DDL statements are statements that create, modify, or delete database objects like tables and stored procedures. Data Manipulation Language (DML) statements work on data only, allowing you to select, insert, update, or delete data for your tables.

The DDL statement we use to create a database is CREATE DATABASE. This statement is huge and has lots of options. We are not going to look at all of these options. We'll just build up the statement we need bit by bit. Start by typing this:

```
CREATE DATABASE AddressBook;
```

Do you think this will work? Try it! Press F5 to run the statement. As Figure 3-7 demonstrates, you should see the message **Command(s) completed successfully**:

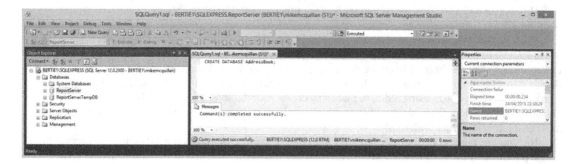

Figure 3-7. *Basic CREATE DATABASE T-SQL statement*

Amazing; it does succeed. Yes, those three simple words are all you need to create a database with the default values (from the **Model** database, referenced earlier). When we opened up the **New Database** dialog earlier and created the database, this is pretty much the statement SQL Server executed in the background.

If you refresh the **Databases** node of your Object Explorer, the **AddressBook** database will be visible. Cool!

THE SEMICOLON

You might have spotted that our CREATE DATABASE statement ended with a semicolon. This is put here to denote the end of a statement. SQL Server doesn't force you to use this at the moment other than in a few unique cases, such as declaring Common Table Expressions (CTEs). It will become required in a future version, so it's best to enter into the habit of finishing all of your statements with a semicolon now. Then you'll be ready for the brave new world! You don't need to put a semicolon after the GO command—if you do the code won't work. This is because GO is technically not part of your code; it separates your code into batches.

Out of curiosity, do you think we can create another database called **AddressBook**? Press F5 to rerun our statement. This time we see an error message—in red, just like a teacher marking our homework (see Figure 3-8)!

Figure 3-8. *"Database already exists" error*

So, we cannot create two databases with the same name. This makes perfect sense, as how would you be able to tell them apart?

The database we have at the moment is not suitable for our requirements, as we want to customize the file names and sizes. We therefore need to drop our database. Replace the CREATE DATABASE statement with:

```
DROP DATABASE AddressBook;
```

Press **F5** to run it. The database will be removed, as Figure 3-9 shows.

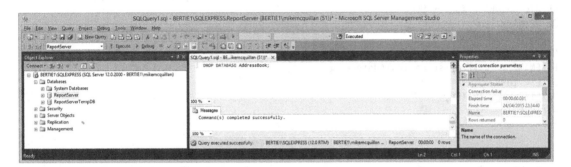

Figure 3-9. *DROP DATABASE in T-SQL*

As you can tell, it is as easy to drop a database as it is to create one. Be careful with the DROP command!

Now, before we write our complete CREATE DATABASE statement, let's consider what we would like to create:

- A database called **AddressBook**

- One data file, 10MB in size

- One log file, 2MB in size

- The data file should autogrow by 50%, and should be able to grow as large as it needs

- The log file should autogrow by 2MB, but should be limited to 100MB in size

MAXIMUM FILE SIZE (MAXSIZE)

There are many schools of thought about the maximum size of database and log files. My view is you should not set size limits on files; you should always let them grow as large as needed. In my experience, when a size limit is set, SQL Server quite often hits it well before the developers or DBAs expected it to be hit. Once that happens the database stops working.

When the transaction log is backed up, it is truncated and all of its space is made available again. This doesn't happen with database files, so you need to be confident about the size of your data. You can set up alerts that will monitor your files proactively, ensuring you are warned when they hit a limit (e.g., only 10% of space is left).

This is a pretty standard database configuration. We'll start by typing in the three words we have already seen, along with ON PRIMARY:

```
CREATE DATABASE AddressBook
ON PRIMARY;
```

This statement will not work; the ON PRIMARY is stating that the file we are about to specify is the primary data file. A database can only have one primary file. We'll add the details for the data file.

```
CREATE DATABASE AddressBook
ON PRIMARY
(
NAME = 'AddressBook',
FILENAME = 'C:\temp\sqlbasics\AddressBook.mdf',
SIZE = 10MB,
MAXSIZE = UNLIMITED,
FILEGROWTH = 50%
);
```

We've now met our requirements for the data file. We've named the file, given it a full file name so SQL Server knows where to create it, and specified its size and growth details. As it is, this is a valid statement and the database would be created, with a default log file, if it was executed. We don't want a default log file, as we can't control where it should be placed. Let's add the log file specification.

```
CREATE DATABASE AddressBook
ON PRIMARY
(
NAME = 'AddressBook',
FILENAME = 'C:\temp\sqlbasics\AddressBook.mdf',
SIZE = 10MB,
MAXSIZE = UNLIMITED,
FILEGROWTH = 50%
)
LOG ON
(
NAME = 'AddressBook_Log',
FILENAME = 'C:\temp\sqlbasics\AddressBook_Log.ldf',
SIZE = 2MB,
MAXSIZE = 100MB,
FILEGROWTH = 2MB
);
```

That's all we need, and as you start out with SQL Server it is likely this is all you need to know about creating a database. There are many more options; search for *T-SQL CREATE DATABASE* on the Internet for a full outline on MSDN (the Microsoft Developer Network web site).

Press F5 and, just like in Figure 3-10, your database will be created.

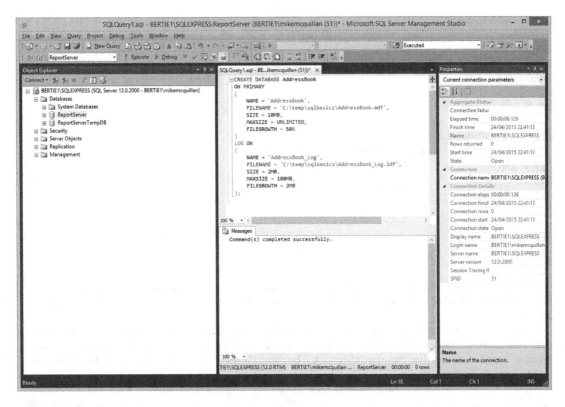

Figure 3-10. *Complete* CREATE DATABASE *in T-SQL*

Press F5 again and you'll see an error, telling you the database already exists.

Now, remember why we've created a script: for reusability purposes. A script allows us to deploy to multiple environments. However, DBAs don't take kindly to scripts failing! So we need to add a mechanism that will allow the script to complete successfully, even if the database already exists.

What we need to do is:

- Check if the database exists

- If it doesn't exist, create it

- If it does exist, do nothing

Do you remember the **Resource** system database? This holds a set of **sys** tables, which hold information about your server and databases. We can use this information to check if the database exists.

Amend your CREATE DATABASE script so it looks like this:

```
USE Master;
IF NOT EXISTS (SELECT 1 FROM sys.databases WHERE [name] = 'AddressBook')
BEGIN

CREATE DATABASE AddressBook
ON PRIMARY
(
```

```
NAME = 'AddressBook',
FILENAME = 'C:\temp\sqlbasics\AddressBook.mdf',
SIZE = 10MB,
MAXSIZE = UNLIMITED,
FILEGROWTH = 50%
)
LOG ON
(
NAME = 'AddressBook_Log',
FILENAME = 'C:\temp\sqlbasics\AddressBook_Log.ldf',
SIZE = 2MB,
MAXSIZE = 100MB,
FILEGROWTH = 2MB
);

END;

GO
```

You can run this as many times as you want. The script will not fail, and the database will only ever be created once. But what is this script doing? It's actually using some concepts we'll be looking at in more detail later on.

Figure 3-11 shows the complete statement. The first line is now USE Master. This gives the focus to the **Master** database, so what we are saying is apply this script using the **Master** database. As this is the parent system database, it makes sense to use this as a default. We'll be using the USE statement much more in later chapters.

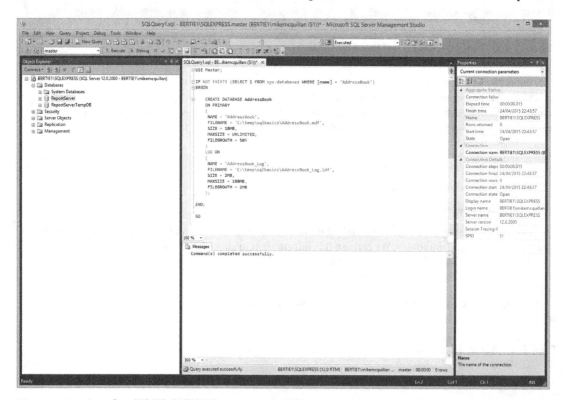

Figure 3-11. *Complete CREATE DATABASE statement in T-SQL*

The next section of code is interesting; it is the code that checks if the database exists.

```
IF NOT EXISTS (SELECT 1 FROM sys.databases WHERE [name] = 'AddressBook')
```

The SELECT 1... statement will return a single column containing the literal numeric value of 1 if a database called **AddressBook** exists on the server. If you highlight that piece of code and run it (in SSMS, if you highlight a block of code and run it, only the highlighted code will be executed), you should see a result of 1 (assuming you have created your database). If the database does not exist, no result is returned.

IF NOT EXISTS says if no result of 1 is returned from the sys.databases query, execute the CREATE DATABASE statement. This is now enclosed in a BEGIN...END block to link it to the IF statement. In short, what we have is:

```
IF (Condition is true)
BEGIN
        Do Something
END
```

We could extend this by adding an ELSE to do something else if the database does already exist, but we'll look at ELSE when we are writing SQL statements in later chapters.

The very last line is GO. SQL Server executes T-SQL code in batches. A batch is just one or more T-SQL statements. The GO command signifies the end of a batch. It is good form to put this in at the end of each batch of commands. When we look at SQLCMD in Chapter 6 you'll see how useful GO can be.

Create a new folder in c:\temp\sqlbasics called apply. Then save this script as c:\temp\sqlbasics\apply\01 - Create AddressBook Database.sql.

Congratulations, you have a database ready to use, and you've just created your first script!

Dropping A Database Using T-SQL

DBAs are very keen on rollback scripts. These are scripts that undo whatever your "apply" scripts did (the CREATE DATABASE script we just created is an apply script).

We'll create a rollback script to drop the database, should it exist. Open a New Query Window (Ctrl+N) and type the following:

```
USE Master;

IF EXISTS (SELECT 1 FROM sys.databases WHERE [name] = 'AddressBook')
BEGIN
DROP DATABASE AddressBook;
END;

GO
```

This is pretty similar to the CREATE DATABASE script, with a few key differences. Instead of IF NOT EXISTS, we now have IF EXISTS. The SELECT 1... query is still the same. So now we are saying that if the query returns 1, perform the action. The action in this case is to drop the database. Run this as many times as you want. It will never fail, but the first time it runs, it will drop the database.

NOT EXISTS AND EXISTS

The EXISTS keyword is used to check if some condition evaluates to true—for example,
IF EXISTS (SELECT 1 FROM sys.databases WHERE [name] = 'AddressBook') returns true
if the **AddressBook** database exists. NOT EXISTS inverts this, so if we have IF NOT EXISTS
(SELECT 1 FROM sys.databases WHERE [name] = 'AddressBook'), the statement will only return
true if the database does not exist. These constructs are very powerful and can help you control the
flow of your code.

To finish off, save this script. In c:\temp\sqlbasics, create a folder called rollback. Save this script as
c:\temp\sqlbasics\rollback\01 - Create AddressBook Database Rollback.sql. It's a good convention
to keep the rollback script file names the same as the apply scripts, but with Rollback either prepended or
appended to the name. This makes it easy for you and others to match the scripts up.

■ **Note** Always ensure your rollbacks leave the system in the same state as your apply script found it.

Advanced Database Scripting

We're all done with database creation. It is worth noting again that the CREATE DATABASE statement is
extremely powerful and has lots of options, so once you are comfortable with basic database creation, please
take a look at the MSDN documentation to check out the more advanced ways you can use this statement
(https://msdn.microsoft.com/en-us/library/ms176061.aspx).

There is also an ALTER DATABASE statement. This can do most of what the CREATE DATABASE statement
does, along with a few other things, but on existing databases. Again, take a look on MSDN
(https://msdn.microsoft.com/en-us/library/ms174269.aspx).

Almost any database object you can create will offer the three statements CREATE, ALTER, and DROP.
You'll see more examples of this pattern later in the book.

Creating Scripts Automatically

If you think writing scripts is going to be a bit onerous, you can use SSMS to automatically generate scripts
for you. Ensure you can see the AddressBook database in Object Explorer and right-click it. Move over the
option that reads **Script Database as**, which is highlighted in Figure 3-12.

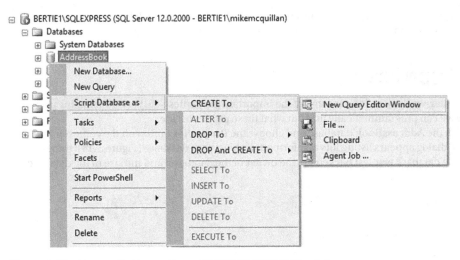

Figure 3-12. *Automatically creating a CREATE DATABASE script*

There are a number of options in here, all of which will create an appropriate script for you. This can be a great time-saver. Move over the **CREATE To** option and choose **New Query Editor Window**. This will open a New Query Window, populated with the T-SQL code. You can choose to save the script as a file, should you wish.

Figure 3-13 shows the generated script. You'll notice that the script generated is much longer and more complicated than the script we created. That's because the script has created statements to set every single database setting; we just accepted the defaults for all of these. But the end result of running this script will be the same; it would create the database. Have a play with this option to determine which scripts you can generate.

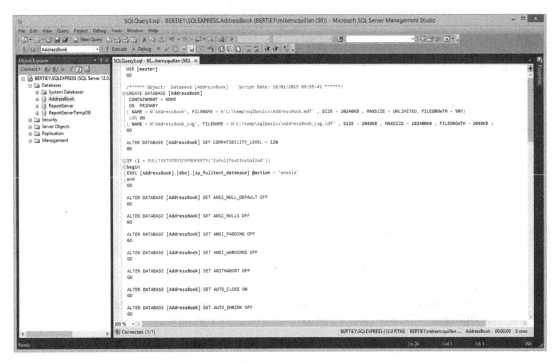

Figure 3-13. *The generated CREATE DATABASE script*

Any scripts you generate will only include the appropriate CREATE, ALTER, or DROP statement; it won't include an IF EXISTS statement like the one we created earlier.

Database Properties

To finish off this chapter, we'll take a look at some of the important properties SQL Server maintains per database, and how we can programmatically find out what these properties are.

If you right-click the **AddressBook** database and choose the **Properties** option on the context menu (it is the last item), a dialog appears listing lots of information about your database (Figure 3-14): things like the date on which the database was last backed up, the owner of the database, and the size of the database.

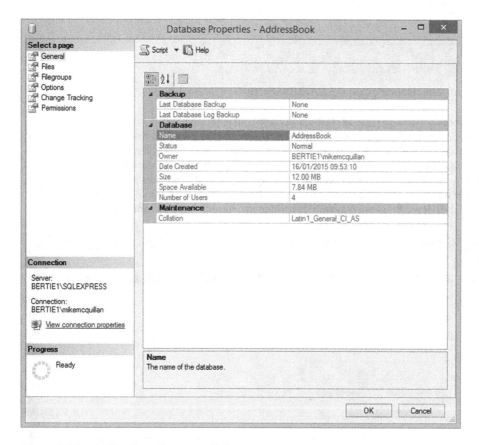

Figure 3-14. *The Database Properties dialog*

We'll take a quick look at three important properties.

- **Status**: The current state of the database. Usually you want this to be **Online**, which means the database is online and available for use. If a database is unavailable it may be **Offline**, and if it is being restored it could be in the **Restoring** state.

- **Recovery Model**: This option is found on the Options page on the left-hand side of the Database Properties dialog. This setting is key. There are three recovery models, and they dictate how the transaction log works. **Full** means all data is written to the transaction log. You won't lose any data if the data file fails. **Bulk Logged** means normal operations are logged, but bulk copy operations (operations involving lots of rows) are minimally logged. You could lose data here if you haven't backed up and a bulk copy operation has occurred. The final option is **Simple**. This doesn't log anything and is usually a bad idea. **Full** is the most common model used and is what should be used in production. If you plan to execute some pretty large inserts/updates/deletes against the database, consider temporarily switching to **Bulk Logged** or **Simple**.

- **Collation**: Collation is shown on the General page, and is also shown on the Options page. On the Options page, it can be changed to a different collation, if desired. Collation dictates how language is used in the database. There are lots of collation options, which dictate things like case sensitivity and accent sensitivity. Collations can affect whether a value like "Dolly" is treated the same as "dolly". It is important to ensure these stay consistent across your servers and databases to prevent issues with cross-database referencing (if required).

These are more advanced topics, but it is important to know they exist. There are lots of other properties available for you to manage. If you need to obtain a particular property value as part of a script, you can use the DATABASEPROPERTYEX system function (we'll talk about functions in Chapter 16). This example returns the Status and the Collation:

```
SELECT  DATABASEPROPERTYEX('AddressBook', 'Status') AS Status,
        DATABASEPROPERTYEX('AddressBook', 'Collation') AS Collation;
```

You can use this to return any database property. Just pass in the name of the database and the name of the property you want. You can find a full list of properties by going to https://msdn.microsoft.com/en-us/library/ms186823.aspx. A demonstration of the executed statement can be seen in Figure 3-15.

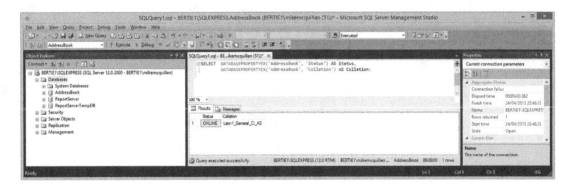

Figure 3-15. *Displaying database properties using T-SQL*

Summary

Well done, you have created a database! In a number of different ways, I might add. Unfortunately, a database without any content is like an empty glass. You need to fill your database up with useful objects that will allow it to store data. We'll take a look at the first and most important of these—tables—in the next chapter.

CHAPTER 4

Tables

Imagine buying a new computer. You bring home the box, full of excitement. You open the box—and it's empty! You have a box, but it's not much use, is it? Databases are exactly the same. If you have a database without tables, it serves no purpose. Tables are the data containers. Everything you might want to store in a database—customer information, order details, your comic collection—has to go into a table. Virtually everything you build in your database will rely on data from tables.

I think it's pretty clear that tables are quite important, so we'd better figure out how they work and how we can create them!

Table Basics

Tables in databases do not consist of four legs and a tabletop. Now that would be interesting! No, database tables consist of two basic elements:

- Columns

- Rows

Together, these two items form a gridlike structure. The columns define the pieces of data we want to store, and the rows hold the values for those columns. A row is just a collection of column values. Here's a quick example:

- We have a table called Customers

- Customers has two columns: FirstName and Surname

- We add a new row: a FirstName of Grace, and a Surname of McQuillan

- We add a second row: a FirstName of Jo, and a Surname of McQuillan

The table now contains two rows of data, one for Grace McQuillan, and one for Jo McQuillan—just like Figure 4-1, in fact.

Figure 4-1. *Two rows of data*

Just having a list of names in a table isn't much good to us. For example, what would happen if a second Grace McQuillan were to be added? How could we tell them apart? How could we link these names to other pieces of data, such as orders made by a customer? How can we prevent duplicate records from being added? The answers to all of these questions and more will become clear as we proceed. Let's have a look at our first table script.

A Starting Point

Use the CREATE TABLE SQL statement to create a table in SQL Server. Take a look at this script.

```
USE AddressBook;

CREATE TABLE dbo.Contacts
(
ContactId INT,
FirstName VARCHAR(40),
LastName VARCHAR(40),
DateOfBirth DATE,
PhoneNumbers VARCHAR(200),
AllowContactByPhone BIT,
FirstAddress VARCHAR(200),
SecondAddress VARCHAR(200),
RoleId INT,
RoleTitle VARCHAR(200),
Notes1 VARCHAR(200),
Notes2 VARCHAR(200),
DrivingLicenseNumber VARCHAR(40),
PassportNumber VARCHAR(40),
ContactVerified BIT,
CreatedDate DATETIME
);

GO
```

First we meet the USE statement we saw in Chapter 3, but this time we are saying USE AddressBook. So whatever we run as part of this batch of T-SQL statements will be executed within the **AddressBook** database. Then we execute a CREATE TABLE statement. This is the only real piece of code in this script. It will create a table called Contacts with the appropriate columns. Then we finish up with our now ubiquitous GO statement.

WHAT IS DBO FOR?

You may have noticed we didn't call the table `Contacts`—rather, we called it `dbo.Contacts`. `dbo` is the default schema. A *schema* is a container that allows you to group together objects in a folder-like way. If you had a set of reporting objects (tables, functions, stored procedures) you could put them all into a schema called `Reporting`.

Schemas are very useful as they allow you to define security permissions for the entire set of objects, rather than one object at a time. They are also great for logically separating your database objects.

Unless you explicitly provide a schema name, all objects you create will be added to the `dbo` schema. The `dbo.` in the preceding example is optional, but it is good practice to be explicit whenever you can.

Schemas are discussed more in Chapter 20.

Save this script to `c:\temp\sqlbasics\apply\02 - Create Contacts Table.sql`. Once saved, run the statement by pressing F5 and the table will be created. To view the table, expand the **Databases** node in the Object Explorer, then **AddressBook**, then **Tables**. As Figure 4-2 shows, you'll see **dbo.Contacts** in the list (you may need to right-click the **Tables** node and choose the **Refresh** option).

Figure 4-2. The Contacts table in Object Explorer

Now right-click `dbo.Contacts` and choose **Edit Top 200 Rows**. The table opens up, awaiting data entry (see Figure 4-3).

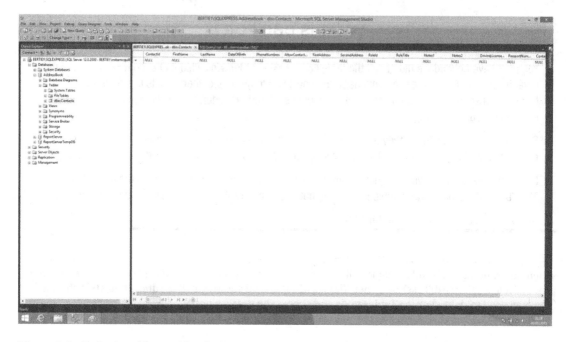

Figure 4-3. Contacts table, awaiting data entry

CHANGING THE NUMBER OF ROWS

You can modify how many rows SSMS will return in the **Edit Top 200 Rows** context menu option. Go to **Tools ➤ Options**, and click **SQL Server Object Explorer** on the left. You can change the values for the appropriate options here—you may choose to display the top 500 rows, for example.

Our first table now exists. You could have used SSMS to create the table had you wished; simply right-click the **Tables** node and choose the **Table** option. This will display the table editor, which is shown in Figure 4-4.

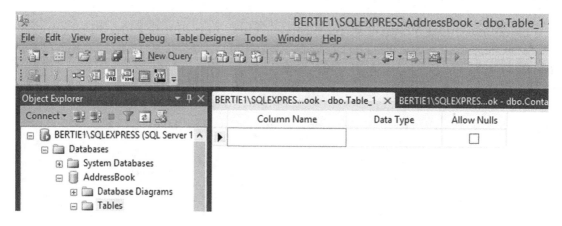

Figure 4-4. Creating a new table using the table editor

56

Of course, using the table editor means our code is not reusable. However, you could create the table using SSMS and script it, as we did with our database in the last chapter. Right-click the Contacts table, select **Script Table as**, then **CREATE To**, and finally click **New Query Editor Window**. As Figure 4-5 shows, the CREATE TABLE statement will appear, again with more detail than we originally provided (remember, CREATE DATABASE did a similar thing).

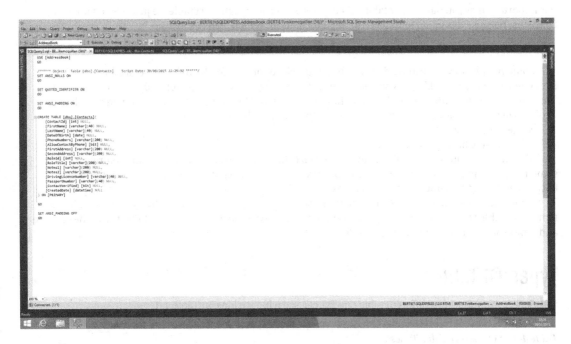

Figure 4-5. *Generating a CREATE TABLE statement*

WHAT'S ALL THAT EXTRA STUFF?

You're probably wondering what SET ANSI_NULLS ON, SET QUOTED_IDENTIFIER ON, the square brackets and so on in Figure 4-5 are for.

SET ANSI_NULLS ON dictates how we find records with NULL values (you'll find out about NULLs in Chapter 7).

SET QUOTED_IDENTIFIER ON determines whether double quotes can be used in SQL statements (so Notes1 works the same as Notes2).

SET ANSI_PADDING ON tells SQL Server how to store text values, and whether spaces at the end of text values should be kept or not.

The square brackets around the various names in the statement in Figure 4-5 are completely optional. They are not needed for any of the preceding terms as they are all fairly simple names. They are required when a name has a special character in it, like a space or parentheses. So the name Role Title would cause an issue, but [Role Title] would work fine. Special characters should be avoided.

Last, each column declaration has the word NULL after it. This means NULL values can be stored in the columns. You'll see more of this in Chapter 7, too.

Okay, you have the extreme basics of `CREATE TABLE` down. Now we need to take a look at what creating a table actually involves.

Naming Tables

It is important that you name your tables accurately. For example, the test table we just created is called `Contacts`, because it is going to house contact information. Which leads us to ask:

To s or not to s, that is the question.

Some people may be reading this and thinking, "Never put a letter S on the end of a table name! Don't pluralize it, you fool!" And you could argue they are right. But other people will be thinking, "Yes, pluralize away." And you could argue they are right, too. The simple answer here is you can choose to pluralize or not, as long as you are consistent. One way isn't better than the other.

Some people like: `Contacts`.

Other people like: `Contact`.

The choice is yours. Personally, I always pluralize. My only rule against this is I don't pluralize when something ends in a Y. So if I had a `Responsibility` table, I would change the name to something like `ResponsibilityItems`, not `Responsibilities`.

Table names can begin with a letter, an underscore, an @ sign, or a # sign. Unless you are creating a temporary table (see the next section), I recommend you always begin with a letter. Keep the names simple and avoid special characters where possible.

Types Of Table

SQL Server supports a few different table types. Let's see what we have in Table 4-1.

Table 4-1. SQL Server Table Types

Table Type	Description
Heap Table	A normal, permanent table, used to store rows of data. The `Contacts` table we just created is a heap table. This is a table without a clustered index (see Chapter 14).
Clustered Table	A normal, permanent table, but with a clustered index (again, see Chapter 14!).
Local Temporary Table	Temporary tables always begin with a # symbol. These are tables that only exist inside a particular block of code. They are temporarily created inside **tempdb** and removed once the code has finished (or the window in which the code is executing is closed).
Global Temporary Table	This begins with ##. It is available to all users of the system until it is destroyed. It must be destroyed manually, unless the system is restarted. Whenever SQL Server restarts it rebuilds **tempdb**, so any temporary tables in there would be removed.
FileTable	These were new in SQL Server 2012. Do you remember our brief discussion on FILESTREAM in Chapter 2? FileTables store FILESTREAM data.

We'll be dealing with clustered tables for the majority of the book.

Columns and Table Data Types

Look at these two lines from our earlier CREATE TABLE statement:

```
ContactId INT,
FirstName VARCHAR(40),
```

These two lines are column declarations. The first defines a ContactId column of type INT (integer), which means the column can store a number. The second, FirstName, is of type VARCHAR(40). This means the value can be any combination of characters, up to a maximum of 40 characters. This is known as a *string* in many programming languages.

The column names make it clear what the purpose of each column is, and this is the thing to remember when naming your columns: always make the meaning clear. Also, avoid special characters if you can; otherwise you may find yourself having to use square brackets. One other point: Always explicitly name columns, especially identifiers. Don't use generic names like ID or Name; use ContactId or ContactName instead. The reason for this will become clear later when we look at relationships. In some special circumstances there may be a valid reason for adding a column called ID, but this is outside the scope of this book.

T-SQL offers many different data types. The table in Appendix A lists them all, but in general you'll find yourself using INT/BIGINT, CHAR/VARCHAR/NVARCHAR, BIT, and the DATETIME options more than anything else. We'll have a quick glance at the data types we are going to use in our examples.

- INT: Numeric values. You can store any whole number in an INT column, from about –2 billion to 2 billion (exact numbers are in Appendix A!). BIGINT is similar but it can store much larger numbers.

- VARCHAR: This stands for variable character. You have to define a number to specify the length of this (between 1 and 8,000) in bytes. You can have strings longer than 8,000 by specifying VARCHAR(MAX) (this allows values up to 2GB in length). You declare a VARCHAR of 25 characters, for example, by specifying it as VARCHAR(25).

  Only the actual data stored in the column takes up room; so if you did have a VARCHAR(25) and the name Dolly was entered, only five characters would be stored. This is different from CHAR(25), which would hold 25 characters (Dolly and 20 spaces). NVARCHAR(25) would also use five characters for Dolly, but it needs double the space to store each character, as the value is stored in Unicode format.

- BIT: This denotes if something is true or false. The value is stored as 0 or 1 (or NULL, if allowed). In a Contacts table, for example, you might have a BIT column for ContactByPhoneAllowed.

THREE-STATE LOGIC

BIT columns support something called three-state logic. Normally, a BIT column only allows two values: TRUE or FALSE. But if you allow NULL values to be stored in the column, too, you can store three different responses. This capability can often come in handy.

- DATETIME: Stores a date and time combination. This is the most commonly used date/time field you'll come across in SQL Server databases, as it was the main date/time storage mechanism until separate Date and Time data types appeared in SQL Server 2012.

UNICODE FORMAT

Unicode is a standardized method that ensures consistency across languages used on computers. It supports multiple characters across many languages, including letters and scripts (e.g., it supports Arabic,).

If your database needs to support multiple languages, you should use Unicode data types like NCHAR, NVARCHAR, and NTEXT. You can use the standard non-Unicode types if you don't have this requirement.

Be careful when deciding how long your string-based columns are going to be. It's fairly easy to make a column bigger, but this has ramifications on other parts of your systems, as we'll see.

Primary Keys

One thing our Contacts table doesn't have is a Primary Key. This is a column (or combination of columns) that can be used to uniquely identify a row. Let's look at an example: me and my dad. Some years ago, we had the same name and address; only our dates of birth differed. As a database record, it would be quite difficult to uniquely identify either of us—you'd need to use name, address, and date of birth. This isn't a good solution. As we develop a database, we add more tables to it and link those tables together using foreign keys, which we'll look at in the next section. It's simpler to use one column in foreign key relationships.

Another thing we want to do is keep primary keys concise. If they are small, this allows us to pull records back from the database faster than if we were using a combination of name, address, and so on. It is standard practice to use numeric fields, like INT or BIGINT, as primary keys. We added a ContactId column to our Contacts table. That column exists to serve one purpose only: to uniquely identify the row. It is there to act as a primary key.

Let's modify our CREATE TABLE T-SQL statement to turn ContactId into a primary key column. First, we'll need to drop the current version of the table. Do you remember the test we added in Chapter 3 to check if a database already existed? We used it to look at sys.databases. Similarly, we'll look at sys.tables to check if our table exists. If it does, we'll drop it, then our code will execute and recreate it.

Open c:\temp\sqlbasics\apply\02 - Create Contacts Table.sql and change it so it looks like this:

```
USE AddressBook;

IF EXISTS (SELECT 1 FROM sys.tables WHERE [Name] = 'Contacts')
BEGIN
DROP TABLE dbo.Contacts;
END;

CREATE TABLE dbo.Contacts
(
ContactId INT,
FirstName VARCHAR(40),
LastName VARCHAR(40),
DateOfBirth DATE,
PhoneNumbers VARCHAR(200),
AllowContactByPhone BIT,
FirstAddress VARCHAR(200),
SecondAddress VARCHAR(200),
RoleId INT,
```

```
RoleTitle VARCHAR(200),
Notes1 VARCHAR(200),
Notes2 VARCHAR(200),
DrivingLicenseNumber VARCHAR(40),
PassportNumber VARCHAR(40),
ContactVerified BIT,
CreatedDate DATETIME
);
```

```
GO
```

Our CREATE TABLE statement remains exactly as it was, but we've added an IF EXISTS check at the top. We are checking if the table exists by looking for its name in sys.tables. If the table does exist, we drop it. Then our CREATE TABLE statement runs without any issues.

Note that I've wrapped the [Name] column in square brackets. Why is this? Didn't I say they were only needed for names with special characters in them, like a space? Indeed I did. But I also recommend using them when column or object names are *reserved words*: words SQL Server uses as part of T-SQL, for example. Name happens to be a SQL Server keyword, so I wrapped it in square brackets to explicitly tell SQL Server I am using it as a column name.

RESERVED WORDS

SQL Server reserves a set of words that have a special meaning within SQL Server—SELECT, for example. Most reserved words act as statements in the T-SQL language, like EXISTS.

I recommend avoiding the use of reserved words wherever possible to avoid confusion. If you have your heart set on a particular word, just remember to wrap the object name (e.g., a table or column) in square brackets, like we did with [Name].

Now that we know we can drop and recreate the table at will, we can add our primary key to it. There are two ways to do this. The first one is to change the ContactId line so it looks like this:

```
ContactId INT PRIMARY KEY,
```

Run the script again. In Object Explorer, right-click **Tables** and then **Refresh**. Expand **Contacts**, then expand **Columns** and **Keys**. You'll see something like Figure 4-6.

```
□ ▦ dbo.Contacts
   □ ▢ Columns
         ⚿ ContactId (PK, int, not null)
         ▤ FirstName (varchar(40), null)
         ▤ LastName (varchar(40), null)
         ▤ DateOfBirth (date, null)
         ▤ PhoneNumbers (varchar(200), null)
         ▤ AllowContactByPhone (bit, null)
         ▤ FirstAddress (varchar(200), null)
         ▤ SecondAddress (varchar(200), null)
         ▤ RoleId (int, null)
         ▤ RoleTitle (varchar(200), null)
         ▤ Notes1 (varchar(200), null)
         ▤ Notes2 (varchar(200), null)
         ▤ DrivingLicenseNumber (varchar(40), null)
         ▤ PassportNumber (varchar(40), null)
         ▤ ContactVerified (bit, null)
         ▤ CreatedDate (datetime, null)
   □ ▢ Keys
         ⚿ PK_Contacts__5C66259B4E1EA027
```

Figure 4-6. *A dynamically named primary key*

Two things of note here. First, the ContactId icon has changed to a small key, and it says PK next to it. This tells us the column is acting as a primary key. Second, we have an entry under **Keys**. This also has a key icon and begins with PK_Contacts, for "primary key." The random letters and numbers have been added by SQL Server to create a unique name.

Now, I don't like this method of creating primary keys. I don't want a load of random letters and numbers at the end of my names; I prefer to exercise more control by explicitly naming my objects. Remove PRIMARY KEY from the ContactId line, so it looks like this again:

```
ContactId INT,
```

Find the CreatedDate line, and add a comma at the end of it. Then, type in the second line in the following script:

```
CreatedDate DATETIME,
CONSTRAINT PK_Contacts PRIMARY KEY (ContactId)
```

Run your script again, refresh **Contacts** in Object Explorer, and expand **Columns** and **Keys**. Now you will see the good primary key name, just like in Figure 4-7:

```
dbo.Contacts
  Columns
      ContactId (PK, int, not null)
      FirstName (varchar(40), null)
      LastName (varchar(40), null)
      DateOfBirth (date, null)
      PhoneNumbers (varchar(200), null)
      AllowContactByPhone (bit, null)
      FirstAddress (varchar(200), null)
      SecondAddress (varchar(200), null)
      RoleId (int, null)
      RoleTitle (varchar(200), null)
      Notes1 (varchar(200), null)
      Notes2 (varchar(200), null)
      DrivingLicenseNumber (varchar(40), null)
      PassportNumber (varchar(40), null)
      ContactVerified (bit, null)
      CreatedDate (datetime, null)
  Keys
      PK_Contacts
```

Figure 4-7. *A primary key named by the developer*

Much better! We now have a concise, to-the-point primary key name. In truth, you can call the primary key anything you want, but using PK is good practice—it tells developers the key's purpose.

Clustered and Nonclustered Keys

Primary keys, whether they use one or more columns (multiple-column primary keys are known as *compound keys*), can be either clustered or nonclustered.

- A *clustered* primary key determines how data are stored on the hard disk

- A *nonclustered* primary key supports fast querying of data, but doesn't dictate how the data are stored on disk

We'll see these terms again when we look at indexes in Chapter 14, where we'll walk through an example of how each of these items can affect how your table stores data. Indeed, a primary key is nothing more than a special type of index. By default, a clustered primary key will be created if you do not explicitly state what type of primary key you want to create.

▓ **Note** You can only have one clustered index per table. This is usually the primary key, but it doesn't have to be, as we've just seen. However, you can have lots of nonclustered indexes on a table, and SQL Server will have you covered.

To explicitly create a nonclustered primary key, change our new CONSTRAINT line to include the NONCLUSTERED keyword:

```
CONSTRAINT pk_Contacts PRIMARY KEY NONCLUSTERED (ContactId)
```

Run this and your table will be recreated. You should use `ContactId` as a clustered column, as you'll be using it to identify lots of pieces of data, and having it in the correct order will speed up queries. So change that line to use the `CLUSTERED` keyword instead:

```
CONSTRAINT pk_Contacts PRIMARY KEY CLUSTERED (ContactId)
```

Run this and save the script. Strictly speaking, we don't need to provide the `CLUSTERED` keyword (this is the default), but it is always better to be explicit—it makes your code easier to understand. Think about the next person!

Foreign Keys and Relationships

I briefly mentioned foreign keys earlier. We use these to link two tables together. One table is a parent and the other is a child. We won't create any foreign keys in this chapter, but it's a good idea to take a look at what they are, to steel yourself for the challenges ahead!

You might think you can create one big table to hold all your data, which is what I did earlier with the `Contacts` table. This is a very bad approach and will make things difficult for you when you need to generate reports or find individual pieces of data. Over the rest of this chapter and the next, you'll see how logically separating data into different tables makes sense.

Say we have two tables: `Contacts` and `ContactPhoneNumbers`. One contact could have many phone numbers. From this simple sentence we can derive that the `Contacts` table (the "one") is the parent, while `ContactPhoneNumbers` (the "many") represents the children. They can have a few types of relationship:

- One to one

- One to many, or many to one

- Many to many

You'll come across lots and lots of one-to-many relationships, and quite a few many-to-manys, too, but not so much on the one-to-one front. Not that it isn't perfectly valid; it just isn't used as much as the other two. Here's what each of these relationships is used for, along with an example for each.

- **One to one**: Normally used to split a large table into several different subtables. Assume a `Contacts` table like the one we saw earlier. Now assume we need to store lots of nationality information. Rather than add those columns to the `Contacts` table, we could create a `ContactVerificationDetails` table and link it to the `Contacts` table. You do this by specifying the same primary key for both tables. Both tables would have `ContactId` as the primary key, which would be used to link the tables together. You can find the primary key in the table by looking for a column name with a key next to it.

  You can see this layout in Figure 4-8. The "one" sides of the relationship are represented by keys at each end of the adjoining line.

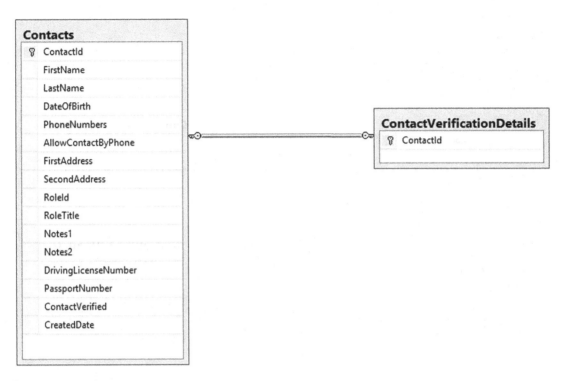

Figure 4-8. *One-to-one relationship diagram*

- **One to many**: This is where a parent record in one table "owns" child records in another table. The records in the "many" table could not exist without the parent. An example here is a record in Contacts as the parent, with a ContactPhoneNumbers table containing the child records. Phone numbers are of no use unless we know to whom they belong.

    We've set this up by defining a different primary key on each table, but including the ContactId column—the parent record's primary key—in both tables. We then define a relationship between those columns to link the tables together.

    Figure 4-9 uses the key we've already seen for the "one" side of the relationship (Contacts), and a figure eight for the "many" side (ContactPhoneNumbers).

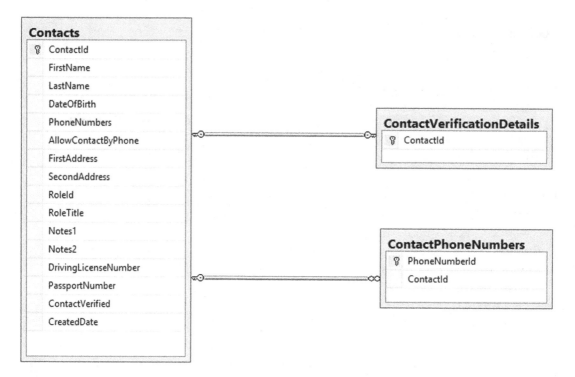

Figure 4-9. *One to many relationship diagram*

- **Many to many**: This is the most complicated, because it requires three tables to implement it correctly. What if Contacts were assigned to Roles? The roles available would stay the same, but they could be assigned to different contacts as they move between different jobs. Indeed, one role may be assigned to multiple contacts—for example, if we had twenty SQL Developers. What we are saying here is one contact can have one or more roles, while one role can be assigned to one or more contacts. We have duality. We cannot link the tables directly, as doing this would necessitate having either Contacts or Roles as the parent—not good, as in this case they are both parents.

  The solution is to add a table in the middle, holding both the Contacts and Roles primary key values as a unique combination. This combination will form a *compound key*: a primary key consisting of more than one column (two in this case). Figure 4-10 shows this implementation.

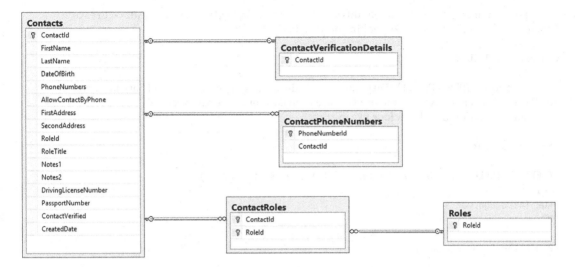

Figure 4-10. *Many-to-many relationship diagram*

Here, we have a one-to-many relationship heading from Contacts to ContactRoles, which is the table facilitating the many-to-many relationship. You can see a key in this table against both ContactId and RoleId; this shows that both columns together are acting as the primary key.

You can see a similar relationship starting at Roles and finishing at ContactRoles, too. Note that both figure eights are linked to ContactRoles, thus defining it as the table holding the many-to-many relationship records.

We're now going to build some tables in our Contacts database and link them together. As we do this you'll see how the concepts we've just covered hang together.

IDENTITY Columns

This has been a big chapter, and we've looked at some really important stuff. We'll continue with our journey into the wacky world of tables in Chapter 5, but we have one more thing to do before our Contacts table is ready for that: we need to add what SQL Server calls an IDENTITY column to it.

An IDENTITY column auto-populates itself with a numeric value. You configure the IDENTITY column's properties to determine what the starting number is and how that number is incremented.

You can create one IDENTITY column per table. IDENTITY columns are almost always created as the primary key. Using an IDENTITY column allows the database to manage primary key values, and removes the responsibility from the developer.

We are going to turn the ContactId column into an IDENTITY column. We'll start assigning values from number 1, and then we'll increment the number by 1 every time. So our first contact should be numbered 1, the second 2, and so on. The IDENTITY column call looks like this:

```
IDENTITY(seed, increment)
```

The seed is the starting number, and the increment dictates what the next number will be. You could have a seed of 2 and an increment of 5, which would generate values of 2, 7, 12, 17 and so on.

Open up our Contacts table script (this should be at c:\temp\sqlbasics\apply\02 - Create Contacts Table.sql). Find the ContactId line and change it to:

```
ContactId INT IDENTITY(1,1),
```

We've added IDENTITY(1,1). These are actually the default values, so we could have just written IDENTITY(). But it is always better to be explicit, as it makes your code easier to read.

Your table script should now look like this:

```
USE AddressBook;

IF EXISTS (SELECT 1 FROM sys.tables WHERE [Name] = 'Contacts')
BEGIN
DROP TABLE dbo.Contacts;
END;

CREATE TABLE dbo.Contacts
(
ContactId INT IDENTITY(1,1),
FirstName VARCHAR(40),
LastName VARCHAR(40),
DateOfBirth DATE,
PhoneNumbers VARCHAR(200),
AllowContactByPhone BIT,
FirstAddress VARCHAR(200),
SecondAddress VARCHAR(200),
RoleId INT,
RoleTitle VARCHAR(200),
Notes1 VARCHAR(200),
Notes2 VARCHAR(200),
DrivingLicenseNumber VARCHAR(40),
PassportNumber VARCHAR(40),
ContactVerified BIT,
CreatedDate DATETIME,
CONSTRAINT PK_Contacts PRIMARY KEY CLUSTERED (ContactId)
);

GO
```

You can easily identify the lines you have changed, as they will have a yellow mark next to them (lines with a green mark are already saved). Press F5 to run this, then open the table for editing (right-click the table in Object Explorer and select **Edit Top 200 Rows**). The eagle-eyed among you may notice the NULL value under ContactId is a slightly different color than the other NULLs. This is because this column's value is now automatically computed for us. Try typing into it—nothing will happen. Now enter a couple of contacts, just the first name and last name (press Enter once you've entered these details for a contact to move to the next line). You'll see the ContactId column's value automatically appear, like in Figure 4-11.

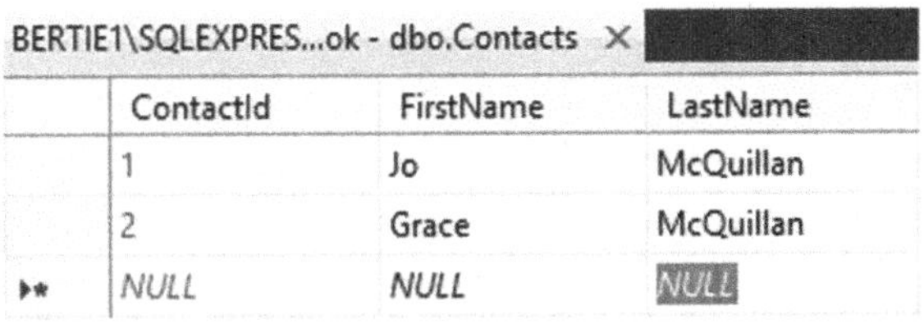

Figure 4-11. *The IDENTITY column in action*

Lovely stuff! Now for one last demonstration. Delete your last contact (so I'd delete ContactId 2 in the table shown above). To delete, right-click the gray box just before the number 2 and choose the **Delete** option from the context menu. You'll be asked to confirm the deletion; click **Yes** to delete the row.

Now, add the row back. What ContactId number do you think will be allocated? Figure 4-12 has the answer:

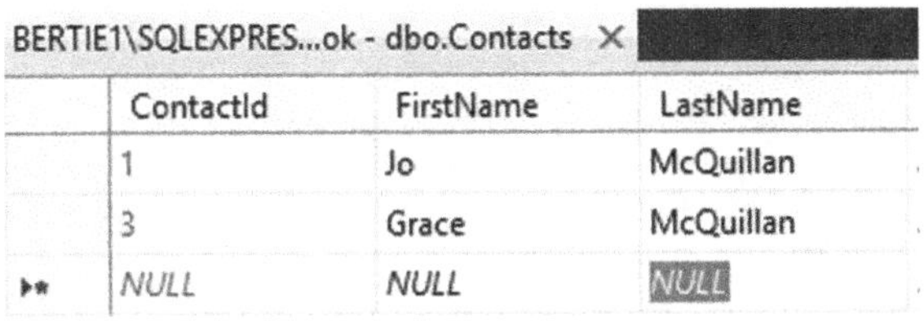

Figure 4-12. *A missing IDENTITY value*

If your answer was 2, I'm afraid you can't pass Go and collect £200 (or $200 if you are in the United States). The IDENTITY column does not reuse values, so the next unused value, 3, is assigned instead.

I highlight this to demonstrate that you should never assume an IDENTITY column's values are sequential. Events like deleting records or failed inserts will cause gaps in your IDENTITY column's values. This isn't a problem, as usually all we are concerned about is the uniqueness of the value.

Now we have everything in place to move on with our design!

Summary

Wow, that was an involved chapter. You've just been through a roller coaster of SQL table details. We began by finding out that a table is the bread and butter of a database, and consists of columns and rows of data. We then met the CREATE TABLE statement and saw how SSMS can be used to create tables.

We had a little look at the data types we can store in tables, such as VARCHAR and INT. We also saw what primary and foreign keys do, why we need them, and how primary keys can be clustered or nonclustered.

Our farewell to this chapter involved finding out what IDENTITY columns do. We ended up with an enhanced version of our Contacts table.

Next, we're going to build on this platform as we continue to refine and improve our **AddressBook** database. Heigh-ho, heigh-ho. . . .

CHAPTER 5

■ ■ ■

Putting Good Tables Together

Now that you have an idea about how tables work, we need to make sure they can store our data in a proper manner. To do this, we use a process called *Database Normalization*. Once this has been applied to our tables, we should have an efficient database structure that minimizes duplicate data. Or to put it simply, everything should just work!

Database Normalization

A database is considered normalized when it meets a set of rules, known as *the three rules of normalization*. All this means is the database is structured in a way that follows recognized good practices and supports efficient data querying. It reduces the amount of duplication in the database and tries to ensure the database is structured correctly.

We'll meet each rule one by one, and apply each to our Contacts table. Normalization should be applied on a table-by-table basis, although you'll often find yourself starting from one table and then normalizing the others from there.

First Normal Form

A table is said to meet First Normal Form (1NF) when it doesn't contain any columns that can be used to store repeating groups. What this means is you should not have any columns that store more than one value, or multiple columns storing similar values. Let's look at our Contacts table in Figure 5-1, populated with some data.

BERTIE1\SQLEXPRES...ok - dbo.Contacts ✕											
ContactId	FirstName	LastName	DateOfBirth	PhoneNumbers	AllowContact...	FirstAddress	SecondAddress	RoleId	RoleTitle	Notes1	
1	Mike	McQuillan	1974-10-03	01200 313131, 07000 100 200	True	Mike's Cool Ho...	Somewhere Ro...	1	Database Person	Mike likes walki...	N
▶*	NULL	NULL	NULL	NULL	NULL	NULL	NULL	NULL	NULL	NULL	P

Figure 5-1. *A Contact record in 1NF*

To add this data, right-click the Contacts table in Object Explorer and click **Edit Top 200 Rows**. A grid will appear and you can type in the values in Figure 5-1. You can enter anything you want; just make sure you specify two phone numbers in the PhoneNumbers column, separated by a comma.

There are two repeating groups in this table. Can you spot them? Take a look at Figure 5-2 for a full list of columns.

- The PhoneNumbers column is being used to store multiple values.

- The Notes1 and Notes2 columns limit us to two notes per contact. This is a poor structure and limits our design.

Column Name	Data Type	Allow Nulls
🔑 ContactId	int	☐
FirstName	varchar(40)	☑
LastName	varchar(40)	☑
DateOfBirth	date	☑
▶ PhoneNumbers	varchar(200)	☑
AllowContactByPhone	bit	☑
FirstAddress	varchar(200)	☑
SecondAddress	varchar(200)	☑
RoleId	int	☑
RoleTitle	varchar(200)	☑
Notes1	varchar(200)	☑
Notes2	varchar(200)	☑
DrivingLicenseNumber	varchar(40)	☑
PassportNumber	varchar(40)	☑
ContactVerified	bit	☑
CreatedDate	datetime	☑
		☐

Column Properties

▲ (General)	
(Name)	PhoneNumbers
Allow Nulls	Yes
Data Type	varchar
Default Value or Binding	
Length	200

Figure 5-2. The SSMS table editor

The PhoneNumbers column is being used to store more than one phone number, so it is a repeating group. You can assume that anything being used to store more than one value is a repeating group. The pluralization of the name is also something of a giveaway. To fix this, we should rename the PhoneNumbers column to PhoneNumber, and then separate the row into two rows.

There are two ways to rename the column: we can use SSMS, or something called a *system stored procedure*. We'll look at both options, as we'll be doing lots of work on stored procedures later in the book.

Let's use SSMS first. Close the table grid if you still have it open—you cannot edit the table if it is open (also, if other users have your table open you'll be prevented from editing it). Right-click the Contacts table and select the **Design** option. The table editor in Figure 5-2 will appear.

You can edit any column in the table here. Clicking a column name will allow you to rename the column, and clicking in a Data Type cell will let you change the data type for a column. The Allow Nulls column determines whether null values can be stored in the column or not. A null value simply means no value is required for this column; it is optional. We'll see much more of NULL in the rest of the book.

You can also change settings by right-clicking columns (see Figure 5-3). If you right-click the little gray square next to ContactId, for example, a dialog appears. From this dialog you can set the selected column as the primary key, insert or delete columns, and create indexes. Note that ContactId has a key next to it, denoting it is already set as the primary key (we did this in Chapter 4). Because of this, the menu option asks us if we want to *remove* the primary key, not set it.

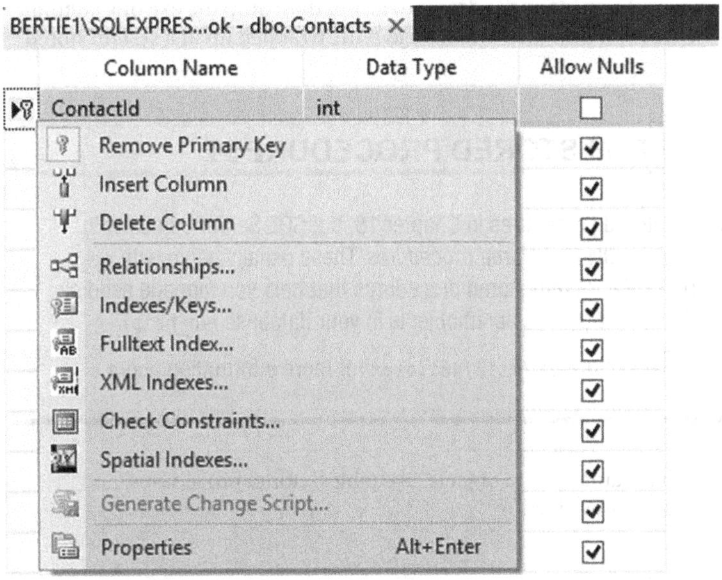

Figure 5-3. *Column options in the SSMS table editor*

For now, we just want to rename the PhoneNumbers column. Click PhoneNumbers and remove the s at the end, so it becomes PhoneNumber. After doing this, go to the **File** menu and click **Save Contacts**, as shown in Figure 5-4.

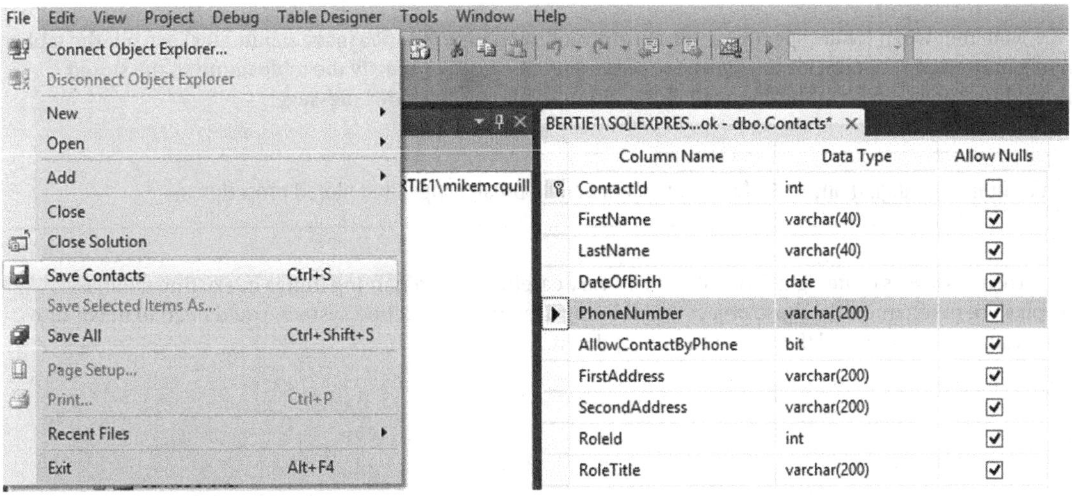

Figure 5-4. *Saving table changes in SSMS*

Note the asterisk in the yellow bar next to dbo.Contacts. This means there are unsaved changes. Once you click **Save Contacts** the asterisk should disappear. Click the **X** to the right of the yellow bar to close the table editor. Now right-click the Contacts table and choose **Edit Top 200 Rows**. The PhoneNumbers column is no more—it is now PhoneNumber!

Remember what we've been talking about though; you can't give a DBA instructions on what they have to do in SSMS—they expect a script! It is not possible using standard SQL statements to rename a column. You would have to create the new column, copy the data into it, and then drop the existing column. Fortunately, we don't need to do this. SQL Server provides a rename feature, wrapped up in a system stored procedure called sp_rename.

WHAT ARE SYSTEM STORED PROCEDURES?

We'll see how you can create your own stored procedures in Chapter 18, but SQL Server comes with a lot of built-in stored procedures, known as *system stored procedures*. These usually begin with sp_, as we've just seen with sp_rename. There are system stored procedures that help you manage sending e-mail from the database, and procedures that tell you about objects in your database (sp_help).

Visit https://msdn.microsoft.com/en-us/library/ms187961.aspx for more information about system stored procedures.

The sp_rename procedure allows us to rename certain objects, like tables, stored procedures, and columns. To put the PhoneNumbers column back we'd write:

```
USE AddressBook;

EXEC sp_rename
@objname = 'dbo.Contacts.PhoneNumber',
@newname = 'PhoneNumbers',
@objtype = 'COLUMN';

GO
```

Note that when we are specifying the existing column name (the @objname parameter), we put the table name in front of it, but not for the @newname parameter. We need to specify the table name so the stored procedure knows which table to look in. After running this you'll see this message:

■ **Caution**   Changing any part of an object name could break scripts and stored procedures.

The message is quite right—you should be very careful about renaming things in existing databases. If you were to rename a database object that is being used in a production system, you'd need to make sure everything that referenced the old name was updated.

We've restored the name to the non-normalized version. You can either design or edit the table to see this. Now we'll correct the name again, by slightly changing the values we are passing to the stored procedure:

```
USE AddressBook;

EXEC sp_rename
@objname = 'dbo.Contacts.PhoneNumbers',
@newname = 'PhoneNumber',
@objtype = 'COLUMN';

GO
```

Don't forget to open `c:\temp\sqlbasics\apply\02 - Create Contacts Table.sql` and rename the PhoneNumbers column to PhoneNumber—we need to keep our script up to date. Fixing the column name in the database will not automatically fix our script for us, and we'll be using that script again very soon.

The PhoneNumber column now meets our 1NF requirements, but the data doesn't. We need to split our current row into two rows, one per phone number. Your data should look like Figure 5-5.

ContactId	FirstName	LastName	DateOfBirth	PhoneNumber	AllowContact...	FirstAddress	SecondAddress	RoleId	RoleTitle	Notes1	Notes2	DrivingLicense...
1	Mike	McQuillan	1974-10-03	01200 313131	True	Mike's Cool Ho...	Somewhere Ro...	1	Database Person	Mike likes walki...	Mike has one d...	1234567
2	Mike	McQuillan	1974-10-03	07000 100 200	True	Mike's Cool Ho...	Somewhere Ro...	1	Database Person	Mike likes walki...	Mike has one d...	1234567
NULL	*NULL*	*NULL*	*NULL*	*NULL*	*NULL*	*NULL*	*NULL*	*NULL*	*NULL*	*NULL*	*NULL*	*NULL*

Figure 5-5. *Contacts data that meets 1NF*

There's a lot of duplication there, especially around the Notes1 and Notes2 columns. Remember that we had two repeating groups: PhoneNumbers and Notes. We'll see what we can do about the repeating Notes group.

Multiple-Column Repeating Groups

The PhoneNumbers column was a single column housing multiple values, so it was easy to bring it to 1NF; all we needed to do was split the rows. You might still think the fix we've made for PhoneNumbers is not quite right, but we'll look at that further on down the road.

The fix for multiple-column repeating groups is not as straightforward. We have two columns:

- Notes1

- Notes2

If you see a table using a similar approach, I can guarantee in no time at all you'll be asked to add a Notes3 column. If you need more than one column to represent the same thing, then you should be putting those columns into their own tables. That's how we'll solve this problem. We'll then link the new table back to the Contacts table via the ContactId primary key. This mechanism will allow us to store as many notes as we want for each contact, because we'll create a one-to-many relationship (one contact can have one or more notes). As we put this into practice we'll see how to:

- create a table using T-SQL,

- create a foreign key using the database diagramming tool, and

- use SSMS to auto-generate the T-SQL for our foreign key.

What do we need in our table? Well, as this is going to be a child table of Contacts, we can immediately see we need a ContactId column. This will not be an IDENTITY column; otherwise we couldn't link it back to the appropriate record in Contacts. We also need a NoteId column of some sort, allowing us to uniquely identify a note. This will be the primary key and will be configured as an IDENTITY column. Finally, we'll need a Notes column to store the actual note details. As both existing Notes columns are VARCHAR(200), that's what we'll use as the data type.

Open a New Query Window (Ctrl+N) and type the following script. We will call this table ContactNotes.

```
USE AddressBook;

IF EXISTS
(SELECT 1 FROM sys.tables WHERE [Name] = 'ContactNotes')
BEGIN
DROP TABLE dbo.ContactNotes;
END;

CREATE TABLE dbo.ContactNotes
(
NoteId INT IDENTITY(1,1),
ContactId INT,
Notes VARCHAR(200),
CONSTRAINT PK_ContactNotes PRIMARY KEY CLUSTERED (NoteId)
);

GO
```

This script doesn't present anything we haven't seen before. We start with what should be our now familiar IF EXISTS...DROP TABLE check. We follow this with a CREATE TABLE statement. Nothing exciting. Now we have two tables: Contacts and ContactNotes.

Save the ContactNotes table script as c:\temp\sqlbasics\apply\03 - Create ContactNotes Table.sql.

We need to join the tables together, so the database can control which notes belong to which contact. We'll do this via the database diagramming tool. This is a useful little item built into SSMS, and it's great for laying out your tables so you can easily see how they relate to each other.

Expand the **AddressBook** database in the Object Explorer. The first item under **AddressBook** should be **Database Diagrams**. Right-click this and choose **New Database Diagram** (shown in Figure 5-6).

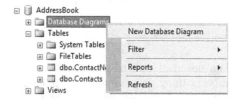

Figure 5-6. *Creating a new database diagram*

When you first click this you may be asked to add database diagramming support to the database. Click **Yes** to do this if you are asked. You should see a screen looking something like Figure 5-7.

Figure 5-7. *Adding tables to a database diagram*

The Add Table dialog in front lists all the tables available in the database. The big blank area behind it is the diagram pane.

REFRESHING THE DIAGRAM TABLES DIALOG

There is a long-standing issue with the Add Table dialog: it doesn't automatically refresh. If we added another table now and then came back to the diagram to add it, the table would not be visible in the Add Table dialog. You need to manually refresh the list by clicking the Refresh button.

To add a table to a diagram, highlight the table name and click the **Add** button. We only have two tables, so just click **Add** twice, then click **Close**. The tables will be displayed on the diagram, which should look similar to Figure 5-8.

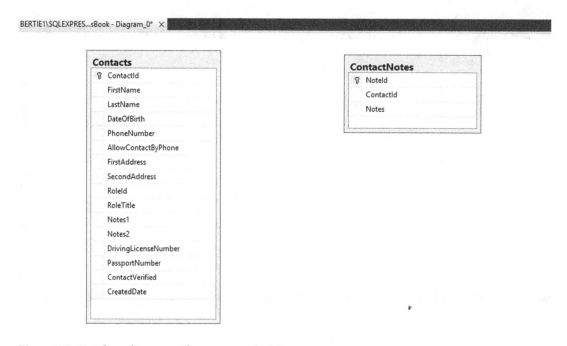

Figure 5-8. *Database diagram with unconnected tables*

The diagramming tool doesn't always lay out tables in the best position, so don't be surprised if the diagram layout is all over the place! You can drag a table anywhere within the diagram pane by dragging it using its title.

At the moment, our two tables are completely unrelated. We are going to change this. We want to make Contacts a parent of ContactNotes. That is, we are saying a ContactNotes record cannot exist unless it is linked to a Contact record. The column both tables share is ContactId. Place your mouse cursor over the grey box next to the ContactId column in the Contacts table. Hold down the left mouse button and drag the cursor over to the ContactId column in the ContactNotes table. A dotted line appears, and when you move the cursor over the ContactId column in ContactNotes it gains a small + sign, denoting a relationship can be created.

Once your cursor is positioned over the ContactId column in ContactNotes, a dotted line will appear. Release the mouse button and wonderful things will happen. Okay, they won't, but you will see a Tables and Columns dialog as per Figure 5-9.

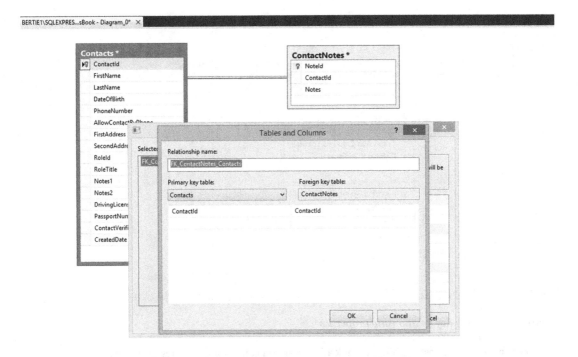

Figure 5-9. *Creating a foreign key in the Database Diagramming tool*

We can see that SQL Server has deduced a relationship name for us: FK_ContactNotes_Contacts. This name is fine and makes sense. FK tells us it is a foreign key, and the rest of it tells us the names of the two tables involved in the relationship, separated by underscores. This is a good convention to use for naming your foreign keys, and it's one we'll return to as we create more relationships.

The dialog also shows us what the **Primary key table** (the parent) is in the relationship, and also the **Foreign key table** (a.k.a. the child). The columns to be linked are shown underneath the tables.

Click the **OK** button. The dialog will disappear and the properties dialog for the Foreign Key Relationship, which has been hiding behind the Tables and Columns dialog, will reveal itself (Figure 5-10).

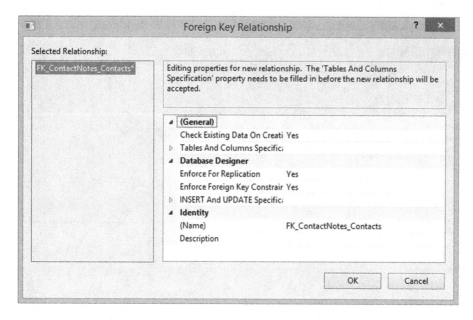

Figure 5-10. *Foreign Key Relationship properties*

There are some interesting things to look at here, as you can tailor quite a few properties for the relationship.

- **Check Existing Data On Creation Or Re-Enabling**: If the tables already have data in them, enabling this option will cause the data to be validated when the relationship is created. If data exists that will not support the relationship (e.g., some ContactIds in ContactNotes that do not exist in Contacts), an error will appear and the relationship will not be created until the offending data has been corrected or removed.

- **INSERT And UPDATE Specification**: If you expand this you'll see:

- **Delete Rule**: No Action

- **Update Rule**: No Action

    This means that if a record in the Contacts table is deleted, any ContactNotes for that contact will not be deleted. Similarly, if the Contacts record is updated the corresponding ContactNotes records will not be updated. We can change this setting. The options are:

- **No Action**: Do nothing. If you try to delete a parent record that has associated children, an error message will be displayed explaining that you cannot delete the parent until the children have been deleted.

- **Cascade**: If the parent record is deleted, the children are deleted. If the parent record is updated, the children are updated, too.

- **Set Null**: If the parent record is deleted, set the foreign key column (ContactId in ContactNotes in this case) to NULL. The same applies to updates if the primary key of the parent table can be manually updated.

- **Set Default**: Same as Set Null, except the column's default value is set on the child records (I'll introduce default column values in the very next chapter). If no default value is set, the foreign key column will be set to NULL.

We won't change any settings. Click **OK** to view your new diagram. You should see the line shown in Figure 5-11 has been added, linking Contacts to ContactNotes.

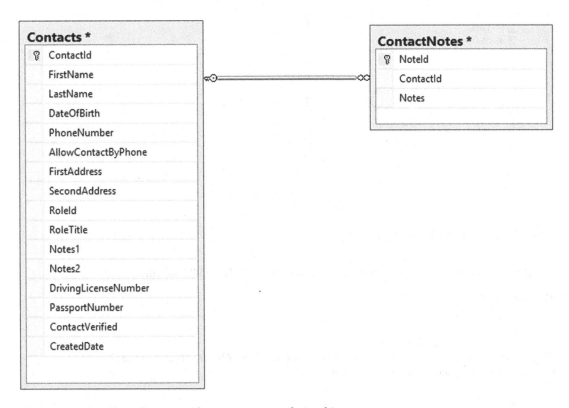

***Figure 5-11.** Database diagram with a one-to-many relationship*

Note the asterisks next to the table names. These indicate the relationship hasn't been saved yet. You should recognize this diagram; it looks similar to the diagrams we saw in the last chapter when we began to investigate foreign keys.

The left-hand side of the line—the Contacts side—begins with a key. This denotes the primary key or parent side of the relationship (the "one" of "one to many"). The right-hand side has the figure eight present, denoting the "many" side—the foreign key or child side.

Go to the **File** menu and click **Save Diagram_0**. You will be asked to give the diagram a name—call it **Contacts**. Click **OK** and you'll see another dialog asking you to confirm the save operation. If you don't want to see this again, uncheck the **Warn about Tables Affected** box in the bottom left-hand corner. Click **Yes** to save the changes. The stars next to the names will disappear and your relationship will be saved.

There's still an issue to resolve: we haven't scripted the creation of our foreign key. Your DBAs won't be pleased with you if you ask them to use the diagramming tool to create a foreign key!

Fortunately, SSMS can come to our rescue here. In the Object Explorer, expand **Databases**, **AddressBook**, **Tables**, **ContactNotes**, and **Keys**. You should see two entries under here: one for the primary key, and one for the foreign key we just created. Right-click the foreign key FK_ContactNotes_Contacts, go to **Script Key as**, then **CREATE To**, and finally **New Query Editor Window**. The full menu is shown in Figure 5-12.

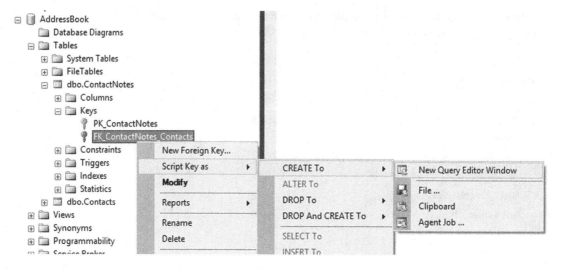

Figure 5-12. *Scripting a foreign key from SSMS*

The query window will appear, populated with a couple of ALTER TABLE statements:

```
USE [AddressBook];
GO

ALTER TABLE [dbo].[ContactNotes]
WITH CHECK ADD CONSTRAINT [FK_ContactNotes_Contacts] FOREIGN KEY([ContactId])
REFERENCES [dbo].[Contacts] ([ContactId]);
GO

ALTER TABLE [dbo].[ContactNotes] CHECK CONSTRAINT [FK_ContactNotes_Contacts];
GO
```

We are only interested in the first ALTER TABLE statement; the second can be ignored. (We'll look at check constraints in Chapter 7.) Tidy up the preceding script so it looks like this:

```
ALTER TABLE dbo.ContactNotes
WITH CHECK
ADD CONSTRAINT FK_ContactNotes_Contacts
FOREIGN KEY (ContactId)
REFERENCES dbo.Contacts (ContactId)
```

We'll have a quick walk through this ALTER TABLE statement:

- ALTER TABLE dbo.ContactNotes tells us that we are altering the ContactNotes table.

- WITH CHECK means the data in the ContactNotes table will be checked to ensure it meets the relationship requirements (i.e., the ContactId column only contains values that are present in the Contacts table).

- ADD CONSTRAINT FK_ContactNotes_Contacts tells SQL Server we want to create a constraint with the name given.

- FOREIGN KEY (ContactId) tells SQL Server the type of constraint we want to create—in this instance, a foreign key. By putting (ContactId) after this we are stating our foreign key will use the ContactId column in the ContactNotes table.

- REFERENCES Contacts (ContactId) completes the statement by adding the parent side of the foreign key relationship. We are linking to the Contacts table via its ContactId column.

We need to cut and paste this statement into our ContactNotes script. We cannot add it to the Contacts script, as when that runs the ContactNotes table would not exist. (We're going to look at the order the scripts run in once we've finished our normalization process.)

Cut the ALTER TABLE statement and paste it into the c:\temp\sqlbasics\apply\03 - Create ContactNotes Table.sql script. Paste the ALTER TABLE statement between the CREATE TABLE and GO statements. The three statements should look like this:

```
CREATE TABLE dbo.ContactNotes
(
NoteId INT IDENTITY(1,1),
ContactId INT,
Notes VARCHAR(200),
CONSTRAINT PK_ContactNotes PRIMARY KEY CLUSTERED (NoteId)
);

ALTER TABLE dbo.ContactNotes
WITH CHECK
ADD CONSTRAINT FK_ContactNotes_Contacts
FOREIGN KEY(ContactId)
REFERENCES dbo.Contacts (ContactId);

GO
```

We're nearly at 1NF! Just one thing left to do: remove the Notes1 and Notes2 columns from the Contacts table. Now that we have the ContactNotes table we don't need them any longer. We can write a quick script to do this. Open a New Query Window and type the following:

```
USE AddressBook;

ALTER TABLE dbo.Contacts
DROP COLUMN Notes1, Notes2;

GO
```

DROPPING COLUMNS IN T-SQL

If you need to drop a column using T-SQL, you use the ALTER TABLE statement, as this code shows. You can specify as many columns as you want when dropping columns in this way, but obviously all columns must exist in the table for the command to execute successfully.

Execute the script and then close it (you don't need to save it). If you close your diagram and reopen it, you'll see the Notes1 and Notes2 columns no longer exist.

We need to remove these columns from the main table script. Open up c:\temp\sqlbasics\apply\02 - Create Contacts Table.sql and remove the following lines:

```
Notes1 VARCHAR(200),
Notes2 VARCHAR(200),
```

This ensures we won't accidentally add the columns back in when we run the scripts in one go. Your CREATE TABLE statement should now look like this:

```
CREATE TABLE dbo.Contacts
(
ContactId INT IDENTITY(1,1),
FirstName VARCHAR(40),
LastName VARCHAR(40),
DateOfBirth DATE,
PhoneNumber VARCHAR(200),
AllowContactByPhone BIT,
FirstAddress VARCHAR(200),
SecondAddress VARCHAR(200),
RoleId INT,
RoleTitle VARCHAR(200),
DrivingLicenseNumber VARCHAR(40),
PassportNumber VARCHAR(40),
ContactVerified BIT,
CreatedDate DATETIME,
CONSTRAINT PK_Contacts PRIMARY KEY CLUSTERED (ContactId)
);
```

Woohoo! We are at 1NF—we've eliminated all repeating groups. Let's step up a level to 2NF.

Second Normal Form

Second Normal Form, or 2NF, is met if the table is in 1NF and all non-key attributes are dependent upon the primary key. That is, all columns in a row depend upon the primary key for their existence. Our primary key is ContactId, so all other columns should be able to be derived from that. FirstName, LastName, DateOfBirth, PhoneNumber, and AllowContactByPhone all seem fine—they certainly belong to a contact. Same for DrivingLicenseNumber, PassportNumber, and ContactVerified (and CreatedDate is just a bit of metadata—we'll discuss that soon). FirstAddress and SecondAddress are dependent upon a contact, although they are a bit ambiguous. Do these represent the first and second lines of an address, as I used them earlier? Or are they supposed to store an address each, such as a home address and a work address? If it's the second option, then this is a repeating group, which we should have resolved during the 1NF phase. For now, we'll assume these are OK.

Next, we have RoleId. I'm not convinced that is reliant on the ContactId. A contact may have a role, but does that mean we care about the RoleId? The next column confirms our thoughts here: RoleTitle. This is what we are interested in for our contacts, but surely RoleTitle is dependent upon RoleId?

RoleId and RoleTitle are preventing us from meeting 2NF. We want to be able to link Contacts to Roles, but we should not be storing these pieces of information in the same table. What we need to do to fix this problem is the following:

- Move RoleId and RoleTitle out into their own table, Roles.

- Create a new table, ContactRoles, to store a ContactId and RoleId.

- Create a one-to-many relationship from Contacts to ContactRoles.

- Create a second one to many relationship from Roles to ContactRoles.

You may be able to tell from this description that we are going to create a many-to-many relationship between Contacts and Roles; that is, one contact may be assigned to multiple roles, and one role may be assigned to multiple Contacts (e.g., your firm might employ 20 SQL developers).

Open a New Query Window and type in the script for the Roles table.

```
USE AddressBook;

IF EXISTS (SELECT 1 FROM sys.tables WHERE [Name] = 'Roles')
BEGIN
DROP TABLE dbo.Roles;
END;

CREATE TABLE dbo.Roles
(
RoleId INT IDENTITY(1,1),
RoleTitle VARCHAR(200),
CONSTRAINT PK_Roles PRIMARY KEY CLUSTERED (RoleId)
);

GO
```

Nothing we haven't seen here before. We add the usual IF EXISTS check, then create the table. We create a clustered primary key, so the roles will be sorted on the disk by RoleId. This makes sense as we are creating a many-to-many relationship using this column.

Run this script and save it as c:\temp\sqlbasics\apply\04 - Create Roles Table.sql. Open another New Query Window and add the script for the ContactRoles table.

```
USE AddressBook;

IF EXISTS (SELECT 1 FROM sys.tables WHERE [Name] = 'ContactRoles')
BEGIN
DROP TABLE dbo.ContactRoles;
END;

CREATE TABLE dbo.ContactRoles
(
ContactId INT,
RoleId INT,
CONSTRAINT PK_ContactRoles PRIMARY KEY CLUSTERED (ContactId, RoleId)
);

GO
```

This is standard stuff until we come to the primary key declaration. The primary key is made up of two columns—a compound key.

What I am saying here is each unique combination of a contact and a role can only exist once in the table. Grace McQuillan can be a developer and she can be a DBA, too, but she can't be a developer and a developer.

Another first for us: this is the first table we've created that contains primary key columns and nothing else. Quite often a many-to-many table will only house primary key columns, as its whole purpose is to provide the link between two other tables.

We're not quite done with this script yet—we need to add the foreign key references to Contacts and Roles. You're going to type these manually this time. Let's do the Contacts foreign key first. After the CREATE TABLE statement (but above the GO statement), type the ALTER TABLE statement.

```
ALTER TABLE dbo.ContactRoles
ADD CONSTRAINT FK_ContactRoles_Contacts
FOREIGN KEY (ContactId)
REFERENCES dbo.Contacts (ContactId)
ON UPDATE NO ACTION
ON DELETE CASCADE;
```

Hmm, this looks slightly different from what we saw earlier. The first four lines are the same, but the last two lines are new. Remember the **INSERT And UPDATE Specification** from the diagramming tool earlier? These lines map to what that was doing.

- **ON UPDATE NO ACTION** states that if we update the Contacts table, we won't make any changes to the ContactRoles table. It is not possible to manually update a ContactId value in the Contacts table (it's an IDENTITY column). As a result, we cannot update it and subsequently cannot update the ContactRoles table via the foreign key, so there is no point in specifying a different option for updates.

- **ON DELETE CASCADE** tells SQL Server to delete any ContactRoles records should we delete the parent contact record.

We'll add a very similar statement to create the relationship between Roles and ContactRoles. Paste this after the previous ALTER TABLE statement (just above the GO):

```
ALTER TABLE dbo.ContactRoles
ADD CONSTRAINT FK_ContactRoles_Roles
FOREIGN KEY (RoleId)
REFERENCES dbo.Roles (RoleId)
ON UPDATE NO ACTION
ON DELETE CASCADE;
```

This is exactly the same as above, except we are linking to Roles instead of Contacts.

Save the script as c:\temp\sqlbasics\apply\05 - Create ContactRoles Table.sql, and run it. You should now have four tables in the database:

- Contacts

- Roles

- ContactNotes

- ContactRoles

We need to remove the RoleId and RoleTitle columns from the Contacts table. Open the script c:\temp\sqlbasics\apply\02 - Create Contacts Table.sql. Remove these two lines:

```
RoleId INT,
RoleTitle VARCHAR(200),
```

Save this script, and open a New Query Window. We need to manually remove the columns from the table. Execute the following DROP COLUMN script in a New Query Window—there's no need to save it:

```
USE AddressBook;

ALTER TABLE dbo.Contacts
DROP COLUMN RoleId, RoleTitle;
```

We'll add our new tables to our diagram, so we can see how everything is linking together. Expand **Database Diagrams** and open the dbo.Contacts diagram we created earlier. The Contacts and ContactNotes tables should already be present. Right-click a white area and click **Add Table**. Click **Refresh** on the dialog that appears, then keep clicking **Add** to add the ContactRoles and Roles tables. Then click the **Close** button.

The diagramming tool is not the greatest when it comes to automatically positioning tables. Drag the tables to a position where you can easily see them and the layout of the relationships. Figure 5-13 shows a nicely laid-out diagram:

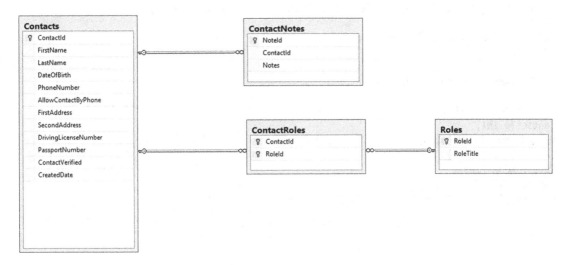

Figure 5-13. *Database diagram with a many-to-many relationship*

You can clearly see how ContactRoles enforces the many-to-many relationship. The Contacts table has drastically changed from our first attempt; we split the columns we've removed from it into three new tables.

We have now reached base camp, also known as 2NF. All non-key attributes are now dependent upon the primary key. Now it's time to head for the summit—yes, it's 3NF time!

Third Normal Form

There are levels of normalization beyond Third Normal Form (3NF), but these are largely theoretical. We'll be stopping our normalization journey here. A table is considered to meet 3NF if it is already in 2NF and every column in the table is dependent upon the primary key and only the primary key. This sounds a bit similar to 2NF, but there is a difference. 2NF was concerned with eliminating columns that depended upon another column, such as RoleTitle being dependent on RoleId. What we are looking for now are columns that don't have a clear dependency on a possible primary key column.

All of our tables except Contacts are pretty simple, and successfully meet 3NF already. Looking at the Contacts table now, it is clear that most columns are dependent upon the ContactId primary key. What are not clear are the dependencies of FirstAddress and SecondAddress.

If we assume FirstAddress should hold the first line of the address and SecondAddress should hold the second line of the address, we can deduce that SecondAddress has a dependency on FirstAddress. This does not meet 3NF. There is an additional issue here: the columns have been named badly, so another developer might think the FirstAddress column stores one entire address (e.g., a home address), and the SecondAddress column should store a second, entirely different address (e.g., a work address).

We need to resolve the address problems. It is entirely possible that a contact may have more than one address, so we need to move address details into their own table. We can then join this table up to Contacts using a one-to-many relationship.

Open a New Query Window and type this script to create the ContactAddresses table:

```
USE AddressBook;

IF EXISTS (SELECT 1 FROM sys.tables WHERE [Name] = 'ContactAddresses')
BEGIN
DROP TABLE dbo.ContactAddresses;
END;

CREATE TABLE dbo.ContactAddresses
(
AddressId INT IDENTITY(1,1),
ContactId INT,
HouseNumber VARCHAR(200),
Street VARCHAR(200),
City VARCHAR(200),
Postcode VARCHAR(20),
CONSTRAINT PK_ContactAddresses PRIMARY KEY NONCLUSTERED (AddressId)
);

GO
```

After the standard IF EXISTS check we create the table. We've made a few changes to how addresses are stored. The AddressId acts as the primary key and ContactId will act as a foreign key, once we've added the relationship. Note that we've declared a NONCLUSTERED primary key here—more on this later. We've then added columns to store HouseNumber, Street, City, and Postcode. This is much more specific than the address detail we've seen so far. We finish up by declaring AddressId as the primary key. All that is left to do is add the foreign key, just above GO:

```
ALTER TABLE dbo.ContactAddresses
ADD CONSTRAINT FK_ContactAddresses_Contacts
FOREIGN KEY (ContactId)
```

```
REFERENCES dbo.Contacts (ContactId)
ON UPDATE NO ACTION
ON DELETE CASCADE;
```

This links ContactAddresses to Contacts. Again, we do nothing on an update, but we will delete any records in ContactAddresses linked to a Contacts record that we delete.

Save this script as c:\temp\sqlbasics\apply\06 - Create ContactAddresses Table.sql. Then press F5 to run it.

We need to open c:\temp\sqlbasics\apply\02 - Create Contacts Table.sql and remove the FirstAddress and SecondAddress lines:

```
FirstAddress VARCHAR(200),
SecondAddress VARCHAR(200),
```

Save and close this. We then need to open up a New Query Window and alter the table to remove the columns (again, no need to save this).

```
USE AddressBook;

ALTER TABLE dbo.Contacts
DROP COLUMN FirstAddress, SecondAddress;
```

Return to your diagram and add this table should you wish. We are now at 3NF and our database is ready to use!

Further Analysis

Let's take a look at the completed diagram in Figure 5-14, so we can see what we have.

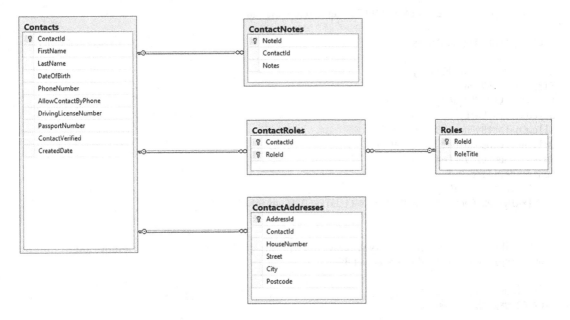

Figure 5-14. *Fully normalized database diagram*

This is looking pretty good. However, I think there are one or two more improvements we can make. These won't affect normalization (all of our tables are now normalized), but they will give our database more flexibility.

Do you remember the first thing we did when we started to normalize our database? We renamed the PhoneNumbers column to the singular PhoneNumber, and we separated out the row with the comma-separated phone numbers into two rows. What this structure does is prevent a contact from having two phone numbers. If we were to do this in the Contacts table now, the same contact would have two different ContactId values, so in essence you would have two different Contacts with the same name, but different phone numbers.

To enhance this structure we will do the following:

- Remove the PhoneNumber column from the Contacts table

- Add a new table, PhoneNumberTypes, to store the types of phone number.

- Add a second new table, ContactPhoneNumbers, to store the phone numbers. We'll add a foreign key to ContactPhoneNumbers to store the type of number.

NEVER PUT EARLY DESIGN DECISIONS OFF

You could argue we don't need to make the PhoneNumber change. But if you spot something during your design phase that you think will become a limitation later on, think about it and fix it straightaway. This will save you a lot of pain in the long run!

Open up the script c:\temp\sqlbasics\apply\02 - Create Contacts Table.sql and remove this line:

```
PhoneNumber VARCHAR(200),
```

This should leave the CREATE TABLE statement looking thus:

```
CREATE TABLE dbo.Contacts
(
ContactId INT IDENTITY(1,1),
FirstName VARCHAR(40),
LastName VARCHAR(40),
DateOfBirth DATE,
AllowContactByPhone BIT,
DrivingLicenseNumber VARCHAR(40),
PassportNumber VARCHAR(40),
ContactVerified BIT,
CreatedDate DATETIME,
CONSTRAINT PK_Contacts PRIMARY KEY CLUSTERED (ContactId)
);
```

Save this, then open a New Query Window and write an ALTER TABLE statement to remove the PhoneNumber column from the Contacts table.

```
ALTER TABLE dbo.Contacts
DROP COLUMN PhoneNumber;
```

Close this window and open another New Query Window, then add this script to create the PhoneNumberTypes table.

```
USE AddressBook;

IF EXISTS (SELECT 1 FROM sys.tables WHERE [Name] = 'PhoneNumberTypes')
BEGIN
DROP TABLE dbo.PhoneNumberTypes;
END;

CREATE TABLE dbo.PhoneNumberTypes
(
PhoneNumberTypeId TINYINT IDENTITY(1,1),
PhoneNumberType VARCHAR(40),
CONSTRAINT PK_PhoneNumberTypes PRIMARY KEY CLUSTERED (PhoneNumberTypeId)
);

GO
```

The CREATE TABLE statement here is pretty simple; the only new thing here is we've used a TINYINT data type instead of an INT. TINYINT can store up to 255 values, so this would allow us 255 phone number types, which is plenty. Save this script as c:\temp\sqlbasics\apply\07 - Create PhoneNumberTypes Table.sql before executing it.

Open another New Query Window and enter this script to create the ContactPhoneNumbers table.

```
USE AddressBook;

IF EXISTS (SELECT 1 FROM sys.tables WHERE [Name] = 'ContactPhoneNumbers')
BEGIN
DROP TABLE dbo.ContactPhoneNumbers;
END;

CREATE TABLE dbo.ContactPhoneNumbers
(
PhoneNumberId INT IDENTITY(1,1),
ContactId INT,
PhoneNumberTypeId TINYINT,
PhoneNumber VARCHAR(30),
CONSTRAINT PK_ContactPhoneNumbers PRIMARY KEY CLUSTERED (PhoneNumberId)
);

ALTER TABLE dbo.ContactPhoneNumbers
ADD CONSTRAINT FK_ContactPhoneNumbers_Contacts
FOREIGN KEY (ContactId)
REFERENCES dbo.Contacts (ContactId)
ON UPDATE NO ACTION
ON DELETE CASCADE;
```

```
ALTER TABLE dbo.ContactPhoneNumbers
ADD CONSTRAINT FK_PhoneNumberTypes_ContactPhoneNumbers
FOREIGN KEY (PhoneNumberTypeId)
REFERENCES dbo.PhoneNumberTypes (PhoneNumberTypeId)
ON UPDATE NO ACTION
ON DELETE CASCADE;

GO
```

Note that the PhoneNumberTypeId column is declared as TINYINT, so it matches the primary key in the PhoneNumberTypes table. We finish off by creating the two relationships we need.

Save this as c:\temp\sqlbasics\apply\08 - Create ContactPhoneNumbers Table.sql. Don't forget to run it!

Looking Things Over

Open the diagram and add the new tables to the diagram. The diagram now looks something like the one shown in Figure 5-15.

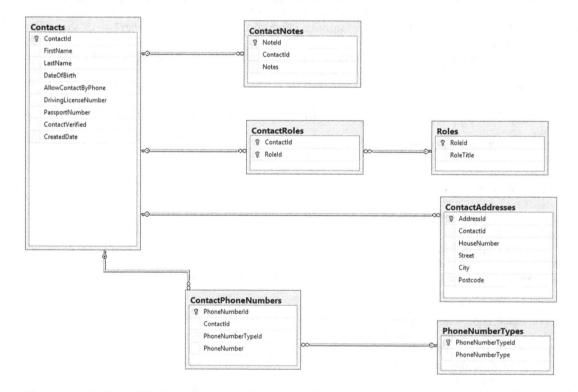

Figure 5-15. *Enhanced database diagram with improved phone numbers*

The ContactPhoneNumbers table looks like it is in the middle of a many-to-many relationship. It isn't. The Contacts table has a one-to-many relationship with ContactPhoneNumbers, via the ContactId column. The PhoneNumberTypes table has a one-to-many relationship with ContactPhoneNumbers via the PhoneNumberTypeId column. It is only a many-to-many relationship if the same column is used in all sides of the relationship.

A Second Enhancement

I mentioned there were one or two enhancements we could make, but so far we've only made one change. Was I telling a fib? Of course not. We can split up our Contacts table into a one-to-one relationship with another table, so we can logically group all of our verification information together. We don't know if the number of verification fields will grow in the future. If they do, having them in their own table will make a lot of sense.

We'll begin by opening c:\temp\sqlbasics\apply\02 - Create Contacts Table.sql. Highlight the lines from DrivingLicenseNumber to ContactVerified, then **cut** them using CTRL-X on your keyboard or the **Edit ➤ Cut** menu option. You can see the highlighted columns in Figure 5-16.

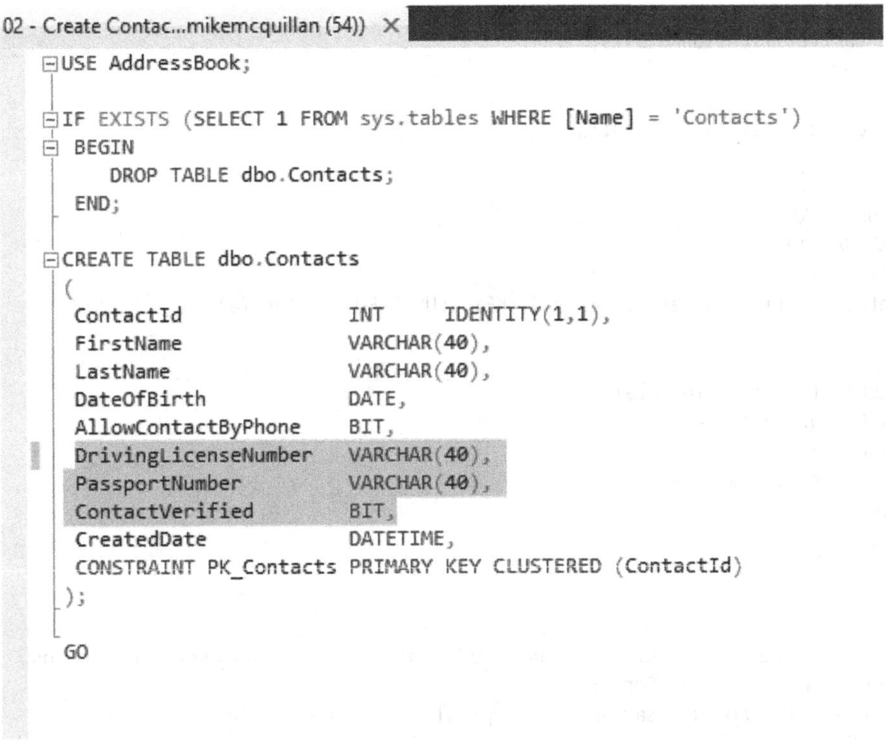

```
02 - Create Contac...mikemcquillan (54)) ×
USE AddressBook;

IF EXISTS (SELECT 1 FROM sys.tables WHERE [Name] = 'Contacts')
 BEGIN
     DROP TABLE dbo.Contacts;
 END;

CREATE TABLE dbo.Contacts
 (
   ContactId              INT     IDENTITY(1,1),
   FirstName              VARCHAR(40),
   LastName               VARCHAR(40),
   DateOfBirth            DATE,
   AllowContactByPhone    BIT,
   DrivingLicenseNumber   VARCHAR(40),
   PassportNumber         VARCHAR(40),
   ContactVerified        BIT,
   CreatedDate            DATETIME,
   CONSTRAINT PK_Contacts PRIMARY KEY CLUSTERED (ContactId)
 );

 GO
```

Figure 5-16. *Highlighting columns for cutting*

The CREATE TABLE statement should be left looking like this:

```
CREATE TABLE dbo.Contacts
(
ContactId INT IDENTITY(1,1),
FirstName VARCHAR(40),
LastName VARCHAR(40),
DateOfBirth DATE,
AllowContactByPhone BIT,
CreatedDate DATETIME,
CONSTRAINT PK_Contacts PRIMARY KEY CLUSTERED (ContactId)
);
```

Open up a New Query Window and type the following script to create the ContactVerificationDetails table. You can paste most of the columns in.

```
USE AddressBook;

IF EXISTS (SELECT 1 FROM sys.tables WHERE [Name] ='ContactVerificationDetails')
BEGIN
DROP TABLE dbo.ContactVerificationDetails;
END;

CREATE TABLE dbo.ContactVerificationDetails
(
ContactId INT,
DrivingLicenseNumber VARCHAR(40),
PassportNumber VARCHAR(40),
ContactVerified BIT,
CONSTRAINT PK_ContactVerificationDetails PRIMARY KEY CLUSTERED (ContactId)
);

ALTER TABLE dbo.ContactVerificationDetails
ADD CONSTRAINT FK_ContactVerificationDetails_Contacts
FOREIGN KEY (ContactId)
REFERENCES dbo.Contacts (ContactId)
ON UPDATE NO ACTION
ON DELETE CASCADE;

GO
```

Nothing we haven't seen before. Note that we declare the ContactId as the primary key, which means we'll have a one-to-one relationship to the Contacts table.

Run this script to create the table, and save it as c:\temp\sqlbasics\09 - Create ContactVerificationDetails Table.sql.

Open a New Query Window and execute this statement to remove the transferred columns from the Contacts table:

```
ALTER TABLE dbo.Contacts
DROP COLUMN DrivingLicenseNumber, PassportNumber, ContactVerified;
```

Close this script without saving it. Now open our `Contacts` diagram and add the `ContactVerificationDetails` table to it. Figure 5-17 shows our completed diagram, with the entire database structure.

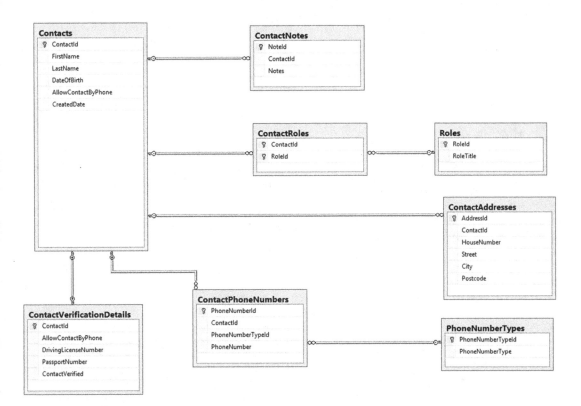

Figure 5-17. *Completed database diagram*

Summary

Well, we've covered a huge amount of ground in the last two chapters. Hopefully, you can now see how vital it is that you correctly structure the tables and how important it is that you take some time to think about how you want your data to be stored.

We're still not quite done with tables, although it's fair to say we've completed the heavy lifting. We've created a bunch of scripts. Now we need to figure out how we can easily execute them in one go. We also need to create some rollback scripts, which will allow us to put the server back to how it was, should we need to.

■ ■ ■

CHAPTER 6

Automating Deployment with SQLCMD

So far, we've created nine scripts: one to create the database, and eight more containing tables and foreign key relationships. You don't want to ask your DBAs to load and execute each script individually. This is where the SQLCMD tool comes in—you can create a simple script that will allow users to execute all of your scripts with a simple press of F5.

You can also use SQLCMD to roll back your changes if necessary, so once you've created the apply SQLCMD script, we'll look at creating some rollback scripts.

What Is SQLCMD?

You were very briefly introduced to SQLCMD way back in Chapter 1. It's a tool, supplied as part of SQL Server, that allows you to manage various aspects of your server. You can also execute T-SQL commands via this tool. SQLCMD can be used in two ways: via the command line, or via SQLCMD Mode in SSMS. We'll use the latter.

We want to use SQLCMD in an extremely simple manner; our intention is to do nothing more than execute multiple scripts in one go. This is the absolute minimum of what SQLCMD is capable of and it's well worth investigating further. Visit https://msdn.microsoft.com/en-us/library/ms162773.aspx for more details on what SQLCMD can do.

Why We Need a SQLCMD Script

Assume we need to make a change to script 02 - Create Contacts Table.sql. We want to rename a column. Open c:\temp\sqlbasics\02 - Create Contacts Table.sql and run it. You'll see a couple of error messages:

```
Msg 3726, Level 16, State 1, Line 5
Could not drop object 'Contacts' because it is referenced by a FOREIGN KEY constraint.
Msg 2714, Level 16, State 6, Line 8
There is already an object named 'Contacts' in the database.
```

The first error happens because the Contacts table cannot be dropped. It cannot be dropped because the Contacts table is linked to other tables via foreign keys. The other tables must be dropped before the Contacts table can be dropped.

The second error happens because the CREATE TABLE statement has tried to execute. It failed because the table already exists, as the table wasn't dropped in the first place.

Close the 02 - Create Contacts Table.sql script, and open a New Query Window.

Rollback Scripts

We've already seen that we cannot run the Contacts Table script, and it's fair to assume there will be other scripts in our apply folder that will not work at the moment. So before we create our SQLCMD scripts we'll create our rollback scripts.

Open Windows Explorer and navigate to c:\temp\sqlbasics\rollback. You should have one script in there, 01 - Create AddressBook Database Rollback.sql. We created this in Chapter 3 to roll back the database creation. It looks like this:

```
USE Master;

IF EXISTS (SELECT 1 FROM sys.databases WHERE [name] = 'AddressBook')
BEGIN
DROP DATABASE AddressBook;
END

GO
```

It does nothing more than check if the **AddressBook** database exists. If it does, the database is dropped.

We need to create eight more rollback scripts, one for each of our table scripts. We'll start from script 02. In the New Query Window you opened, type the rollback script:

```
USE AddressBook;

IF EXISTS (SELECT 1 FROM sys.tables WHERE [Name] = 'Contacts')
BEGIN
DROP TABLE dbo.Contacts;
END;

GO
```

This is pretty much the same as the apply script, except it doesn't have the CREATE TABLE statement in it. Save this script as c:\temp\sqlbasics\rollback\02 - Create Contacts Table Rollback.sql. Then, for all the other scripts, follow these steps:

- Open New Query Window

- Enter the script:

  ```
  USE AddressBook;

  IF EXISTS (SELECT 1 FROM sys.tables WHERE [Name] = 'ContactNotes')
  BEGIN
  DROP TABLE dbo.ContactNotes;
  END;

  GO
  ```

- Save the script as c:\temp\sqlbasics\rollback\03 - Create ContactNotes Table Rollback.sql

- Open New Query Window

- Enter the script:

```
USE AddressBook;

IF EXISTS (SELECT 1 FROM sys.tables WHERE [Name] = 'Roles')
BEGIN
DROP TABLE dbo.Roles;
END;

GO
```

- Save the script as c:\temp\sqlbasics\rollback\04 - Create Roles Table Rollback.sql

- Open New Query Window

- Enter the script:

```
USE AddressBook;

IF EXISTS (SELECT 1 FROM sys.tables WHERE [Name] = 'ContactRoles')
BEGIN
DROP TABLE dbo.ContactRoles;
END;

GO
```

- Save the script as c:\temp\sqlbasics\rollback\05 - Create ContactRoles Table Rollback.sql

- Open New Query Window

- Enter the script:

```
USE AddressBook;

IF EXISTS (SELECT 1 FROM sys.tables WHERE [Name] = 'ContactAddresses')
BEGIN
DROP TABLE dbo.ContactAddresses;
END;

GO
```

- Save the script as c:\temp\sqlbasics\rollback\06 - Create ContactAddresses Table Rollback.sql

- Open New Query Window

- Enter the script:

```
USE AddressBook;

IF EXISTS (SELECT 1 FROM sys.tables WHERE [Name] = 'PhoneNumberTypes')
BEGIN
DROP TABLE dbo.PhoneNumberTypes;
END;

GO
```

- Save the script as c:\temp\sqlbasics\rollback\07 - Create PhoneNumberTypes Table Rollback.sql

- Open New Query Window

- Enter the script:

```
USE AddressBook;

IF EXISTS (SELECT 1 FROM sys.tables WHERE [Name] = 'ContactPhoneNumbers')
BEGIN
DROP TABLE dbo.ContactPhoneNumbers;
END;

GO
```

- Save the script as c:\temp\sqlbasics\rollback\08 - Create ContactPhoneNumbers Table Rollback.sql

- Open New Query Window

- Enter the script:

```
USE AddressBook;

IF EXISTS (SELECT 1 FROM sys.tables WHERE [Name] = 'ContactVerificationDetails')
BEGIN
DROP TABLE dbo.ContactVerificationDetails;
END;

GO
```

- Save the script as c:\temp\sqlbasics\rollback\09 - Create ContactVerificationDetails Table Rollback.sql

That was a fair bit of typing. If you look at your rollback folder in Windows Explorer you should see nine files, which are shown in Figure 6-1.

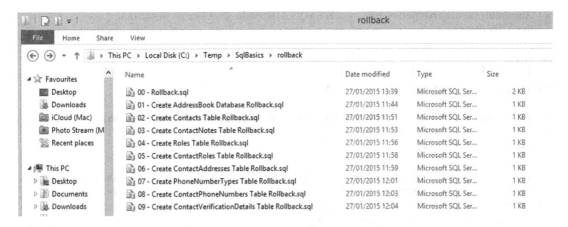

Figure 6-1. Rollback files

We have nine apply files and nine rollback files. Now we can look at creating a SQLCMD file for rollback purposes.

Creating the SQLCMD Rollback Script

In SSMS, press Ctrl+N to open a New Query Window. Go to the **Query** menu and click the **SQLCMD Mode** option you can see in Figure 6-2.

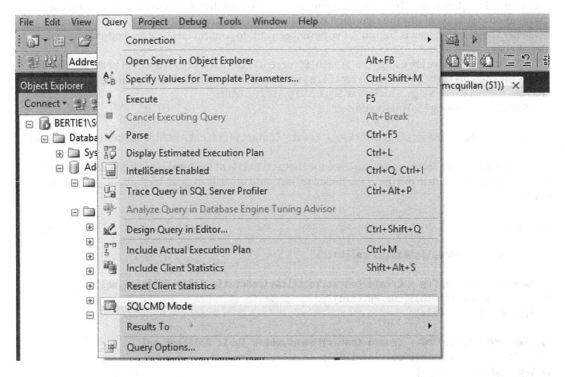

Figure 6-2. Turning on SQLCMD mode in SSMS

Absolutely nothing happens when you click SQLCMD mode. Don't worry about that.
Type this code:

```
USE master;
```

```
:setvar path "C:\temp\sqlbasics\rollback\"
```

```
:setvar currentFile "09 - Create ContactVerificationDetails Table Rollback.sql"
PRINT 'Executing $(path)$(currentFile)';
:r $(path)$(currentFile)
```

The USE statement we've seen before, but everything else is brand new. The lines beginning with a colon are bold (they will be highlighted gray on screen) and do not end with a semicolon. This shows they are SQLCMD commands. If you turn SQLCMD mode off the highlighting will disappear and red underlines will appear instead, showing the code is not valid T-SQL.

The first line begins with :setvar. This declares a variable, called path, and we assign the value c:\temp\sqlbasics\rollback\ to it. This holds the path in which our rollback files reside. The end \ is very important, as we'll concatenate the file name to the end of the path when we execute the script in a moment.

The next three lines are grouped together, indicating they all act together to perform an action. We start with another :setvar, this time setting the name of the file we want to process—in this case, script 09 to roll back the creation of the ContactVerificationDetails table. The following line starts with :r. This is a little more difficult to figure out by looking at it; :setvar can be seen as a shortened version of *set variable*. What could :r mean?

Next, we have a PRINT statement. This just outputs the contents of the variables. It is here to tell us what the :r statement is going to do.

Finally, we have the :r command. :r appends the contents of the specified file to the statement cache. In other words, SQL Server will execute the contents of the file provided. This tells us what :r does, but it gives us no indication of why the command is called :r. My best guess is *r* stands for "run" (one other developer I know says it means "return"). I've never been able to confirm this, so if anybody has any other ideas feel free to e-mail me!

The :r command we are using—:r $(path)$(currentFile)—will obtain the path to the SQL file by joining the contents of the path and currentFile variables. Note that we had to wrap the variable names in brackets, preceded by a $ sign. This is how SQLCMD parses variables.

Run this by pressing F5. You should see:

```
Executed C:\temp\SqlBasics\rollback\09 - Create ContactVerificationDetails Table Rollback.sql
```

If you refresh your Tables node, you'll see the ContactVerificationDetails table has disappeared. We'll complete this script to roll the entire database back. Add the following under the code you've already entered.

```
USE master;
```

```
:setvar path "C:\temp\SqlBasics\rollback\"
```

```
:setvar currentFile "09 - Create ContactVerificationDetails Table Rollback.sql"
PRINT 'Executing $(path)$(currentFile)';
:r $(path)$(currentFile)
```

```
:setvar currentFile "08 - Create ContactPhoneNumbers Table Rollback.sql"
PRINT 'Executing $(path)$(currentFile)';
:r $(path)$(currentFile)
```

```
:setvar currentFile "07 - Create PhoneNumberTypes Table Rollback.sql"
PRINT 'Executing $(path)$(currentFile)';
:r $(path)$(currentFile)

:setvar currentFile "06 - Create ContactAddresses Table Rollback.sql"
PRINT 'Executing $(path)$(currentFile)';
:r $(path)$(currentFile)

:setvar currentFile "05 - Create ContactRoles Table Rollback.sql"
PRINT 'Executing $(path)$(currentFile)';
:r $(path)$(currentFile)

:setvar currentFile "04 - Create Roles Table Rollback.sql"
PRINT 'Executing $(path)$(currentFile)';
:r $(path)$(currentFile)

:setvar currentFile "03 - Create ContactNotes Table Rollback.sql"
PRINT 'Executing $(path)$(currentFile)';
:r $(path)$(currentFile)

:setvar currentFile "02 - Create Contacts Table Rollback.sql"
PRINT 'Executing $(path)$(currentFile)';
:r $(path)$(currentFile)

:setvar currentFile "01 - Create AddressBook Database Rollback.sql"
PRINT 'Executing $(path)$(currentFile)';
:r $(path)$(currentFile)

PRINT 'All rollback scripts successfully executed.';

USE master;
```

This is the same code we've already seen, just repeated for each file we want to process. Note we're processing the files in reverse order, 09 to 01. Remember this is a rollback, so we need to remove each database object in the order we added it. When we apply, we'll apply from 01 to 09, so we need to roll back from 09 to 01.

THE IMPORTANCE OF ORDER

Numbering your scripts is completely optional, but it is a really good idea and will make managing script execution much easier. By numbering, you can clearly see the order in which scripts should be executed. Likewise, you can simply reverse the numeric order to create a rollback script.

We finish up with a USE master statement. This gives the focus back to the master database at the end of the script.

Save this script to `c:\temp\sqlbasics\rollback\00 - Rollback.sql`. When you feel brave enough, run it—this will delete the entire **AddressBook** database. Figure 6-3 shows a successful execution of the rollback script.

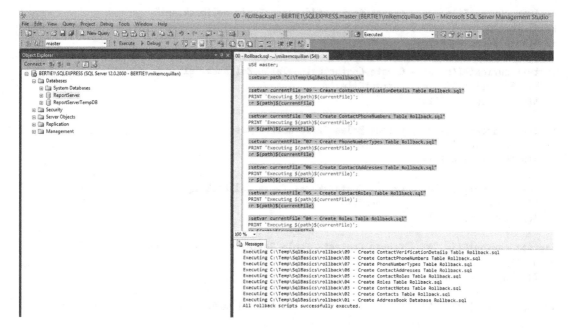

Figure 6-3. *Executing a rollback script in SQLCMD mode*

On to the apply version!

Creating the SQLCMD Apply Script

This is pretty much exactly the same script, except we point it at the apply path and execute the scripts in ascending numerical order. It should be obvious now why we've been numbering the scripts as we go: it makes it easy to identify the order in which they should be executed.

Here's the apply script; type this into a New Query Window. Don't forget to turn on SQLCMD mode.

```
USE master;

:setvar path "C:\temp\SqlBasics\apply\"

:setvar currentFile "01 - Create AddressBook Database.sql"
PRINT 'Executing $(path)$(currentFile)';
:r $(path)$(currentFile)

:setvar currentFile "02 - Create Contacts Table.sql"
PRINT 'Executing $(path)$(currentFile)';
:r $(path)$(currentFile)
```

```
:setvar currentFile "03 - Create ContactNotes Table.sql"
PRINT 'Executing $(path)$(currentFile)';
:r $(path)$(currentFile)

PRINT 'Executing $(path)$(currentFile)';
:setvar currentFile "04 - Create Roles Table.sql"
:r $(path)$(currentFile)

:setvar currentFile "05 - Create ContactRoles Table.sql"
PRINT 'Executing $(path)$(currentFile)';
:r $(path)$(currentFile)

:setvar currentFile "06 - Create ContactAddresses Table.sql"
PRINT 'Executing $(path)$(currentFile)';
:r $(path)$(currentFile)

:setvar currentFile "07 - Create PhoneNumberTypes Table.sql"
PRINT 'Executing $(path)$(currentFile)';
:r $(path)$(currentFile)

:setvar currentFile "08 - Create ContactPhoneNumbers Table.sql"
PRINT 'Executing $(path)$(currentFile)';
:r $(path)$(currentFile)

:setvar currentFile "09 - Create ContactVerificationDetails Table.sql"
PRINT 'Executing $(path)$(currentFile)';
:r $(path)$(currentFile)

PRINT 'All apply scripts successfully executed.';

USE master;
```

Save this as c:\temp\sqlbasics\apply\00 - Apply.sql. Run it and, as in Figure 6-4, your database will magically be restored!

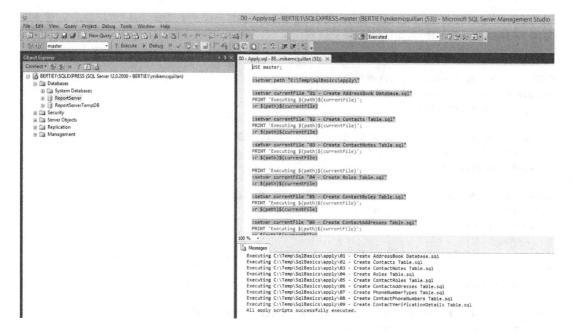

Figure 6-4. Executing an apply script in SQLCMD mode

You can run the apply and rollback scripts as many times as you want. Run the rollback to drop the database, then run the apply to restore it. Repeat this as many times as you like!

Summary

Thanks to SQLCMD, you now have the ability to create and drop our database with ease. SQLCMD can do much more than you've seen here and is a tool that you should learn to love. Read up on the MSDN documentation at https://msdn.microsoft.com/en-us/library/ms162773.aspx and turn yourself into a SQLCMD expert!

We will now finish off our tables, by ensuring only good data can be entered into the tables. We'll use a combination of NULL and constraints to do this.

■ ■ ■

CHAPTER 7

NULLs and Table Constraints

You've done brilliantly. You've created an entire database with a normalized table structure. You've even created specialized scripts so you can build or drop the database easily. Now we're going to look at how we can help to ensure—as far as we can—that only good data is entered into our tables. As you might imagine, SQL Server provides a few tools that can help. We're going to look at the following:

- NULLS: what they are, and how we can specify whether a column supports them or not

- **Default Constraints**: why and how to use them

- **Table Constraints**: You've actually already met some of these, when we created primary keys and foreign keys in Chapter 4 There are two other types we'll look at: CHECK and UNIQUE.

NULL Constraints

I've mentioned NULL a few times in this book now. But just what is NULL? NULL is nothing. Nada. Zip. NULL means no value has been provided for a particular column. Look at this record in Figure 7-1.

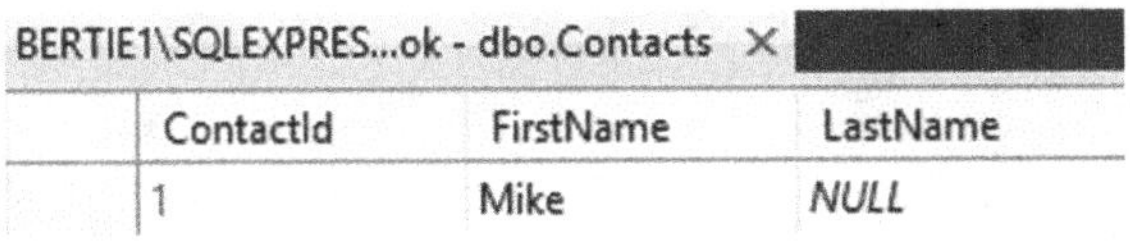

BERTIE1\SQLEXPRES...ok - dbo.Contacts ✕		
ContactId	FirstName	LastName
1	Mike	NULL

Figure 7-1. A record with a NULL LastName value

We have a record here with a FirstName, but no LastName. It's important to understand that this is very different from the record in Figure 7-2.

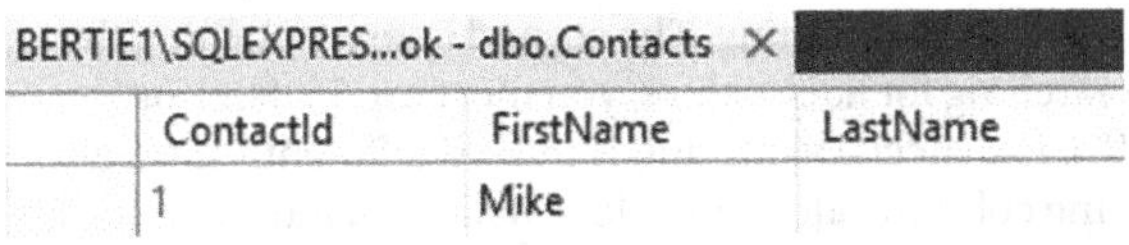

BERTIE1\SQLEXPRES...ok - dbo.Contacts ✕		
ContactId	FirstName	LastName
1	Mike	

Figure 7-2. A record with an empty-string LastName value

107

This record has a blank LastName. NULL means no value has been provided for LastName; blank means an empty string has been provided. Let's see how these values affect our queries. If you want to find records for which a LastName has *not* been specified, use the special IS keyword, as the script in Figure 7-3 demonstrates.

```
SQLQuery12.sql - B...ikemcquillan (51))*  ×
USE AddressBook;

SELECT ContactId, FirstName, LastName
    FROM dbo.Contacts
WHERE LastName IS NULL;
```

Figure 7-3. *Filtering for NULL values using* IS NULL

As Figure 7-4 shows, we can simply use the = operator if a value has been specified, such as an empty string.

```
SQLQuery12.sql - B...ikemcquillan (51))*  ×
USE AddressBook;

SELECT ContactId, FirstName, LastName
    FROM dbo.Contacts
WHERE LastName IS NULL;

SELECT ContactId, FirstName, LastName
    FROM dbo.Contacts
WHERE LastName = ''
```

100 % ▾

| Results | Messages |

ContactId	FirstName	LastName

	ContactId	FirstName	LastName
1	1	Mike	

Figure 7-4. *Filtering for empty string values using* =

The first query, which returned a record before, now returns nothing. The second query, matching the empty string, successfully returns the record. When searching for NULL values, you must use IS NULL or IS NOT NULL—you cannot use = NULL or != NULL. NULL is a special value and is treated differently from all other values. Be aware that if you want to change a string column value in SSMS to NULL, you must either type NULL in uppercase or press Ctrl+0 (make sure you select the column first).

NULL = NULL

You might think NULL = NULL would return TRUE. It doesn't, because NULL means an indistinct value. So NULL never equals NULL. The only way you can make NULL = NULL at the moment is to run the command SET ANSI_NULLS OFF, which will turn off ISO-compliant treatment of NULL in SQL Server. This functionality is deprecated and will be disabled in a future version of SQL Server, so using it is not advised. Also, NULL doesn't equal NULL, so you shouldn't use it anyway!

Don't worry about the details of these queries—you'll be introduced to them soon enough. For now, just remember that NULL means no value has been provided. In a Contacts table I don't think it's a good idea to allow NULL values for the FirstName and LastName columns—surely every contact has a name? Let's quickly revisit the CREATE TABLE statement for the Contacts table:

```
CREATE TABLE dbo.Contacts
(
ContactId INT IDENTITY(1,1),
FirstName VARCHAR(40),
LastName VARCHAR(40),
DateOfBirth DATE,
AllowContactByPhone BIT,
CreatedDate DATETIME,
CONSTRAINT PK_Contacts PRIMARY KEY CLUSTERED (ContactId)
);
```

What we want to do here is force the user to supply FirstName and LastName values. We don't necessarily need a DateOfBirth value, so we'll allow NULLs for that. We probably do want values to be supplied for the other columns. Open up script 02 and change the CREATE TABLE statement so it looks like this:

```
CREATE TABLE dbo.Contacts
(
ContactId INT IDENTITY(1,1) NOT NULL,
FirstName VARCHAR(40) NOT NULL,
LastName VARCHAR(40) NOT NULL,
DateOfBirth DATE NULL,
AllowContactByPhone BIT NOT NULL,
CreatedDate DATETIME NOT NULL,
CONSTRAINT PK_Contacts PRIMARY KEY CLUSTERED (ContactId)
);
```

We've added either NULL or NOT NULL to the end of each column declaration. The DateOfBirth column has NULL next to it, denoting NULL values are allowed. The other columns all specify NOT NULL, which means a value must be supplied when a row is being inserted into the table.

Save the script. Then run the 00 - Rollback.sql script in the rollback folder, and then run the 00 - Apply.sql file in the apply folder (don't forget to turn on SQLCMD mode before running these). The database will be recreated, along with the NULL constraints on the Contacts table. Refresh the **AddressBook** database in the Object Explorer, find the Contacts table, and open it for editing (right-click the Contacts table and choose **Edit Top 200 Rows**).

Enter a name into the FirstName column, and then press Enter. Lo and behold, the error message in Figure 7-5 is displayed.

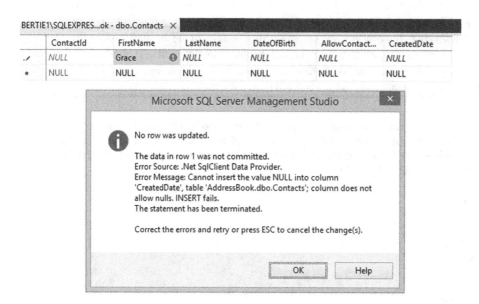

Figure 7-5. *NOT NULL constraint preventing a new row insert*

This is interesting—SQL Server would not let us add our new row. The error message states it's because no value was provided for the CreatedDate column. We'll keep seeing these errors until all columns that do not allow NULLs have been populated. If you populate all columns except DateOfBirth you should be allowed to add your row. The AllowContactByPhone column can accept TRUE, FALSE, 1 (for TRUE), or 0 (for FALSE). The CreatedDate column requires a date, in the format YYYY-MM-DD. You can add a time, too if you want, in the format YYYY-MM-DD HH:MM:SS. Once all values have been correctly specified you'll see a new row, just like the one in Figure 7-6.

	ContactId	FirstName	LastName	DateOfBirth	AllowContactByPhone	CreatedDate
	2	Grace	McQuillan	*NULL*	False	2015-01-27 23:11:23.000

BERTIE1\SQLEXPRES...ok - dbo.Contacts ✕

Figure 7-6. *Adding a new row after creating NULL constraints*

That's all there is to NULL constraints. We didn't need to specify NULL on the ContactId column, as it's a primary key and is therefore required anyway. But as I've said many times already, always be explicit so it's obvious what you are trying to do.

We need to add appropriate NULL constraints for the other tables in our database. Modify the apply scripts as directed (no need to touch the rollback scripts).

- 03 - Create ContactNotes Table.sql

  All columns should be NOT NULL—there isn't much point in a NULL note.

```
CREATE TABLE dbo.ContactNotes
(
NoteId INT IDENTITY(1,1) NOT NULL,
ContactId INT NOT NULL,
Notes VARCHAR(200) NOT NULL,
CONSTRAINT PK_ContactNotes PRIMARY KEY CLUSTERED (NoteId)
);
```

- 04 - Create Roles Table.sql

  Again, make all columns NOT NULL. A role must have a title and an ID.

```
CREATE TABLE dbo.Roles
(
RoleId INT IDENTITY(1,1) NOT NULL,
RoleTitle VARCHAR(200) NOT NULL,
CONSTRAINT PK_Roles PRIMARY KEY CLUSTERED (RoleId)
);
```

- 05 - Create ContactRoles Table.sql

  Yet again, all columns should be NOT NULL. The many-to-many link record is useless without both values.

```
CREATE TABLE dbo.ContactRoles
(
ContactId INT NOT NULL,
RoleId INT NOT NULL,
CONSTRAINT PK_ContactRoles PRIMARY KEY CLUSTERED (ContactId, RoleId)
);
```

- 06 - Create ContactAddresses Table.sql

  It's difficult to determine the values a user may provide for an address, so we'll make all of the address columns optional. Just the keys are required.

```
CREATE TABLE dbo.ContactAddresses
(
AddressId INT IDENTITY(1,1) NOT NULL,
ContactId INT NOT NULL,
HouseNumber VARCHAR(200) NULL,
Street VARCHAR(200) NULL,
City VARCHAR(200) NULL,
Postcode VARCHAR(20) NULL,
CONSTRAINT PK_ContactAddresses PRIMARY KEY NONCLUSTERED (AddressId)
);
```

- 07 - Create PhoneNumberTypes Table.sql

  There's no point in having a NULL phone number type, so all columns here are required.

  ```
  CREATE TABLE dbo.PhoneNumberTypes
  (
  PhoneNumberTypeId TINYINT IDENTITY(1,1) NOT NULL,
  PhoneNumberType VARCHAR(40) NOT NULL,
  CONSTRAINT PK_PhoneNumberTypes PRIMARY KEY CLUSTERED (PhoneNumberTypeId)
  );
  ```

- 08 - Create ContactPhoneNumbers Table.sql

  Again, a phone number record is useless without a phone number! We want all columns populated.

  ```
  CREATE TABLE dbo.ContactPhoneNumbers
  (
  PhoneNumberId INT IDENTITY(1,1) NOT NULL,
  ContactId INT NOT NULL,
  PhoneNumberTypeId TINYINT NOT NULL,
  PhoneNumber VARCHAR(30) NOT NULL
  CONSTRAINT PK_ContactPhoneNumbers PRIMARY KEY CLUSTERED (PhoneNumberId)
  );
  ```

- 09 - Create ContactVerificationDetails Table.sql

  Our final table, and this has some optional values. We don't know what the user will enter for verification purposes, so we'll make DrivingLicenseNumber and PassportNumber both optional.

  ```
  CREATE TABLE dbo.ContactVerificationDetails
  (
  ContactId INT NOT NULL,
  DrivingLicenseNumber VARCHAR(40) NULL,
  PassportNumber VARCHAR(40) NULL,
  ContactVerified BIT NOT NULL
  CONSTRAINT PK_ContactVerificationDetails PRIMARY KEY CLUSTERED (ContactId));
  ```

Excellent! Close all open windows and roll back the database (execute the 00 - Rollback.sql script). In certain circumstances this may fail—SSMS keeps a background process connected to the database, preventing it from being dropped. If you see an error saying **Cannot drop database AddressBook because it is currently in use**, you need to close SSMS, reopen it, open the rollback script, and then execute it again. This time it will work fine.

Once you've successfully rolled back, open and run 00 - Apply.sql. The database is now locked down to prevent NULL values where necessary. Do you see how easy SQL Server makes it for you to tighten up data entry?

And we're not finished yet!

Constraints

We are now going to take a look at two types of constraint: *default constraints* and *table constraints*. Both are useful, as you'll see.

Default Constraints

A default constraint is assigned to a column when a new row is inserted into a table and no value has been specified for that column. Say the CreatedDate column in the Contacts table had a specific date assigned to it as a default value. Inserting a new row would cause that date to be set as the CreatedDate column value, unless an alternative value was specified.

You shouldn't assign default values to every column; just where it makes sense. Defaults usually work well for BIT columns (defaulting them to TRUE or FALSE), and columns like CreatedDate, which are generally used for auditing purposes.

There are only two tables we want to assign default values for in our database: Contacts and ContactVerificationDetails. We'll assign the following defaults:

- Contacts: set a default of FALSE on AllowContactByPhone

- Contacts: set a default of the current date/time on CreatedDate

- ContactVerificationDetails: set a default of FALSE on ContactVerified

Note that none of these columns allow NULL values, which is another good reason for using default values (bear in mind that a NULL value can be manually supplied via an INSERT statement).

Creating a Default Constraint

Open up c:\temp\sqlbasics\apply\02 - Create Contacts Table.sql. Find the AllowContactByPhone line and change it by adding a DEFAULT clause:

```
AllowContactByPhone BIT NOT NULL DEFAULT 0,
```

That's all you need to do—the 0 means FALSE. Rebuild the database (run the 00 - Rollback.sql script, then the 00 - Apply.sql script—whenever I mention rebuilding the database going forward, this is what you should do) and then add a new record to the Contacts table (using the **Edit Top 200 Rows** option), *without* specifying a value for the AllowContactByPhone column. Before you press Enter, you should see something like Figure 7-7.

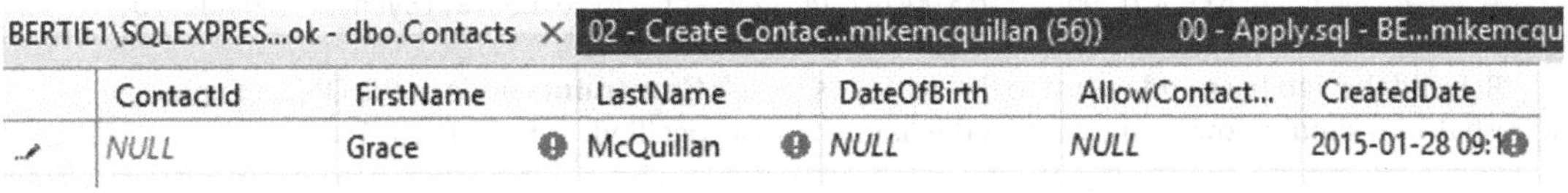

ContactId	FirstName	LastName	DateOfBirth	AllowContact...	CreatedDate
NULL	Grace	❶ McQuillan	❶ NULL	NULL	2015-01-28 09:1❶

Figure 7-7. About to commit a new row with default values

Now press Enter to commit the row. The row will change—AllowContactByPhone still displays NULL, but there's a red exclamation mark to the left of the row (you can see this in Figure 7-8). This indicates we are not looking at the current version of the row.

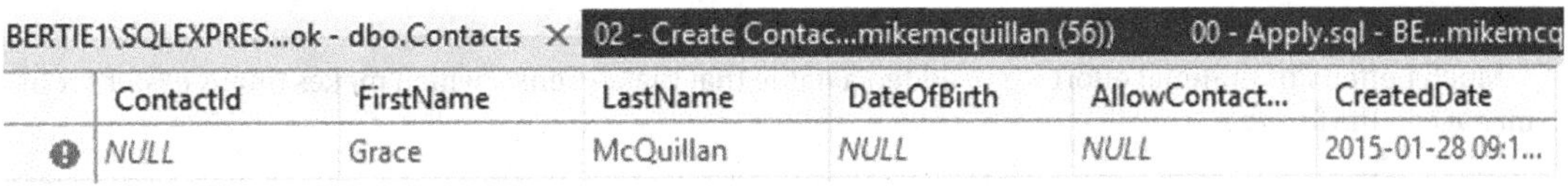

ContactId	FirstName	LastName	DateOfBirth	AllowContact...	CreatedDate
❶ NULL	Grace	McQuillan	NULL	NULL	2015-01-28 09:1...

Figure 7-8. A newly committed row that needs refreshing

Press Ctrl+R on your keyboard to refresh the table's contents. The red exclamation mark should disappear, the ContactId column should be populated, and the AllowContactByPhone column should change to FALSE (Figure 7-9).

BERTIE1\SQLEXPRES...ok - dbo.Contacts ×		02 - Create Contac...mikemcquillan (56))		00 - Apply.sql - BE...mikemcq		
ContactId	FirstName	LastName	DateOfBirth	AllowContact...	CreatedDate	
1	Grace	McQuillan	NULL	False	2015-01-28 09:1...	

Figure 7-9. The new row, refreshed with default values

Great, isn't it? But it's not a bed of roses just yet. In the Object Explorer, expand the Contacts table (**Databases ➤ AddressBook ➤ Tables ➤ Contacts**), and expand **Constraints**. Uh-oh—as Figure 7-10 shows, things don't look pleasant.

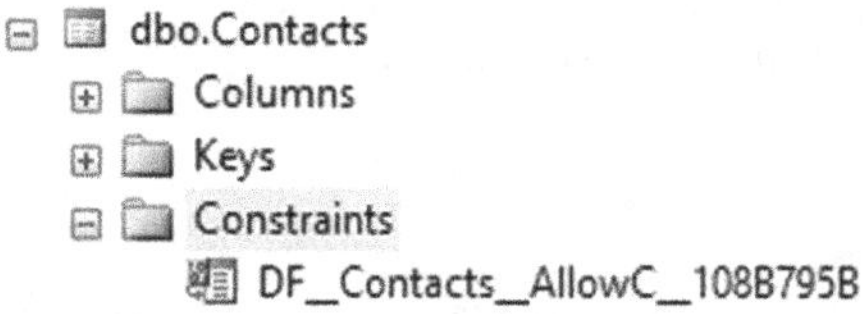

⊟ ▦ dbo.Contacts
  ⊞ 🗀 Columns
  ⊞ 🗀 Keys
  ⊟ 🗀 Constraints
      ▨ DF_Contacts_AllowC_108B795B

Figure 7-10. A badly named default constraint

Can you remember when we first created a primary key? SQL Server appended a weird combination of letters and numbers to the end of the primary key name, making it difficult to maintain should we need to amend it in the future. A similar thing has happened here. We didn't provide a name for the constraint, so SQL Server has provided one for us. This name is of no use. We'd never remember it, and it isn't explicit—we want to stay in control of the names of our objects. So we need to return to our 02 - Create Contacts Table.sql script. Change the AllowContactByPhone line:

```
AllowContactByPhone BIT NOT NULL CONSTRAINT DF_Contacts_AllowContactByPhone DEFAULT 0,
```

Rebuild the database and return to the Contacts table's **Constraints** node in the Object Explorer. Refresh this; it should now be showing us the name we just specified, as in Figure 7-11.

⊟ ▦ dbo.Contacts
  ⊞ 🗀 Columns
  ⊞ 🗀 Keys
  ⊟ 🗀 Constraints
      ▨ DF_Contacts_AllowContactByPhone

Figure 7-11. A well-named default constraint

Much better! For minimal effort we've added a name that makes sense, which makes things easier for us to manage in the future.

We can now go ahead and modify the CreatedDate column in the same script. This is a value used purely for auditing, so there is need to ask the person creating the record to supply it. Change the CreatedDate line:

```
CreatedDate DATETIME NOT NULL CONSTRAINT DF_Contacts_CreatedDate DEFAULT GETDATE()
```

This looks very similar to the AllowContactByPhone default constraint, except we specify GETDATE() as the value (you always specify the value you want as the default after the DEFAULT keyword). GETDATE() is one of SQL Server's system functions (there's a list of some of the more useful functions in Appendix C). It returns the current date and time.

Save the 02 - Create Contacts Table.sql script. Before we rebuild the database, we may as well modify the 09 - Create ContactVerificationDetails Table.sql script. We want to specify a default value on the ContactVerified column.

```
ContactVerified BIT NOT NULL CONSTRAINT
DF_ContactVerificationDetails_ContactVerified DEFAULT 0
```

Save this script, too, and then rebuild the database. Try adding a new record to Contacts, but specify just a FirstName and LastName (as I've done in Figure 7-12).

BERTIE1\SQLEXPRES...ok - dbo.Contacts ×		00 - Apply.sql - BE...mikemcquillan (55))		00 - Rollback.sql -...\mikemcc	
	ContactId	FirstName	LastName	DateOfBirth	AllowContact...	CreatedDate
➤	NULL	Grace	❶ McQuillan	❶ NULL	NULL	NULL

Figure 7-12. *Creating a new row with default constraints*

Press Enter, then Ctrl+R to refresh the rows. As Figure 7-13 demonstrates, you should be left with just a NULL DateOfBirth.

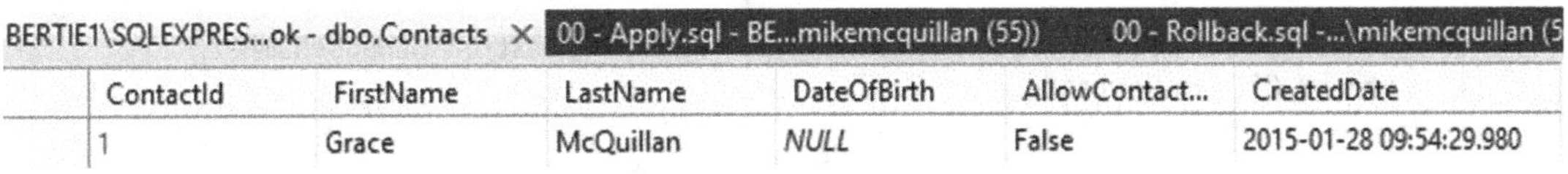

BERTIE1\SQLEXPRES...ok - dbo.Contacts ×		00 - Apply.sql - BE...mikemcquillan (55))		00 - Rollback.sql -...\mikemcquillan (5	
	ContactId	FirstName	LastName	DateOfBirth	AllowContact...	CreatedDate
	1	Grace	McQuillan	NULL	False	2015-01-28 09:54:29.980

Figure 7-13. *A new row displaying default values*

We're all done with default values. Just remember that defaults are only applied when you create a row, not when you update it. But they are very useful, especially when used in conjunction with stored procedures, as we'll see later.

Table Constraints Part 1—Check Constraints

A Check constraint is very different from a default, and it will be applied to new rows and existing rows that are being updated. Use a Check constraint to ensure valid values are entered into your rows—the insert or update operation is rejected if the Check constraint is not met.

When we were looking at NULL earlier, you may remember we added a record with a blank LastName value. This isn't a NULL value, but rather an empty string. Try it—you can still do this (Figure 7-14 shows the proof!).

BERTIE1\SQLEXPRES...ok - dbo.Contacts	×	
ContactId	FirstName	LastName
1	Mike	

Figure 7-14. *Specifying an empty LastName value*

You can also enter an empty FirstName should you wish. This is not good—we'll use a Check constraint to solve this problem. The rules for Check constraints are the following:

- Check constraints can be applied to multiple columns (by specifying them at the table level), or to just one column (by specifying them at the column level).

- The expression you specify must return TRUE or FALSE.

- Multiple Check constraints can be applied to a single column.

- Any valid T-SQL expression can be used as part of a Check constraint, as long as it returns TRUE or FALSE.

If the Check constraint returns FALSE, the constraint has failed and the insert or update operation is rejected. Because of this, you need to ensure any programs you or other developers may write to insert or update data are aware that an error may occur should the constraints not be met. Of course, preventing bad data and allowing systems to do something logical when bad data is provided is the main reason why we implement Check constraints.

We are going to add the following Check constraints to our database:

- Contacts: Ensure that valid FirstName and LastName values are provided.

- Contacts: Limit DateOfBirth to values greater than January 1, 1850.

- ContactAddresses: Ensure a valid value is provided for at least one of HouseNumber, Street, City, or Postcode.

Creating a Table Constraint

Because the first and third constraints I mentioned involve multiple columns, these constraints will be created at the table level. The second constraint, to limit DateOfBirth, will be a column constraint.

Open the 02 - Create Contacts Table.sql script from the apply folder. Add a new line to the bottom of the CREATE TABLE statement.

```
CREATE TABLE dbo.Contacts
(
ContactId INT IDENTITY(1,1) NOT NULL,
FirstName VARCHAR(40) NOT NULL,
LastName VARCHAR(40) NOT NULL,
DateOfBirth DATE NULL,
```

```
AllowContactByPhone BIT NOT NULL CONSTRAINT DF_Contacts_AllowContactByPhone DEFAULT 0,
CreatedDate DATETIME NOT NULL CONSTRAINT DF_Contacts_CreatedDate DEFAULT GETDATE(),
CONSTRAINT PK_Contacts PRIMARY KEY CLUSTERED (ContactId),
CONSTRAINT CK_Contacts_FirstNameLastName CHECK (FirstName != '' OR LastName != '')
);
```

We give the Check constraint a name, beginning with CK for Check—yes, sensible naming strikes again! Then we have the keyword CHECK, followed by some text wrapped up in brackets. The text within the brackets is your *check expression*. This is what SQL Server will evaluate whenever a value is provided for the FirstName or LastName columns. You can use virtually any valid T-SQL expression in a Check constraint.

Save the script and rebuild your database. If you'd rather not rebuild the database, you can run the following ALTER TABLE statement:

```
ALTER TABLE dbo.Contacts
ADD CONSTRAINT CK_Contacts_FirstNameLastName CHECK (FirstName != '' OR LastName != '');
```

Note the name clearly describes the table and columns involved with the constraint. If you have multiple constraints for the same columns, consider adding an extra piece of information to the end of the name.

REBUILDING VS. ALTERING

We've been consistently rebuilding the database throughout this chapter. This is fine, as our database doesn't contain any data yet. Once a database is put into production it will contain data, and rebuilding it ceases to be an option.

When this happens, you will need to write scripts that ALTER existing objects, rather than CREATE them.

If you ran the ALTER TABLE statement, you'll see the now familiar **Command(s) completed successfully** message. Let's go ahead and test our constraint.

Open up the Contacts table for editing and add a row. Make sure you enter a blank value for the FirstName column (just press Delete to clear out the NULL), and a valid value for the LastName column. Your row should look something like the second row in Figure 7-15.

BERTIE1\SQLEXPRES...ok - dbo.Contacts ✕		SQLQuery1.sql - BE...ikemcquillan (57))*		02 - Create Contac...mikemcq	
ContactId	FirstName	LastName	DateOfBirth	AllowContact...	CreatedDate
1	Grace	McQuillan	*NULL*	False	2015-01-28 09:5...
NULL		❶ Potter	❶ *NULL*	*NULL*	*NULL*

Figure 7-15. About to commit a new row with a blank FirstName value

Once you are ready, press Enter—all other columns have defaults or allow NULLs. We are expecting to see an error message appear, rejecting the row.

What actually happens is a red exclamation mark appears to the left of the row, shown in Figure 7-16.

	ContactId	FirstName	LastName	DateOfBirth	AllowContact...	CreatedDate
	1	Grace	McQuillan	NULL	False	2015-01-28 09:5...
❶	NULL		Potter	NULL	NULL	NULL

Figure 7-16. *A committed new row awaiting a refresh*

We saw this earlier. Press Ctrl+R to refresh the table. As Figure 7-17 shows, the row has been accepted!

	ContactId	FirstName	LastName	DateOfBirth	AllowContact...	CreatedDate
	1	Grace	McQuillan	NULL	False	2015-01-28 09:5...
	3		Potter	NULL	False	2015-01-28 13:0...

Figure 7-17. *A refreshed row with an empty* FirstName *value*

This isn't good. We've (well, I've) done something wrong. Just as a test, blank out the LastName column, too, and press Enter. Do you see the error message in Figure 7-18?

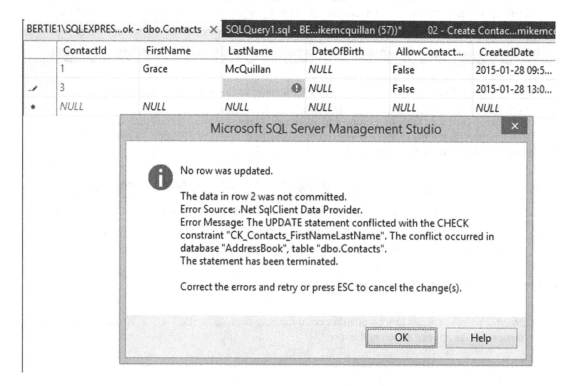

Figure 7-18. *Attempting to update a row with blank* FirstName *and* LastName *entries*

Ah-ha! The error message in Figure 7-18 is what we were expecting to see earlier, an error telling us there is a conflict with the CK_Contacts_FirstNameLastName constraint. So things work if we leave both values empty. What the heck is going on?

I'll analyze the constraint expression. FirstName != '' checks if an empty string has been provided for FirstName. != means NOT EQUAL TO. So if FirstName is Mike, this will return TRUE, as Mike is NOT EQUAL TO an empty string. If FirstName is an empty string, this will return FALSE.

The check for LastName is exactly the same. They are joined by the keyword OR. This means only one of these conditions has to be met. So if FirstName is an empty string but LastName isn't, the constraint has been met. And vice versa—if we have a FirstName but no LastName, we have one of the values, so the constraint has been met.

This isn't what we want—we want the constraint to ensure both values have been provided. Let's drop the constraint and change it to use AND instead. Open a New Query Window and type in this code:

```
ALTER TABLE dbo.Contacts DROP CONSTRAINT CK_Contacts_FirstNameLastName;

ALTER TABLE dbo.Contacts ADD CONSTRAINT CK_Contacts_FirstNameLastName CHECK (FirstName != ''
AND LastName != '');
```

This is a subtle but important change. This expression is saying both FirstName and LastName must not be empty strings for the insert or update to fail. So if one of them is empty, the check will not be met.

Run this. If you have a row in the table with either a blank FirstName or LastName column value, the constraint won't be created—you'll see a red warning message, just like the one in Figure 7-19.

Figure 7-19. *A failed attempt to create a Check constraint*

This is because the data currently in the table don't meet the constraint. This is good; SQL Server is telling us to clean up our data before creating the constraint. To delete the offending row, return to the Contacts table in the table editor, right-click the gray box to the left of the row, and choose the **Delete** option as shown in Figure 7-20.

| | Potter | NULL | False | 2015-01-28 13:0... |
| | NULL | NULL | NULL | NULL |

Execute SQL   Ctrl+R
Cut   Ctrl+X
Copy   Ctrl+C
Paste   Ctrl+V
Delete   Del
Pane
Clear Results
Properties   Alt+Enter

Figure 7-20. *Deleting the noncompliant row*

You will be asked to confirm the deletion. Do so, then return to the query window containing the constraint code.

CREATING CHECK CONSTRAINTS WHEN NONCOMPLIANT DATA EXISTS

Often, you'll want to introduce new Check constraints after a system has been live for a while. The table you are adding the constraint to may contain rows that don't meet the new Check constraint, and editing or deleting them may not be an option. Fear not—you can use the WITH CHECK and WITH NOCHECK options when creating the constraint. WITH CHECK is the default and will cause data to be validated against the new constraint. If you don't want to validate the existing data, use WITH NOCHECK. The constraint will only apply to new and updated rows.

These clauses apply to foreign keys too.

Highlight the ALTER TABLE ADD CONSTRAINT code (like I've done in Figure 7-21) and then press F5. This is a very nice feature of SSMS; if you have highlighted some code, it will only execute that code. We don't want to execute the ALTER TABLE DROP CONSTRAINT code—that executed earlier when we first tried to recreate the constraint. The DROP CONSTRAINT succeeded, but the ADD CONSTRAINT failed because of the bad data in the table.

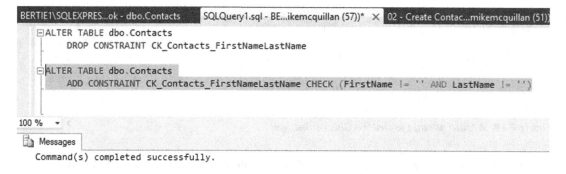

Figure 7-21. *Creating a modified Check constraint*

Now return to the table editor and try to add a new row, with a blank FirstName and a valid LastName. Press Enter to commit the row. What happens? The error message appears, telling us the constraint has not been met. Hurrah! Click **OK** on the error message and blank out the LastName, too. Press Enter again. You should still see the error message. Now try specifying a valid FirstName, but no LastName. Press Enter, and again you should see the error message. Everything seems fine. Finally, enter a valid FirstName and LastName. The row should be accepted this time. Press Ctrl+R to refresh the table. You should see the two rows in Figure 7-22.

	ContactId	FirstName	LastName	DateOfBirth	AllowContact...	CreatedDate
	1	Grace	McQuillan	*NULL*	False	2015-01-28 09:5...
	7	Dennis	Potter	*NULL*	False	2015-01-28 13:2...

Figure 7-22. *Inserting a valid row*

Great, our constraint is working! This is a pretty simple constraint we've added, but it serves to illustrate how powerful Check constraints can be.

Creating a Column Constraint

Make sure you amend the 02 - Create Contacts Table.sql script with the change we made to the CK_Contacts_FirstNameLastName constraint. While you're there, add a new constraint at the bottom to check if DateOfBirth values are greater than January 1, 1850. Here's the full CREATE TABLE statement:

```
CREATE TABLE dbo.Contacts
(
ContactId INT IDENTITY(1,1) NOT NULL,
FirstName VARCHAR(40) NOT NULL,
LastName VARCHAR(40) NOT NULL,
DateOfBirth DATE NULL,
AllowContactByPhone BIT NOT NULL CONSTRAINT DF_Contacts_AllowContactByPhone DEFAULT 0,
CreatedDate DATETIME NOT NULL CONSTRAINT DF_Contacts_CreatedDate DEFAULT GETDATE(),
CONSTRAINT PK_Contacts PRIMARY KEY CLUSTERED (ContactId),
CONSTRAINT CK_Contacts_FirstNameLastName CHECK (FirstName != '' AND LastName != ''),
CONSTRAINT CK_Contacts_DateOfBirth CHECK (DateOfBirth > '1850-01-01')
);
```

You can either rebuild the database, or run this ALTER TABLE statement:

```
ALTER TABLE dbo.Contacts ADD CONSTRAINT CK_Contacts_DateOfBirth CHECK (DateOfBirth > '1850-01-01');
```

Return to the Contacts table's table editor and add a new row, leaving NULL as the DateOfBirth value. The row should be created as normal, even though we didn't specify a DateOfBirth. You can see it in Figure 7-23.

	ContactId	FirstName	LastName	DateOfBirth	AllowContact...	CreatedDate
	1	Grace	McQuillan	NULL	False	2015-01-28 09:5...
	7	Dennis	Potter	NULL	False	2015-01-28 13:2...
▶	8	Richard	Adams	NULL	False	2015-01-28 13:3...
*	NULL	NULL	NULL	NULL	NULL	NULL

Figure 7-23. Inserting a new row without a DateOfBirth

This is correct, as we have configured DateOfBirth to allow NULL values. Now, modify your new row—enter a DateOfBirth after January 1, 1850. This should be saved, too. Enter the date in the format YYYY-MM-DD (e.g., 1938-05-01 for May 1, 1938). Figure 7-24 shows the updated row.

ContactId	FirstName	LastName	DateOfBirth	AllowContact...	CreatedDate
1	Grace	McQuillan	NULL	False	2015-01-28 09:5...
7	Dennis	Potter	NULL	False	2015-01-28 13:2...
8	Richard	Adams	1938-05-01	False	2015-01-28 13:3...
NULL	NULL	NULL	NULL	NULL	NULL

Figure 7-24. *Updating the row with a* DateOfBirth *value*

Wonderful. We'll change that date to December 29, 1849 (1849-12-29). As expected, our Check constraint raises a complaint, which is displayed in Figure 7-25.

ContactId	FirstName	LastName	DateOfBirth	AllowContact...	CreatedDate
1	Grace	McQuillan	NULL	False	2015-01-28 09:5...
7	Dennis	Potter	NULL	False	2015-01-28 13:2...
8	Richard	Adams	1849-12-29	False	2015-01-28 13:3...
NULL	NULL	NULL	NULL	NULL	NULL

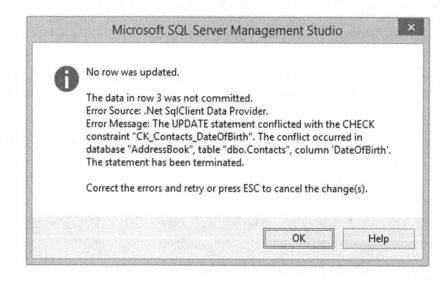

Figure 7-25. *Updating the row with an out-of-range* DateOfBirth

Click **OK** and press Esc to reject the changes. The DateOfBirth will revert back to 1938-05-01. Another Check constraint successfully created, this time as a column constraint. Now we only accept contacts who are roughly less than 165 years old!

One last example—we said we'd create a Check constraint on the ContactAddresses table, to ensure a valid value is provided for at least one of HouseNumber, Street, City, or Postcode. Note we only require one of these values, not all of them. We still use AND to check this. Open up 06 - Create ContactAddresses Table.sql from the apply folder. Change the CREATE TABLE statement to include the Check constraint.

```
CREATE TABLE dbo.ContactAddresses
(
AddressId INT IDENTITY(1,1) NOT NULL,
ContactId INT NOT NULL,
HouseNumber VARCHAR(200) NULL,
Street VARCHAR(200) NULL,
City VARCHAR(200) NULL,
Postcode VARCHAR(20) NULL,
CONSTRAINT PK_ContactAddresses PRIMARY KEY NONCLUSTERED (AddressId),
CONSTRAINT CK_ContactAddresses_HouseNumberStreetCityPostcode
CHECK (HouseNumber != '' AND Street != '' AND City != '' AND Postcode != '')
);
```

Here's the ALTER TABLE statement so you don't need to rebuild your database:

```
ALTER TABLE dbo.ContactAddresses ADD CONSTRAINT
  CK_ContactAddresses_HouseNumberStreetCityPostcode CHECK
  (HouseNumber != '' AND Street != '' AND City != '' AND Postcode != '');
```

Make a note of a valid ContactId from the Contacts table, then open the table editor for the ContactAddresses table. Try adding addresses with all NULL values—this will be allowed, as will adding an address with at least one valid value specified (as long as the other values are not empty strings). But try adding an address with an empty string and it will be rejected, with the error message shown in Figure 7-26.

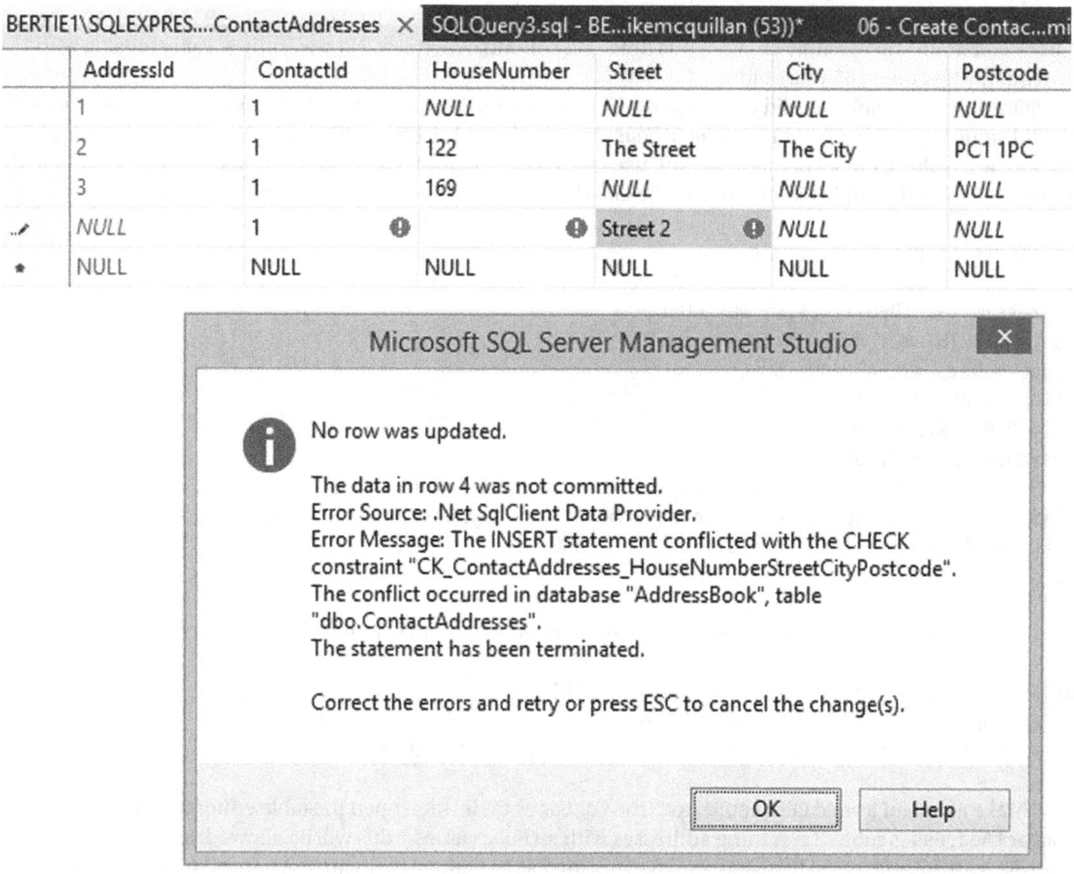
BERTIE1\SQLEXPRES....ContactAddresses
SQLQuery3.sql - BE...ikemcquillan (53))*
06 - Create Contac...mi
AddressId
ContactId
HouseNumber
Street
City
Postcode
1
1
NULL
NULL
NULL
NULL
2
1
122
The Street
The City
PC1 1PC
3
1
169
NULL
NULL
NULL
NULL
1
Street 2
NULL
NULL
NULL
NULL
NULL
NULL
NULL
NULL
Microsoft SQL Server Management Studio
No row was updated.
The data in row 4 was not committed.
Error Source: .Net SqlClient Data Provider.
Error Message: The INSERT statement conflicted with the CHECK constraint "CK_ContactAddresses_HouseNumberStreetCityPostcode". The conflict occurred in database "AddressBook", table "dbo.ContactAddresses".
The statement has been terminated.
Correct the errors and retry or press ESC to cancel the change(s).
OK
Help

Figure 7-26. *Inserting an address without a `HouseNumber` value*

Congratulations, you've just made bad data entry much harder!

Table Constraints Part 2—Unique Constraints

To finish this chapter, we'll create a unique constraint. This is a special type of constraint that ensures a particular column, or combination of columns, in each row is unique. We'll add one unique constraint to the `ContactPhoneNumbers` table, which will ensure each `ContactId` and `PhoneNumber` combination is unique.

Open script `08 - Create ContactPhoneNumbers Table.sql` and modify the `CREATE TABLE` statement to include the `Unique` constraint.

```
CREATE TABLE dbo.ContactPhoneNumbers
(
PhoneNumberId INT IDENTITY(1,1) NOT NULL,
ContactId INT NOT NULL,
PhoneNumberTypeId TINYINT NOT NULL,
PhoneNumber VARCHAR(30) NOT NULL
CONSTRAINT PK_ContactPhoneNumbers PRIMARY KEY CLUSTERED (PhoneNumberId),
CONSTRAINT UQ_ContactIdPhoneNumber UNIQUE (ContactId, PhoneNumber)
);
```

This looks very similar to the constraints we've added already. It's more akin to a primary key constraint than a Check constraint. We give the constraint a name—beginning with UQ for Unique this time—and then declare the UNIQUE keyword, with the columns to check for uniqueness in brackets.

Here's the ALTER TABLE script for you to run:

```
ALTER TABLE dbo.ContactPhoneNumbers ADD CONSTRAINT
    UQ_ContactIdPhoneNumber UNIQUE (ContactId, PhoneNumber);
```

To test this, we must add a record to the PhoneNumberTypes table—the PhoneNumberTypeId column in the ContactPhoneNumbers table does not allow NULLs, and is a foreign key. Open the table editor for PhoneNumberTypes and add a PhoneNumberType of *Home*. Press Enter and make a note of the PhoneNumberTypeId given to this record. This value will probably be 1, as you can see in Figure 7-27.

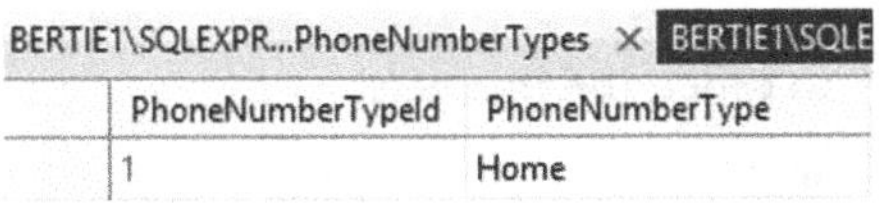

Figure 7-27. Inserting a Home PhoneNumberType record

Next, make sure you have two contacts present in the Contacts table. Make a note of their ContactIds and try adding phone numbers for them in the ContactPhoneNumbers table. For the same contact, try adding the same phone number two times. The second time, you'll see the error message shown in Figure 7-28.

	PhoneNumber...	ContactId		PhoneNumberTypeId	PhoneNumber	
	1	1		1	0100 100 100	
	2	1		1	0100 100 200	
✎	NULL	1	❶	1	❶ 0100 100 100 ❶	
✶	NULL	NULL		NULL	NULL	

> **Microsoft SQL Server Management Studio** ✕
>
> ❶ No row was updated.
>
> The data in row 3 was not committed.
> Error Source: .Net SqlClient Data Provider.
> Error Message: Violation of UNIQUE KEY constraint
> 'UQ_ContactIdPhoneNumber'. Cannot insert duplicate key in object
> 'dbo.ContactPhoneNumbers'. The duplicate key value is (1, 0100 100
> 100).
> The statement has been terminated.
>
> Correct the errors and retry or press ESC to cancel the change(s).
>
> [OK]   [Help]

Figure 7-28. *A unique constraint in action*

The error message tells us that the unique constraint is working exactly as expected—the same contact cannot have the same phone number more than once. However, we can specify the same number for a different contact, as Figure 7-29 proves.

PhoneNumber...	ContactId	PhoneNumberTypeId	PhoneNumber
1	1	1	0100 100 100
2	1	1	0100 100 200
4	7	1	0100 100 100

Figure 7-29. *Specifying the same phone number for two contacts*

This is correct, as the unique constraint applies to the combination of ContactId and PhoneNumber. We've now guaranteed that each contact will not have duplicate phone numbers.

Some Constraints Are Really Indexes

We haven't spoken about indexes yet—that will happen in Chapter 14. We've been merrily creating constraints in this chapter—or have we? Not quite. In the Object Explorer, expand **Databases ➤ AddressBook ➤ ContactPhoneNumbers ➤ Constraints**. Expand **Indexes**, too. There will be nothing under **Constraints**—eh?—but there will be some items beneath **Indexes**, which you can see in Figure 7-30.

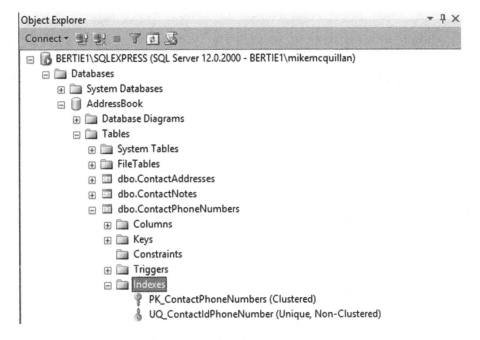

Figure 7-30. *Constraints that are actually indexes*

Both the primary key and the unique constraint have been created as indexes. This is because they *are* indexes! Check constraints and default constraints will be created as constraints, and will exist below the **Constraints** node. Primary keys are created as either a clustered or nonclustered index, and unique constraints are created as a unique index.

I mention this now just to avoid confusion should you go looking for your constraints! We'll talk about it in more detail later.

Summary

That was a marathon of a chapter. We've locked our database down pretty well. We started by determining which columns could accept NULL values, and then assigned some default values to certain columns. We continued to improve our database by adding some Check constraints, limiting the values supplied by users for certain columns. We finished off by introducing a unique constraint to the ContactPhoneNumbers table, preventing the same number from being provided multiple times for the same contact.

Everything has come together wonderfully, so much so that we've finished our table structure. Yes, our tables are now ready to be populated with some data—which means it's Data Manipulation Language time!

CHAPTER 8

■ ■ ■

DML (or Inserts, Updates, and Deletes)

We've created a solid database structure, but just as a database is useless without tables, so a table is useless without data. We've been using the table editor to add data to tables, but it's time to introduce the power of the T-SQL language. We'll look at how we can add data to our tables, edit it, and how we can remove it. We'll even do a little bit of querying, which will take us nicely into the next chapter.

Let's add some records!

Reference Data vs. Real Data

Before we add anything to the database, it's important to understand the difference between reference data and what I call real data. The **AddressBook** database contains two reference tables:

- Roles
- PhoneNumberTypes

and six real data tables:

- Contacts
- ContactAddresses
- ContactNotes
- ContactPhoneNumbers
- ContactRoles
- ContactVerificationDetails

Reference data represents data that you need, but that doesn't actually form part of your main data set. The intention of the **AddressBook** database is to store contact information. It doesn't have the aim of storing types of role or phone numbers—the fact that we are storing this information is a by-product of storing contact data. We store these types so we can link them to contacts, allowing us to determine whether a phone number is a work or home number, for example. But we could still use our contact data without this information—it is just used as a reference to embellish our contact data.

The real data tables hold the data we actually built the system for—in this case, contact data. If we built a stock control system we'd have a set of real data tables related to stock and order information, and then some reference tables storing things like item type, supplier category, and so on.

Okay, now that we've cleared that up, we can take a look at inserting some reference data, in preparation for adding real data.

Inserting Data

To prepare ourselves, let's rebuild the database. Close any query windows you may have open, and open `c:\temp\sqlbasics\rollback\00 - Rollback.sql`. Switch into SQLCMD mode (**Query ➤ SQLCMD Mode**) and run the script. Next, open `c:\temp\sqlbasics\apply\00 - Apply.sql`, go back into SQLCMD mode, and run it to recreate the database.

Okay, it's clean slate time. We'll start by adding some phone number types. We want to add:

- Home
- Work
- Mobile
- Other

We have four phone number types to deal with. So far, we've been using the table editor to add records to tables. Now we are going to start using SQL DML statements.

WHAT IS DML?

DML stands for Data Manipulation Language. It represents a group of SQL statements that can be used to manage your data. There are four DML statements—SELECT, to retrieve data; INSERT, to add data; UPDATE, to update data (big surprise); and DELETE, to remove data (even bigger surprise). We'll look at SELECT in detail in the next chapter.

These statements are also known in the industry as CRUD—Create (INSERT), Read (SELECT), Update (UPDATE), Delete (DELETE). If somebody says CRUD to you, they're probably referring to the acronym, not the quality of your code!

Open up a New Query Window and type in and run the query shown in Figure 8-1.

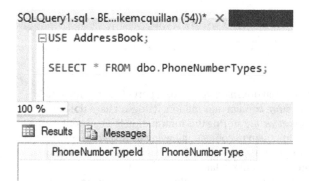

Figure 8-1. *Querying an empty PhoneNumberTypes table*

As expected, no results are returned by the SELECT statement (if you did see some data, you need to recreate the database). We'll take a look at the SELECT statement in some detail in the next chapter, so for now just be aware that we use it to retrieve data from tables—specifically, here, the PhoneNumberTypes table.

There are three ways to use the INSERT INTO statement. The most common method of use is to use the VALUES keyword. In between the two statements in Figure 8-1, type this INSERT INTO statement:

```
INSERT INTO dbo.PhoneNumberTypes (PhoneNumberType) VALUES ('Home');
```

INSERT INTO tells SQL Server what type of command we want to run—a record insert, in this case. dbo.PhoneNumberTypes is the name of the table we are inserting into, and we then add the names of the columns we want to insert into in parentheses. PhoneNumberTypes only has two columns, and the PhoneNumberTypeId is a calculated IDENTITY column for which we don't need to provide a value. So we just declare the PhoneNumberType column for insert. The next keyword is VALUES, which tells SQL Server we are now going to start providing the values for INSERT. These are also wrapped in parentheses, and we must provide the same number of columns and values. We have specified one column, so we must provide one value. If we tried to supply two values, we'd see:

```
Msg 110, Level 15, State 1, Line 3
```

There are fewer columns in the INSERT statement than values specified in the VALUES clause. The number of values in the VALUES clause must match the number of columns specified in the INSERT statement.

A simpler breakdown of the INSERT INTO statement we've just created is:

```
INSERT INTO TableName (Columns) VALUES (ValuesToInsert);
```

If there are multiple columns and values, you separate them with a comma. We'll see this shortly.

Now that we have added the INSERT statement to our script, run it. This time, the one record shown in Figure 8-2 should be returned.

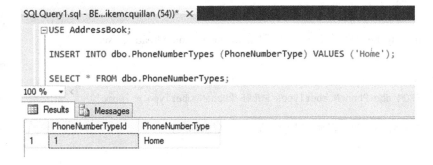

Figure 8-2. *Inserting a Home record into PhoneNumberTypes*

If we run this again, what do you think will happen? You may be surprised—a second record for Home will be inserted (Figure 8-3).

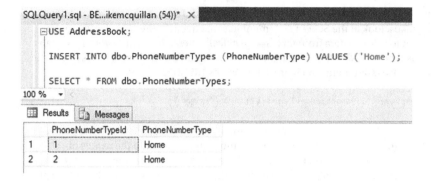

Figure 8-3. Inserting a duplicate Home PhoneNumberType record

Eh? That wasn't in the script! Well actually, it was. There were a couple of ways we could have prevented this:

- Put a unique constraint on the PhoneNumberType column.
- Check if the value exists in the table before we try to insert it.

We've seen both of these techniques in the book already. We created a Unique index on the ContactPhoneNumbers table in the last chapter, and we've already used IF statements to check if particular databases and tables exist.

We're not going to add a Unique constraint to prevent this; instead, we'll add a check to determine if the record already exists. Before we do this, we need to remove the duplicate record. Run this statement in its own window:

```
DELETE dbo.PhoneNumberTypes WHERE PhoneNumberTypeId = 2;
```

This will remove the duplicate—you should see this message:

```
(1 row(s) affected)
```

Close that window and modify the INSERT script to check if the Home record already exists.

```
USE AddressBook;

IF NOT EXISTS (SELECT 1 FROM dbo.PhoneNumberTypes WHERE PhoneNumberType = 'Home')
BEGIN
INSERT INTO dbo.PhoneNumberTypes (PhoneNumberType) VALUES ('Home');
END;

SELECT * FROM dbo.PhoneNumberTypes;
```

Run this as many times as you want—it won't insert a duplicate. The IF NOT EXISTS statement is something we saw first in Chapter 3. All it does is check if a "Home" record exists—if it does, the INSERT INTO statement will not be executed.

We'll add the second record—Work—using a slightly different mechanism. Enhance the script to include the Work insert:

```
USE AddressBook;

IF NOT EXISTS (SELECT 1 FROM dbo.PhoneNumberTypes WHERE PhoneNumberType = 'Home')
BEGIN
INSERT INTO dbo.PhoneNumberTypes (PhoneNumberType) VALUES ('Home');
END;

IF NOT EXISTS (SELECT 1 FROM dbo.PhoneNumberTypes WHERE PhoneNumberType = 'Work')
BEGIN
INSERT INTO dbo.PhoneNumberTypes (PhoneNumberType)
SELECT 'Work';
END;

SELECT * FROM dbo.PhoneNumberTypes;
```

We've added another IF NOT EXISTS check, this time for Work. But the INSERT INTO statement is slightly different. Instead of the VALUES keyword with brackets, this time we have SELECT 'Work'. Huh?

It's possible to insert multiple records in one go using the SELECT statement. We're going to investigate the SELECT statement in the very next chapter, but it can be used as part of the INSERT statement to insert one or more records (there's no real limit to the number of records you can insert using this). You can insert records from other tables, or specific values as we've done here.

If you highlight SELECT 'Work' in your Query Window and run it, one record will be returned, as shown in Figure 8-4:

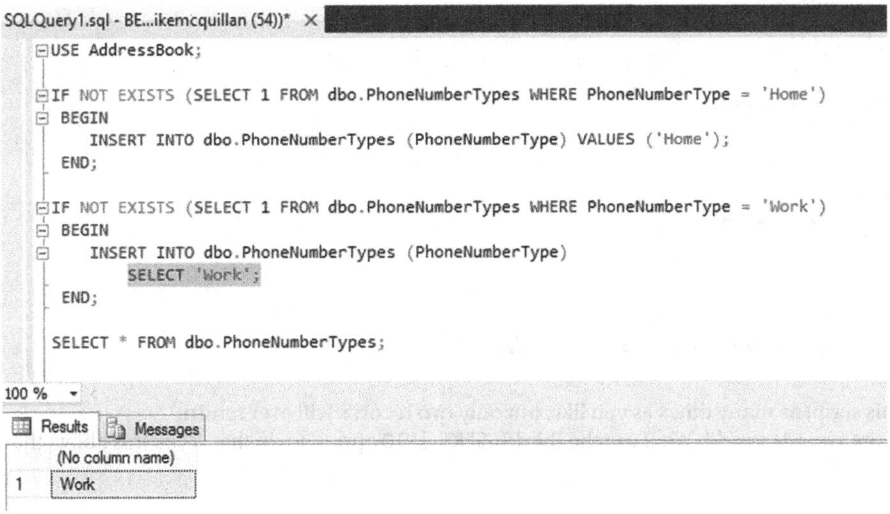

Figure 8-4. Checking if records exist before inserting them

It really is just a normal SELECT statement. We'll use this again soon.

USING SELECT IN INSERT STATEMENTS

The preceding statement is using a literal value, Work. It is not inserting data from another table, as there is no FROM statement (we'll meet FROM in Chapter 11). When we use SELECT with a string enclosed in single quotes as we've done here, only the literal string is returned. Do not use double quotes, as this will return an error. You don't have to use literal strings—for instance, if you wanted to insert the current date/time into a column, you could use SELECT GETDATE(); to insert it using the built-in SQL date/time function.

You can think of it as:

```
INSERT INTO TableName (Columns) SELECT ValuesToInsert
```

Click in your Query Window to unhighlight the code, and then run the entire script. The two records in Figure 8-5 should be returned.

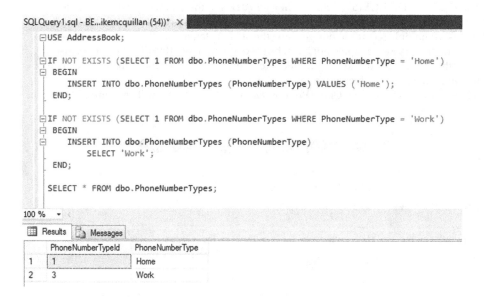

Figure 8-5. *Only inserting records when they don't already exist*

You may run this script as many times as you like, but only two records will ever return.

We have two more records to add. We'll use the third INSERT INTO option to do that. Type this above the SELECT statement:

```
IF NOT EXISTS (SELECT 1 FROM dbo.PhoneNumberTypes WHERE PhoneNumberType IN ('Mobile', 'Other'))
BEGIN
INSERT INTO dbo.PhoneNumberTypes (PhoneNumberType)
VALUES ('Mobile'), ('Other');
END;
```

There are two things here we haven't seen. The first occurs in the SELECT statement used by IF NOT EXISTS. It uses IN, not =. The equals operator can be used to check for the existence of one value; the IN operator can check multiple values at the same time. We need to do this because the INSERT INTO statement is trying to insert two values, not one. You can provide multiple values by wrapping them up in their own set of parentheses, as you did earlier.

Run the entire script and you'll see four values have been inserted (Figure 8-6).

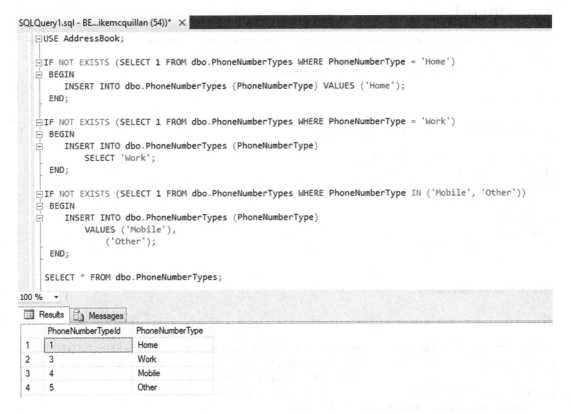

Figure 8-6. *Inserting four PhoneNumberType records*

Again, you can keep running this—you'll only ever see four values returned.

We've now populated our PhoneNumberTypes table, and introduced the three different ways in which the INSERT INTO statement can be used. Before we create a script to insert records into the Roles table, finish this script off. Remove the SELECT statement and add a GO to the end of the script (we remove the SELECT as we don't need it when we rebuild the database). Save it as c:\temp\sqlbasics\apply\10 - Insert PhoneNumberTypes.sql. Then open up the 00 - Apply.sql script and add this code to the end of the script, so the records will be inserted if we rebuild the database again:

```
:setvar currentFile "10 - Insert PhoneNumberTypes.sql"
PRINT 'Executing $(path)$(currentFile)';
:r $(path)$(currentFile)
```

This should go above the line:

```
PRINT 'All apply scripts successfully executed.'
```

Wonderful! Now we'll create a new script to populate the Roles table.

More Inserts

Remember that roles are part of a many-to-many relationship with contacts, so one contact can hold one or more roles. We'll create a selection of roles that we can use in our system.

Open a New Query Window and add the role insert script.

```
USE AddressBook;

IF ((SELECT COUNT(1) FROM dbo.Roles) = 0)
BEGIN
INSERT INTO dbo.Roles (RoleTitle)
VALUES ('Developer'),
('DBA'),
('IT Support Specialist'),
('Manager'),
('Directors'),
('Database Administrator');
END;

SELECT * FROM dbo.Roles;

GO
```

We start with something new—there's no IF NOT EXISTS statement, just an IF. The SELECT COUNT(1) statement returns the number of rows in the Roles table. This line says if the number of rows found in the Roles table is zero, then insert the new rows. So if at least one row is present in Roles then nothing will be inserted. We're using the VALUES clause with multiple values to perform the inserts.

Run this and six rows should be inserted (Figure 8-7).

Figure 8-7. *An insert script for the* Roles *table*

Once you've seen this working, remove the SELECT from the script—again, we don't need it when rebuilding the database. Save the script as c:\temp\sqlbasics\apply\11 - Insert Roles.sql.

We're done with our reference data—or are we?

The UPDATE Statement

Oh no—we made a mistake when we inserted our records into the Roles table. Specifically, in record 5—it has the wrong RoleTitle. Nobody is going to have a RoleTitle of Directors—it should be Director. Darn! Well, our first fix is to open c:\temp\sqlbasics\apply\11 - Insert Roles.sql and remove the s from Directors (don't forget to save):

```
INSERT INTO dbo.Roles (RoleTitle)
VALUES ('Developer'),
('DBA')
('IT Support Specialist'),
('Manager'),
('Director'),
('Database Administrator');
```

The problem is, we've already executed this script. If we run it again, we still see Directors next to RoleId 5. This is because we added a check to the start of the script, preventing any inserts from occurring should at least one row exist. So how can we fix it? With an UPDATE statement! An UPDATE statement takes the form:

```
UPDATE TableName
SET ColumnName1 = NewValue1,
ColumnName2 = NewValue2,
ColumnNameN = NewValueN
WHERE RequiredColumnName = RequiredValue;
```

This is a pretty simple example, and the WHERE line is actually optional. You can specify as many columns for update as required. Here's our UPDATE script to fix Directors. Enter this into a New Query Window.

```
USE AddressBook;

UPDATE dbo.Roles
SET RoleTitle = 'Director'
WHERE RoleTitle = 'Directors';

SELECT * FROM dbo.Roles;
```

The first line is UPDATE dbo.Roles. This tells SQL Server the name of the table we want to update. The SET line is more granular, and informs the DBMS of the names of the columns we are changing, along with the new values. So we are setting the RoleTitle column to the value of Director.

The last line, the WHERE line, is key. The statement would run without this but would update the RoleTitle to Director *for every row in the table*. The WHERE clause limits the rows SQL Server will update. So here, we've told SQL Server to update rows where the RoleTitle column's value is equal to Directors. Run this and watch what happens—hopefully something similar to Figure 8-8.

Figure 8-8. Updating the Directors role

All fixed! You can run this again and again and the results won't change, as no rows now match the criteria we specified (RoleTitle = 'Directors'). Very nifty!

There are more complex versions of the UPDATE statement, but this example covers the basics. We'll meet those more complex versions in later chapters. The key thing to remember with UPDATE statements is to ensure your WHERE clauses are correct. Our later chapters will also show you how to check this.

As a final task here, modify the 00 - Apply.sql script to include script 11. Here's the code you need to add above the final PRINT statement:

```
:setvar currentFile "11 - Insert Roles.sql"
PRINT 'Executing $(path)$(currentFile)';
:r $(path)$(currentFile)
```

Deleting Records

We've added records and updated them. Logically, there's only one more thing we can do: remove them. Sometimes you do need to delete data from a database, perhaps for records that were mistakenly created. This is where the DELETE statement comes into play. This works in a very similar manner to the UPDATE statement. The format of the UPDATE statement is:

```
UPDATE TableName
SET ColumnName1 = NewValue1,
ColumnName2 = NewValue2,
ColumnNameN = NewValueN
WHERE RequiredColumnName = RequiredValue;
```

The DELETE statement is structured as:

```
DELETE FROM TableName
WHERE RequiredColumnName = RequiredValue;
```

We don't have the SET section, as you can't delete individual column values—you delete the entire row.

Now, if you look back at the image of our Roles table, you'll see an error still remains. We've fixed the Directors problem, but we have duplicate items. Item 2 is DBA and item 6 is Database Administrator. These are one and the same thing, and having two separate items will knock out any reports we try to run in the future for DBAs. The solution is to delete one of these items. "DBA" is the standard industry term, so we'll delete the last item—Database Administrator. In a New Query Window, type in the DELETE script:

```
USE AddressBook;

DELETE FROM dbo.Roles
WHERE RoleTitle = 'Database Administrator';

SELECT * FROM dbo.Roles;
```

I should point out that the SELECT statements we are running at the end of each batch are purely optional—we're using them to inspect that our expected value has been deleted. Run this statement and just the five rows in Figure 8-9 will be returned.

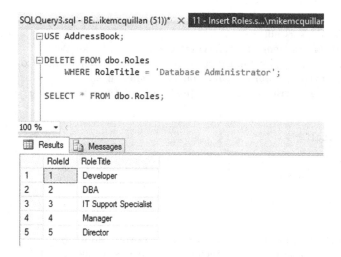

Figure 8-9. *Deleting the* Database Administrator *role*

We need to remove the invalid record from our main INSERT script. Open up c:\temp\sqlbasics\ apply\11 - Insert Roles.sql. Delete the Database Administrator line, and replace the ending comma on the Director line with a semicolon. Here's the updated script:

```
USE AddressBook;

IF ((SELECT COUNT(1) FROM dbo.Roles) = 0)
BEGIN
INSERT INTO dbo.Roles (RoleTitle)
VALUES ('Developer'),
('DBA'),
('IT Support Specialist'),
('Manager'),
('Director');
END;

GO
```

We're nearly done; we just need to create rollback scripts to clear out the PhoneNumberTypes and Rules tables. These are pretty easy, as all we have to do is empty each table (neither table contained any data before we put it in there with our preceding scripts). Create script c:\temp\sqlbasics\rollback\10 - Insert PhoneNumberTypes Rollback.sql first:

```
USE AddressBook;

DELETE FROM dbo.PhoneNumberTypes;

GO
```

Not much to that, is there? We don't need a WHERE clause, as we want to empty the entire table. Of course, you should always be careful when running DELETE statements like this. I've accidentally emptied out tables more times than I care to remember! Never in production, though (a manager of mine did that once—it wasn't good!).

Save this script as c:\temp\sqlbasics\rollback\11 - Insert Roles Rollback.sql.

```
USE AddressBook;

DELETE FROM dbo.Roles;

GO
```

Another simple script. Finish off by adding both of these scripts to the top of the SQLCMD 00 - Rollback.sql script, under the :setvar path line.

```
:setvar currentFile "11 - Insert Roles Rollback.sql"
PRINT 'Executing $(path)$(currentFile)';
:r $(path)$(currentFile)

:setvar currentFile "10 - Insert PhoneNumberTypes Rollback.sql"
PRINT 'Executing $(path)$(currentFile)';
:r $(path)$(currentFile)
```

Try running rollback scripts 10 and 11. You won't see any rows displayed, as we've not included a SELECT statement. You can tell the script has worked by the information message SQL Server returns to you. As Figure 8-10 shows, for instance, running the Roles rollback script (script 11) deletes five rows:

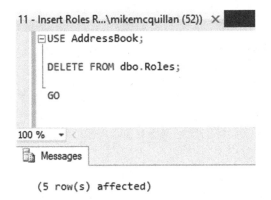

Figure 8-10. *Deleting all records from the Roles table*

Magnificent!

Summary

This was an interesting chapter, as we moved from the creation of objects that store data to the creation of the data itself. We've covered how to insert, update, and delete data from tables, using a variety of options. We've also seen how we can use the SELECT statement to check if data already exists in the table before we try to insert it.

We've now populated our reference data, so our next job is to add some contact information to the system. And the BULK INSERT command is going to help us do just that!

■ ■ ■

CHAPTER 9

Bulk Inserting Data

In the last chapter, we saw how we can manipulate records using INSERT INTO, UPDATE, and DELETE, and we used these statements to populate our reference data tables. Now let's add some contacts and their related information to our database. We could do this with these three statements—and we will—but we can also use SQL Server's BULK INSERT statement to add records via external files.

We'll start by adding some data using the BULK INSERT statement, and then we'll create a script to manually add a contact. We'll cover a lot of SQL Server functionality in this chapter, so hang on to your hat!

The BULK INSERT Statement

The BULK INSERT statement imports a data file into a database table (you can also import into a view, but that's something we won't look at in this book).

The basic structure of the BULK INSERT statement is:

```
BULK INSERT TableName FROM 'Full Path To FileName' WITH (Specify Options Here);
```

We are only interested in a couple of the options the statement provides, but if you want to see the full list, visit https://msdn.microsoft.com/en-us/library/ms188365.aspx.

Two things need to exist for the BULK INSERT statement to work:

- a table, into which data can be inserted

- a file containing data that will be imported into the table

The number of columns in the data file must correlate to the number of columns in the data file. We're going to start by importing a file into the Contacts table.

Preparing the Data File

Figure 9-1 gives us a look at the columns in our Contacts table.

ContactId	FirstName	LastName	DateOfBirth	AllowContactByPhone	CreatedDate

Figure 9-1. *Columns in the Contacts table*

And Figure 9-2 shows our Contacts data file as a table:

ContactId	FirstName	LastName	DateOfBirth	AllowContactByPhone	CreatedDate
0	Stephen	Gerrard	1980-05-30	1	
0	Dennis	Potter	1935-05-17	0	
0	Richard	Adams	1920-05-09	0	
0	Bertie	McQuillan	2001-06-30	1	
0	Walt	Disney	1966-12-05	1	
0	Barbara	Gordon	1952-01-11	0	
0	Josephine	Bailey	1949-05-31	1	
0	Linda	Canoglu	1959-07-11	1	
0	Grace	McQuillan	1993-09-27	0	
0	Vera	Black	1984-08-03	0	
0	Angelica	Jones	1981-02-04	1	
0	Steve	Davis	1957-08-22	1	
0	Allison	Fisher	1968-02-24	1	
0	julius	Marx	1990-10-02	0	
0	george	formby	1944-05-26	1	
0	Alan	Partridge	1965-04-14	0	
0	Harper	Lee	1986-04-28	1	
0	Robert	Burns	1959-01-25	0	
0	Michael	Jackson	1967-06-31	0	
0	Roald Dahl		1916-09-13	1	

Figure 9-2. Contacts *data file contents*

The first row contains the column names, and these map to the columns held in our Contacts table. The other rows contain data. You can download this file from www.mcqtech.com/books/introducingsql/files. Save it to c:\temp\sqlbasics\importfiles\01_Contacts.csv. You may need to create the **importfiles** folder if it doesn't already exist.

Having the column names in the file is completely optional, and if they are specified they don't even have to have the same names as the table. We have them in the file purely so we can see to which table column the data file column should map. BULK INSERT uses the position of the data file columns to map to the table columns. So column 1 in the file is imported into table column 1, column 2 maps to table column 2, and so on.

If we look at the rows of data in our file, we can see that the ContactId column contains 0. This is because the database will automatically calculate ContactId values for us, as ContactId is an IDENTITY column. CreatedDate is blank as this has a default value. We could have left AllowContactByPhone as a blank value, too, as this has a default value, but we want some of these values to be TRUE, so we specify the actual values as 1 (for TRUE) or 0 (for FALSE).

FirstName and LastName are self-explanatory. In the last row, you should note there is no LastName specified; don't worry about this. Remember that we have a Check constraint configured to prevent blank values from being inserted into the LastName column.

There's also an error in the DateOfBirth column: Michael Jackson has an invalid value in this column (there is no 31st day in June!). Note the format of the DateOfBirth column: YYYY-MM-DD. It is important you use the date format expected by SQL Server, otherwise the import will fail (there are ways around this, but they are outside of our scope).

The BULK INSERT statement uses text files. These can be created with a variety of tools, such as Notepad, Word, and Excel. Excel is quite often the best way of creating your data files, as it makes the construction of rows of data straightforward.

A text file may have any extension you care to give it, but these are the two most common types of text file you'll deal with:

- **TXT**: a text file

- **CSV**: a comma separated file

We are going to use a CSV file, which consists of rows, and column values separated by commas. Here's an example:

```
ContactId,FirstName,LastName,DateOfBirth,AllowContactByPhone,DateCreated
0,Stephen,Gerrard,1980-05-30,1,
```

You can use any type of separator you wish—commas are the most common, but you'll see tabs and pipes used regularly. The BULK INSERT statement allows you to specify what character you are using as the column terminator. Similarly, the newline character built into Windows is usually used as the row terminator (this is written as \r\n). If you receive files from other companies they may not follow these conventions, which is why you can specify your own characters if necessary.

The default column terminator is actually the tab character (\t). \r\n is the default row terminator.

To save a file in Excel as a comma-separated file, go to **File ➤ Save As**, and in the **Save as type** drop-down list, choose **CSV (Comma delimited) (*.csv)**. Figure 9-3 shows what the dialog looks like in Excel 2013.

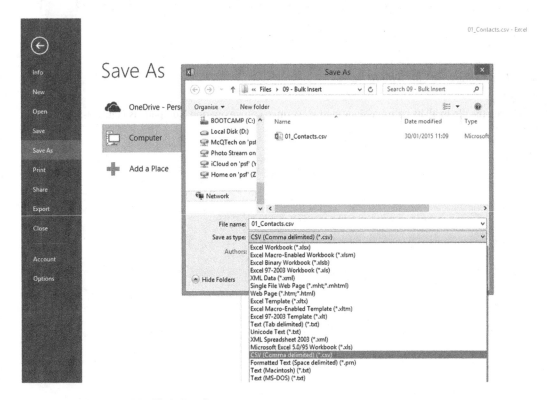

Figure 9-3. *Saving a CSV file in Excel*

If you have created the file manually rather than downloading it, make sure you save it as
c:\temp\sqlbasics\importfiles\01_Contacts.csv.

To view the file, make sure you've closed Excel (if you have it open). Open Windows Explorer and
navigate to c:\temp\sqlbasics\importfiles. Right-click 01_Contacts.csv and choose **Open with**. If
Open with has a submenu containing **Notepad** (as seen in Figure 9-4), click Notepad to open the file in that
program. If there is no submenu, click **Open with** and choose **Notepad** from the options that appear.

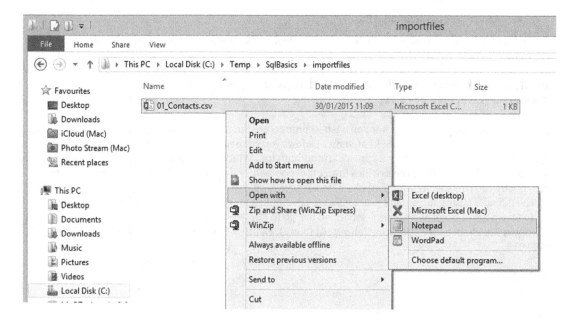

Figure 9-4. *Opening a CSV file with Notepad*

You'll see the file in all its comma-separated glory once you've opened Notepad, as Figure 9-5
demonstrates.

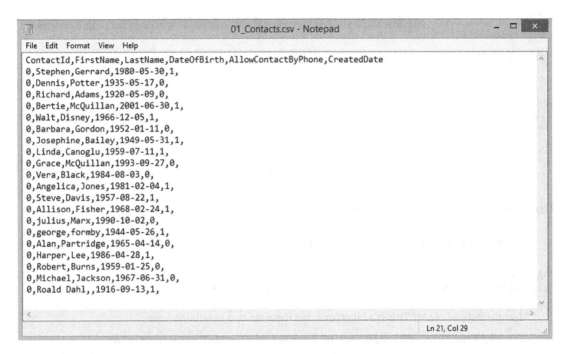

Figure 9-5. *A CSV file opened in Notepad*

The file is now ready for import. Time to type a BULK INSERT statement.

Importing the Data File

Open SSMS, connect to your server, and open up a New Query Window. Type in the BULK INSERT script:

```
USE AddressBook;

BULK INSERT dbo.Contacts FROM 'C:\temp\sqlbasics\importfiles\01_Contacts.csv';
GO
```

This is all pretty simple. We are saying to import the file 01_Contacts.csv to the Contacts table. But when we hit F5 to run it, things go wrong (Figure 9-6)!

```
SQLQuery2.sql - BE...ikemcquillan (52))*  ×
  ⊟USE AddressBook;

  ⊟BULK INSERT dbo.Contacts
       FROM 'C:\temp\sqlbasics\importfiles\01_Contacts.csv';

   GO
```

```
100 %   ▼
 ┠ Messages
  Msg 4832, Level 16, State 1, Line 3
  Bulk load: An unexpected end of file was encountered in the data file.
  Msg 7399, Level 16, State 1, Line 3
  The OLE DB provider "BULK" for linked server "(null)" reported an error. The provider did not give any information about the error.
  Msg 7330, Level 16, State 2, Line 3
  Cannot fetch a row from OLE DB provider "BULK" for linked server "(null)".
```

Figure 9-6. *A failed BULK INSERT statement*

Huh? THREE errors?! Well, the first error actually tells us the problem:

```
Msg 4832, Level 16, State 1, Line 3
Bulk load: An unexpected end of file was encountered in the data file.
```

"Unexpected end of file." This is a bit cryptic, but there are two possible causes:

- BULK INSERT is using the wrong row terminator for our file (\r\n instead of \n)

- BULK INSERT is using the wrong column terminator for our file (\t instead of ,)

The upshot is BULK INSERT cannot figure out where our rows or columns start and end.

We'll have to add a WITH clause to specify the row and column terminators. Column terminators are known as field terminators by the BULK INSERT statement. Replace the line:

```
BULK INSERT dbo.Contacts FROM 'C:\temp\sqlbasics\importfiles\01_Contacts.csv';
```

with:

```
BULK INSERT dbo.Contacts FROM 'C:\temp\sqlbasics\importfiles\01_Contacts.csv'
WITH (ROWTERMINATOR = '\n', FIELDTERMINATOR = ',');
```

There are a number of values you can provide for the ROWTERMINATOR clause, but \r\n and \n are the most common (\r is a carriage return, \n is a newline—these come from the C programming language).

Run this. Oh no, another error! Well, two actually.

```
Msg 4864, Level 16, State 1, Line 3
Bulk load data conversion error (type mismatch or invalid character for the specified
codepage) for row 1, column 1 (ContactId).
Msg 8114, Level 16, State 10, Line 3
Error converting data type DBTYPE_DBDATE to date.
```

The first error informs us that the ContactId value in the first row is invalid. The second error tells us there's an invalid date in the file.

Concentrating on the first error, let's take a look at the first row in our file (Figure 9-7).

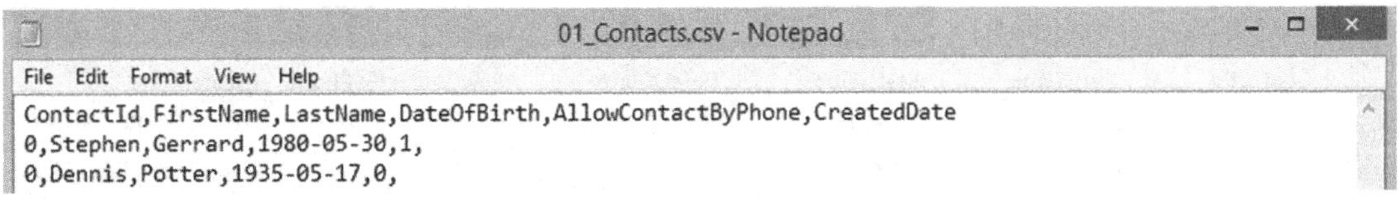

ContactId,FirstName,LastName,DateOfBirth,AllowContactByPhone,CreatedDate
0,Stephen,Gerrard,1980-05-30,1,
0,Dennis,Potter,1935-05-17,0,

Figure 9-7. The first row contains headers.

The first line of data for Stephen Gerrard looks okay; it has a 0 in it. ContactId is an IDENTITY column; specifying a 0 should allow the BULK INSERT statement to ignore the 0 and just assign the next value. When specifying a value for an IDENTITY column in a BULK INSERT statement, you must specify a value in the correct format (i.e., an integer value). We've specified 0 for every row, but we could have put any number we wished to in there and it should still work. If you want BULK INSERT to use the actual values we provide for an IDENTITY column, then you need to specify the KEEPIDENTITY clause inside the WITH declaration.

The Stephen Gerrard row isn't raising the error; this has a valid ContactId value. Row 1 has the error, and that is the row containing the column headers. Unless we specifically tell it, BULK INSERT will assume any row containing column headers is a data row. To solve this issue, we need to tell BULK INSERT to ignore the first row, by starting the import at row 2. Replace the existing BULK INSERT...WITH statement with this new version:

```
BULK INSERT dbo.Contacts FROM 'C:\temp\sqlbasics\importfiles\01_Contacts.csv'
WITH (ROWTERMINATOR = '\n', FIELDTERMINATOR = ',', FIRSTROW = 2);
```

There is also a LASTROW option, which lets you specify the number of the last row you want to import. If you had a 20-row file but just wanted to import 10 rows, you could specify LASTROW = 11 (assuming the first data row was row 2).

Run this and you should be left with just the DBTYPE_DBDATE error we saw earlier. This is being caused by our Michael Jackson row, which has a date of 1967-06-31. As we mentioned earlier, June has only 30 days!

There is an ERRORFILE clause we can add; maybe that will help? This copies any rows that fail to import into the error file specified.

```
BULK INSERT dbo.Contacts FROM 'C:\temp\sqlbasics\importfiles\01_Contacts.csv'
WITH (ROWTERMINATOR = '\n', FIELDTERMINATOR = ',', FIRSTROW = 2, ERRORFILE =
'c:\temp\sqlbasics\importfiles\01_Contacts_Errors.csv');
```

Still no joy:

```
Msg 8114, Level 16, State 10, Line 3
Error converting data type DBTYPE_DBDATE to date.
```

Unfortunately, no import can be attempted because the value specified doesn't meet the format of the column—a date in this case. To resolve the issue, we need to modify the file. Change Michael Jackson's DateOfBirth from 1967-06-31 to 1967-06-30. Save the file and run the BULK INSERT statement again.

Hopefully all will go well, and you'll see this message:

```
(19 row(s) affected)
```

Excellent, we've imported some contacts. But hang on (dramatic music here)! We have 20 rows in our file. What's happened to one of our rows? Open the table editor for the Contacts table to display the rows, like in Figure 9-8.

ContactId	FirstName	LastName	DateOfBirth	AllowContactByPhone	CreatedDate
1	Stephen	Gerrard	1980-05-30	True	2015-01-30 14:23:41.857
2	Dennis	Potter	1935-05-17	False	2015-01-30 14:23:41.857
3	Richard	Adams	1920-05-09	False	2015-01-30 14:23:41.857
4	Bertie	McQuillan	2001-06-30	True	2015-01-30 14:23:41.857
5	Walt	Disney	1966-12-05	True	2015-01-30 14:23:41.857
6	Barbara	Gordon	1952-01-11	False	2015-01-30 14:23:41.857
7	Josephine	Bailey	1949-05-31	True	2015-01-30 14:23:41.857
8	Linda	Canoglu	1959-07-11	True	2015-01-30 14:23:41.857
9	Grace	McQuillan	1993-09-27	False	2015-01-30 14:23:41.857
10	Vera	Black	1984-08-03	False	2015-01-30 14:23:41.857
11	Angelica	Jones	1981-02-04	True	2015-01-30 14:23:41.857
12	Steve	Davis	1957-08-22	True	2015-01-30 14:23:41.857
13	Allison	Fisher	1968-02-24	True	2015-01-30 14:23:41.857
14	julius	Marx	1990-10-02	False	2015-01-30 14:23:41.857
15	george	formby	1944-05-26	True	2015-01-30 14:23:41.857
16	Alan	Partridge	1965-04-14	False	2015-01-30 14:23:41.857
17	Harper	Lee	1986-04-28	True	2015-01-30 14:23:41.857
18	Robert	Burns	1959-01-25	False	2015-01-30 14:23:41.857
19	Michael	Jackson	1967-06-30	False	2015-01-30 14:23:41.857

Figure 9-8. Nineteen successful rows

Who is missing? It's the last row, for Roald Dahl. If you recall, this row didn't have a LastName value.

0,Roald Dahl,,1916-09-13,1,

We added a Check constraint to prevent blank FirstName and LastName values in Chapter 7. This constraint has correctly stopped the bad data from coming in. Hurray for us!

BULK INSERT AND CHECK CONSTRAINTS

The behavior we've just encountered isn't SQL Server's expected behavior. The BULK INSERT documentation states that Check constraints will be ignored by the BULK INSERT statement, unless the CHECK_CONSTRAINTS clause is specified. So the Roald Dahl row should have been inserted. Any rows that fail because of a Check constraint will not be added to the ERRORFILE, either.

My view is this is a bug in BULK INSERT. To be on the safe side, you should specify CHECK_CONSTRAINTS if you want constraints to be enforced. You'll see this clause on the rest of the BULK INSERT statements in this chapter.

We've finished with our BULK INSERT, and have successfully inserted 19 contact rows. Our complete BULK INSERT script follows; save this as c:\temp\sqlbasics\apply\12 - Bulk Insert Contacts.sql.

```
USE AddressBook;

BULK INSERT dbo.Contacts FROM 'C:\temp\sqlbasics\importfiles\01_Contacts.csv'
WITH
(ROWTERMINATOR = '\n', FIELDTERMINATOR = ',', FIRSTROW = 2, ERRORFILE =
'c:\temp\sqlbasics\importfiles\01_Contacts_Errors.csv', CHECK_CONSTRAINTS);
GO
```

Add a call to this file in the 00 - Apply.sql script, so SQLCMD will execute the script whenever we rebuild the database. Put this above the PRINT statement near the bottom of the script.

```
:setvar currentFile "12 - Bulk Insert Contacts.sql"
PRINT 'Executing $(path)$(currentFile)';
:r $(path)$(currentFile)
```

Great; now for the other tables.

More Bulk Insert Escapades

We have five more tables we need to populate:

- ContactAddresses
- ContactNotes
- ContactPhoneNumbers
- ContactRoles
- ContactVerificationDetails

We'll use BULK INSERT to help us with the population. Except for ContactVerificationDetails, which extends the Contacts table, all of these are child tables, which presents us with a different set of problems.

Populating these tables is not as easy as you might expect. They all need a ContactId value to be provided. Without a ContactId, not one record can be created in any of these tables. Until we run script 12 to BULK INSERT the Contacts table, none of our records will have a ContactId value. We have two options here; assume the same ContactIds will always be assigned to the same contacts when the database is created, or create custom scripts to insert the values.

The custom script is tempting, but it is the long way around in this case. We'll take a look at creating a custom script to add our missing Roald Dahl record a bit later. For now, it's pretty safe to assume the same ContactIds will always be assigned to the same contact records when the database is created. After all, the scripts are always executed in the same order, against a clean database. So we'll import CSV files to all five tables. You can download the files from www.mcqtech.com/books/introducingsql/files. Save them to c:\temp\sqlbasics\importfiles. As displayed in Figure 9-9, you should finish up with six files in the folder.

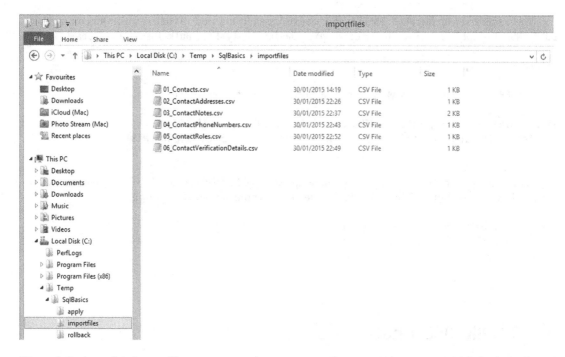

Figure 9-9. *A set of six import files*

The files we are about to import are going to include the ID values for records we assume will already exist, such as Contacts, PhoneNumberTypes, and Roles. To be on the safe side, rebuild your database before running these import files. This is a good checkpoint to ensure your 00 - Apply.sql and 00 - Rollback.sql files are working as expected (don't forget to turn on SQLCMD mode from the **Query** menu before trying to run these scripts). After you have rebuilt your database, create this script:

```
USE AddressBook;

BULK INSERT dbo.ContactAddresses FROM 'c:\temp\sqlbasics\importfiles\02_ContactAddresses.csv'
WITH
(ROWTERMINATOR = '\n', FIELDTERMINATOR = ',', FIRSTROW = 2,
ERRORFILE = 'c:\temp\sqlbasics\importfiles\02_ContactAddresses_Errors.csv',
CHECK_CONSTRAINTS);

GO
```

Save this as c:\temp\sqlbasics\apply\13 - Bulk Insert Contact Addresses.sql. Now copy this code into a New Query Window, and change the following two lines:

- BULK INSERT dbo.ContactAddresses FROM
  'c:\temp\sqlbasics\importfiles\02_ContactAddresses.csv'

- ERRORFILE = c:\temp\sqlbasics\importfiles\02_ContactAddresses_Errors.csv',

To:

- BULK INSERT dbo.ContactNote FROM 'c:\temp\sqlbasics\importfiles\
  03_ContactNotes.csv'

- ERRORFILE = 'c:\temp\sqlbasics\importfiles\03_ContactNotes_Errors.csv',

Save this script as c:\temp\sqlbasics\apply\14 - Bulk Insert ContactNotes.sql. Follow these steps for the next three scripts:

- Change the preceding two lines to:

  ```
  BULK INSERT dbo.ContactPhoneNumbers FROM 'c:\temp\sqlbasics\importfiles\04_
  ContactPhoneNumbers.csv'
  ERRORFILE = 'c:\temp\sqlbasics\importfiles\04_ContactPhoneNumbers_Errors.csv',
  ```

- Save the script as c:\temp\sqlbasics\apply\15 - Bulk Insert
  ContactPhoneNumbers.sql.

- Change the two lines to:

  ```
  BULK INSERT dbo.ContactRoles FROM 'c:\temp\sqlbasics\importfiles\05_ContactRoles.csv'
  ERRORFILE = 'c:\temp\sqlbasics\importfiles\05_ContactRoles_Errors.csv',
  ```

- Save the script as c:\temp\sqlbasics\apply\16 - Bulk Insert ContactRoles.sql

- Change the two lines to:

  ```
  BULK INSERT dbo.ContactVerificationDetails FROM 'c:\temp\sqlbasics\
  importfiles\06_ContactVerificationDetails.csv'
  ERRORFILE = 'c:\temp\sqlbasics\importfiles\06_ContactVerificationDetails_Errors.csv',
  ```

- Save the script as c:\temp\sqlbasics\apply\17 - Bulk Insert
  ContactVerificationDetails.sql

You should now have the 18 files shown in Figure 9-10 in your apply folder (including the 00 - Apply.sql script).

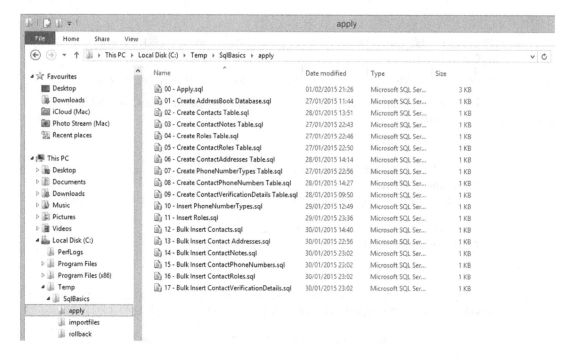

Figure 9-10. *The complete set of apply scripts so far*

You may have noted that scripts 12 to 17 all include the exact same code; the only things that change are the paths to the import file and the output error file, should any errors occur. We could have placed all of these calls into one script file, but adding them separately makes it easier for us to drop an import should we need to.

Let's quickly look at Figure 9-11, which displays the contents of the 02_ContactAddresses.csv file.

AddressId	ContactId	HouseNumber	Street	City	Postcode
0	1	47	Madryn Avenue	Liverpool	L1 1PR
0	1	29	Formby Road	Formby	L21 1DD
0	2	169	Portobello Road	London	SW19 2AK
0	3	Nadallo	Los Ramblas	Barcelona	11223
0	4	2	Thornycroft	Chester	CH8 4PA
0	5	Walt Disney World	Florida	USA	45689
0	6	11	Knight Road	Gotham	99331
0	7	123	Gladwyn Street	Pottersville	PT9 5GA
0	8	265	Princes Road	Edinburgh	EH1 2EW
0	9	122	Stirling Crescent	Prescot	L32 9TY
0	10	198	Dartmoor Road	Yelverton	PL20 6RR
0	11	Maesdu Park	Builder Street West	Llandudno	LL30 1HH
0	12	10	South Street	Romford	RM1 6TV
0	13	1	St George's Avenue	Northampton	NN2 6JD
0	14	24	Mission Hill	Los Angeles County	78944
0	15	Beryldene	The Front	Lytham St Annes	BL1 1LX
0	16	Partridge House	Royal Arcade	Norwich	NR2 1NQ
0	17	Atticus Ranch	Maycomb County	Alabama	91210
0	18	Burns Cottage	Ayr	Alloway	KA1 1WK
0	19	Neverland Ranch	Santa Barbara	California	93441

Figure 9-11. The ContactAddresses.csv file contents

The last four columns contain address information, but the first two columns are a bit different. AddressId is the primary key of the ContactAddresses table, and it's also an IDENTITY column. So just as we did with the ContactId column in the 01_Contacts.csv import file, we set this value to 0. Doing this will cause the BULK INSERT statement to assign IDENTITY values in the AddressId column to the new records.

The really interesting column is ContactId. This is populated with a set of numbers. These are the ContactIds we know will be assigned to the contact records when they are created. We know what the IDs will be based on the record's location in the file. The Stephen Gerrard record is the first record in the 01_Contacts.csv import file, so when the database has been rebuilt and is awaiting an import, it will be assigned the ContactId value of 1. The first two addresses in 02_ContactAddresses.csv are for ContactId 1, meaning they will both be linked to Stephen Gerrard. All other records work in a similar manner for their appropriate contacts.

GENERATING IMPORT FILES

Normally, you would not have ID values present in a file; you'd have a different piece of information, such as a customer number. You would create something called a *staging table* to which the data would be imported via the BULK INSERT statement. A staging table is just a table that exactly mirrors the contents of the import file. This is what we've just done—we've actually treated our data tables as staging tables.

Once you have data in the staging tables you would have another piece of code ready to run that could look up the correct ContactId for a record, then insert the record into the appropriate table (e.g., ContactAddresses). One of the exercises suggested in Appendix D asks you to modify the database to implement this type of import.

Open the 00 - Apply.sql script, and above this line:

```
PRINT 'All apply scripts successfully executed.';
```

add the lines:

```
:setvar currentFile "13 - Bulk Insert Contact Addresses.sql"
PRINT 'Executing $(path)$(currentFile)';
:r $(path)$(currentFile)

:setvar currentFile "14 - Bulk Insert ContactNotes.sql"
PRINT 'Executing $(path)$(currentFile)';
:r $(path)$(currentFile)

:setvar currentFile "15 - Bulk Insert ContactPhoneNumbers.sql"
PRINT 'Executing $(path)$(currentFile)';
:r $(path)$(currentFile)

:setvar currentFile "16 - Bulk Insert ContactRoles.sql"
PRINT 'Executing $(path)$(currentFile)';
:r $(path)$(currentFile)

:setvar currentFile "17 - Bulk Insert ContactVerificationDetails.sql"
PRINT 'Executing $(path)$(currentFile)';
:r $(path)$(currentFile)
```

Save this, and then rebuild the database (run the 00 - Rollback.sql script first, then the updated 00 - Apply.sql script). If you take a look at any of the contact tables now, you'll find data in them. Figure 9-12 shows the ContactPhoneNumberstable:

BERTIE1\SQLEXPRE...tactPhoneNumbers ✕ 00 - Rollback.sql -...\mikemcquillan (54)) 00 - Apply.sql - BE...mikemcquillan (51))

PhoneNumberId	ContactId	PhoneNumberTypeId	PhoneNumber
1	1	2	0151 264 2500
2	3	1	01565 100 100
3	7	3	07000 200 200
4	8	3	07000 300 300
5	12	1	01928 150 150
6	12	3	07500 350 350
7	14	1	01606 250 250
8	14	2	01606 260 260
9	16	1	01782 400 400
10	16	2	01782 410 410
11	16	3	07600 420 420
12	16	4	01782 430 430
13	18	3	07700 500 500
14	18	4	01244 520 520
15	19	4	0161 900 900
►* NULL	NULL	NULL	NULL

Figure 9-12. *Imported* ContactPhoneNumbers *records*

Operation Data Import successfully completed, Sergeant Major! Now for the rollback.

Truncating Tables

The rollbacks for these scripts are fairly simple. Each rollback script just needs to clear out the table it's corresponding apply script has populated, ensuring the IDENTITY value is reset back to 1. This is actually a breeze for all tables except the Contacts table.

Here's the script; there isn't much to it:

```
USE AddressBook;

TRUNCATE TABLE dbo.ContactAddresses;

GO
```

The TRUNCATE TABLE is a special type of DELETE command. If you think back to our earlier look at the DELETE statement, we could delete an entire table if we didn't specify a WHERE clause. TRUNCATE TABLE does the same thing, the principal difference being TRUNCATE TABLE *always* clears out a table. You cannot tell a TRUNCATE TABLE statement which records you want to delete—it's all or nothing.

The preceding script will clear out the ContactAddresses table. TRUNCATE TABLE is a very useful alternative to DELETE FROM when you want to clear out a table:

- TRUNCATE TABLE resets IDENTITY columns back to the seed value; DELETE FROM doesn't do this, and IDENTITY will pick up from where it left off.

- DELETE FROM logs every single row deletion, which can quickly fill up your log. TRUNCATE TABLE logs just the TRUNCATE TABLE command, taking up less log space.

- TRUNCATE TABLE is faster than DELETE FROM.

One key thing to remember is TRUNCATE TABLE cannot be used on tables that are referenced by a foreign key. ContactAddresses participates in a foreign-key relationship with the Contacts table, but it is the child in that relationship; the TRUNCATE TABLE restriction applies to the parent tables. So we are good to use ContactAddresses with TRUNCATE TABLE.

As I said earlier, creating the rollback script is a breeze for all tables except the Contacts table. The foreign-key restriction is the reason we can't use TRUNCATE TABLE with the Contacts table. We'll come back to Contacts in a moment after we've created the other rollback scripts.

Enter the script for ContactAddresses given earlier and save it as c:\temp\sqlbasics\rollback\13 - Bulk Insert Contact Addresses Rollback.sql. Now you can create the rollback scripts for the other tables:

- c:\temp\sqlbasics\rollback\14 - Bulk Insert ContactNotes Rollback.sql

  ```
  USE AddressBook;

  TRUNCATE TABLE dbo.ContactNotes;

  GO
  ```

- c:\temp\sqlbasics\rollback\15 - Bulk Insert ContactPhoneNumbers Rollback.sql

  ```
  USE AddressBook;

  TRUNCATE TABLE dbo.ContactPhoneNumbers;

  GO
  ```

- c:\temp\sqlbasics\rollback\16 - Bulk Insert ContactRoles Rollback.sql

  ```
  USE AddressBook;

  TRUNCATE TABLE dbo.ContactRoles;

  GO
  ```

- c:\temp\sqlbasics\rollback\17 - Bulk Insert ContactVerificationDetails Rollback.sql

  ```
  USE AddressBook;

  TRUNCATE TABLE dbo.ContactVerificationDetails;

  GO
  ```

We're missing rollback script 12! We need this to clear out the Contacts table. As mentioned, we can't use TRUNCATE TABLE here, so we'll replace this with DELETE FROM instead.

```
USE AddressBook;

DELETE FROM dbo.Contacts;

GO
```

Hold on, though—this only fulfills half of our requirement! Yes, it will clear the table out. But it won't reset the ContactId IDENTITY column to 1. To do that, we need to add something called a DBCC command.

```
USE AddressBook;

DELETE FROM dbo.Contacts;
DBCC CHECKIDENT('dbo.Contacts', RESEED, 1);

GO
```

Save this script as c:\temp\sqlbasics\rollback\12 - Bulk Insert Contacts Rollback.sql.

The DBCC command—DBCC CHECKIDENT—resets the IDENTITY column to its seed value. In brackets, we specify the table name, the RESEED command, and the value we want to reseed to—1, in this case. DBCC stands for Database Console Command, and a number of these commands are available to you in SQL Server; look up what is on offer at https://msdn.microsoft.com/en-us/library/ms188796.aspx.

DBCC COMMANDS

Database Console Commands are often used by DBAs. They can be used to check the status of a database (DBCC CHECKDB) or to shrink a file (DBCC SHRINKFILE). It's well worth taking a look at what can be done with DBCC commands; you never know when they'll come in handy.

We've successfully created a full set of rollback scripts. As with the apply folder, the rollback folder should now contain 18 files (you can see these in Figure 9-13).

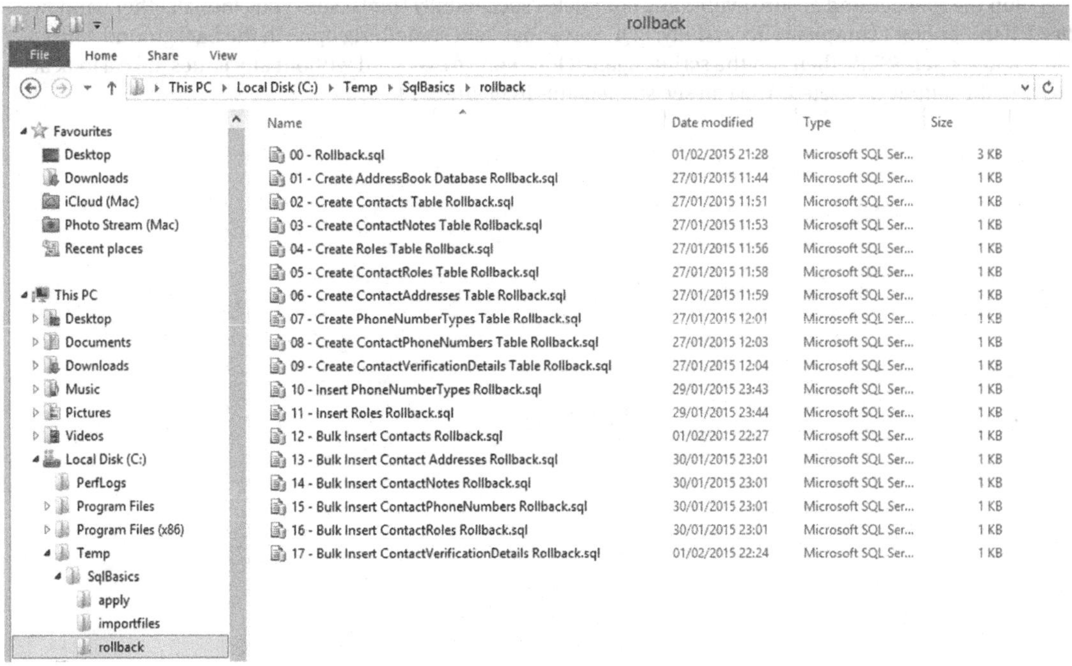

Figure 9-13. *The complete set of rollback scripts so far*

The final step is to include our new files in the 00 - Rollback.sql SQLCMD script. Add these lines to the top of the script, underneath the :setvar path line.

```
:setvar currentFile "17 - Bulk Insert ContactVerificationDetails Rollback.sql"
PRINT 'Executing $(path)$(currentFile)';
:r $(path)$(currentFile)

:setvar currentFile "16 - Bulk Insert ContactRoles Rollback.sql"
PRINT 'Executing $(path)$(currentFile)';
:r $(path)$(currentFile)

:setvar currentFile "15 - Bulk Insert ContactPhoneNumbers Rollback.sql"
PRINT 'Executing $(path)$(currentFile)';
:r $(path)$(currentFile)

:setvar currentFile "14 - Bulk Insert ContactNotes Rollback.sql"
PRINT 'Executing $(path)$(currentFile)';
:r $(path)$(currentFile)

:setvar currentFile "13 - Bulk Insert Contact Addresses Rollback.sql"
PRINT 'Executing $(path)$(currentFile)';
:r $(path)$(currentFile)

:setvar currentFile "12 - Bulk Insert Contacts Rollback.sql"
PRINT 'Executing $(path)$(currentFile)';
:r $(path)$(currentFile)
```

Run the rollback and ensure everything completes successfully (make sure you close all other windows first). If things don't complete successfully, SQL Server has kept something open in the background—just close and reopen SSMS, then run the scripts again. Once you've executed without any issues, take a look at some of the output generated. You can see some of this in Figure 9-14.

```
Messages
   Executing C:\Temp\SqlBasics\rollback\17 - Bulk Insert ContactVerificationDetails Rollback.sql
   Executing C:\Temp\SqlBasics\rollback\16 - Bulk Insert ContactRoles Rollback.sql
   Executing C:\Temp\SqlBasics\rollback\15 - Bulk Insert ContactPhoneNumbers Rollback.sql
   Executing C:\Temp\SqlBasics\rollback\14 - Bulk Insert ContactNotes Rollback.sql
   Executing C:\Temp\SqlBasics\rollback\13 - Bulk Insert Contact Addresses Rollback.sql
   Executing C:\Temp\SqlBasics\rollback\12 - Bulk Insert Contacts Rollback.sql

   (19 row(s) affected)
   Checking identity information: current identity value '19'.
   DBCC execution completed. If DBCC printed error messages, contact your system administrator.
   Executing C:\Temp\SqlBasics\rollback\11 - Insert Roles Rollback.sql

   (5 row(s) affected)
   Executing C:\Temp\SqlBasics\rollback\10 - Insert PhoneNumberTypes Rollback.sql

   (4 row(s) affected)
   Executing C:\Temp\SqlBasics\rollback\09 - Create ContactVerificationDetails Table Rollback.sql
   Executing C:\Temp\SqlBasics\rollback\08 - Create ContactPhoneNumbers Table Rollback.sql
   Executing C:\Temp\SqlBasics\rollback\07 - Create PhoneNumberTypes Table Rollback.sql
   Executing C:\Temp\SqlBasics\rollback\06 - Create ContactAddresses Table Rollback.sql
   Executing C:\Temp\SqlBasics\rollback\05 - Create ContactRoles Table Rollback.sql
   Executing C:\Temp\SqlBasics\rollback\04 - Create Roles Table Rollback.sql
   Executing C:\Temp\SqlBasics\rollback\03 - Create ContactNotes Table Rollback.sql
   Executing C:\Temp\SqlBasics\rollback\02 - Create Contacts Table Rollback.sql
```

Figure 9-14. *Output of the rollback script*

All scripts should execute as normal, but look at the lines that show row(s) affected. This tells you how many rows were deleted from the appropriate tables. There is also a message telling you that the DBCC command has executed, and what the current value was before the DBCC CHECKIDENT command ran.

After rollback has completed, run the 00 - Apply.sql script to recreate the database. Make sure the scripts have completed successfully. Once completed, you'll see we have a **Results** tab displayed, instead of the **Messages** tab. Figure 9-15 shows the contents of the **Results** tab.

	PhoneNumberTypeId	PhoneNumberType
1	1	Home
2	2	Work
3	3	Mobile
4	4	Other

	RoleId	RoleTitle
1	1	Developer
2	2	DBA
3	3	IT Support Specialist
4	4	Manager
5	5	Director

Figure 9-15. *Results output of the apply script*

This is because we left SELECT statements in at the end of the PhoneNumberTypes and Roles record creation scripts—the **Results** tab shows us the results of those SELECT statements. Click the **Messages** tab to see the output generated by the scripts (shown in Figure 9-16):

```
▦ Results   ▤ Messages
   Executing C:\Temp\SqlBasics\apply\01 - Create AddressBook Database.sql
   Executing C:\Temp\SqlBasics\apply\02 - Create Contacts Table.sql
   Executing C:\Temp\SqlBasics\apply\03 - Create ContactNotes Table.sql
   Executing C:\Temp\SqlBasics\apply\04 - Create Roles Table.sql
   Executing C:\Temp\SqlBasics\apply\05 - Create ContactRoles Table.sql
   Executing C:\Temp\SqlBasics\apply\06 - Create ContactAddresses Table.sql
   Executing C:\Temp\SqlBasics\apply\07 - Create PhoneNumberTypes Table.sql
   Executing C:\Temp\SqlBasics\apply\08 - Create ContactPhoneNumbers Table.sql
   Executing C:\Temp\SqlBasics\apply\09 - Create ContactVerificationDetails Table.sql
   Executing C:\Temp\SqlBasics\apply\10 - Insert PhoneNumberTypes.sql

   (1 row(s) affected)

   (1 row(s) affected)

   (2 row(s) affected)

   (4 row(s) affected)
   Executing C:\Temp\SqlBasics\apply\11 - Insert Roles.sql

   (5 row(s) affected)

   (5 row(s) affected)
   Executing C:\Temp\SqlBasics\apply\12 - Bulk Insert Contacts.sql

   (19 row(s) affected)
   Executing C:\Temp\SqlBasics\apply\13 - Bulk Insert Contact Addresses.sql

   (20 row(s) affected)
   Executing C:\Temp\SqlBasics\apply\14 - Bulk Insert ContactNotes.sql

   (11 row(s) affected)
   Executing C:\Temp\SqlBasics\apply\15 - Bulk Insert ContactPhoneNumbers.sql
```

Figure 9-16. *Messages output of the apply script*

Again, we can see lots of row(s) affected messages, telling us how many rows were added to each table by the appropriate script. Not bad; now we have a database with some data in it!

Summary

That was an epic journey, much like Bilbo's trek to Dale in *The Hobbit*. Of course, Bilbo's adventures don't end when he reaches Dale, and our adventures in data import haven't finished with this chapter, either.

Do you remember Roald Dahl? Not in the sense that he was an author who wrote some fantastic books, but rather in the sense that we had to take his record out of our Contacts import file. Our last data task is to create an import script to bring Roald Dahl to life in our database, and we'll look at doing this in the very next chapter. Keep walking!

CHAPTER 10

■ ■ ■

Creating Data Import Scripts

We've just seen, in some detail, how the BULK INSERT statement can be used to import files into database tables. Unfortunately, there are some limitations with BULK INSERT, which meant we had to remove one of our contact records from the appropriate files.

Fortunately, T-SQL can come to our rescue. In this chapter, we are going to create a script to insert a contact record and its associated child records (addresses, phone numbers, and so on). I'll introduce lots of new T-SQL terms in this chapter, so hold your nose and jump in!

Purpose of the Import Script

Our aim is to successfully add Roald Dahl to the database, along with all his related records. The records we want to add are:

- Contacts record
- ContactVerificationDetails record
- ContactRoles record, adding Roald as a developer
- ContactAddresses record
- ContactNotes record
- Two ContactPhoneNumbers records, one for a mobile phone, and one for a work phone number

Roald failed to import as part of our BULK INSERT statement, as the LastName column had incorrectly been left blank. We could have created a second comma-separated file containing a fixed version of Roald Dahl's record, but then we wouldn't have fun creating this script, would we?

Starting the Script with Variables

In SSMS, open a New Query Window and add this T-SQL code:

```
USE AddressBook;

DECLARE @ContactId INT;
```

The USE statement is familiar to us, but the DECLARE statement is new. This declares a variable. A *variable* is a temporary object that can hold a value for us. The line breaks down as follows:

- **DECLARE**: Tells SQL Server we are declaring a variable.

- **@ContactId**: The name of the variable. Almost every variable in T-SQL must begin with an @ symbol (there is the odd exception, but these exceptions are outside the scope of this book). A variable cannot be a reserved word (e.g., a word in the T-SQL language).

- **INT**: The type of variable. This can be a valid SQL Server data type, such as VARCHAR(200) or DATETIME.

Variables are very useful as they can give seemingly random values a meaningful name and purpose. They only exist for the lifetime of the script (at which point they are destroyed), and they can hold transitory information until it is needed. Variables will become an important part of your T-SQL toolkit. We'll expand the DECLARE statement to include a few other variables.

```
DECLARE @ContactId INT,
@DeveloperRoleId INT,
@MobilePhoneNumberTypeId TINYINT,
@WorkPhoneNumberTypeId TINYINT,
@NumberOfVerificationRecords INT,
@NumberOfContactRoleRecords INT,
@NumberOfContactAddressRecords INT,
@NumberOfContactNoteRecords INT,
@NumberOfContactPhoneNumberRecords INT;
```

Now we have nine variables. Nearly all of these are INTs, except for the two phone number type variables, which are TINYINTs. You should be able to figure out what each variable is for from its name. We could have written:

```
DECLARE @ContactId INT;
DECLARE @DeveloperRoleId INT;
DECLARE @MobilePhoneNumberTypeId TINYINT;
```

This is a lot more typing and not as succinct. It won't change the performance either way. We have a set of variables in place. Now we have to look up the reference data values we are interested in.

Reference Data Lookups

Do you remember our discussion about "real" data versus reference data in Chapter 8? Reference data was the stuff you add to the database that is used as metadata, such as phone number types and roles. We're not interested in these particular things themselves, but we are interested in them as part of a wider contact record.

We aim to add Roald Dahl as a developer, with mobile and work phone numbers. This necessitates looking up the appropriate reference data values. We need the ID values of the preceding records to be able to insert them into the appropriate tables. We are going to populate three of our variables with these values:

- @DeveloperRoleId

- @MobilePhoneNumberTypeId

- @WorkPhoneNumberTypeId

Add these lines under the variable declarations:

```
-- Obtain lookup values
SELECT @DeveloperRoleId = RoleId FROM dbo.Roles WHERE RoleTitle = 'Developer';
SELECT @MobilePhoneNumberTypeId = PhoneNumberTypeId FROM dbo.PhoneNumberTypes
WHERE PhoneNumberType = 'Mobile';
SELECT @WorkPhoneNumberTypeId = PhoneNumberTypeId FROM dbo.PhoneNumberTypes
WHERE PhoneNumberType = 'Work';
```

The first line begins with --. The text following it looks a bit odd—it reads like English. That's because it *is* English! This is what is known as a comment—something the developer adds to explain what a particular piece of code is doing. A comment is not part of the code, but instead helps to describe the code. We've helpfully stated here that the lines below the comment will obtain some lookup values. Comments are very useful and we'll sprinkle this script with them. Note there are two ways of declaring comments:

- Single-line comments can be created with -- (two hyphens)

- Multi-line comments should be created using /* to start, and */ to finish

So you could have:

```
-- Obtain lookup values
/* Obtain lookup values */
```

Use whatever suits you best.

The second line is an almost typical SELECT statement:

```
SELECT @DeveloperRoleId = RoleId FROM dbo.Roles WHERE RoleTitle = 'Developer';
```

SELECT @DeveloperRoleId = RoleId says set the @DeveloperRoleId variable to the value of the RoleId column in the specified table.

FROM dbo.Roles WHERE RoleTitle = 'Developer' tells SQL Server to obtain RoleId from the Roles table, using the ID for the record where the role title is equal to "Developer". This statement must only return one row, otherwise it will fail—you cannot assign multiple values to a variable.

We still haven't looked at SELECT in any great depth yet, but we did see it in basic use earlier, selecting out the contents of a table. Here we use it to assign a value to a variable. This is a pretty common piece of code and one you'll come across often. We could have written:

```
SELECT @DeveloperRoleId = 1;
```

This has same end result, but how do you know the ID of the developer role is 1? And what happens if the developer role was added using a different ID? The first version is better—it tells us what it is trying to do and will always find the correct ID, thanks to the WHERE clause.

The two other SELECT statements are exactly the same, but populate the two phone number type variables.

Now add these lines.

```
PRINT 'Developer Role ID: ' + CAST(@DeveloperRoleId AS VARCHAR(20));
PRINT 'Mobile Phone Number Type ID: ' + CAST(@MobilePhoneNumberTypeId AS VARCHAR(20));
PRINT 'Work Phone Number Type ID: ' + CAST(@WorkPhoneNumberTypeId AS VARCHAR(20));
```

The PRINT statement is something else we've already met, but there is some new stuff, too. It's all normal at first—PRINT 'Developer Role ID: '. But then we have a + sign. What's that for? It is telling the PRINT statement to add whatever comes after the + sign to the 'Developer Role ID: ' string we've already declared (this is how SQL Server handles string concatenation). What comes after the plus sign is:

```
CAST(@DeveloperRoleId AS VARCHAR(20));
```

The PRINT statement can only display strings. @DeveloperRoleId is an INT. So if we had written this:

```
PRINT 'Developer Role ID: ' + @DeveloperRoleId;
```

The statement would have failed with an error. We need to change the type temporarily from INT to VARCHAR. The terminology to do this is to CAST the value from one type to another. So we cast the integer variable to a string using the CAST function.

THE CAST FUNCTION

You can cast most types from one to another, as long as they make sense. If you have a string value of "2015-01-02" you could cast it to a DATETIME, using CAST('2015-01-02' AS DATETIME). But you couldn't cast "Hello" as a DATETIME.

When casting, think about what you are trying to do and whether you need the cast.

Also, take a look at the CONVERT function. This can be used like CAST, but it gives you more control over dates.

The two other PRINT statements are very similar to the statement we've just worked through.
We can run what we have so far by pressing F5. If you see the following output, everything is working!

```
Developer Role ID: 1
Mobile Phone Number Type ID: 3
Work Phone Number Type ID: 2
```

Splendid, our reference data lookups are working. Now to add some real data.

Inserting the Contact Record

We don't want to insert the contact record and its associated subrecords—*unless it doesn't already exist*. We already know how to check for the existence of a record: we use the IF NOT EXISTS statement we've been using throughout the book. This time, we want to check if Roald Dahl already exists, so we write the following line at the bottom of our script:

```
IF NOT EXISTS (SELECT 1 FROM dbo.Contacts WHERE FirstName = 'Roald' AND LastName = 'Dahl')
BEGIN;
```

If a Contacts record exists with a FirstName of 'Roald' and a LastName of 'Dahl', we won't execute the code under the BEGIN block. BEGIN and END enclose the code that will execute if the condition required to fulfil the IF NOT EXISTS statement has been met.

We'll now add the INSERT under the BEGIN; statement we just added.

```
-- No need to specify AllowContactByPhone or CreatedDate, as they have
-- default values
-- and Roald has said we cannot contact him by phone
INSERT INTO dbo.Contacts(FirstName, LastName, DateOfBirth) VALUES ('Roald', 'Dahl',
'1916-09-13');
```

Nothing new here, we're just adding a record to Contacts. The next line is new, though:

```
SELECT @ContactId = @@IDENTITY;
```

The ContactId column in the Contacts table is an IDENTITY column. To be able to insert records into ContactAddresses and other subtables, we need the ContactId. Specifically, we need to store the ContactId value assigned to Roald Dahl's record in the @ContactId variable. This is where @@IDENTITY comes in. This is a SQL Server global variable. It holds the last identity value generated by the database, no matter which table generated it.

If you insert a record into ContactAddresses and it is given AddressId 6 by its IDENTITY column, @@IDENTITY will hold the value 6. If you insert a record into Roles and the RoleId is assigned 97, @@IDENTITY will hold the value 97.

When we insert Roald Dahl into the Contacts table, the record will be given an ID value. This will be assigned to @@IDENTITY. We then store the value of @@IDENTITY in @ContactId for future use.

WHY DON'T WE JUST USE @@IDENTITY ALL THE TIME?

You might be asking why we bother assigning @@IDENTITY to @ContactId. After all, @@IDENTITY is holding the value we need anyway, right? Well, maybe.

The first reason we use @ContactId is because it makes more sense for a developer to see @ContactId than @@IDENTITY peppered throughout our script.

The second reason is much more important. As soon as we *or anybody else* adds a new record that generates an IDENTITY value, the contents of @@IDENTITY will change. Imagine if our script runs and inserts a contact. Around the same time, another script ran and inserted a role. If we were using @@IDENTITY, our script would try inserting use the RoleId, which would lead to some pretty unpleasant errors. Always assign the contents of global variables you want to use to local variables immediately— then you can be confident the values are not going to change.

You can find out more about global variables in Appendix C.

Award yourself a prize if you noticed we haven't added an END to this block of code. We don't want to do this just yet—there are more inserts to come.

Adding Subrecords

Now that we have a main record, we can add the subrecords. We'll only do this if a valid value was assigned to the @ContactId variable. Here's the code to add the subrecords. This should go directly under the SELECT @ContactId line.

```
IF (@ContactId IS NOT NULL)
BEGIN

-- Add verification details
INSERT INTO dbo.ContactVerificationDetails(ContactId, DrivingLicenseNumber, ContactVerified)
VALUES (@ContactId, '1031', 0);

SELECT @NumberOfVerificationRecords = @@ROWCOUNT;

-- Add developer role to contact
IF (@DeveloperRoleId IS NOT NULL)
BEGIN
INSERT INTO dbo.ContactRoles(ContactId, RoleId) VALUES (@ContactId, @DeveloperRoleId);

SELECT @NumberOfContactRoleRecords = @@ROWCOUNT;
END;

-- Add an address
INSERT INTO dbo.ContactAddresses(ContactId, HouseNumber, Street, City, Postcode)
VALUES (@ContactId, '200', 'Shaftsbury Avenue', 'Hastings', 'TN38 8EZ');

SELECT @NumberOfContactAddressRecords = @@ROWCOUNT;

-- Add a note
INSERT INTO dbo.ContactNotes(ContactId, Notes)
VALUES (@ContactId, 'Roald Dahl is a famous author. He is best known for books aimed
at children, such as the BFG.');

SELECT @NumberOfContactNoteRecords = @@ROWCOUNT;

-- Add phone numbers
IF (@MobilePhoneNumberTypeId IS NOT NULL AND @WorkPhoneNumberTypeId IS NOT NULL)
BEGIN
INSERT INTO dbo.ContactPhoneNumbers(ContactId, PhoneNumberTypeId, PhoneNumber)
VALUES (@ContactId, @MobilePhoneNumberTypeId, '07100 988 199'),
 (@ContactId, @WorkPhoneNumberTypeId, '01424 700 700');

SELECT @NumberOfContactPhoneNumberRecords = @@ROWCOUNT;
END;

END;
```

There looks to be quite a bit here, but it's all pretty similar. Five inserts are happening in this code block:

- Adding a record to ContactVerificationDetails

- Adding a record to ContactRoles, if @DeveloperRoleId is valid

- Adding a record to ContactAddresses

- Adding a record to ContactNotes

- Adding two records to ContactPhoneNumbers, if both @MobilePhoneNumberTypeId and @WorkPhoneNumberTypeId are valid

The first line is IF (@ContactId IS NOT NULL). This does nothing more than check if a valid value was assigned to the @ContactId variable through @@IDENTITY. If a valid value is present, the code enters the IF block, which is all of the code wrapped between the BEGIN and END.

The first insert is to the ContactVerificationDetails table. This is a typical INSERT, with nothing notable about it other than we are using @ContactId to specify the ContactId value to insert. The next line is interesting, though:

```
SELECT @NumberOfVerificationRecords = @@ROWCOUNT;
```

We are using another global variable here (all global variables begin with @@). This time it's @@ROWCOUNT. This holds the number of the rows that were processed by the last DML statement to execute. We've just inserted one row into ContactVerificationDetails, so we would expect @@ROWCOUNT to hold a value of one. We assign this to the @NumberOfVerificationRecords variable, so we can check at the end what the script did.

@@ROWCOUNT is a handy little variable and can be used to check if you have inserted, updated, or deleted the correct number of rows. It is reset after each statement, so you must assign it to a variable in the statement immediately after the DML command you executed.

Our next block of code combines everything we've seen so far.

```
-- Add developer role to contact
IF (@DeveloperRoleId IS NOT NULL)
BEGIN
INSERT INTO dbo.ContactRoles(ContactId, RoleId) VALUES (@ContactId, @DeveloperRoleId);

SELECT @NumberOfContactRoleRecords = @@ROWCOUNT;
END;
```

This code will add a record into ContactRoles, which you will recall is a many-to-many table. The INSERT only executes if the @DeveloperRoleId is not null; that is, it contains a valid value. If the INSERT succeeds we again store the @@ROWCOUNT value, this time in a different variable.

The next two INSERTs add records to both ContactAddresses and ContactNotes.

```
-- Add an address
INSERT INTO dbo.ContactAddresses(ContactId, HouseNumber, Street, City, Postcode)
VALUES (@ContactId, '200', 'Shaftsbury Avenue', 'Hastings', 'TN38 8EZ');

SELECT @NumberOfContactAddressRecords = @@ROWCOUNT;

-- Add a note
INSERT INTO dbo.ContactNotes(ContactId, Notes)
VALUES (@ContactId, 'Roald Dahl is a famous author. He is best known for books aimed at
children, such as the BFG.');

SELECT @NumberOfContactNoteRecords = @@ROWCOUNT;
```

These execute in exactly the same manner as the ContactVerificationDetails INSERT. The final INSERT, for ContactPhoneNumbers, is a little different from the others: it adds two records.

```
-- Add phone numbers
IF (@MobilePhoneNumberTypeId IS NOT NULL AND @WorkPhoneNumberTypeId IS NOT NULL)
BEGIN
INSERT INTO dbo.ContactPhoneNumbers(ContactId, PhoneNumberTypeId, PhoneNumber)
VALUES (@ContactId, @MobilePhoneNumberTypeId, '07100 988 199'),
(@ContactId, @WorkPhoneNumberTypeId, '01424 700 700');

SELECT @NumberOfContactPhoneNumberRecords = @@ROWCOUNT;
END;
```

The INSERTs only occur if the reference lookups successfully populated the two phone-number-type variables.

With all the INSERTs completed, you just need to add an END to the very end of the script, to close the IF NOT EXISTS block.

Displaying the Outcome

We finish the script with a SELECT statement, to display the ContactId we created, along with the number of records we inserted into each table.

```
-- Return what we've done
SELECT @ContactId AS ContactId,
@NumberOfVerificationRecords AS NumberOfVerificationRecordsAdded,
@NumberOfContactRoleRecords AS NumberOfContactRoleRecords,
@NumberOfContactAddressRecords AS NumberOfContactAddressRecords,
@NumberOfContactNoteRecords AS NumberOfContactNoteRecords,
@NumberOfContactPhoneNumberRecords AS NumberOfContactPhoneNumberRecords;
```

This is a fairly simple SELECT statement, as it doesn't use a table to obtain its data—it just displays the values of variables. Interestingly, each line has an extra AS clause at the end of it (e.g. @ContactId AS ContactId). This is a *column alias*, and is the column name that will be displayed on screen. We'll learn more about aliases in Chapter 11.

To complete the script, add a GO at the end. Here's the complete script.

```
USE AddressBook;

DECLARE @ContactId INT,
@DeveloperRoleId INT,
@MobilePhoneNumberTypeId TINYINT,
@WorkPhoneNumberTypeId TINYINT,
@NumberOfVerificationRecords INT,
@NumberOfContactRoleRecords INT,
@NumberOfContactAddressRecords INT,
@NumberOfContactNoteRecords INT,
@NumberOfContactPhoneNumberRecords INT;
```

```sql
-- Obtain lookup values
SELECT @DeveloperRoleId = RoleId FROM dbo.Roles WHERE RoleTitle = 'Developer';
SELECT @MobilePhoneNumberTypeId = PhoneNumberTypeId FROM dbo.PhoneNumberTypes WHERE
PhoneNumberType = 'Mobile';
SELECT @WorkPhoneNumberTypeId = PhoneNumberTypeId FROM dbo.PhoneNumberTypes WHERE
PhoneNumberType = 'Work';

PRINT 'Developer Role ID: ' + CAST(@DeveloperRoleId AS VARCHAR(20));
PRINT 'Mobile Phone Number Type ID: ' + CAST(@MobilePhoneNumberTypeId AS VARCHAR(20));
PRINT 'Work Phone Number Type ID: ' + CAST(@WorkPhoneNumberTypeId AS VARCHAR(20));

IF NOT EXISTS (SELECT 1 FROM dbo.Contacts WHERE FirstName = 'Roald' AND LastName = 'Dahl')
BEGIN

-- No need to specify AllowContactByPhone or CreatedDate,
-- as they have default values
-- and Roald has said we cannot contact him by phone
INSERT INTO dbo.Contacts(FirstName, LastName, DateOfBirth) VALUES ('Roald', 'Dahl',
'1916-09-13');

SELECT @ContactId = @@IDENTITY;

IF (@ContactId IS NOT NULL)
BEGIN

-- Add verification details
INSERT INTO dbo.ContactVerificationDetails(ContactId, DrivingLicenseNumber, ContactVerified)
VALUES (@ContactId, '1031', 0);

SELECT @NumberOfVerificationRecords = @@ROWCOUNT;

-- Add developer role to contact
IF (@DeveloperRoleId IS NOT NULL)
BEGIN
INSERT INTO dbo.ContactRoles(ContactId, RoleId) VALUES (@ContactId, @DeveloperRoleId);

SELECT @NumberOfContactRoleRecords = @@ROWCOUNT;
END;

-- Add an address
INSERT INTO dbo.ContactAddresses(ContactId, HouseNumber, Street, City, Postcode)
VALUES (@ContactId, '200', 'Shaftsbury Avenue', 'Hastings', 'TN38 8EZ');

SELECT @NumberOfContactAddressRecords = @@ROWCOUNT;

-- Add a note
INSERT INTO dbo.ContactNotes(ContactId, Notes)
VALUES (@ContactId, 'Roald Dahl is a famous author. He is best known for books aimed
at children, such as the BFG.');
```

171

```
SELECT @NumberOfContactNoteRecords = @@ROWCOUNT;

-- Add phone numbers
IF (@MobilePhoneNumberTypeId IS NOT NULL AND @WorkPhoneNumberTypeId IS NOT NULL)
BEGIN
INSERT INTO dbo.ContactPhoneNumbers(ContactId, PhoneNumberTypeId, PhoneNumber)
VALUES (@ContactId, @MobilePhoneNumberTypeId, '07100 988 199'),
(@ContactId, @WorkPhoneNumberTypeId, '01424 700 700');

SELECT @NumberOfContactPhoneNumberRecords = @@ROWCOUNT;
END;

END;

END;

-- Return what we've done
SELECT @ContactId AS ContactId,
@NumberOfVerificationRecords AS NumberOfVerificationRecordsAdded,
@NumberOfContactRoleRecords AS NumberOfContactRoleRecords,
@NumberOfContactAddressRecords AS NumberOfContactAddressRecords,
@NumberOfContactNoteRecords AS NumberOfContactNoteRecords,
@NumberOfContactPhoneNumberRecords AS NumberOfContactPhoneNumberRecords;

GO
```

Run this and you'll see a table of results that hopefully match Figure 10-1.

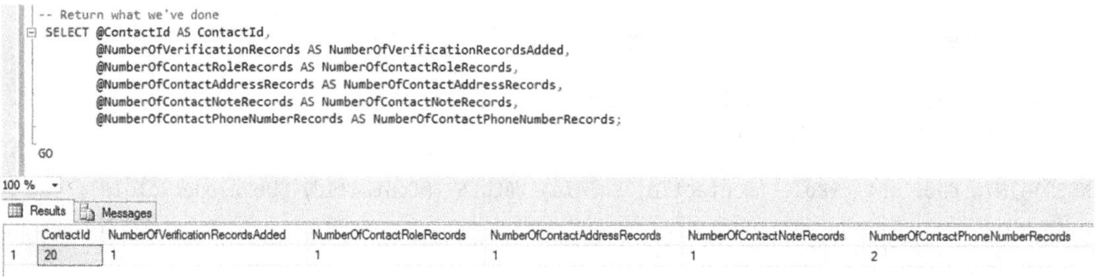

Figure 10-1. *Results of the import script*

Those numbers look good to me! Save this script as c:\temp\sqlbasics\apply\18 - Insert Contact Record.sql, and add this code to the end of the 00 - apply.sql script:

```
:setvar currentFile "18 - Insert Contact Record.sql"
PRINT 'Executing $(path)$(currentFile)';
:r $(path)$(currentFile)
```

Try running script 18 again. It will execute successfully, but you'll have a different set of results, which can be seen in Figure 10-2.

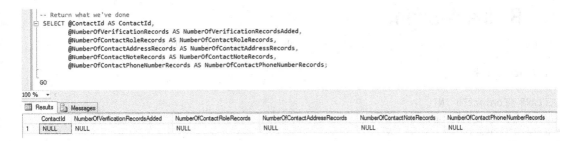

Figure 10-2. *Second set of results from the import script*

This is because we are checking if the record already exists. We've already executed the script once, so the second time it runs there is nothing for it to do. Hence the NULL values in every column.

As we are happy with the script, we no longer require the SELECT statement—it will just interfere with the output when we run our main apply script. Comment it out. Start by highlighting the code, then choose one of these SSMS options:

- Press Ctrl+K, then Ctrl+C (to uncomment, press Ctrl+K, then Ctrl+U)

- In the **Edit** menu, select **Advanced ➤ Comment Selection** (choose **Uncomment Selection** to uncomment the code)

Run the script again to prove that the SELECT statement no longer executes (Figure 10-3). If you ever need to put it back you can simply uncomment the code.

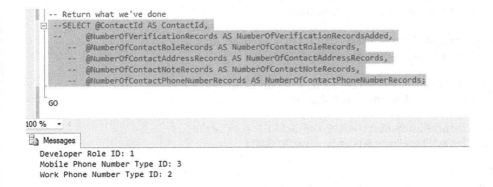

Figure 10-3. *Commented out code doesn't run*

Save your changes. Now we need to create a rollback script that will remove Roald Dahl.

The Rollback Script

The rollback script is much easier to write than the apply script. Here it is in all its glory.

```
USE AddressBook;

DECLARE @ContactId INT,
@NumberOfVerificationRecords INT,
@NumberOfContactRoleRecords INT,
@NumberOfContactAddressRecords INT,
@NumberOfContactNoteRecords INT,
@NumberOfContactPhoneNumberRecords NT;

IF EXISTS (SELECT 1 FROM dbo.Contacts WHERE FirstName = 'Roald' AND LastName = 'Dahl')
BEGIN

-- Obtain the contact ID value
SELECT @ContactId = ContactId FROM dbo.Contacts WHERE FirstName = 'Roald' AND LastName =
'Dahl';

-- Delete sub-records
DELETE FROM dbo.ContactVerificationDetails WHERE ContactId = @ContactId;
SELECT @NumberOfVerificationRecords = @@ROWCOUNT;

DELETE FROM dbo.ContactRoles WHERE ContactId = @ContactId;
SELECT @NumberOfContactRoleRecords = @@ROWCOUNT;

DELETE FROM dbo.ContactAddresses WHERE ContactId = @ContactId;
SELECT @NumberOfContactAddressRecords = @@ROWCOUNT;

DELETE FROM dbo.ContactNotes WHERE ContactId = @ContactId;
SELECT @NumberOfContactNoteRecords = @@ROWCOUNT;

DELETE FROM dbo.ContactPhoneNumbers WHERE ContactId = @ContactId;
SELECT @NumberOfContactPhoneNumberRecords = @@ROWCOUNT;

-- Delete main record
DELETE FROM dbo.Contacts WHERE ContactId = @ContactId;

END;

--SELECT @ContactId AS DeletedContactId,
-- @NumberOfVerificationRecords AS NumberOfVerificationRecordsAdded,
-- @NumberOfContactRoleRecords AS NumberOfContactRoleRecords,
-- @NumberOfContactAddressRecords AS NumberOfContactAddressRecords,
-- @NumberOfContactNoteRecords AS NumberOfContactNoteRecords,
-- @NumberOfContactPhoneNumberRecords AS NumberOfContactPhoneNumberRecords;

GO
```

We have a commented-out SELECT statement at the end. This is the same as our apply script—we've added the SELECT for any troubleshooting we might need to do at a later date.

Save this to c:\temp\sqlbasics\rollback\18 - Insert Contact Record Rollback.sql, and add the execution code to the top of the 00 - Rollback.sql script.

```
:setvar currentFile "18 - Insert Contact Record Rollback.sql"
PRINT 'Executing $(path)$(currentFile)';
:r $(path)$(currentFile)
```

We've seen everything this script does before. The variable declarations are very similar to those we saw in the apply script; we just don't have as many of them as we don't need to look up reference data values.

The next line is the key to the entire script:

```
IF EXISTS (SELECT 1 FROM dbo.Contacts WHERE FirstName = 'Roald' AND LastName = 'Dahl')
```

This tells us the script will only do something if a record called Roald Dahl exists in the Contacts table. If it doesn't, the script will execute the SELECT statement after the END statement and a lot of NULL values will be displayed. If it does exist, the code enters the IF block and obtains the ContactId value for Roald Dahl, assigning it to the @ContactId variable.

```
-- Obtain the contact ID value
SELECT @ContactId = ContactId FROM dbo.Contacts WHERE FirstName = 'Roald' AND LastName =
'Dahl';
```

We then execute DELETE statements against each table, storing the number of rows processed by each statement. Note that we don't check if @ContactId has a valid value here. We could do that but it doesn't matter. If the @ContactId variable is NULL the DELETE statements will execute but they won't do anything, as no ContactId with a NULL value can possibly exist.

The final DELETE statement removes the main record from the Contacts table.

```
-- Delete main record
DELETE FROM dbo.Contacts WHERE ContactId = @ContactId;
```

And as with the apply script, we have a SELECT statement that shows us how many records were deleted.

Uncomment the SELECT statement at the bottom and run the script. We should see that ContactId 20 is the DeletedContactId, along with numbers in the other columns that denote how many records we removed from each table. In other words, your results should look like those in Figure 10-4.

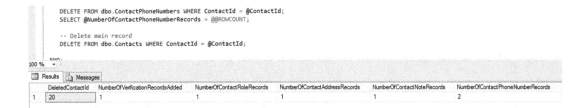

Figure 10-4. *Showing what was deleted*

Run it again, and just like the apply statement, a lot of NULL values will be returned (you can see these in Figure 10-5). This is because of the IF EXISTS check at the top of the script—the script will only attempt to delete if Roald Dahl exists. He doesn't, as we deleted him when we first ran the script.

Figure 10-5. *Running the delete when it has already been executed*

Comment the SELECT statement back out, save the script, and we're all done! Rebuild the database so you are ready for the next chapter.

Summary

This chapter has concluded our look at data imports. Strictly speaking, what we did in this chapter wasn't a data import per se, but rather a look at how an individual record, along with its child records, can be added to a database. But we've now seen how to import using files and how to add data using scripts.

We used the SELECT statement a few times in this chapter, and indeed we've come across this statement before. It's now time to take a proper look at the SELECT statement. Let's see what powers it can grant us!

CHAPTER 11

■ ■ ■

The SELECT Statement

You will use the SELECT statement more than any other T-SQL statement in your database career. This is an axiom that applies to DBAs as much as it does to developers. SELECT is your friend, your assistant, your sidekick. Whenever you have a question about your database, chances are SELECT will give you the answer. That said, SELECT in the wrong hands can be evil. Evil! It's easier to make SELECT give you the wrong data than the right data (much easier, usually). Let's see if we can keep SELECT on the side of the good guys.

What Is the SELECT Statement For?

The SELECT statement can be used for a number of purposes, but its main aim is to return a set of data. A *set* is a collection of rows, and in SQL, thinking in sets is very important. Many developers focus on working on one row of data at a time, but SQL Server makes it very easy to work on sets of data, meaning you can insert, update, and delete multiple records with one statement, rather than processing one record at a time. I'll talk about this more in Chapter 19. The SELECT statement is very important when dealing with sets, as it usually the SELECT statement that generates the set of data for you.

SELECT can also be used to modify rows, in conjunction with the aforementioned INSERT INTO, UPDATE, and DELETE statements.

The Simple SELECT Statement

Let's begin by taking a look at the simplest form of SELECT statement. We'll write a SELECT that shows all records in the Contacts table.

```
USE AddressBook;

SELECT * FROM dbo.Contacts;
```

If you rebuilt your database at the end of the last chapter, this should return the 20 rows displayed in Figure 11-1.

```
SQLQuery2.sql - BE...ikemcquillan (54))*  ×
    ⊟USE AddressBook;

    SELECT * FROM dbo.Contacts;
```

100 % ▼

▦ Results ▤ Messages

	ContactId	FirstName	LastName	DateOfBirth	AllowContactByPhone	CreatedDate
1	1	Stephen	Gerrard	1980-05-30	1	2015-05-05 22:22:55.403
2	2	Dennis	Potter	1935-05-17	0	2015-05-05 22:22:55.403
3	3	Richard	Adams	1920-05-09	0	2015-05-05 22:22:55.403
4	4	Bertie	McQuillan	2001-06-30	1	2015-05-05 22:22:55.403
5	5	Walt	Disney	1966-12-05	1	2015-05-05 22:22:55.403
6	6	Barbara	Gordon	1952-01-11	0	2015-05-05 22:22:55.403
7	7	Josephine	Bailey	1949-05-31	1	2015-05-05 22:22:55.403
8	8	Linda	Canoglu	1959-07-11	1	2015-05-05 22:22:55.403
9	9	Grace	McQuillan	1993-09-27	0	2015-05-05 22:22:55.403
10	10	Vera	Black	1984-08-03	0	2015-05-05 22:22:55.403
11	11	Angelica	Jones	1981-02-04	1	2015-05-05 22:22:55.403
12	12	Steve	Davis	1957-08-22	1	2015-05-05 22:22:55.403
13	13	Allison	Fisher	1968-02-24	1	2015-05-05 22:22:55.403
14	14	julius	Marx	1990-10-02	0	2015-05-05 22:22:55.403
15	15	george	formby	1944-05-26	1	2015-05-05 22:22:55.403
16	16	Alan	Partridge	1965-04-14	0	2015-05-05 22:22:55.403
17	17	Harper	Lee	1986-04-28	1	2015-05-05 22:22:55.403
18	18	Robert	Burns	1959-01-25	0	2015-05-05 22:22:55.403
19	19	Michael	Jackson	1967-06-30	0	2015-05-05 22:22:55.403
20	20	Roald	Dahl	1916-09-13	0	2015-05-05 22:22:55.513

Figure 11-1. *A simple SELECT statement*

This statement is about as simple as it can be. SELECT * tells SQL Server to return every column in whatever table (or tables) we specify. The * is a shorthand way of saying "give me every column." The * is actually very bad and we'll be ditching it shortly!

FROM tells SQL Server that we are about to give it the names of the tables from which we want data. We write FROM dbo.Contacts, so this SELECT statement is saying to display every column for every row in the Contacts table—which is exactly what we can see in Figure 11-1.

WHY IS * A BAD THING?

SELECT * won't usually pass the steely gaze of a weatherworn DBA. This is because it's good practice only to return what you need from your SELECT statements, and also because it isn't explicit about what your SELECT statement is doing. If you always return every column, you could be sending lots of extra data across the network whenever a program calls your SELECT statement. Always be explicit—we'll be (mostly!) explicit from this point onward.

We are going to write a SELECT statement that only lists those contacts who agreed we could contact them via their phone number. Before we do that, we should implement best practice and remove the * from our statement, replacing it with the names of the columns we are interested in.

```
USE AddressBook;

SELECT ContactId, FirstName, LastName, DateOfBirth, AllowContactByPhone, CreatedDate
FROM dbo.Contacts;
```

Press F5 to run this; the results (partly shown in Figure 11-2) will be exactly the same.

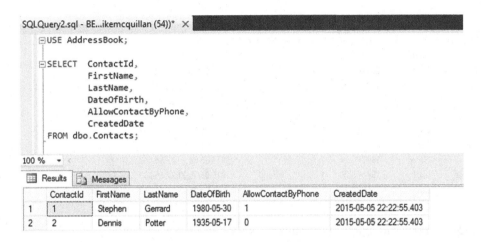

Figure 11-2. *Explicitly declaring columns with a SELECT statement*

Obviously, * can be used if you are just writing a quick SELECT statement for your own use, or to inspect a table for some reason or other. Just make sure you never use it in production code. Always think of the next person!

The WHERE Clause

It is possible to filter the results of the SELECT statement in a variety of ways, but the most common method is to use the WHERE clause. This allows you to tell SQL Server only to return rows that meet a particular set of criteria. The criteria must use columns that are present in the result set returned by the tables in the SELECT statement. Our current SELECT statement only uses the Contacts table, so we could filter based on any of those columns.

We want to filter on the AllowContactByPhone column. We are looking for records where the value of that column is set to 1. In the following code, add the WHERE line in bold:

```
SELECT ContactId, FirstName, LastName, DateOfBirth, AllowContactByPhone, CreatedDate FROM
dbo.Contacts WHERE AllowContactByPhone = 1;
```

This is the same SELECT statement we wrote earlier, except we've added a WHERE clause to the end. The WHERE clause is saying only to return records where the AllowContactByPhone column's value is set to 1. Exactly 10 of our contacts have this particular value in that particular column. You can see these contacts in Figure 11-3.

```
SQLQuery2.sql - BE...ikemcquillan (54))*  ×
  USE AddressBook;

  SELECT  ContactId,
          FirstName,
          LastName,
          DateOfBirth,
          AllowContactByPhone,
          CreatedDate
     FROM dbo.Contacts
  WHERE AllowContactByPhone = 1;
```

100 % ▾

	ContactId	First Name	Last Name	DateOfBirth	AllowContactByPhone	CreatedDate
1	1	Stephen	Gerrard	1980-05-30	1	2015-05-05 22:22:55.403
2	4	Bertie	McQuillan	2001-06-30	1	2015-05-05 22:22:55.403
3	5	Walt	Disney	1966-12-05	1	2015-05-05 22:22:55.403
4	7	Josephine	Bailey	1949-05-31	1	2015-05-05 22:22:55.403
5	8	Linda	Canoglu	1959-07-11	1	2015-05-05 22:22:55.403
6	11	Angelica	Jones	1981-02-04	1	2015-05-05 22:22:55.403
7	12	Steve	Davis	1957-08-22	1	2015-05-05 22:22:55.403
8	13	Allison	Fisher	1968-02-24	1	2015-05-05 22:22:55.403
9	15	george	formby	1944-05-26	1	2015-05-05 22:22:55.403
10	17	Harper	Lee	1986-04-28	1	2015-05-05 22:22:55.403

Figure 11-3. A SELECT statement using a WHERE clause

Look carefully at the AllowContactByPhone column; all values are set to 1. We can extend the WHERE clause to specify multiple conditions—for instance, we might say give me contacts whom I can phone who were born in the 1980s. (I want to talk to them about Hanson! Look them up on Wikipedia.) There is absolutely no limit to the number of clauses you can add to a WHERE clause; you can specify as many as you like.

The AND Operator

We'll use the AND operator to add our 1980s clause:

```
SELECT ContactId, FirstName, LastName, DateOfBirth, AllowContactByPhone, CreatedDate
FROM dbo.Contacts
WHERE AllowContactByPhone = 1
AND DateOfBirth BETWEEN '1980-01-01' AND '1989-12-31';
```

The AND operator is saying that both condition 1 (allowing contact by phone) and condition 2 (the date of birth should be in the 1980s) must be met for a row to be returned. As you can see in Figure 11-4, three records match our WHERE clause.

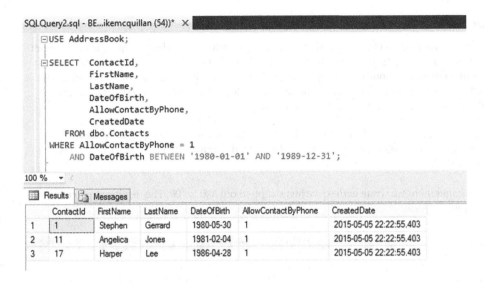

Figure 11-4. *Enhanced SELECT statement using AND*

We used the BETWEEN operator to specify a range that our criteria had to meet—in this instance, a date range. A *range* tells SQL Server that you are looking for records that have a value that falls on or between the values you've specified. We entered the first and the last dates of the 1980s, so any record with a date of birth on or between those would have been picked up.

There are also some other useful operators to be aware of, as shown in Table 11-1.

Table 11-1. *T-SQL Operators*

Operator	Description
>	Greater than
>=	Greater than or equal to
=	Equal to
<	Less than
<=	Less than or equal to
!= or <>	Not equal to
IN (values)	Required value must meet one of the specified values
BETWEEN Value1 AND Value2	Value must fall on or between the two specified values

BETWEEN is the better option in our example (simply because it is easier to read and maintain), but it also could have been written as:

```
SELECT ContactId, FirstName, LastName, DateOfBirth, AllowContactByPhone, CreatedDate FROM
dbo.Contacts WHERE AllowContactByPhone = 1 AND DateOfBirth >= '1980-01-01' AND DateOfBirth
<= '1989-12-31';
```

The results are the same, but the query is not as elegant—we've had to specifically state that both the >= and <= apply to the DateOfBirth column. We only needed to specify the column name once using BETWEEN.

181

The OR Operator

Now, we've decided that we want to change the query to return all contacts who have either allowed contact by phone or who were born in the 1980s. To be clear: if the contact was born in the 1980s, it doesn't matter whether we can contact them by phone or not—they should be returned. If the contact was not born in the 1980s, they should only be returned if they can be contacted by telephone. The AND BETWEEN statement we wrote earlier will not suffice here, so we change the AND to OR.

```
SELECT ContactId, FirstName, LastName, DateOfBirth, AllowContactByPhone, CreatedDate
FROM dbo.Contacts WHERE AllowContactByPhone = 1 OR DateOfBirth BETWEEN '1980-01-01' AND
'1989-12-31';
```

This is the same statement we wrote earlier; we just swapped out AND for OR. The results, as you can see in Figure 11-5, are quite different.

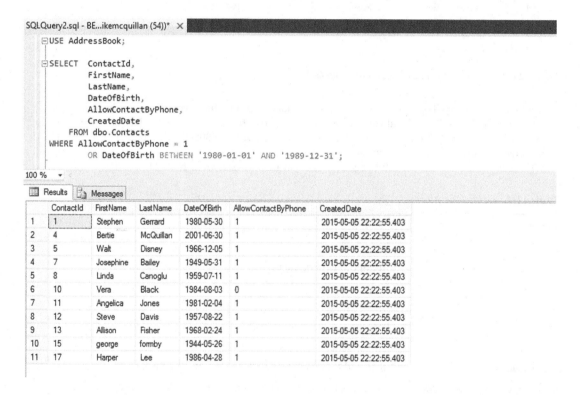

Figure 11-5. *Using the OR operator*

Eleven rows are now returned. Ten of them we've already seen—they match the first criteria regarding AllowContactByPhone = 1. Row 6 contains a record that has AllowContactByPhone set to 0. It doesn't match the first criteria but it does match the second, as the contact was born in the 1980s.

What we were saying when we were using AND was:

- Find me contacts that allow contact by phone, and who were born in the 1980s

What we are now saying with OR is:

- Find me contacts that either allow contact by phone, or were born in the 1980s

With the AND operator, all of the criteria had to be matched. With the OR operator, any one of the criteria needs a match. This is an important distinction.

The IN Operator

BETWEEN allows you to filter using a range of values, but IN allows you to filter using specific values. Say we only want to find contacts whose surname is one of McQuillan, Partridge, or Formby.

```
SELECT ContactId, FirstName, LastName, DateOfBirth, AllowContactByPhone, CreatedDate FROM
dbo.Contacts WHERE LastName IN ('McQuillan', 'Partridge', 'Formby');
```

We tell the IN operator which values we are interested in by specifying them in the parentheses. You can place as many values as you want in the parentheses. Running it brings back the four expected results (shown in Figure 11-6).

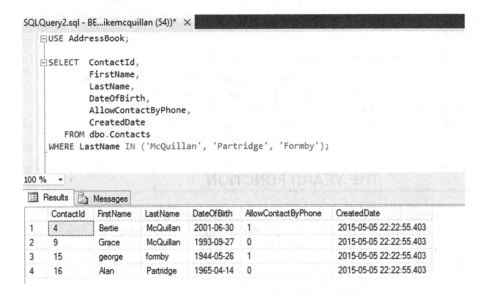

Figure 11-6. *Using IN to filter*

This statement is equivalent to specifying two OR operators instead:

```
SELECT ContactId, FirstName, LastName, DateOfBirth, AllowContactByPhone, CreatedDate FROM
dbo.Contacts WHERE LastName = 'McQuillan' OR LastName = 'Partridge' OR LastName = 'Formby';
```

I'm sure you'll agree that the IN version is much easier to read and extend if necessary!

Mixing Operators

We've covered a huge amount of ground already, yet we've hardly scratched the surface of the SELECT statement's capabilities. Let's look at something a little more advanced. We've seen how to use operators like AND, OR, and IN. But we can actually mix and match these in the same statement should we wish.

USE PARENTHESES TO GROUP CONDITIONS

When specifying multiple conditions that use OR statements, I recommend using parentheses to logically group them. I've often been stumped with OR statements when I haven't used parentheses!

Here's a more complicated WHERE clause.

```
SELECT ContactId, FirstName, LastName, DateOfBirth, AllowContactByPhone, CreatedDate
FROM dbo.Contacts WHERE (AllowContactByPhone = 1 AND YEAR(DateOfBirth) > 1969) OR
(AllowContactByPhone = 0 AND YEAR(DateOfBirth) < 1970) OR (LastName IN ('Fisher', 'Formby'));
```

Note there are two parentheses at the end there. This returns 13 rows, broken down as follows:

- Four rows match the first criteria: allow contact by phone and born in 1970 or after.

- Seven rows match the second criteria: do not allow contact by phone and born before 1970.

- The last two rows match the surnames specified in the final clause.

Note that we've linked two conditions together using AND, and enclosed those in parentheses. The enclosure makes it clear what the statement is trying to do. If the parentheses were not there, the statement would be much harder to read—try taking them out and see what you think.

This statement will work with or without the parentheses, but quite often not using them will produce misleading results, so be very careful. I always add them when I'm using OR; it's good practice.

THE YEAR() FUNCTION

The preceding example uses the built-in T-SQL function YEAR(). This accepts a date (which comes from the DateOfBirth column in the example) and returns the year specified in that date. So a date of 1974-10-03 would return 1974. There are many date functions in SQL Server, including the obvious MONTH() and DAY(). Take a look at what's on offer—there's some powerful stuff available.

More information on system functions can be found in Appendix C.

Ordering Data

We're pretty conversant with the SELECT statement now. We can pull the data from a table and filter it in many wild and wonderful ways. Now we need to figure out how to order that data. If we run a SELECT statement without any filters, the records in the Contacts table are returned ordered by the ContactId column. Figure 11-7 proves this:

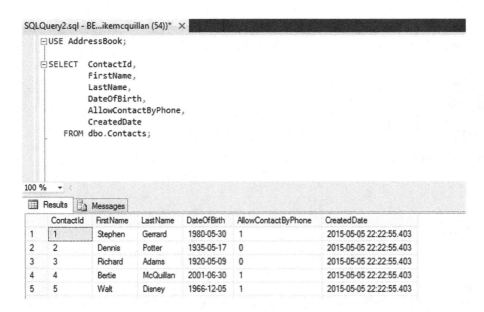

Figure 11-7. *A naturally ordered SELECT statement*

We can actually order by any column or combination of columns we choose, using the ORDER BY clause. We'll modify the SELECT statement to order by the LastName column, in alphabetical order.

```
SELECT ContactId, FirstName, LastName, DateOfBirth, AllowContactByPhone, CreatedDate FROM
dbo.Contacts ORDER BY LastName ASC;
```

ASC is short for ascending. This is actually the default and we could have omitted it, but it's always best to be explicit—remember, think about the next person! Lo and behold, by the magic of SQL Server, our results are returned, sorted by the LastName column. Check out Figure 11-8.

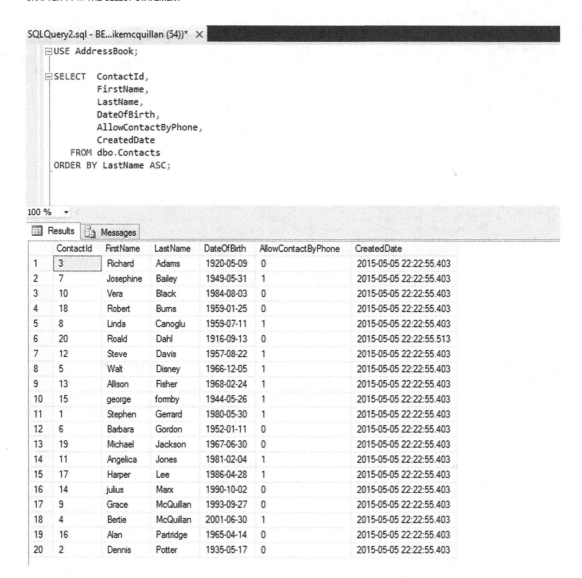

Figure 11-8. A SELECT statement in ascending order using ORDER BY

Not bad, eh? Now change ASC to DESC. You've guessed it—this will reverse the order, sorting by LastName using Z-A ordering. You can see the reversed rows in Figure 11-9.

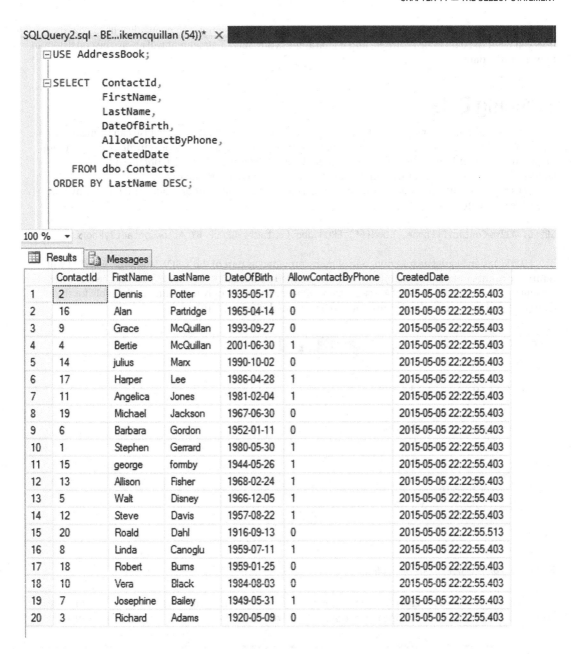

Figure 11-9. *A SELECT statement in descending order using ORDER BY*

You can sort one column in ascending order and another in descending order, as in this example:

```
SELECT ContactId, FirstName, LastName, DateOfBirth, AllowContactByPhone, CreatedDate FROM
dbo.Contacts WHERE LastName = 'McQuillan' ORDER BY LastName ASC, ContactId DESC;
```

If you change the ContactId DESC to ContactId ASC, you'll notice the order of the two records change.

It's often wise to specify an ORDER BY clause in your SELECT statements. It explicitly tells the database how you want the data to be returned, and it guarantees your SELECT statement will always be consistent in how it returns data.

Grouping Data

We're motoring along nicely, and it is time for a quick look at how the GROUP BY clause can aggregate data for us. With GROUP BY, we can break our data down into groups, and a row will be returned for each group displaying whatever information we have requested. GROUP BY is usually used to obtain some kind of statistical information, such as the number of records that match a particular type.

Let's say we wanted to know how many contacts we had that allow phone calls, and how many that don't. We can write:

```
SELECT AllowContactByPhone, COUNT(*) FROM dbo.Contacts GROUP BY AllowContactByPhone;
```

COUNT() is an aggregate function, one of many provided as part of the T-SQL language. COUNT() will return the number of rows matching the criteria specified by the GROUP BY clause, so in this case it will return a count for each different value of AllowContactByPhone. There are only two values in the table for this column: 1 and 0. So we can expect two rows to be returned (Figure 11-10).

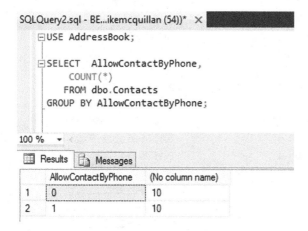

Figure 11-10. A GROUP BY using COUNT()

There are 10 records of each type in the Contacts table. You can group on more than one column; the only rule is whatever columns appear in the SELECT...FROM must also appear in the GROUP BY clause.

AGGREGATE FUNCTIONS

T-SQL provides a number of aggregate functions that can greatly enhance your queries. Many of these are designed to work with or without a GROUP BY clause.

You can find a list of all the aggregate functions at https://msdn.microsoft.com/en-us/library/ms173454.aspx. Some of these are outlined in Appendix C.

The COUNT() function can be used to obtain a total count of all rows in a table, by simply executing:

```
SELECT COUNT(*) FROM dbo.Contacts;
```

If you specify a column name, as we did earlier, you *must* specify a GROUP BY clause. If you do not specify the GROUP BY clause, like in this statement:

```
SELECT AllowContactByPhone, COUNT(*) FROM dbo.Contacts;
```

you'll see a message along these lines:

```
Msg 8120, Level 16, State 1, Line 3
Column 'dbo.Contacts.AllowContactByPhone' is invalid in the select list because it is not
contained in either an aggregate function or the GROUP BY clause.
```

GROUP BY can be used in conjunction with the WHERE and ORDER BY statements. It actually goes above the ORDER BY. Here's an example, bringing together all of our elements so far:

```
SELECT LastName, COUNT(*) FROM dbo.Contacts WHERE YEAR(DateOfBirth) BETWEEN 1980 AND 2010
GROUP BY LastName ORDER BY LastName ASC;
```

We are asking for the number of contacts born between 1980 and 2010 to be returned, broken down by their last name and also ordered by their last name. There are two McQuillans in this period, so as their names match it returns a count of 2 for that particular row (look at row 6 in Figure 11-11).

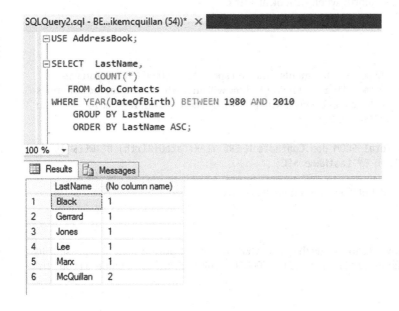

Figure 11-11. *GROUP BY using WHERE and ORDER BY*

The GROUP BY clause has a few optional extras, the most commonly used of which is the HAVING clause. This acts as a WHERE clause for the GROUP BY clause. You can use it to limit results based on the output of the GROUP BY clause (you can also filter the results using ungrouped columns).

189

Modify our statement so it only returns results that had a count higher than 1:

```
SELECT LastName, COUNT(*) FROM dbo.Contacts WHERE YEAR(DateOfBirth) BETWEEN 1980 AND 2010
GROUP BY LastName HAVING COUNT(*) > 1 ORDER BY LastName ASC;
```

Voila, only the McQuillan record now meets our criteria (see Figure 11-12). AND, OR, and other operators can be used in the HAVING clause, just like in the WHERE clause. It's powerful stuff!

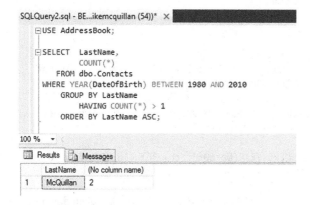

Figure 11-12. *GROUP BY with HAVING clause*

We'll revisit the GROUP BY clause shortly when we look at JOINs.

Column Aliases

There was a problem in our various GROUP BY statements—did you spot it? The COUNT(*) column was displayed with the title (No column name). That's not helpful—how will anybody know what the column is for? Fortunately, column aliases, which we met briefly in Chapter 10, can come to our rescue. To specify an alias, you use the AS keyword, followed by a name:

```
SELECT LastName, COUNT(*) AS Total FROM dbo.Contacts WHERE YEAR(DateOfBirth) BETWEEN 1980
AND 2010 GROUP BY LastName ORDER BY LastName ASC;
```

To be truthful, the AS is optional, but if it weren't there you'd have:

```
COUNT(*) Total;
```

I find this confusing, so I always like to specify the AS so what I'm doing is obvious. It is also possible to alias tables, which we'll see in Chapter 12. Run this and the COUNT(*) column will have a name, as you can see in Figure 11-13. Cool!

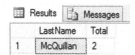

Figure 11-13. *Giving a name to a calculated column*

Limiting Rows with TOP

We've seen how we can filter the rows returned using the WHERE and GROUP BY clauses. We've also seen how the result sets can be ordered with ORDER BY. What do you do if you want to specify a maximum number of results? Say we want to grab the first five results from the Contacts table? No problem, we can specify a TOP clause.

The TOP clause does nothing more than say "Give me however many rows I ask for." If I say TOP (10), I will receive 10 rows back. If the result set contains less than 10 rows, I'll receive however many were returned, but I will never, ever receive more than 10.

Happily, TOP is as easy to implement as column aliases. This very simple query gives us the first five contacts in first name order:

```
SELECT TOP (5) ContactId, FirstName, LastName, DateOfBirth, AllowContactByPhone, CreatedDate
FROM dbo.Contacts ORDER BY FirstName ASC;
```

Execute this and just five rows are returned, which you can see in Figure 11-14.

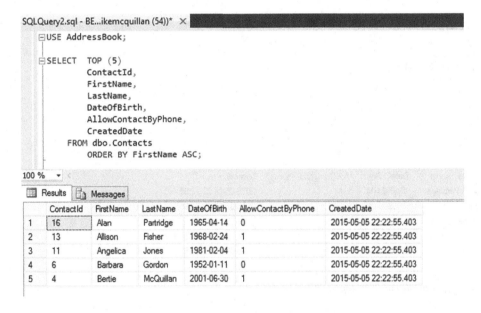

Figure 11-14. Limiting result sets using TOP

Note that the parentheses in TOP (5) are optional—we could have written TOP 5 and the SELECT would have worked just as well. You can use TOP with INSERT, UPDATE, and DELETE, but for these you *must provide the parentheses*. It's also ANSI compliant, so it makes sense to be consistent.

As a final TOP test, try changing ORDER BY FirstName ASC; to ORDER BY FirstName DESC;. The query will still return five rows, but you'll see five different rows because you have switched the order. TOP will only ever return the number of rows you specify, in the order you specify.

Merging Columns

Another nice trick you can use to make your SELECT statements stand out from the crowd is to combine multiple columns into one. This is pleasantly straightforward. What if we wanted to display a ContactName column instead of separate FirstName and LastName columns? Easy, we just concatenate the columns:

```
SELECT TOP (5) ContactId, FirstName + ' ' + LastName AS ContactName, DateOfBirth,
AllowContactByPhone, CreatedDate FROM dbo.Contacts ORDER BY FirstName ASC;
```

We are using the + sign to concatenate the value in the FirstName column with a space followed by the value in the LastName column. We use the AS keyword to specify a column alias, giving the column a name. Apart from the column alias this is very similar to what we saw when using the PRINT statement in Chapter 10. Run this and you'll have a ContactName column, as shown in Figure 11-15.

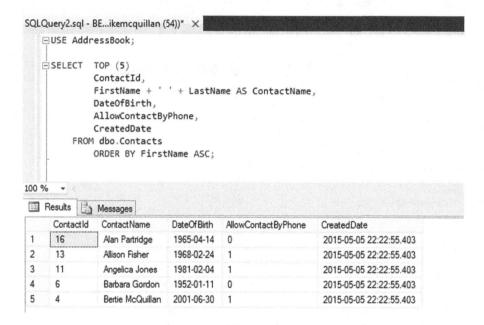

Figure 11-15. *Merging multiple columns together*

Columns you create in this manner are known as *derived columns* or *computed columns*. We'll see some more examples during our discussion of JOINs in Chapter 12.

Summary

We've begun our travels in the world of SELECT statements. We haven't done anything particularly complicated yet, but we have covered all of the basics. We're not done with SELECT just yet, though—there's plenty more to come, starting in the very next chapter.

CHAPTER 12

■ ■ ■

Joining Tables

Up to this point, all of our SELECT statements have used the Contacts table. This may seem thrilling enough, but we're about to take the octane level up to Jason Statham movie territory. The Contacts table we've been looking at doesn't offer us much information—really, just the name and date of birth. If we wanted to phone a contact, how would we identify that contact's phone number? Based on the approach we've used so far, we could write a SELECT to find a record in the Contacts table using FirstName and LastName. From there, we could make a note of the ContactId and then use this to write a SELECT against the ContactPhoneNumbers table, to list that particular contact's phone numbers.

This is all well and good, but talk about going the long way around! We'll look at how joins can be used to solve this very problem. Joins let you link related tables together, allowing their contents to be displayed as a single result set. We could join Contacts to ContactPhoneNumbers, and display the various phone numbers alongside the contact names. The foreign keys we implemented earlier give our tables the means to link to each other.

SQL Server offers five types of join. In practice, I've found INNER JOIN and LEFT OUTER JOIN are used regularly, with RIGHT OUTER JOIN used semiregularly. The remaining two, FULL OUTER JOIN and CROSS JOIN, are seldom used. They can be very handy to know about when the need arises, though. We'll begin by seeing how joins can be applied to SELECT statements, but we'll also see how they can be used to INSERT, UPDATE, and DELETE data too.

INNER JOIN

An INNER JOIN will only return data that exists in both tables specified in the join. You specify which column (or columns) you want to join on. If there is a match in both tables, a row will be returned. The black area in Figure 12-1 shows the rows that match.

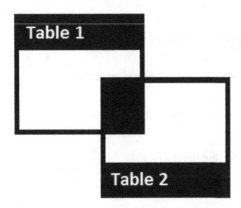

Figure 12-1. *Data returned by an INNER JOIN*

If Table 1 contains a record with an ID that is not present in Table 2, that record will not be returned. Similarly, if Table 2 contains a record with an ID that is not present in Table 1, it will not be returned.

If the ID is present on a record in both Table 1 and Table 2, it will be included in the result set. Here's our first attempt at an INNER JOIN, using SELECT * for now (naughty me!).

```
SELECT * FROM dbo.Contacts
INNER JOIN dbo.ContactPhoneNumbers
ON dbo.Contacts.ContactId = dbo.ContactPhoneNumbers.ContactId;
```

Note that the INNER JOIN is so called because it only returns rows that exist in both tables. The inner data is highlighted in the diagram above, showing how the data intersects. Anything outside of this intersected area is termed OUTER data.

The query above returns the 17 rows displayed in Figure 12-2.

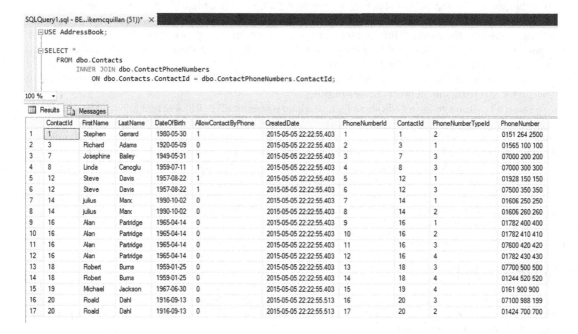

Figure 12-2. *Data returned by an INNER JOIN—for real!*

Hmm, this query and its results seem to bring up more questions than answers. If I saw this I'd be asking:

- Why does the query specify the table names multiple times? Isn't there a cleaner way of writing the code?

- Why is the PhoneNumberId column included in the results? It's of no interest to me.

- Why do the results contain two ContactId columns?

- The PhoneNumberTypeId just lists numbers. How can I find out the real PhoneNumberType?

- Can I display something more user friendly than 1 or 0 in the AllowContactByPhone column?

- Why aren't all of my contacts included in this report? I can tell by the ContactId values that some of them are missing, like ContactId 2.

- Can I filter this to just include the contacts who have said I can phone them?

Whew, there's a lot to look at here! I'll try to answer and resolve each question one by one.

To start with, the query is unnecessarily long. Do you remember the column aliases we just looked at? Well, you can alias tables, too. We need to use table aliases here. We assign the alias to the table when we first declare it in the SELECT statement, and we can then reference it from anywhere in the query using its alias. We'll change Contacts to C, and ContactPhoneNumbers to CPN.

```
SELECT * FROM dbo.Contacts AS C
INNER JOIN dbo.ContactPhoneNumbers AS CPN
ON C.ContactId = CPN.ContactId;
```

This is much easier to understand and much shorter to write, too. So now we know that anywhere we see C it represents the Contacts table, and anywhere we see CPN it represents the ContactPhoneNumbers table.

The next two questions involve the columns we are showing in this query. We're using * at the moment, so every column from both tables is being returned. We should limit the set to just the useful columns. PhoneNumberId isn't useful, so we won't include that. ContactId might be useful—but we don't want two ContactIds. Why are there two of them? Don't worry, nothing sinister is going on! The first one comes from the Contacts table, and the second comes from the ContactPhoneNumbers table. We can use our aliases to just return the Contacts version.

Without further ado, let's reduce the columns.

```
SELECT C.ContactId, C.FirstName, C.LastName, C.DateOfBirth, C.AllowContactByPhone,
    CPN.PhoneNumberTypeId, CPN.PhoneNumber FROM dbo.Contacts AS C
INNER JOIN dbo.ContactPhoneNumbers AS CPN
ON C.ContactId = CPN.ContactId;
```

If we run this, things look better, as you can see in Figure 12-3.

```
SQLQuery1.sql - BE...ikemcquillan (51))*  ×
    USE AddressBook;

    SELECT  C.ContactId,
            C.FirstName,
            C.LastName,
            C.DateOfBirth,
            C.AllowContactByPhone,
            CPN.PhoneNumberTypeId,
            CPN.PhoneNumber
        FROM dbo.Contacts AS C
            INNER JOIN dbo.ContactPhoneNumbers AS CPN
                ON C.ContactId = CPN.ContactId;

100 %   ▼
    Results    Messages
```

	ContactId	FirstName	LastName	DateOfBirth	AllowContactByPhone	PhoneNumberTypeId	PhoneNumber
1	1	Stephen	Gerrard	1980-05-30	1	2	0151 264 2500
2	3	Richard	Adams	1920-05-09	0	1	01565 100 100
3	7	Josephine	Bailey	1949-05-31	1	3	07000 200 200
4	8	Linda	Canoglu	1959-07-11	1	3	07000 300 300
5	12	Steve	Davis	1957-08-22	1	1	01928 150 150
6	12	Steve	Davis	1957-08-22	1	3	07500 350 350
7	14	julius	Marx	1990-10-02	0	1	01606 250 250
8	14	julius	Marx	1990-10-02	0	2	01606 260 260
9	16	Alan	Partridge	1965-04-14	0	1	01782 400 400
10	16	Alan	Partridge	1965-04-14	0	2	01782 410 410
11	16	Alan	Partridge	1965-04-14	0	3	07600 420 420
12	16	Alan	Partridge	1965-04-14	0	4	01782 430 430
13	18	Robert	Burns	1959-01-25	0	3	07700 500 500
14	18	Robert	Burns	1959-01-25	0	4	01244 520 520
15	19	Michael	Jackson	1967-06-30	0	4	0161 900 900
16	20	Roald	Dahl	1916-09-13	0	3	07100 988 199
17	20	Roald	Dahl	1916-09-13	0	2	01424 700 700

Figure 12-3. *Using table aliases and targeted columns*

What do you think would happen if you hadn't put a C. in front of ContactId? SQL Server would have thrown an error:

```
Msg 209, Level 16, State 1, Line 3
Ambiguous column name 'ContactId'.
```

This is because the table containing ContactId cannot be identified without the alias. To say the alias is important to making your code easy to understand is an understatement, especially as SQL Server allows you to be very loose in most cases with your aliases. This version of the query works equally as well as the preceding amended version.

```
SELECT C.ContactId, FirstName, LastName, DateOfBirth, AllowContactByPhone,
    PhoneNumberTypeId, PhoneNumber
FROM dbo.Contacts AS C
INNER JOIN dbo.ContactPhoneNumbers AS CPN
ON C.ContactId = CPN.ContactId;
```

BE CONSISTENT!

Just because you *can* do something, doesn't mean that you *should*. Make your code as consistent as you possibly can at all times, even if this sometimes means a little extra typing. If your query uses more than one table, use table aliases against every column—it really will make your query easier to read.

Note that only ContactId has an alias. We have no idea which table the other columns are coming from—it could be either table in the join. Not too much of a problem when you are only joining two tables, but if you add more joins to the mix it will become very difficult to manage. Always prefix column names with the table alias.

On to the next problem: replacing the PhoneNumberTypeId. To obtain the human-readable version of a phone number type, we need to join to the PhoneNumberTypes table. The ContactPhoneNumbers table has a foreign key to this table via the PhoneNumberTypeId column. We'll add another INNER JOIN to our query, and replace the CPN.PhoneNumberTypeId column with the PhoneNumberType column from the PhoneNumberTypes table, which we've aliased as PNT.

```
SELECT C.ContactId, C.FirstName, C.LastName, C.DateOfBirth, C.AllowContactByPhone,
    PNT.PhoneNumberType, CPN.PhoneNumber
FROM dbo.Contacts AS C
INNER JOIN dbo.ContactPhoneNumbers AS CPN
ON C.ContactId = CPN.ContactId
INNER JOIN dbo.PhoneNumberTypes PNT
ON CPN.PhoneNumberTypeId = PNT.PhoneNumberTypeId;
```

■ **Note**   You can include as many joins and tables as you want in a query (SQL Server 2005 had a limit of 256 tables; now you are only constrained by local resources). I've never seen a query with more than 40 tables, and that wasn't very well written or thought out!

We're working our way through the questions; things aren't looking too bad at all now. Figure 12-4 shows our current position.

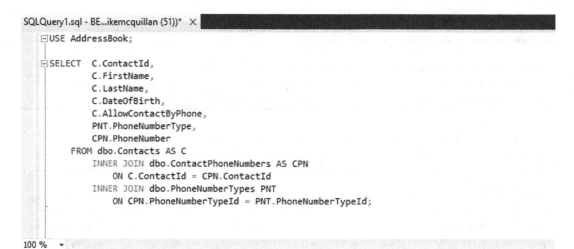

Figure 12-4. *Including the PhoneNumberTypeId join*

Our next problem involves the `AllowContactByPhone` column—can we make it more user friendly? Yes, we can. This is not a join problem, but it is typical of the kind of question you'll come up against when writing reporting queries for users. We can amend the values to `'Yes'` or `'No'` using something called a CASE statement. We'll display `Yes` for values of 1, and `No` for values of 0. Replace the line `C.AllowContactByPhone` with this:

```
CASE C.AllowContactByPhone
    WHEN 1 THEN 'Yes'
    ELSE 'No'
END AS AllowContactByPhone,
```

The CASE statement works in a similar fashion to the IF statement, but it operates on each row. This example says if AllowContactByPhone is 1, display Yes. If it is anything else, display No. We could have written this as:

```
CASE C.AllowContactByPhone
    WHEN 1 THEN 'Yes'
    WHEN 0 THEN 'No'
    ELSE 'No'
END AS AllowContactByPhone,
```

You can specify as many WHEN clauses as required, but you can only have one ELSE clause. The optional ELSE clause performs the mopping up of any values you didn't include in the WHEN clauses for any reason. If you don't specify an ELSE clause and you don't explicitly specify a WHEN clause for a value, the column will contain a NULL value.

Our code doesn't include the WHEN 0 clause, as it is redundant. If the value is 1, display Yes. If it is anything else, we are not allowed to make a phone call, so just display No. The ELSE clause handles the No values.

Run the query now, and you'll see Yes and No in the AllowContactByPhone column (Figure 12-5).

```
SQLQuery1.sql - BE...ikemcquillan (51))*  ×
  USE AddressBook;

  SELECT  C.ContactId,
          C.FirstName,
          C.LastName,
          C.DateOfBirth,
          CASE C.AllowContactByPhone
              WHEN 1 THEN 'Yes'
              ELSE 'No'
          END AS AllowContactByPhone,
          PNT.PhoneNumberType,
          CPN.PhoneNumber
      FROM dbo.Contacts AS C
          INNER JOIN dbo.ContactPhoneNumbers AS CPN
              ON C.ContactId = CPN.ContactId
          INNER JOIN dbo.PhoneNumberTypes PNT
              ON CPN.PhoneNumberTypeId = PNT.PhoneNumberTypeId;
```

100 %

Results | Messages

	ContactId	FirstName	LastName	DateOfBirth	AllowContactByPhone	PhoneNumberType	PhoneNumber
1	1	Stephen	Gerrard	1980-05-30	Yes	Work	0151 264 2500
2	3	Richard	Adams	1920-05-09	No	Home	01565 100 100
3	7	Josephine	Bailey	1949-05-31	Yes	Mobile	07000 200 200
4	8	Linda	Canoglu	1959-07-11	Yes	Mobile	07000 300 300
5	12	Steve	Davis	1957-08-22	Yes	Home	01928 150 150
6	12	Steve	Davis	1957-08-22	Yes	Mobile	07500 350 350
7	14	julius	Marx	1990-10-02	No	Home	01606 250 250
8	14	julius	Marx	1990-10-02	No	Work	01606 260 260
9	16	Alan	Partridge	1965-04-14	No	Home	01782 400 400
10	16	Alan	Partridge	1965-04-14	No	Work	01782 410 410
11	16	Alan	Partridge	1965-04-14	No	Mobile	07600 420 420
12	16	Alan	Partridge	1965-04-14	No	Other	01782 430 430
13	18	Robert	Burns	1959-01-25	No	Mobile	07700 500 500
14	18	Robert	Burns	1959-01-25	No	Other	01244 520 520
15	19	Michael	Jackson	1967-06-30	No	Other	0161 900 900
16	20	Roald	Dahl	1916-09-13	No	Mobile	07100 988 199
17	20	Roald	Dahl	1916-09-13	No	Work	01424 700 700

Figure 12-5. *Adding a CASE statement*

We had to add a column alias at the end. If we hadn't done this, no name would have been assigned to the column. This is because the CASE statement generates a derived column.

This is a very simple introduction to CASE statements. You can do a lot with them and they'll become a useful part of your arsenal. Used wisely, CASE statements can greatly reduce your code in certain places.

Back to INNER JOINs. Two questions left. First, why can't I see all of my contacts? If you look at the results in Figure 12-5, only 10 of the contacts are included in the results. Why is this? Are the results correct? Indeed, yes, the results are correct.

The ContactPhoneNumbers table contains 17 phone numbers, but several of these belong to the same contact. For example:

Contact ID	No. of Phone Numbers
1	1
3	1
7	1
8	1
12	2
14	2
16	4
18	2
19	1
20	2

Our query contains 17 results, one for each phone number. If we want to include all of our contacts, regardless of whether they have a phone number or not, we'll need to use a LEFT JOIN. We'll change our query a little later to do this.

Time to answer our final question. Can we filter the list so just those contacts who have agreed to be contacted by phone are included? Of course we can, using a WHERE clause:

```
SELECT C.ContactId, C.FirstName, C.LastName, C.DateOfBirth,
    CASE C.AllowContactByPhone WHEN 1 THEN 'Yes' ELSE 'No' END AS AllowContactByPhone,
    PNT.PhoneNumberType, CPN.PhoneNumber
FROM dbo.Contacts AS C
INNER JOIN dbo.ContactPhoneNumbers AS CPN
ON C.ContactId = CPN.ContactId
INNER JOIN dbo.PhoneNumberTypes PNT
ON CPN.PhoneNumberTypeId = PNT.PhoneNumberTypeId
WHERE C.AllowContactByPhone = 1;
```

We specified the alias in front of the column name—we always use the alias now for consistency. And we still use 1 to match values, even though we display Yes in the result set. Using the CASE statement in the WHERE clause is possible, but adds unnecessary overhead. Here's how you do it, though:

```
WHERE CASE C.AllowContactByPhone WHEN 1 THEN 'Yes' ELSE 'No' END = 'Yes'
```

We've done well here; this is a pretty useful query. If you run it, the five results in Figure 12-6 should be returned.

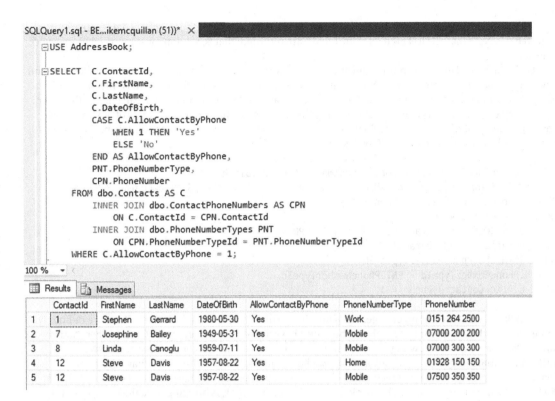

```
SQLQuery1.sql - BE...ikemcquillan (51))*  ×
  ☐USE AddressBook;

  ☐SELECT  C.ContactId,
           C.FirstName,
           C.LastName,
           C.DateOfBirth,
           CASE C.AllowContactByPhone
               WHEN 1 THEN 'Yes'
               ELSE 'No'
           END AS AllowContactByPhone,
           PNT.PhoneNumberType,
           CPN.PhoneNumber
       FROM dbo.Contacts AS C
           INNER JOIN dbo.ContactPhoneNumbers AS CPN
               ON C.ContactId = CPN.ContactId
           INNER JOIN dbo.PhoneNumberTypes PNT
               ON CPN.PhoneNumberTypeId = PNT.PhoneNumberTypeId
       WHERE C.AllowContactByPhone = 1;
100 %  ▾
```

Results | Messages

	ContactId	FirstName	LastName	DateOfBirth	AllowContactByPhone	PhoneNumberType	PhoneNumber
1	1	Stephen	Gerrard	1980-05-30	Yes	Work	0151 264 2500
2	7	Josephine	Bailey	1949-05-31	Yes	Mobile	07000 200 200
3	8	Linda	Canoglu	1959-07-11	Yes	Mobile	07000 300 300
4	12	Steve	Davis	1957-08-22	Yes	Home	01928 150 150
5	12	Steve	Davis	1957-08-22	Yes	Mobile	07500 350 350

Figure 12-6. *The Completed INNER JOIN Query*

We've had a good introduction to INNER JOINs. The key to understanding them is remembering that matching records must exist in both tables involved in the join—unlike our next contestant. . . .

LEFT OUTER JOIN

LEFT OUTER JOINs—or LEFT JOINs as I'll refer to them—return every row from the left-hand table, but only matching rows from the right-hand table. Figure 12-7 illustrates how data are matched.

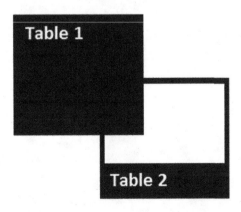

Figure 12-7. *Data returned by a LEFT JOIN*

Everything comes back from Table 1, but only the overlapping data—the matching data—are returned from Table 2. Note that all OUTER data from Table 1 are returned; that is, we don't just returned intersected data here.

Our INNER JOIN query currently returns all records from Contacts that have ContactPhoneNumbers and have stated that we are allowed to contact them by phone. The first part of the problem is solved using an INNER JOIN, and the WHERE clause is used to check if contact is allowed by phone. We can change this query to return all contact records that have stated they can be contacted by phone, regardless of whether they have a phone number or not (maybe they plan to provide one in future?). Make one simple modification: change the first INNER JOIN to a LEFT OUTER JOIN.

```
SELECT C.ContactId, C.FirstName, C.LastName, C.DateOfBirth,
    CASE C.AllowContactByPhone WHEN 1 THEN 'Yes' ELSE 'No' END AS AllowContactByPhone,
    PNT.PhoneNumberType, CPN.PhoneNumber
FROM dbo.Contacts AS C
LEFT OUTER JOIN dbo.ContactPhoneNumbers AS CPN
ON C.ContactId = CPN.ContactId
INNER JOIN dbo.PhoneNumberTypes PNT
ON CPN.PhoneNumberTypeId = PNT.PhoneNumberTypeId
WHERE C.AllowContactByPhone = 1;
```

Run this . . . and there is no change. The same five results come back. Why is that? There are definitely some contacts that allow contact by phone, but don't have a matching record in the ContactPhoneNumbers table. Where are they? Don't worry, they are still in the database. The problem is the second INNER JOIN. This is matching records in ContactPhoneNumbers and PhoneNumberTypes that have the same PhoneNumberTypeId. Our contact records that don't have a phone number have a PhoneNumberTypeId of NULL, which cannot be matched. The first join, the LEFT OUTER JOIN, is bringing back the records, but the second INNER JOIN is filtering them out. The solution is to change the second INNER JOIN into a LEFT OUTER JOIN, too.

```
SELECT C.ContactId, C.FirstName, C.LastName, C.DateOfBirth,
    CASE C.AllowContactByPhone WHEN 1 THEN 'Yes' ELSE 'No' END AS AllowContactByPhone,
    PNT.PhoneNumberType, CPN.PhoneNumber
FROM dbo.Contacts AS C
LEFT OUTER JOIN dbo.ContactPhoneNumbers AS CPN
ON C.ContactId = CPN.ContactId
LEFT OUTER JOIN dbo.PhoneNumberTypes PNT
ON CPN.PhoneNumberTypeId = PNT.PhoneNumberTypeId
WHERE C.AllowContactByPhone = 1;
```

And now our results make a bit more sense, as Figure 12-8 tells us.

```
SQLQuery1.sql - BE...ikemcquillan (51))*  ×
    USE AddressBook;

    SELECT  C.ContactId,
            C.FirstName,
            C.LastName,
            C.DateOfBirth,
            CASE C.AllowContactByPhone
                WHEN 1 THEN 'Yes'
                ELSE 'No'
            END AS AllowContactByPhone,
            PNT.PhoneNumberType,
            CPN.PhoneNumber
        FROM dbo.Contacts AS C
            LEFT OUTER JOIN dbo.ContactPhoneNumbers AS CPN
                ON C.ContactId = CPN.ContactId
            LEFT OUTER JOIN dbo.PhoneNumberTypes PNT
                ON CPN.PhoneNumberTypeId = PNT.PhoneNumberTypeId
        WHERE C.AllowContactByPhone = 1;
```

100 % ▾

▦ Results ▤ Messages

	ContactId	FirstName	LastName	DateOfBirth	AllowContactByPhone	PhoneNumberType	PhoneNumber
1	1	Stephen	Gerrard	1980-05-30	Yes	Work	0151 264 2500
2	4	Bertie	McQuillan	2001-06-30	Yes	NULL	NULL
3	5	Walt	Disney	1966-12-05	Yes	NULL	NULL
4	7	Josephine	Bailey	1949-05-31	Yes	Mobile	07000 200 200
5	8	Linda	Canoglu	1959-07-11	Yes	Mobile	07000 300 300
6	11	Angelica	Jones	1981-02-04	Yes	NULL	NULL
7	12	Steve	Davis	1957-08-22	Yes	Home	01928 150 150
8	12	Steve	Davis	1957-08-22	Yes	Mobile	07500 350 350
9	13	Allison	Fisher	1968-02-24	Yes	NULL	NULL
10	15	george	formby	1944-05-26	Yes	NULL	NULL
11	17	Harper	Lee	1986-04-28	Yes	NULL	NULL

Figure 12-8. *Data returned after specifying LEFT JOINs*

Five of these records have phone numbers and phone number types; the rest all show NULL.

I've used the phrase LEFT OUTER JOIN in the query. I could easily have written LEFT JOIN instead. This is an area where I have no real preference—for me, LEFT JOIN is just as descriptive as LEFT OUTER JOIN. I'll continue to use LEFT OUTER JOIN and so on throughout the book, but just remember to be consistent. Plump for one or the other, and stick with it.

Let's look at another LEFT OUTER JOIN. This is a bit simpler than our previous example.

```
SELECT C.ContactId, C.FirstName, C.LastName, C.DateOfBirth,
    CASE C.AllowContactByPhone WHEN 1 THEN 'Yes' ELSE 'No' END AS AllowContactByPhone,
    CPN.PhoneNumber
FROM dbo.Contacts AS C
LEFT OUTER JOIN dbo.ContactPhoneNumbers AS CPN
ON C.ContactId = CPN.ContactId
ORDER BY C.ContactId ASC;
```

We've removed the extra LEFT OUTER JOIN and the WHERE clause. Now every record in Contacts will be returned regardless of whether a phone number record is available or not. That's 27 records in total. You can see most of these in Figure 12-9.

```
SQLQuery2.sql - BE...ikemcquillan (55))*  ×  SQLQuery1.sql - BE...ikemcquillan (51))*
  USE AddressBook;

  SELECT  C.ContactId,
          C.FirstName,
          C.LastName,
          C.DateOfBirth,
          CASE C.AllowContactByPhone
              WHEN 1 THEN 'Yes'
              ELSE 'No'
          END AS AllowContactByPhone,
          CPN.PhoneNumber
      FROM dbo.Contacts AS C
          LEFT OUTER JOIN dbo.ContactPhoneNumbers AS CPN
              ON C.ContactId = CPN.ContactId
      ORDER BY C.ContactId ASC;
```

100 %

Results   Messages

	ContactId	FirstName	LastName	DateOfBirth	AllowContactByPhone	PhoneNumber
1	1	Stephen	Gerrard	1980-05-30	Yes	0151 264 2500
2	2	Dennis	Potter	1935-05-17	No	NULL
3	3	Richard	Adams	1920-05-09	No	01565 100 100
4	4	Bertie	McQuillan	2001-06-30	Yes	NULL
5	5	Walt	Disney	1966-12-05	Yes	NULL
6	6	Barbara	Gordon	1952-01-11	No	NULL
7	7	Josephine	Bailey	1949-05-31	Yes	07000 200 200
8	8	Linda	Canoglu	1959-07-11	Yes	07000 300 300
9	9	Grace	McQuillan	1993-09-27	No	NULL
10	10	Vera	Black	1984-08-03	No	NULL
11	11	Angelica	Jones	1981-02-04	Yes	NULL
12	12	Steve	Davis	1957-08-22	Yes	01928 150 150
13	12	Steve	Davis	1957-08-22	Yes	07500 350 350
14	13	Allison	Fisher	1968-02-24	Yes	NULL
15	14	julius	Marx	1990-10-02	No	01606 250 250
16	14	julius	Marx	1990-10-02	No	01606 260 260
17	15	george	formby	1944-05-26	Yes	NULL
18	16	Alan	Partridge	1965-04-14	No	01782 400 400
19	16	Alan	Partridge	1965-04-14	No	01782 410 410
20	16	Alan	Partridge	1965-04-14	No	01782 430 430
21	16	Alan	Partridge	1965-04-14	No	07600 420 420
22	17	Harper	Lee	1986-04-28	Yes	NULL

Figure 12-9. Records returned regardless of phone number

Say we want to display all contact records regardless of whether we have a phone number for them or not, and we only want to display their phone number if it is a home phone number. Any ideas how we may do that? What's that? Add a WHERE clause, you say? Okay, here's that very query with the LEFT OUTER JOIN to PhoneNumberTypes reintroduced, too.

```
SELECT C.ContactId, C.FirstName, C.LastName, C.DateOfBirth,
    CASE C.AllowContactByPhone WHEN 1 THEN 'Yes' ELSE 'No' END AS AllowContactByPhone,
    PNT.PhoneNumberType, CPN.PhoneNumber
FROM dbo.Contacts AS C
LEFT OUTER JOIN dbo.ContactPhoneNumbers AS CPN
ON C.ContactId = CPN.ContactId
LEFT OUTER JOIN dbo.PhoneNumberTypes AS PNT
ON CPN.PhoneNumberTypeId = PNT.PhoneNumberTypeId
WHERE PNT.PhoneNumberType = 'Home'
ORDER BY C.ContactId ASC;
```

Does this work? No! Only the home numbers are returned. Records without a home number have been removed (check out Figure 12-10).

	ContactId	FirstName	LastName	DateOfBirth	AllowContactByPhone	PhoneNumberType	PhoneNumber
1	3	Richard	Adams	1920-05-09	No	Home	01565 100 100
2	12	Steve	Davis	1957-08-22	Yes	Home	01928 150 150
3	14	julius	Marx	1990-10-02	No	Home	01606 250 250
4	16	Alan	Partridge	1965-04-14	No	Home	01782 400 400

Figure 12-10. *Only home phone numbers returned*

The problem is the WHERE clause limits what is displayed. The query is executing in this manner:

- FROM dbo.Contacts AS C returns all contacts. There are 20 records in the set at this point.

- LEFT OUTER JOIN dbo.ContactPhoneNumbers returns all contacts, and any matching phone numbers. The set now contains 27 records.

- LEFT OUTER JOIN dbo.PhoneNumberTypes includes each phone number's phone number type. The set still contains 27 records.

- WHERE PNT.PhoneNumberType = 'Home' tells the query to remove all records from the set that don't have a phone number type of 'Home'. Only 4 records meet this criteria

Okay, that doesn't work, then. How about removing the WHERE clause and adding it to the last LEFT OUTER JOIN?

```
SELECT C.ContactId, C.FirstName, C.LastName, C.DateOfBirth, CASE C.AllowContactByPhone WHEN 1
THEN 'Yes' ELSE 'No' END AS AllowContactByPhone, PNT.PhoneNumberType, CPN.PhoneNumber FROM
dbo.Contacts AS C LEFT OUTER JOIN dbo.ContactPhoneNumbers AS CPN ON C.ContactId =
CPN.ContactId LEFT OUTER JOIN dbo.PhoneNumberTypes AS PNT ON CPN.PhoneNumberTypeId =
PNT.PhoneNumberTypeId AND PNT.PhoneNumberType = 'Home' ORDER BY C.ContactId ASC;
```

We've now told the second LEFT OUTER JOIN that two conditions must be fulfilled for records to be returned. Unfortunately, this is still wrong! Twenty-seven rows are returned now (Figure 12-11 shows some of these rows)—that's all contacts and their phone numbers.

	ContactId	FirstName	LastName	DateOfBirth	AllowContactByPhone	PhoneNumberType	PhoneNumber
1	1	Stephen	Gerrard	1980-05-30	Yes	NULL	0151 264 2500
2	2	Dennis	Potter	1935-05-17	No	NULL	NULL
3	3	Richard	Adams	1920-05-09	No	Home	01565 100 100
4	4	Bertie	McQuillan	2001-06-30	Yes	NULL	NULL
5	5	Walt	Disney	1966-12-05	Yes	NULL	NULL
6	6	Barbara	Gordon	1952-01-11	No	NULL	NULL
7	7	Josephine	Bailey	1949-05-31	Yes	NULL	07000 200 200
8	8	Linda	Canoglu	1959-07-11	Yes	NULL	07000 300 300
9	9	Grace	McQuillan	1993-09-27	No	NULL	NULL
10	10	Vera	Black	1984-08-03	No	NULL	NULL
11	11	Angelica	Jones	1981-02-04	Yes	NULL	NULL
12	12	Steve	Davis	1957-08-22	Yes	Home	01928 150 150

Figure 12-11. *All contacts and phone numbers are returned—not good!*

Yes, the PhoneNumberType column correctly shows nothing except the 'Home' value, but there are several rows with a PhoneNumber value and no PhoneNumberType. What the heck happened here?

- FROM dbo.Contacts AS C returns all contacts. There are 20 records in the set at this point.

- LEFT OUTER JOIN dbo.ContactPhoneNumbers returns all contacts, and any matching phone numbers. The set now contains 27 records.

- LEFT OUTER JOIN dbo.PhoneNumberTypes has been limited to only return the 'Home' phone number type. The set still contains 27 records. The 'Home' filter only applies to records returned from the PhoneNumberTypes table—it's in the wrong place.

This result set is actually worse than our first effort, as the data are inconsistent. A user would ask why we have phone numbers without phone number types. To successfully return all contacts and only the home phone numbers, we need to obtain all contacts, and then only records from ContactPhoneNumbers that have a PhoneNumberTypeId of 1. The PhoneNumberTypes table is irrelevant in terms of limiting the result set. This query should do the trick; Figure 12-12 has the result.

```
SELECT C.ContactId, C.FirstName, C.LastName, C.DateOfBirth,
    CASE C.AllowContactByPhone WHEN 1 THEN 'Yes' ELSE 'No' END AS AllowContactByPhone,
    PNT.PhoneNumberType, CPN.PhoneNumber
FROM dbo.Contacts AS C
LEFT OUTER JOIN dbo.ContactPhoneNumbers AS CPN
ON C.ContactId = CPN.ContactId AND CPN.PhoneNumberTypeId = 1
LEFT OUTER JOIN dbo.PhoneNumberTypes AS PNT
ON CPN.PhoneNumberTypeId = PNT.PhoneNumberTypeId
ORDER BY C.ContactId ASC;
```

	ContactId	First Name	Last Name	DateOfBirth	AllowContactByPhone	PhoneNumberType	PhoneNumber
1	1	Stephen	Gerrard	1980-05-30	Yes	NULL	NULL
2	2	Dennis	Potter	1935-05-17	No	NULL	NULL
3	3	Richard	Adams	1920-05-09	No	Home	01565 100 100
4	4	Bertie	McQuillan	2001-06-30	Yes	NULL	NULL
5	5	Walt	Disney	1966-12-05	Yes	NULL	NULL
6	6	Barbara	Gordon	1952-01-11	No	NULL	NULL
7	7	Josephine	Bailey	1949-05-31	Yes	NULL	NULL
8	8	Linda	Canoglu	1959-07-11	Yes	NULL	NULL
9	9	Grace	McQuillan	1993-09-27	No	NULL	NULL
10	10	Vera	Black	1984-08-03	No	NULL	NULL
11	11	Angelica	Jones	1981-02-04	Yes	NULL	NULL
12	12	Steve	Davis	1957-08-22	Yes	Home	01928 150 150
13	13	Allison	Fisher	1968-02-24	Yes	NULL	NULL
14	14	julius	Marx	1990-10-02	No	Home	01606 250 250
15	15	george	formby	1944-05-26	Yes	NULL	NULL
16	16	Alan	Partridge	1965-04-14	No	Home	01782 400 400
17	17	Harper	Lee	1986-04-28	Yes	NULL	NULL
18	18	Robert	Burns	1959-01-25	No	NULL	NULL
19	19	Michael	Jackson	1967-06-30	No	NULL	NULL
20	20	Roald	Dahl	1916-09-13	No	NULL	NULL

Figure 12-12. *A perfect record set!*

Eureka!

As Figure 12-12 highlights, all 20 contacts are returned, and just the home phone numbers are displayed. Why did this query work when the others failed?

- `FROM dbo.Contacts AS C` returns all contacts. There are 20 records in the set at this point.

- `LEFT OUTER JOIN dbo.ContactPhoneNumbers` returns all contacts, and any matching phone numbers that are of type `'Home'` (PhoneNumberTypeId = 1). The set still contains 20 records.

- `LEFT OUTER JOIN dbo.PhoneNumberTypes` returns the phone number type for matching records. As the set only contains blank phone numbers or home phone numbers, only the `'Home'` type will be displayed. The set still contains 20 records.

These examples illustrate just how important it is to think about how you construct your JOINs. With great power comes great responsibility!

We have one last example to look at for LEFT OUTER JOIN. We can use LEFT OUTER JOIN to figure out how many phone numbers we have per contact, using GROUP BY. Pop this query into SSMS and run it.

```
SELECT C.ContactId, C.FirstName, C.LastName, C.DateOfBirth, COUNT(*) AS PhoneNumberTotal
FROM dbo.Contacts AS C LEFT OUTER JOIN dbo.ContactPhoneNumbers AS CPN ON C.ContactId =
CPN.ContactId GROUP BY C.ContactId, C.FirstName, C.LastName, C.DateOfBirth ORDER BY
C.ContactId ASC;
```

Figure 12-13 has the results.

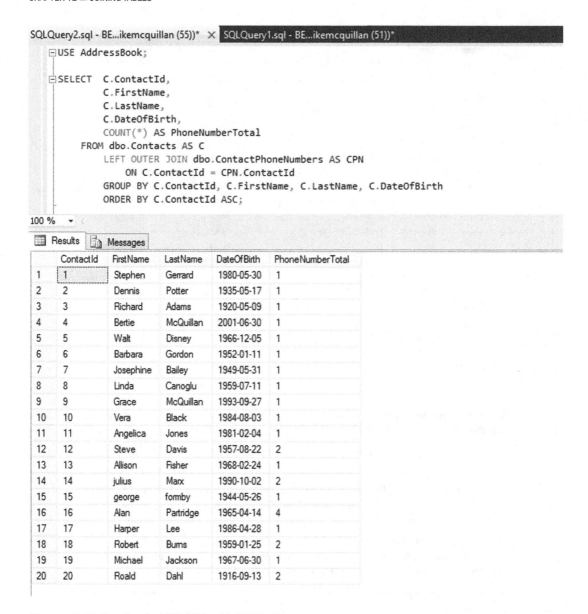

Figure 12-13. *Results of a LEFT JOIN with GROUP BY*

This doesn't look right—the PhoneNumberTotal column is showing at least one phone number exists for every contact. We know this isn't the case. Why has this happened? Well, in this particular instance the fault doesn't lie with the LEFT OUTER JOIN; it lies with the COUNT(*) statement. COUNT(*) tells SQL Server to include every row when counting. Because every contact exists in the result set at least once, regardless of whether they have a phone number or not, a value of at least 1 will always be returned. Higher numbers will be seen for those records that have more than one phone number. Figure 12-14 shows the set without the GROUP BY.

	ContactId	FirstName	LastName	DateOfBirth	PhoneNumber
1	1	Stephen	Gerrard	1980-05-30	0151 264 2500
2	2	Dennis	Potter	1935-05-17	NULL
3	3	Richard	Adams	1920-05-09	01565 100 100
4	4	Bertie	McQuillan	2001-06-30	NULL
5	5	Walt	Disney	1966-12-05	NULL
6	6	Barbara	Gordon	1952-01-11	NULL
7	7	Josephine	Bailey	1949-05-31	07000 200 200
8	8	Linda	Canoglu	1959-07-11	07000 300 300
9	9	Grace	McQuillan	1993-09-27	NULL
10	10	Vera	Black	1984-08-03	NULL
11	11	Angelica	Jones	1981-02-04	NULL
12	12	Steve	Davis	1957-08-22	01928 150 150
13	12	Steve	Davis	1957-08-22	07500 350 350
14	13	Allison	Fisher	1968-02-24	NULL
15	14	julius	Marx	1990-10-02	01606 250 250
16	14	julius	Marx	1990-10-02	01606 260 260
17	15	george	formby	1944-05-26	NULL
18	16	Alan	Partridge	1965-04-14	01782 400 400
19	16	Alan	Partridge	1965-04-14	01782 410 410
20	16	Alan	Partridge	1965-04-14	01782 430 430
21	16	Alan	Partridge	1965-04-14	07600 420 420
22	17	Harper	Lee	1986-04-28	NULL
23	18	Robert	Burns	1959-01-25	01244 520 520
24	18	Robert	Burns	1959-01-25	07700 500 500
25	19	Michael	Jackson	1967-06-30	0161 900 900
26	20	Roald	Dahl	1916-09-13	01424 700 700
27	20	Roald	Dahl	1916-09-13	07100 988 199

Figure 12-14. Phone number data grouped by contact

Most of these groups contain one record. We can see a few with two, and Alan Partridge has four records. The key to fixing our GROUP BY is the PhoneNumber column. Some of the records have a NULL PhoneNumber value—we need to COUNT using this column. The NULL will cause a zero value to be returned. If we change COUNT(*) to COUNT(CPN.PhoneNumber):

```
SELECT C.ContactId, C.FirstName, C.LastName, C.DateOfBirth, COUNT(CPN.PhoneNumber) AS
PhoneNumberTotal
FROM dbo.Contacts AS C
LEFT OUTER JOIN dbo.ContactPhoneNumbers AS CPN
ON C.ContactId = CPN.ContactId GROUP BY C.ContactId, C.FirstName, C.LastName, C.DateOfBirth
ORDER BY C.ContactId ASC;
```

Our query will work as expected. You can see the outcome in Figure 12-15.

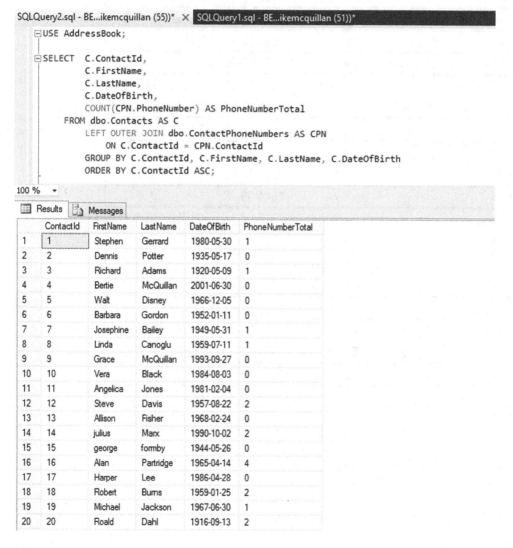

Figure 12-15. *Returning home number counts with LEFT JOIN*

We've covered some pretty interesting stuff here. The crucial thing to understand is how easy it is to output the wrong results, even when the query appears at face value to be correct. Now that we've thoroughly explored the LEFT OUTER JOIN, we'll take a look at its twin brother, RIGHT OUTER JOIN.

RIGHT OUTER JOIN

LEFT OUTER JOINs return everything from the left-hand table along with matching records from the right-hand table. As you might have guessed, RIGHT OUTER JOINs return everything from the right-hand table, along with matching records from the left-hand table. The black area in Figure 12-16 shows how data is returned from a RIGHT OUTER JOIN.

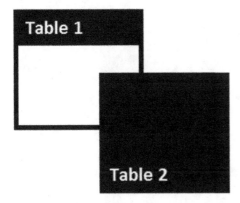

Figure 12-16. *Data returned by a RIGHT JOIN*

To demonstrate how this works, we first need to add a new Role record.

```
INSERT INTO dbo.Roles (RoleTitle) VALUES ('Sales');
```

This leaves us with the six roles you can see in Figure 12-17.

	RoleId	RoleTitle
1	1	Developer
2	2	DBA
3	3	IT Support Specialist
4	4	Manager
5	5	Director
6	6	Sales

Figure 12-17. *A new Sales role*

Our aim here is to return how many contacts there are per role in the database. We'll start off with an INNER JOIN to create this.

```
SELECT R.RoleTitle, COUNT(CR.RoleId) AS Total
FROM dbo.ContactRoles CR INNER JOIN dbo.Roles R
ON CR.RoleId = R.RoleId GROUP BY R.RoleTitle
ORDER BY R.RoleTitle ASC;
```

This returns the five results displayed in Figure 12-18.

Figure 12-18. *Showing the number of contacts per role—no Sales*

We are missing the total for the new Sales role we just added. This is because we are using an INNER JOIN, and no records in ContactRoles are linked to this new role. Changing to a LEFT JOIN brings back exactly the same result, as it brings back everything from the left-hand table—ContactRoles—and matching records from the Roles table on the right-hand side.

The fix for this is to change to a RIGHT OUTER JOIN. This will return all records from the right-hand table—Roles—before executing the GROUP BY on the matching records returned by the left-hand table, ContactRoles.

```
SELECT R.RoleTitle, COUNT(CR.RoleId) AS Total
FROM dbo.ContactRoles CR
RIGHT OUTER JOIN dbo.Roles R
ON CR.RoleId = R.RoleId
GROUP BY R.RoleTitle
ORDER BY R.RoleTitle ASC;
```

This time, success (see Figure 12-19). We rock!

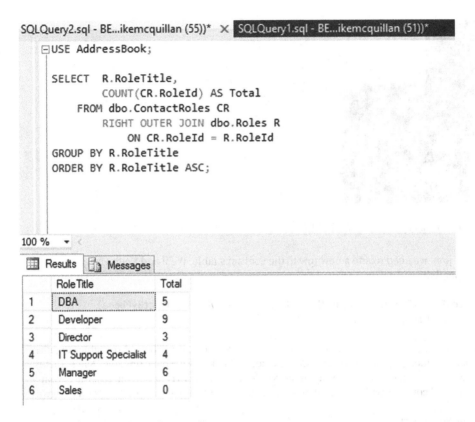

SQLQuery2.sql - BE...ikemcquillan (55))* ✕ SQLQuery1.sql - BE...ikemcquillan (51))*

```
USE AddressBook;

SELECT   R.RoleTitle,
         COUNT(CR.RoleId) AS Total
    FROM dbo.ContactRoles CR
         RIGHT OUTER JOIN dbo.Roles R
             ON CR.RoleId = R.RoleId
GROUP BY R.RoleTitle
ORDER BY R.RoleTitle ASC;
```

100 %   ▼   ◁

Results   Messages

	Role Title	Total
1	DBA	5
2	Developer	9
3	Director	3
4	IT Support Specialist	4
5	Manager	6
6	Sales	0

Figure 12-19. RIGHT JOIN shows Sales!

If you want to delve further into RIGHT OUTER JOINs, try changing the queries we wrote when exploring LEFT OUTER JOINs to use RIGHT OUTER JOINs. As I mentioned earlier, you'll usually use a LEFT OUTER JOIN rather than a RIGHT OUTER JOIN if you are writing a query from scratch. I tend to use RIGHT OUTER JOINs when I'm refactoring an existing query and using a RIGHT OUTER JOIN will save me from moving tables around.

One OUTER JOIN type left to look at. . . .

FULL OUTER JOIN

This type of join is seldom used, but when it's needed it can be a real time saver. So far, the joins we've seen allow us to

- return exact matches from two tables (INNER JOIN), and

- return all records from one table, and matching records from another (LEFT and RIGHT OUTER JOINs).

FULL OUTER JOIN does something different. It returns every row from both tables (represented by the completely black squares in Figure 12-20). We can bring back all contacts and all roles that match, but we can also return contacts that are not associated with a role, and roles that are not associated with a contact.

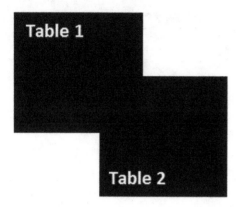

Figure 12-20. *Data returned by a* FULL OUTER JOIN

To illustrate this join, we need to add a new row to the Contacts table. We'll add Keith Chegwin ("Cheggers" to his friends):

```
INSERT INTO dbo.Contacts(FirstName, LastName, DateOfBirth, AllowContactByPhone)
VALUES ('Keith', 'Chegwin', '1957-01-17', 1);
```

We'll use three tables in our example: ContactRoles, Contacts, and Roles. These three tables together form a many-to-many relationship between Contacts and Roles. We know we have one role (Sales) that is not linked to any Contacts. And we now have a contact (Keith Chegwin) who is not linked to a role. What we want to do is return all contacts with their matching roles, but also the Sales role and the Keith Chegwin contact.

We'll handle the Roles part first.

```
SELECT CR.RoleId, R.RoleTitle
FROM dbo.ContactRoles CR FULL OUTER JOIN dbo.Roles R
ON CR.RoleId = R.RoleId;
```

As it stands, this query returns all records that match in ContactRoles and Roles, as well as any records in Roles that do not exist in ContactRoles (you can see the results in Figure 12-21). We could have done the same thing with a RIGHT OUTER JOIN.

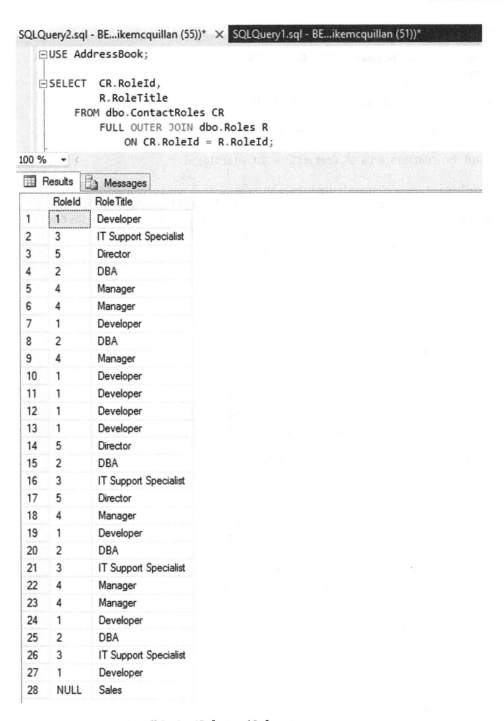

Figure 12-21. *Returning all ContactRoles and Roles*

Note the NULL RoleId in the final record, for Sales. This is because no records exist for Sales in the ContactRoles table.

Now it's time to introduce the power of FULL OUTER JOIN. Add a second FULL OUTER JOIN, linking to Contacts this time.

```
SELECT C.ContactId, CR.RoleId, R.RoleTitle, C.FirstName,
    C.LastName, C.DateOfBirth, C.AllowContactByPhone
FROM dbo.ContactRoles CR FULL OUTER JOIN dbo.Roles R
ON CR.RoleId = R.RoleId
FULL OUTER JOIN dbo.Contacts C ON CR.ContactId = C.ContactId;
```

What should happen now is all records that exist in all three tables should be returned. The Sales record in the Roles table should be returned with mostly NULL values, and the Keith Chegwin record in Contacts should also be returned, again with NULL values in all columns except for columns returned via the Contacts table. The full result set is shown in Figure 12-22; the last two rows show the unmatched records.

	ContactId	RoleId	Role Title	First Name	Last Name	DateOfBirth	AllowContactByPhone
1	1	1	Developer	Stephen	Gerrard	1980-05-30	1
2	2	3	IT Support Specialist	Dennis	Potter	1935-05-17	0
3	2	5	Director	Dennis	Potter	1935-05-17	0
4	3	2	DBA	Richard	Adams	1920-05-09	0
5	4	4	Manager	Bertie	McQuillan	2001-06-30	1
6	5	4	Manager	Walt	Disney	1966-12-05	1
7	6	1	Developer	Barbara	Gordon	1952-01-11	0
8	6	2	DBA	Barbara	Gordon	1952-01-11	0
9	6	4	Manager	Barbara	Gordon	1952-01-11	0
10	7	1	Developer	Josephine	Bailey	1949-05-31	1
11	8	1	Developer	Linda	Canoglu	1959-07-11	1
12	9	1	Developer	Grace	McQuillan	1993-09-27	0
13	10	1	Developer	Vera	Black	1984-08-03	0
14	10	5	Director	Vera	Black	1984-08-03	0
15	11	2	DBA	Angelica	Jones	1981-02-04	1
16	12	3	IT Support Specialist	Steve	Davis	1957-08-22	1
17	13	5	Director	Allison	Fisher	1968-02-24	1
18	14	4	Manager	julius	Marx	1990-10-02	0
19	15	1	Developer	george	formby	1944-05-26	1
20	15	2	DBA	george	formby	1944-05-26	1
21	15	3	IT Support Specialist	george	formby	1944-05-26	1
22	15	4	Manager	george	formby	1944-05-26	1
23	16	4	Manager	Alan	Partridge	1965-04-14	0
24	17	1	Developer	Harper	Lee	1986-04-28	1
25	18	2	DBA	Robert	Burns	1959-01-25	0
26	19	3	IT Support Specialist	Michael	Jackson	1967-06-30	0
27	20	1	Developer	Roald	Dahl	1916-09-13	0
28	NULL	NULL	Sales	NULL	NULL	NULL	NULL
29	21	NULL	NULL	Keith	Chegwin	1957-01-17	1

Figure 12-22. *The last two rows are unmatched*

All of the matched records have returned just as an INNER JOIN would. You can think of the FULL OUTER JOIN as executing all three of INNER JOIN, LEFT OUTER JOIN, and RIGHT OUTER JOIN. Very useful at times.

CROSS JOIN

Our final join is not used on a regular basis. A CROSS JOIN is usually used to generate test data—it has few other practical uses. There is no image for this join as it's quite difficult to show graphically—going straight to an example will work better here. I've rebuilt my database, so any records I've added during this chapter are gone now.

Assume the Contacts table has 20 records in it, and the ContactPhoneNumbers table has 17 records in it. We've already seen via our other joins how we can return this information, ensuring the correct parent is mapped to the correct children by specifying a join condition. There's no such condition here—a CROSS JOIN doesn't allow you to specify one. Write this:

```
SELECT * FROM dbo.Contacts AS C
CROSS JOIN dbo.ContactPhoneNumbers AS CPN;
```

Without any criteria specified to dictate how the tables should be joined, how many rows do you think will be returned here? Go on, try it. Make sure you look at the row count returned in the bottom right-hand corner (I've put a box around it in Figure 12-23).

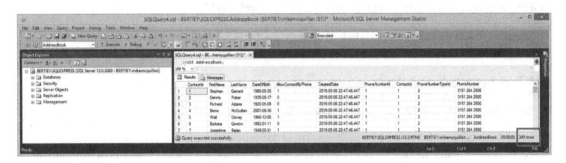

Figure 12-23. *A Cartesian Product via CROSS JOIN*

It returns 340 rows! Why, when we should have no more than 20? Well, 20 rows in Contacts, and 17 in ContactPhoneNumbers: 20 * 17 = 340. This join returns every possible combination of the two tables, so for every row in the Contacts table, 17 combinations are returned—one for each ContactPhoneNumbers record.

Obviously this is not good, as we have no way of telling which phone number belongs to which contact. But it is only not good if we were trying to use the data in a realistic scenario (i.e., we wanted to call the contact)—we'd use one of the other join types for that. This join would be useful for us if we were trying to generate lots and lots of contacts so we could test the database. Keep this join in mind if you are ever asked to generate some test data.

CARTESIAN PRODUCTS

The result set the CROSS JOIN returned is known as a *Cartesian Product*. A Cartesian Product occurs when a database query returns every possible row combination across two tables. It is easy to accidentally create Cartesian Product result sets, so ensure you test your queries thoroughly for accidental duplicates.

217

Using JOINs In DML Statements

I've covered all the various join types available to us in SQL Server. I'm sure you'll agree there's been quite a bit to take in. Before I wrap up this chapter, we'll look at how JOINs can be used as part of the INSERT INTO, UPDATE and DELETE statements.

Whenever I'm tasked with writing a DML statement, I always begin by writing a SELECT statement. Let's say I've been asked to insert a new Senior Developer record into the Roles table. Once this is available, I need to change all developers in the database into senior developers. I then have to remove the Developer role from these senior developers. Last, I've been asked to change IT Support Specialists to Developers. Let's break this down into the statements we need to write:

- INSERT a new Senior Developer record into the Roles table

- INSERT Senior Developer records into ContactRoles, for those Contacts who currently hold the Developer role

- DELETE all ContactRoles records that have the Developer role assigned to them

- UPDATE all ContactRoles records that have the IT Support Specialist role assigned to them, and change them to Developer

Let's do the easy part first: adding the new Senior Developer record.

```
INSERT INTO dbo.Roles(RoleTitle) VALUES ('Senior Developer');
```

Run this to add the new role. Now, before we write the INSERT Senior Developers statement, we'll write a SELECT to obtain the existing Developer ContactRoles records. Do this in a New Query Window.

```
SELECT CR.ContactId, CR.RoleId
FROM dbo.Roles AS R INNER JOIN dbo.ContactRoles AS CR
ON R.RoleId = CR.RoleId WHERE R.RoleTitle = 'Developer';
```

This returns the nine ContactRoles records. Using JOINs in INSERTs is as simple as including a SELECT statement under the INSERT INTO statement. So we just change the SELECT statement to output the ContactId and the RoleId of the Senior Developer role.

```
SELECT CR.ContactId,
    (SELECT RoleId FROM dbo.Roles WHERE RoleTitle = 'Senior Developer') AS RoleTitle
FROM dbo.Roles AS R INNER JOIN dbo.ContactRoles AS CR
ON R.RoleId = CR.RoleId WHERE R.RoleTitle = 'Developer';
```

We've used something new here—a subquery, to return the RoleId of the Senior Developer role. It's possible to embed queries inside other queries as part of SELECT statements. We have no easy way of using a JOIN to obtain the Senior Developer RoleId (because none of the records we are modifying currently have a Senior Developer role), so we just embedded the SELECT statement to pull it back into our main query. The subquery is seen as a column within the result set (RoleTitle in Figure 12-24).

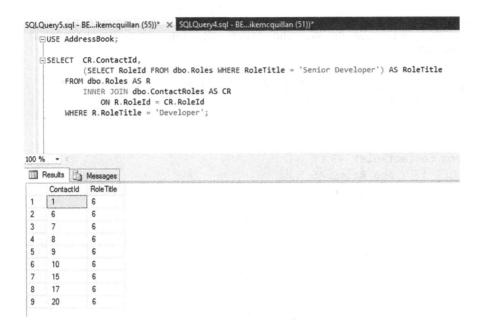

SQLQuery5.sql - BE...ikemcquillan (55))* ✕ SQLQuery4.sql - BE...ikemcquillan (51))*

```
USE AddressBook;

SELECT  CR.ContactId,
        (SELECT RoleId FROM dbo.Roles WHERE RoleTitle = 'Senior Developer') AS RoleTitle
    FROM dbo.Roles AS R
        INNER JOIN dbo.ContactRoles AS CR
            ON R.RoleId = CR.RoleId
    WHERE R.RoleTitle = 'Developer';
```

100 %

Results | Messages

	ContactId	RoleTitle
1	1	6
2	6	6
3	7	6
4	8	6
5	9	6
6	10	6
7	15	6
8	17	6
9	20	6

Figure 12-24. SELECT statement preparation for an INSERT

Now we can just prepend an INSERT over the top of the SELECT statement.

```
INSERT INTO dbo.ContactRoles(ContactId, RoleId) SELECT CR.ContactId, (SELECT RoleId FROM
dbo.Roles WHERE RoleTitle = 'Senior Developer') AS RoleTitle FROM dbo.Roles AS R INNER JOIN
dbo.ContactRoles AS CR ON R.RoleId = CR.RoleId WHERE R.RoleTitle = 'Developer';
```

Run this and you should see 9 row(s) affected.

Now we need to implement our DELETE statement. We want to delete all Developer records from the ContactRoles table. Again, we begin by writing a SELECT statement to obtain the relevant records. Another reason for writing a SELECT statement to do this is it allows you to check that you are obtaining the correct data. If you just run an UPDATE or DELETE statement without checking the data first, you could process the wrong data.

The SELECT statement is pretty simple.

```
SELECT CR.ContactId, CR.RoleId
FROM dbo.ContactRoles AS CR INNER JOIN dbo.Roles AS R
ON CR.RoleId = R.RoleId WHERE R.RoleTitle = 'Developer';
```

This also returns nine rows. This makes perfect sense; we were switching the Developers to Senior Developers. To change this SELECT statement into a DELETE statement, you replace everything above the FROM line with the DELETE statement. As multiple tables are involved in the statement, you must provide the alias of the table you wish to delete from.

```
DELETE FROM CR FROM dbo.ContactRoles AS CR
INNER JOIN dbo.Roles AS R
ON CR.RoleId = R.RoleId WHERE R.RoleTitle = 'Developer';
```

Remember, once you have specified a table alias, you should always use that to reference the table in the query. Run this and the same nine rows that were returned by the SELECT statement will be deleted (look at the message in Figure 12-25).

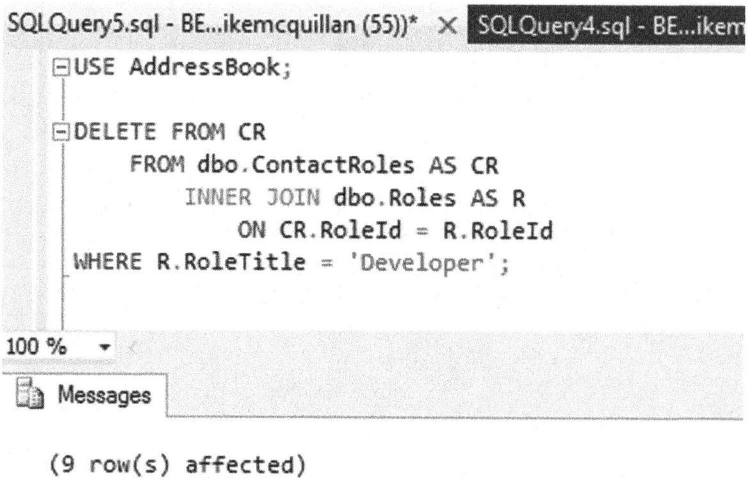

```
SQLQuery5.sql - BE...ikemcquillan (55))*  ×  SQLQuery4.sql - BE...ikem
    ☐USE AddressBook;

    ☐DELETE FROM CR
          FROM dbo.ContactRoles AS CR
                INNER JOIN dbo.Roles AS R
                   ON CR.RoleId = R.RoleId
      WHERE R.RoleTitle = 'Developer';

100 %    ▼
    Messages

    (9 row(s) affected)
```

Figure 12-25. *Deleting data using INNER JOIN*

If you change this back to a SELECT statement now, no rows will be returned. All is as it should be. We can move on to the last task: updating IT Support Specialists to make them Developers. Again, we begin by creating the SELECT statement to obtain the IT Support Specialists.

```
SELECT CR.ContactId, CR.RoleId
FROM dbo.ContactRoles AS CR
INNER JOIN dbo.Roles AS R ON CR.RoleId = R.RoleId
WHERE R.RoleTitle = 'IT Support Specialist';
```

This returns the four records shown in Figure 12-26.

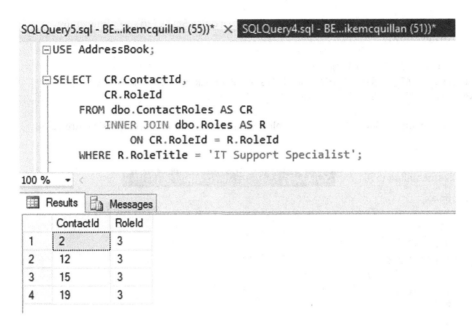

Figure 12-26. *More SELECT statement preparation for an INSERT*

Now we remove the SELECT part and replace it with an UPDATE, again using the table alias. We also use a subquery again, to obtain the RoleId of the Developer record.

```
UPDATE CR SET CR.RoleId = (SELECT RoleId FROM dbo.Roles WHERE RoleTitle = 'Developer')
    FROM dbo.ContactRoles AS CR INNER JOIN dbo.Roles AS R ON CR.RoleId = R.RoleId
    WHERE R.RoleTitle = 'IT Support Specialist';
```

We already know that everything in the statement from FROM onwards will ensure the correct records are processed. We've specified that we want to update CR (ContactRoles), setting the RoleId to Developer. We don't need to change the ContactId value. Running this tells us four records have been updated (Figure 12-27).

```
⊟UPDATE CR
    SET CR.RoleId =
        (SELECT RoleId FROM dbo.Roles WHERE RoleTitle = 'Developer')
  FROM dbo.ContactRoles AS CR
    INNER JOIN dbo.Roles AS R
        ON CR.RoleId = R.RoleId
  WHERE R.RoleTitle = 'IT Support Specialist';
```

100 % ▾

🔣 Messages

(4 row(s) affected)

Figure 12-27. *The SELECT statement converted to an UPDATE*

We've successfully modified our data using JOINs. We can run a quick SELECT to show how many records of each type we have now.

```
SELECT R.RoleTitle, COUNT(CR.RoleId) AS Total
    FROM dbo.ContactRoles AS CR RIGHT JOIN dbo.Roles AS R ON CR.RoleId = R.RoleId
    GROUP BY R.RoleTitle ORDER BY R.RoleTitle ASC;
```

We should have no IT Support Specialists, four Developers, and nine Senior Developers. Figure 12-28 confirms this.

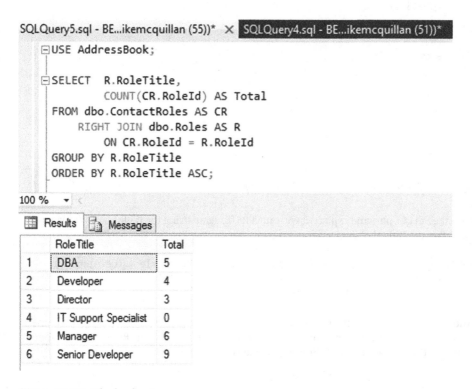

Figure 12-28. *The final outcome*

Summary

Well done, you've learned how one of the most important aspects of SQL Server development works. Joins are essential if you want to do anything useful with SQL Server, especially when it comes to querying. We've actually gone beyond querying, looking at how joins can help us to insert, update, and delete multiple records.

You have many of the pieces you need to become proficient with SQL Server in place. There is still more to learn (isn't there always?). We'll continue to improve our SELECT skills by delving into views. Let's walk into the distance. . . .

CHAPTER 13

Views

Contrary to popular opinion, a view isn't something you see out of a window. Not in database terms, anyway. I'm afraid it's much more mundane! A view in a database can be thought of as a virtual table. It allows you to view data in a particular way, by utilizing other database objects.

You may not be aware of it, but we've already done most of the hard work involved in creating views by understanding how to use the SELECT statement and the various joins available to us. We'll create a couple of useful views to improve our database.

What Are Views For?

I've already mentioned that a view can be thought of as a virtual table. You may be debating why you would need virtual tables when you have real ones. There are a few reasons:

- **Efficiency**: You can display data from multiple tables and not write the same queries over and over again.

- **Performance**: You can cache the query a view uses, and you can even create something called an *indexed view*, which further improves speed.

- **Security**: You can limit the amount of data certain users can see.

- **Less coding**: Views reduce the amount of code you need to write and can be referenced in other queries using joins.

Sometimes a view just makes things easier. Think of all those SELECT statements we were writing earlier. Some of those were eminently reusable. Had we enclosed them in views, we wouldn't need to reenter the code, and that view would be available to all users of our database.

Creating Views

Creating views is one of the simpler things you can do in SQL Server. You use the CREATE VIEW statement, which at its most basic looks like this:

```
CREATE VIEW ViewName AS SELECT...
```

We'll create a view to return verified contacts. Open a New Query Window and enter this script:

```
USE AddressBook;

CREATE VIEW dbo.VerifiedContacts AS
SELECT C.ContactId, C.FirstName, C.LastName, C.DateOfBirth, CASE C.AllowContactByPhone
WHEN 1 THEN 'Yes' ELSE 'No' END AS AllowContactByPhone, CVD.DrivingLicenseNumber,
CVD.PassportNumber FROM dbo.Contacts C INNER JOIN dbo.ContactVerificationDetails CVD ON
C.ContactId = CVD.ContactId WHERE CVD.ContactVerified = 1;

GO
```

Press F5 to run this. The script fails! The error is:

```
Msg 111, Level 15, State 1, Line 3
'CREATE VIEW' must be the first statement in a query batch.
```

All this means is we need to put a GO after the USE AddressBook line. The batch has to begin with CREATE VIEW.

After adding the GO, run this again. You should now see **Command(s) completed successfully**. But no data is displayed at all. Did you think the SELECT statement would run? That's not what you've done here. You've created a database object, just like you did when we created our tables all those chapters ago.

Save this script as c:\temp\sqlbasics\apply\19 - Create VerifiedContacts View.sql. Don't forget to add it to the end of our 00 - Apply.sql script, too:

```
:setvar currentFile "19 - Create VerifiedContacts View.sql"
PRINT 'Executing $(path)$(currentFile)';
:r $(path)$(currentFile)
```

Now you can use the view just like you would use any other table. Open a New Query Window and type this query:

```
USE AddressBook;
SELECT * FROM dbo.VerifiedContacts;
```

As you can see in Figure 13-1, just the verified contacts are returned, and the columns we specified are displayed.

SQLQuery7.sql - BE...ikemcquillan (55))* ✕ 19 - Create Verifie...\mikemcquillan (51))

```
USE AddressBook;

SELECT * FROM dbo.VerifiedContacts;
```

100 % ▾

Results Messages

	ContactId	First Name	Last Name	DateOfBirth	AllowContactByPhone	DrivingLicenseNumber	Passport Number
1	1	Stephen	Gerrard	1980-05-30	Yes	1001	PP4000
2	2	Dennis	Potter	1935-05-17	No	1002	PP4010
3	4	Bertie	McQuillan	2001-06-30	Yes	1004	NULL
4	5	Walt	Disney	1966-12-05	Yes	NULL	PP4030
5	6	Barbara	Gordon	1952-01-11	No	1010	PP4040
6	9	Grace	McQuillan	1993-09-27	No	1013	NULL
7	10	Vera	Black	1984-08-03	No	1014	PP4070
8	11	Angelica	Jones	1981-02-04	Yes	NULL	NULL
9	12	Steve	Davis	1957-08-22	Yes	1020	PP4080
10	14	julius	Marx	1990-10-02	No	1022	PP4100
11	15	george	formby	1944-05-26	Yes	1023	PP4110
12	17	Harper	Lee	1986-04-28	Yes	1025	PP4130
13	19	Michael	Jackson	1967-06-30	No	1027	PP4150

Figure 13-1. *Returning everything from the* VerifiedContacts *view*

dbo.VerifiedContacts is underlined in Figure 13-1. This is because Intellisense—the technology built into SSMS to auto-complete table names and so on as you type—doesn't know the view exists yet.

REFRESHING INTELLISENSE

You can refresh your local Intellisense cache immediately by pressing Ctrl+Shift+R on your keyboard, or clicking **Edit ➤ Intellisense ➤ Refresh Local Cache**.

The view has worked exactly as a table would. As Figure 13-2 shows, we can even filter the view.

SQLQuery7.sql - BE...ikemcquillan (55))* ✕ 19 - Create Verifie...\mikemcquillan (51))

```
USE AddressBook;

SELECT * FROM dbo.VerifiedContacts
    WHERE YEAR(DateOfBirth) > 1980;
```

100 % ▾

Results Messages

	ContactId	First Name	Last Name	DateOfBirth	AllowContactByPhone	DrivingLicenseNumber	Passport Number
1	4	Bertie	McQuillan	2001-06-30	Yes	1004	NULL
2	9	Grace	McQuillan	1993-09-27	No	1013	NULL
3	10	Vera	Black	1984-08-03	No	1014	PP4070
4	11	Angelica	Jones	1981-02-04	Yes	NULL	NULL
5	14	julius	Marx	1990-10-02	No	1022	PP4100
6	17	Harper	Lee	1986-04-28	Yes	1025	PP4130

Figure 13-2. *Filtering the* VerifiedContacts *view*

225

Adding Columns to Views

Let's say we need to add a new column, AddressVerified, to the ContactVerificationDetails table, to hold a flag denoting if a contact's address has been confirmed. Executing this script in a New Query Window adds the column without difficulty:

```
ALTER TABLE dbo.ContactVerificationDetails ADD AddressVerified  BIT NULL;
```

If you run the SELECT statement against the view again, you'll note the new column doesn't appear. Return to the CREATE VIEW script and change it to an ALTER VIEW statement, with the new column included in a CASE statement:

```
USE AddressBook;

GO


ALTER VIEW dbo.VerifiedContacts
AS
SELECT C.ContactId, C.FirstName, C.LastName, C.DateOfBirth, CASE C.AllowContactByPhone
WHEN 1 THEN 'Yes' ELSE 'No' END AS AllowContactByPhone, CVD.DrivingLicenseNumber, CVD.
PassportNumber, -- New column
CASE CVD.AddressVerified WHEN 1 THEN 'Yes' ELSE 'No' END AS AddressVerified FROM dbo.
Contacts C INNER JOIN dbo.ContactVerificationDetails CVD ON C.ContactId = CVD.ContactId
WHERE CVD.ContactVerified = 1;

GO
```

Run this and return to the SELECT statement, which will now display the column (you can see it in Figure 13-3).

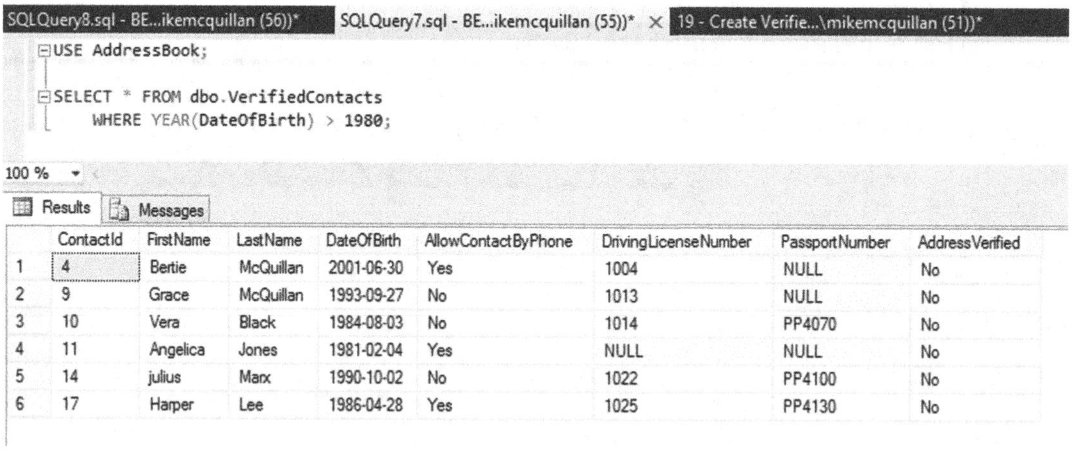

Figure 13-3. *The updated VerifiedContacts view*

Checking If a View Already Exists

ALTER VIEW makes it easy for you to change an existing view. However, using ALTER VIEW will fail should we rebuild our database; the view has to exist for ALTER VIEW to work, and the view will not exist during a database rebuild, as no CREATE VIEW command has been exercised.

Fortunately, our old friends, system views, come to our rescue yet again. Modify script 19 - Create VerifiedContacts View.sql to check if the view exists, and restore the CREATE VIEW statement while you are there, too.

```
USE AddressBook;

IF EXISTS (SELECT 1 FROM sys.views WHERE [Name] = 'VerifiedContacts')
BEGIN
DROP VIEW dbo.VerifiedContacts;
END;

GO

CREATE VIEW dbo.VerifiedContacts
AS
SELECT C.ContactId, C.FirstName, C.LastName, C.DateOfBirth, CASE C.AllowContactByPhone WHEN
1 THEN 'Yes' ELSE 'No' END AS AllowContactByPhone, CVD.DrivingLicenseNumber,
CVD.PassportNumber, -- New column
CASE CVD.AddressVerified WHEN 1 THEN 'Yes' ELSE 'No' END AS AddressVerified FROM
dbo.Contacts C INNER JOIN dbo.ContactVerificationDetails CVD ON C.ContactId = CVD.ContactId
WHERE CVD.ContactVerified = 1;

GO
```

We use the sys.views system view to check if the view exists, in the same way we checked if a table existed. The DROP VIEW command will drop the view if the view exists. DROP VIEW can be used to drop any view, and it will not prompt you when doing so. Be careful!

Save this script, rerun the view, and rerun your SELECT statement. Everything should be hunky-dory.

CAN I USE VIEWS TO INSERT AND UPDATE DATA?

You can use views should you wish to insert and update data. However, I recommend against doing this. It leads to confusion. It isn't too bad if a view only represents one table, but usually a view joins multiple tables together. Which table should the view insert to if there are multiple tables present?

Just use views to SELECT data from your tables. Think of them as read-only tables and use them for their intended purpose!

Broken Views

Some bright spark has decided we don't need an AddressVerified column in the ContactVerificationDetails table after all. Some people! Not to worry. We whiz off to a New Query Window, and execute the command:

```
USE AddressBook;

ALTER TABLE dbo.ContactVerificationDetails
DROP COLUMN AddressVerified;
```

Bang! The column has gone, obliterated by the confirmation message of **Command(s) completed successfully**. We ring the bright spark to confirm the deed is done and put our feet up, feeling pretty good about life.

Five minutes later the phone rings—the system isn't working! You take a look at it and indeed, there is some kind of database error. After investigating you narrow it down to the VerifiedContacts view. You run a SELECT statement against the view and are shocked to see it fail (the errors are shown in Figure 13-4).

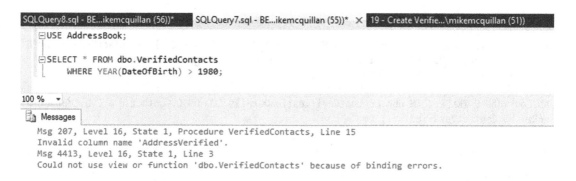

Figure 13-4. *A broken view*

The first message tells you that the view is using the AddressVerified column you just dropped. The second error states that the view cannot be used because of binding errors. The binding error occurs because the columns the view is expecting to find in its SELECT statement no longer exist.

Why didn't SQL Server tell you about this? How did it let you delete the column when you are using it?

SCHEMABINDING

As usual, SQL Server isn't at fault when we incorrectly remove a column—we're at fault (could it be any other way?). We should have told SQL Server it must check if the table is being used by any other objects before it allows the table's structure to be modified. We can do this by using the SCHEMABINDING directive.

SCHEMABINDING tells SQL Server to link the view directly to the table. When SCHEMABINDING is not specified, the view just exists as an entity in its own right. Even though it uses one or more tables, it has no relationship with those tables—the tables have no idea that the view exists. By specifying SCHEMABINDING we bind the view to the tables. This means that if anybody tries to modify a column in the table and the view will be affected by that change, the change will be prevented.

Execute the script to add the AddressVerified column back to the database, in order to fix the view:

```
ALTER TABLE dbo.ContactVerificationDetails
ADD AddressVerified     BIT NULL;
```

To modify the CREATE VIEW statement, add WITH SCHEMABINDING immediately after the view name. Change your CREATE VIEW script to include WITH SCHEMABINDING:

```
CREATE VIEW dbo.VerifiedContacts
WITH SCHEMABINDING
AS...
```

Run this and the view will be created. Execute the SELECT statement to make sure everything is still working as expected (hopefully your results will match Figure 13-5).

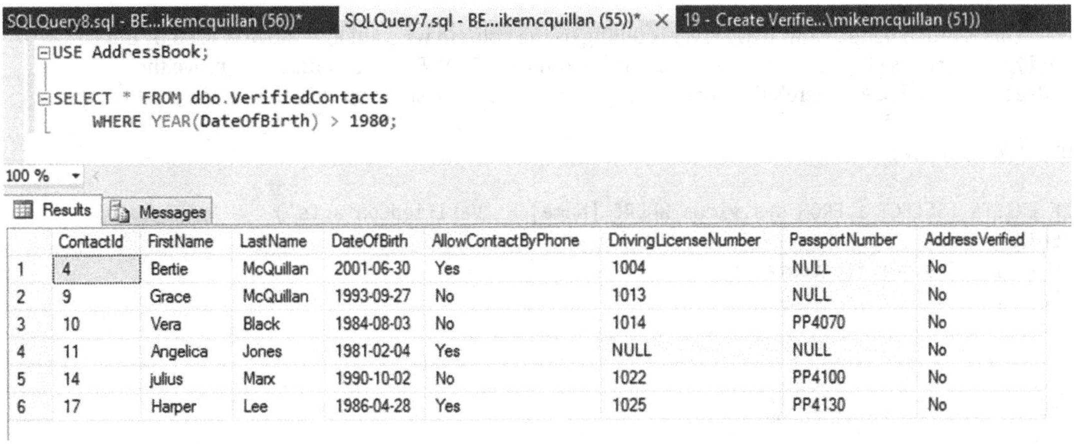

	ContactId	FirstName	LastName	DateOfBirth	AllowContactByPhone	DrivingLicenseNumber	PassportNumber	AddressVerified
1	4	Bertie	McQuillan	2001-06-30	Yes	1004	NULL	No
2	9	Grace	McQuillan	1993-09-27	No	1013	NULL	No
3	10	Vera	Black	1984-08-03	No	1014	PP4070	No
4	11	Angelica	Jones	1981-02-04	Yes	NULL	NULL	No
5	14	julius	Marx	1990-10-02	No	1022	PP4100	No
6	17	Harper	Lee	1986-04-28	Yes	1025	PP4130	No

Figure 13-5. *Making sure the view works*

Now return to the query window containing your DROP COLUMN statement and run it (or type it back in if necessary).

```
ALTER TABLE dbo.ContactVerificationDetails
DROP COLUMN AddressVerified;
```

This time the attempt to remove the column fails. Figure 13-6 shows the errors.

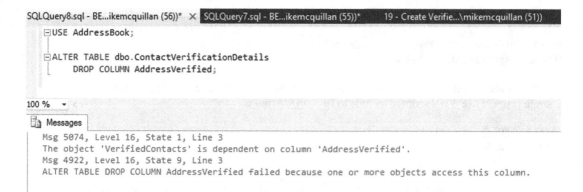

Figure 13-6. *Attempting to remove a schema-bound column*

This is much better. Now SQL Server is telling us the column we want to remove is used by our VerifiedContacts view. To remove it, we return to our CREATE VIEW statement, and remove the AddressVerified piece. Here's the final version of the view. Make sure you save this as script 19.

```
USE AddressBook;

IF EXISTS (SELECT 1 FROM sys.views WHERE [Name] = 'VerifiedContacts')
BEGIN
DROP VIEW dbo.VerifiedContacts;
END;

GO

CREATE VIEW dbo.VerifiedContacts
WITH SCHEMABINDING
AS
SELECT C.ContactId, C.FirstName, C.LastName, C.DateOfBirth, CASE C.AllowContactByPhone
WHEN 1 THEN 'Yes' ELSE 'No' END AS AllowContactByPhone, CVD.DrivingLicenseNumber,
CVD.PassportNumber FROM dbo.Contacts C INNER JOIN dbo.ContactVerificationDetails CVD ON
C.ContactId = CVD.ContactId WHERE CVD.ContactVerified = 1;

GO
```

Run this, and then try to drop the column again. This time, it succeeds (Figure 13-7)!

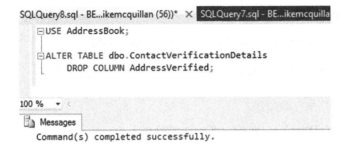

Figure 13-7. *Column dropped successfully after view modification*

Using Views in Joins

You can use views in any SELECT statement you care to write, including joins. It's no different to using a table. Here's a SELECT statement that joins our ContactVerificationDetails view to the ContactRoles and Roles tables.

```
USE AddressBook;

SELECT VC.ContactId, VC.FirstName, VC.LastName, VC.DateOfBirth, VC.AllowContactByPhone,
VC.DrivingLicenseNumber, VC.PassportNumber, R.RoleTitle FROM dbo.VerifiedContacts VC INNER
JOIN dbo.ContactRoles CR ON VC.ContactId = CR.ContactId INNER JOIN dbo.Roles R ON CR.RoleId =
R.RoleId WHERE YEAR(VC.DateOfBirth) > 1980;
```

Figure 13-8 shows that this returns the expected results.

```
USE AddressBook;

SELECT  VC.ContactId,
        VC.FirstName,
        VC.LastName,
        VC.DateOfBirth,
        VC.AllowContactByPhone,
        VC.DrivingLicenseNumber,
        VC.PassportNumber,
        R.RoleTitle
FROM dbo.VerifiedContacts VC
    INNER JOIN dbo.ContactRoles CR
        ON VC.ContactId = CR.ContactId
    INNER JOIN dbo.Roles R
        ON CR.RoleId = R.RoleId
WHERE YEAR(VC.DateOfBirth) > 1980;
```

	ContactId	FirstName	LastName	DateOfBirth	AllowContactByPhone	DrivingLicenseNumber	PassportNumber	RoleTitle
1	4	Bertie	McQuillan	2001-06-30	Yes	1004	NULL	Manager
2	9	Grace	McQuillan	1993-09-27	No	1013	NULL	Senior Developer
3	10	Vera	Black	1984-08-03	No	1014	PP4070	Director
4	10	Vera	Black	1984-08-03	No	1014	PP4070	Senior Developer
5	11	Angelica	Jones	1981-02-04	Yes	NULL	NULL	DBA
6	14	julius	Marx	1990-10-02	No	1022	PP4100	Manager
7	17	Harper	Lee	1986-04-28	Yes	1025	PP4130	Senior Developer

Figure 13-8. *Joining the view to other tables*

Using Views in Other Views

Much as you can use any table in any view, you can use any view you've already created in other views. We've just written a SELECT statement to join the VerifiedContacts view to the ContactRoles and Roles tables. Let's convert this into a view, removing the WHERE clause while we're at it.

```
USE AddressBook;

IF EXISTS (SELECT 1 FROM sys.views WHERE [Name] = 'VerifiedContactRoles')
BEGIN
DROP VIEW dbo.VerifiedContactRoles;
END;

GO

CREATE VIEW dbo.VerifiedContactRoles
WITH SCHEMABINDING
AS
SELECT VC.ContactId, VC.FirstName, VC.LastName, VC.DateOfBirth, VC.AllowContactByPhone,
VC.DrivingLicenseNumber, VC.PassportNumber, R.RoleTitle FROM dbo.VerifiedContacts VC INNER
JOIN dbo.ContactRoles CR ON VC.ContactId = CR.ContactId INNER JOIN dbo.Roles R ON CR.RoleId =
R.RoleId;

GO
```

Save this as c:\temp\sqlbasics\apply\20 - Create VerifiedContactRoles View.sql. Run the script, open a New Query Window, and execute a SELECT statement.

```
USE AddressBook;

SELECT * FROM dbo.VerifiedContactRoles WHERE YEAR(DateOfBirth) BETWEEN 1940 AND 1960 AND
RoleTitle = 'Developer';
```

As demonstrated in Figure 13-9, the query runs without issue.

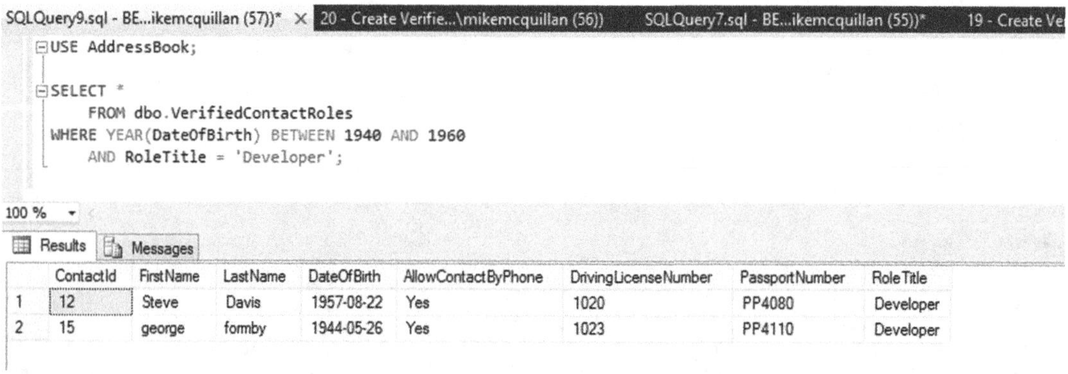

Figure 13-9. *Querying using the VerifiedContactRoles view*

Add the CREATE VIEW script to the bottom of the 00 - Apply.sql script:

```
:setvar currentFile "20 - Create VerifiedContactRoles View.sql"
PRINT 'Executing $(path)$(currentFile)'
:r $(path)$(currentFile)
```

Remember, you can use views to greatly reduce your code. If you find yourself constantly writing the same joins, consider putting them in a view to reduce your code.

Indexed Views

It's possible to improve view performance by indexing views. We'll take a look at indexing views in the very next chapter.

Dropping the Views

Dropping a view works in the same way as dropping a table or database. The command to use is DROP VIEW, followed by the view name. To drop our VerifiedContacts view we'd write:

```
DROP VIEW dbo.VerifiedContacts;
```

If you did want to drop this view, you'd need to drop the VerifiedContactRoles view first, as it references the VerifiedContacts view.

We need to create some rollback scripts for the two views we created, so let's incorporate DROP VIEW into those. Here is c:\temp\sqlbasics\rollback\19 - Create VerifiedContacts View Rollback.sql:

```
USE AddressBook;

IF EXISTS (SELECT 1 FROM sys.views WHERE [Name] = 'VerifiedContacts')
BEGIN
DROP VIEW dbo.VerifiedContacts;
END;

GO
```

And here is c:\temp\sqlbasics\rollback\20 - Create VerifiedContactRoles View Rollback.sql:

```
USE AddressBook;

IF EXISTS (SELECT 1 FROM sys.views WHERE [Name] = 'VerifiedContactRoles')
BEGIN
DROP VIEW dbo.VerifiedContactRoles;
END;

GO
```

To finish off, just add the relevant SQLCMD calls to the top of the 00 - Rollback.sql script.

```
:setvar currentFile "20 - Create VerifiedContactRoles View Rollback.sql"
PRINT 'Executing $(path)$(currentFile)';
:r $(path)$(currentFile)

:setvar currentFile "19 - Create VerifiedContacts View Rollback.sql"
PRINT 'Executing $(path)$(currentFile)';
:r $(path)$(currentFile)
```

Summary

Views offer a fantastic mechanism that is often underused (I include myself here!). They can save you a world of pain and make queries easier to understand by hiding complexity.

I mentioned it is possible to index views for better performance. That's something we'll see in our next chapter, as we take a look at indexing.

CHAPTER 14

Indexes

We've already met indexes during our database travels to date. We were creating clustered indexes when we created primary keys, and we also created unique indexes when we created unique constraints.

Indexes are important because they can greatly affect how well your database performs. The benefits of an index become apparent once your database contains a certain number of rows; it's possible to reduce queries that can take 20 minutes (in some cases) to just two seconds. That's how important they are.

We'll take a tour of the various types of index you can create, look at some examples, and see how to create an indexed view. This is a big subject, so hold on to your hat!

What Is an Index?

A database index is not particularly different from an index in a book. Just as you might use a book index to lookup a particular word or phrase (e.g., CREATE VIEW), SQL Server uses an index to quickly find records based on search criteria you supply to it.

Think what happens if you ask SQL Server to bring back all contacts who are developers. If there is an index on the RoleTitle column, SQL Server can use the index to find the rows that match the search criteria. If no index exists, SQL Server has to inspect every single row to find a match.

Why Are Indexes Useful?

Whenever it executes a query, SQL Server uses something called the *Query Optimizer*. This is a built-in component of SQL Server that takes the T-SQL code you provide and figures out the fastest way of executing it. Indexes can help the Query Optimizer decide on the best path to take. This often helps to avoid disk input/output operations (disk I/O)—operations in which data has to be read from disk instead of memory.

Disk I/O operations are expensive from a time-taken perspective, as disks are slower to access than memory. Indexes help to reduce disk I/O, as SQL Server can access the data it needs with fewer steps, especially as the data in the index is sorted according to the indexed columns, resulting in faster lookups.

What Do Indexes Affect?

Indexes affect SELECT, UPDATE, and DELETE statements. They also affect the MERGE statement, which I won't cover in this book. Anything that uses joins or WHERE conditions might benefit from an index.

Identifying Which Columns to Index

Quite often you'll come to a database and find a lot of indexes have been created that make no sense. While I could probably write a thesis on all of the ways you can identify what you should index, and how to develop a good indexing strategy, there are actually a couple of basic rules of thumb that you can apply to determine whether a column should be included in an index or not.

We'll use this statement as a basis for our discussion:

```
SELECT C.ContactId, C.FirstName, C.LastName, C.DateOfBirth, PNT.PhoneNumberType, CPN.
PhoneNumber FROM Contacts C INNER JOIN dbo.ContactPhoneNumbers CPN ON C.ContactId =
CPN.ContactId INNER JOIN dbo.PhoneNumberTypes PNT ON CPN.PhoneNumberTypeId =
PNT.PhoneNumberTypeId WHERE C.DateOfBirth BETWEEN '1950' AND '2010' AND
PNT.PhoneNumberType = 'Home';
```

The basic steps to index identification are:

- Write or obtain the SQL statements that will be used to return data from the database. This includes any UPDATE or DELETE statements that use joins or WHERE conditions.

- Once you have the statements, make a note of the columns used in joins. Contrary to popular belief, a foreign key column is *not* automatically included in an index. (I've been told this by many non-SQL developers down the years—it isn't true!)

- Look for any WHERE conditions used by the queries and identify the columns used by such queries.

- Finally, make a note of the columns returned by the SELECT statements.

The statement returns six columns. We join on:

- Contacts.ContactId (this is the primary key and is clustered),

- ContactPhoneNumbers.ContactId (a non-indexed foreign key),

- ContactPhoneNumbers.PhoneNumberTypeId (a non-indexed foreign key), and

- PhoneNumberTypes.PhoneNumberTypeId (a clustered primary key).

Finally, the WHERE clause uses two conditions, each of which uses a different column:

- Contacts.DateOfBirth and

- PhoneNumberTypes.PhoneNumberType

An index can only apply to one table. You cannot spread an index over two tables (Indexed Views offer a kind of workaround to this problem, as we'll see later). This means you cannot create a single index to optimize the preceding query—you'll have to create appropriate indexes on all of the tables involved in the query.

How Indexes Work

I've already mentioned why indexes are useful. Before we create any indexes, we'll take a glance at how they work. This will help you understand why indexes help queries run faster.

Imagine we have 30 rows in a table, and we write a query that will cause row 17 to be returned. Without an index, SQL Server finds the row we are interested in by executing something called a *Table Scan* (Figure 14-1).

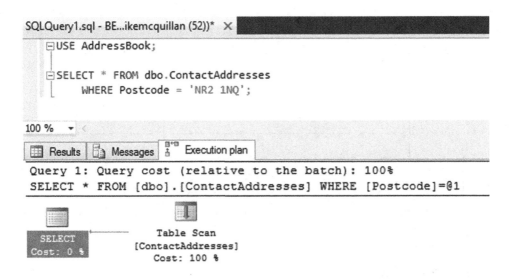

Figure 14-1. Executing a query with a Table Scan

Figure 14-1 shows something called an *Execution Plan*. You can turn these on to help you determine if SQL Server is executing your queries in the most efficient manner. *Table Scans are bad, and most definitely not efficient.* To turn execution plans on, click the **Include Actual Execution Plan** option in the **Query** menu of SSMS (or press Ctrl+M). The **Execution Plan** tab will appear after your query completes.

Table Scans

Why is a table scan bad? Because they mean *every single row in your table is being interrogated.* Our query looks for a particular postcode, which can be found in row 17 of 30. To find that row, SQL Server inspected the first 16 rows before finding the match. It marked row 17 as a match, then carried on inspecting rows 18 to 30 to check if any of those matched. This isn't too bad when only 30 rows exist, but imagine if a million rows existed!

B-Trees

Indexes offer a much more efficient method of finding data by using something called a *B-Tree*, more formally known as a *Balanced Tree*. This is a structure that causes data to be split into different levels, allowing for very fast data querying. The B-Tree for a clustered index consists of three levels. Figure 14-2 shows how the levels are structured.

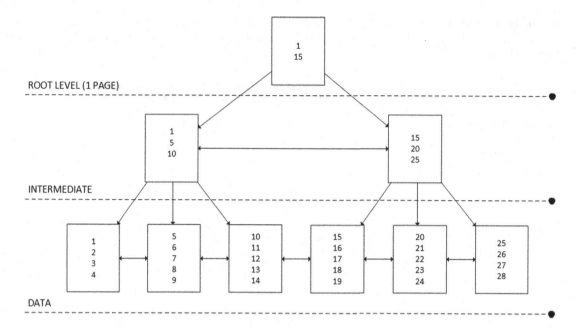

Figure 14-2. *A clustered index B-Tree*

There is only ever one root level, and it only ever contains one page. There can be multiple intermediate levels, depending upon the amount of data the index holds. Finally, there is only ever one data level, and the pages in this level hold the actual data, sorted as per the clustered index.

You are probably wondering what these pages I've mentioned are. I'm not going to delve deeply into how SQL Server structures its data in this book, but here's a quick overview. Do you remember how a SQL Server database can consist of one or more files? Tables may be contained within one of those files, or spread across multiple files. Each file is split into *extents*. You could think of an extent as a folder. Each extent contains eight *pages*. Pages hold rows. If an extent is a folder, a page is a sheet of paper, and a row is a line on that sheet of paper. These pages that hold the data rows are what we are talking about with regards to indexes.

Now, let's say we've added a clustered index on the Postcode column, and we're again looking for postcode NR2 1NQ. Figure 14-3 has the execution plan.

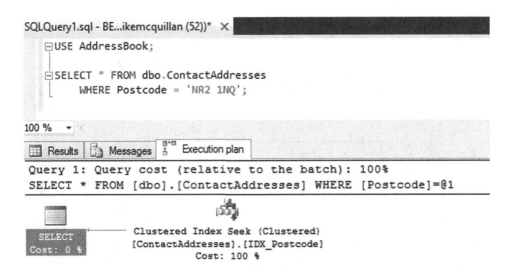

Figure 14-3. *Running the same query after adding a clustered index*

Now we have a Clustered Index Seek instead of a Table Scan (you may see a Clustered Index Scan—don't worry about it if you do). Is this any better? Let's see. Data is now ordered by the postcode. For simplicity, we'll assume the row we are interested in is still at position 17. We'll also assume the data is ordered using numbers, so we can use our earlier diagram (in reality, it would be sorted by postcode). Here's what SQL Server will do:

- Start at the root page and look at the value of the record at the start of the page. We have the value 1. The next value is 15. Seventeen is not between 1 and 15, so the index navigates to the page in the intermediate level that begins with value 15.

- The same process occurs. The start value is 15 and the next value is 20. Seventeen is between these two values, so the search now drops down to the data page level.

- The data page contains the index identifier for row 17. As this is a clustered index, it also holds the data. We're done!

We only had to navigate three times to find the value using the clustered index, rather than checking all 30 rows to see if they matched. Much more efficient, especially when you consider what could happen if the table contained many more rows.

This is a much-simplified explanation of how indexes work, but it should demonstrate that indexes can be very effective when used correctly.

Non-Clustered Indexes And B-Trees

Non-clustered indexes work in a very similar manner to clustered indexes, except the data is not stored in a sorted order, and indeed is not stored on the data pages. The data pages in a non-clustered index store an identifier that points at the row containing the data. So once the B-Tree has done its work and found the correct data page, there is an additional step as the index hops over to the actual row to retrieve the columns you have requested. You can see this extra step in Figure 14-4.

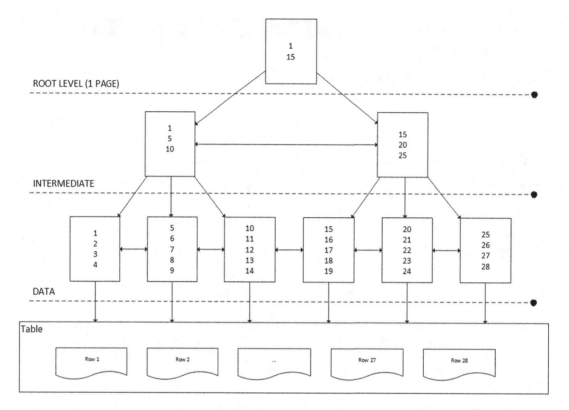

Figure 14-4. *A non-clustered index B-Tree*

Included columns can work around this; you can include columns in an index and the values for those columns will be stored right inside the index. This can avoid the additional step required for non-clustered indexes if all of the relevant columns are available. We'll see how this works in a few pages' time, in the section "Indexed Columns vs. Included Columns".

Basics Of The CREATE INDEX Statement

Rather unsurprisingly, the CREATE INDEX statement is used to create indexes. The basic structure of this command is:

```
CREATE INDEX IndexName ON TableName (Columns);
```

To create a clustered index you'd write:

```
CREATE CLUSTERED INDEX IndexName ON TableName (Columns);
```

Creating non-clustered indexes is very similar:

```
CREATE NONCLUSTERED INDEX IndexName ON TableName (Columns);
```

Including additional columns with the index is as simple as adding the INCLUDES keyword:

```
CREATE INDEX IndexName ON TableName (Columns) INCLUDE (Columns);
```

You can also create something called a *filtered index*, which works on a subset of data (more to come on this, in the section Filtered Indexes). The command to create a filtered index is:

```
CREATE INDEX IndexName ON TableName (Columns) WHERE (Conditions);
```

We'll delve into all these commands starting right now.

Clustered Indexes

A clustered index dictates how the data in a table is sorted on disk. As it's only possible to sort data on disk in one particular way, you can only have one clustered index per table. Clustered indexes are often the most performant kind of index because the data is returned as soon as it is located by the index. This is because the data is stored with the index.

To determine how a clustered index works, think of a telephone book (if this seems too old-fashioned for you, think of the Contacts app on your mobile phone). Say you want to look up Grace McQuillan's phone number. You open your phone book (or app) and scan for Grace McQuillan. All data is stored alphabetically. As soon as you find Grace McQuillan you have access to her phone number. The data was there as soon as you located Grace McQuillan. This is different to a non-clustered index, which will tell you where to locate the data.

Creating a Clustered Index

Most of the tables in our **AddressBook** database already have clustered indexes—we created all tables with clustered primary keys—so we cannot create additional clustered indexes on those tables. However, there is one exception: the ContactAddresses table, shown in Figure 14-5. This was created with a non-clustered primary key.

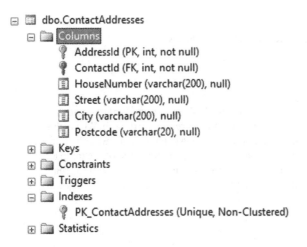

Figure 14-5. ContactAddresses with a non-clustered primary key

Why did we do this? The primary key on this table is `AddressId`. This column exists purely to give a unique, fast primary key to the table. As a piece of data the users are interested in, it is utterly irrelevant. Users will never see it and we are unlikely to use it to find addresses; we are more likely to use the `ContactId` or the `Postcode` when searching for addresses. It therefore makes infinitely more sense to have the data sorted by these columns—lookups will be much faster.

Before creating the index, open up a New Query Window and execute the T-SQL shown in Figure 14-6. We can see that the data is sorted by `AddressId`.

SQLQuery3.sql - BE...ikemcquillan (54))* ✕

```
USE AddressBook;

SELECT * FROM dbo.ContactAddresses;
```

100 % ▼

▦ Results | 🔿 Messages

	AddressId	ContactId	HouseNumber	Street	City	Postcode
1	1	1	47	Madryn Avenue	Liverpool	L1 1PR
2	2	1	29	Formby Road	Formby	L21 1DD
3	3	2	169	Portobello Road	London	SW19 2AK
4	4	3	Nadallo	Los Ramblas	Barcelona	11223
5	5	4	2	Thornycroft	Chester	CH8 4PA
6	6	5	Walt Disney World	Florida	USA	45689
7	7	6	11	Knight Road	Gotham	99331

Figure 14-6. *Query showing how the primary key orders data*

Open up another New Query Window and enter this script (don't run it yet).

```
USE AddressBook;
CREATE CLUSTERED INDEX IX_C_ContactAddresses_ContactIdPostcode ON
dbo.ContactAddresses(Postcode, ContactId);

GO
```

The statement is pretty simple. The `CLUSTERED` keyword informs SQL Server we want to create a clustered index—if this weren't present, a `NONCLUSTERED` index would be created by default. We've given the index a descriptive name, so future developers coming to our database can easily see what its purpose is. The `IX_C` at the start indicates the object is a clustered index. We then have the name of the table for which we are creating the index, followed by the columns we are indexing. Execute this script to create the clustered index, then return to the `SELECT * FROM dbo.ContactAddresses` script and run it again (Figure 14-7).

```
USE AddressBook;

SELECT * FROM dbo.ContactAddresses;
```

100 %

Results | Messages

	AddressId	ContactId	HouseNumber	Street	City	Postcode
1	4	3	Nadallo	Los Ramblas	Barcelona	11223
2	6	5	Walt Disney World	Florida	USA	45689
3	15	14	24	Mission Hill	Los Angeles County	78944
4	18	17	Atticus Ranch	Maycomb County	Alabama	91210
5	20	19	Neverland Ranch	Santa Barbara	California	93441
6	7	6	11	Knight Road	Gotham	99331
7	16	15	Beryldene	The Front	Lytham St Annes	BL1 1LX
8	5	4	2	Thornycroft	Chester	CH8 4PA
9	9	8	265	Princes Road	Edinburgh	EH1 2EW
10	19	18	Burns Cottage	Ayr	Alloway	KA1 1WK
11	1	1	47	Madryn Avenue	Liverpool	L1 1PR
12	2	1	29	Formby Road	Formby	L21 1DD

Figure 14-7. *The same query after adding a clustered index*

Wow, Figure 14-7 shows us that the order has changed somewhat! AddressId, which was neatly ordered earlier, is now all over the place. So is ContactId. If you look at the Postcode column you'll see it is nicely ordered. This makes sense, as it was the first column specified in our index.

Take a look at rows 11 and 12—these are both addresses for ContactId 1, and they are ordered by Postcode in ascending order. At a glance, the data in Figure 14-7 looks oddly ordered, because the ID columns are jumbled up. But the rows are sorted according to our index. It's because of indexes like the one we've just implemented that query results sometimes seem to be arbitrarily ordered.

So we've created a clustered index. We can see the results of the index simply by executing a SELECT * statement. Do you think this is a good index? It's *almost* a good index. To figure out why, we need to assess how this table is likely to be used. This table is probably going to be used in two ways:

- Obtain address information when a contact is being viewed through an app of some description, so address details can be displayed alongside the contact details (this will use a join of some sort)

- Support searching for addresses via a search interface (e.g., searching by postcode)

Of these two use cases, the most common is probably going to be the first. The likely user interface will ask the operator to ask for the contact's name or date of birth, from which their record will be found and displayed on-screen. A join will then be executed to return the contact's addresses using the ContactId. It seems ContactId is likely to be used more than Postcode, so we'll make ContactId the first field in the index, with Postcode the second.

Return to the window containing your CREATE INDEX statement. Swap the field names around and execute the CREATE INDEX statement again. As Figure 14-8 tells us, it all goes wrong!

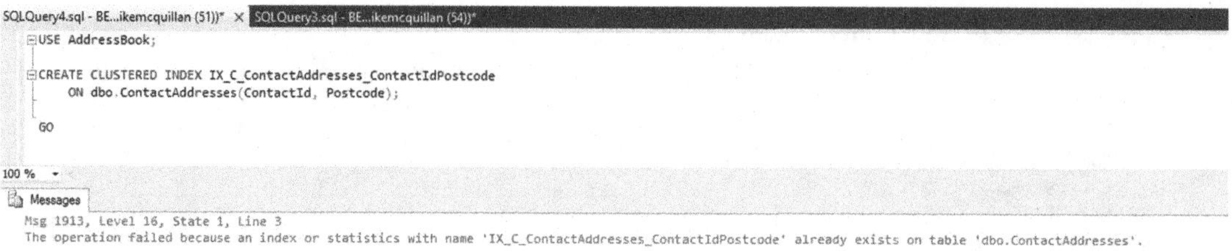

Figure 14-8. *The index already exists*

We have a couple of options here.

- Modify the index using SSMS

- Check if the index exists, drop it if it does, then recreate it

ALTER INDEX is not like other ALTER statements, as it doesn't allow modification of the index's definition. It is used to change index options, and we'll look at what it can do a bit later.

Modifying using SSMS isn't a good idea, as it breaks our principle of providing DBAs with a set of scripts they can execute on any environment. Still, let's take a look at what we could do here.

Modifying an Index Using SSMS

In the Object Explorer, right-click the ContactAddresses table and refresh it. Then expand the **Indexes** node. You should see the two indexes shown in Figure 14-9: our new index and the primary key index.

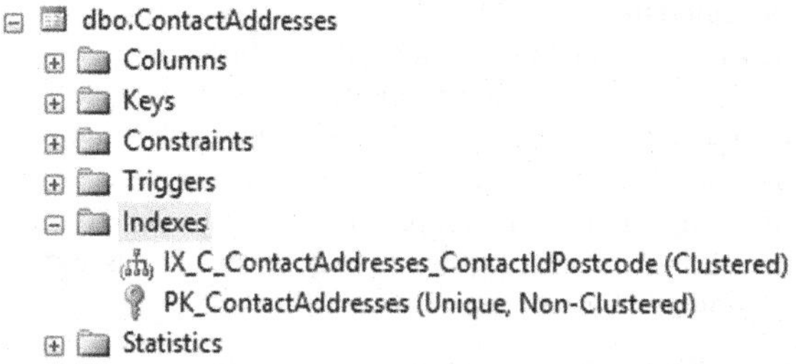

Figure 14-9. *The indexes present for ContactAddresses*

Right-click **IX_C_ContactAddresses_ContactIdPostcode** and choose the **Properties** option from the context menu (alternatively, double-click the index name). The index properties dialog in Figure 14-10 opens up.

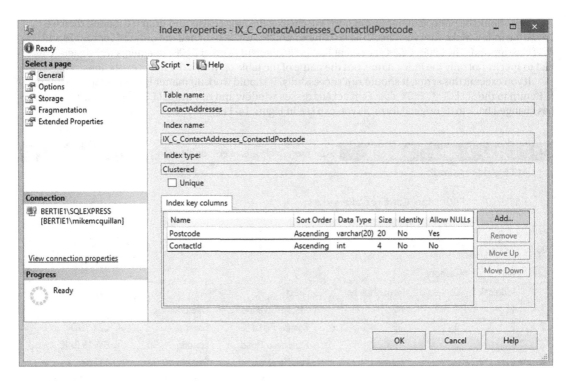

Figure 14-10. *Index properties dialog*

Note the **Index key columns** section. You could use the **Move Up/Move Down** buttons to change the order of the index columns. There are other options on the right that allow you to customize various aspects of the index—we'll take a look at one or two of those using T-SQL later. You'd also see this screen if you chose to create a new index using SSMS.

It's worth pointing out that you can right-click an index in the Object Explorer and script it to a file or New Query Window, just as we did with tables and databases earlier.

For me, using SSMS involves a lot more work! Let's modify our script to check if the index already exists.

Checking If an Index Exists with T-SQL

Return to our CREATE INDEX script window. We'll add a check to see if the index exists, very similar to the checks we've already added for tables and views. We used sys.tables and sys.views to check if a table or view existed, so no prizes for guessing that the system table holding the indexes is called sys.indexes. Let's add that check!

```
USE AddressBook;

IF EXISTS (SELECT 1 FROM sys.indexes WHERE [name] =
'IX_C_ContactAddresses_ContactIdPostcode')
BEGIN
DROP INDEX IX_C_ContactAddresses_ContactIdPostcode ON dbo.ContactAddresses;
END;

CREATE CLUSTERED INDEX IX_C_ContactAddresses_ContactIdPostcode ON
dbo.ContactAddresses(ContactId, Postcode);

GO
```

This should be pretty familiar to you now. We check if the index exists and drop it if it does, then we create the index. Make sure you check the last line carefully—we've switched the order of ContactId and Postcode around. The DROP INDEX statement is slightly different to other DROP statements we've met—we had to specify not only the index name, but the name of the table on which the index exists, too.

If you execute this script, it should run successfully. It should work no matter how many times you run it. Return to the SELECT * FROM dbo.ContactAddresses window and run the SELECT statement. The order has changed back to its original form, as you can see in Figure 14-11.

	AddressId	ContactId	HouseNumber	Street	City	Postcode
1	1	1	47	Madryn Avenue	Liverpool	L1 1PR
2	2	1	29	Formby Road	Formby	L21 1DD
3	3	2	169	Portobello Road	London	SW19 2AK
4	4	3	Nadallo	Los Ramblas	Barcelona	11223
5	5	4	2	Thornycroft	Chester	CH8 4PA
6	6	5	Walt Disney World	Florida	USA	45689
7	7	6	11	Knight Road	Gotham	99331
8	8	7	123	Gladwyn Street	Pottersville	PT9 5GA
9	9	8	265	Princes Road	Edinburgh	EH1 2EW
10	10	9	122	Stirling Crescent	Prescot	L32 9TY

Figure 14-11. ContactAddresses with ContactId in the clustered index

The fact that AddressId is in order is actually a coincidence—the table is now sorted by ContactId, then Postcode. If we added a new address for ContactId 1 it would appear in the top three rows, depending upon the postcode provided.

Save the index script as c:\temp\sqlbasics\apply\21 - Create ContactAddresses Clustered Index.sql. Then add a call to the bottom of the 00 - Apply.sql script.

```
:setvar currentFile "21 - Create ContactAddresses Clustered Index.sql"
PRINT 'Executing $(path)$(currentFile)';
:r $(path)$(currentFile)
```

Now that we have a handle on clustered indexes, we'll move on to creating some indexes of the non-clustered variety.

Non-Clustered Indexes

You can have pretty much all the non-clustered indexes you want on any table in your database—you can add up to 999 of them (in SQL Server 2008 and later you were previously limited to "only" 249). These are the indexes your queries will normally use. Clustered indexes are great, but they are limited because you can only have one of them. You also need to keep the key as small and efficient as possible, which can limit their effectiveness in queries.

Non-clustered indexes can exist with or without a clustered index. A table will generally work better if a clustered index exists, as will its non-clustered indexes. But it isn't a deal breaker.

We've already seen how a non-clustered index differs from a clustered index, in that it doesn't dictate the order in which table data is stored. Rather, the keys in the index are stored in a separate structure, which is used to identify the rows we are interested in. Once the rows have been identified, a link held within the non-clustered index is used to obtain the appropriate data from the appropriate rows.

We'll use the phone number tables to demonstrate non-clustered indexes. We want to find all contacts who have a home phone number. Not a problem; we can write that query in a jiffy!

```
USE AddressBook;

SELECT C.ContactId, C.FirstName, C.LastName, C.AllowContactByPhone, PNT.PhoneNumberType,
CPN.PhoneNumber FROM dbo.Contacts C INNER JOIN dbo.ContactPhoneNumbers CPN ON C.ContactId =
CPN.ContactId INNER JOIN dbo.PhoneNumberTypes PNT ON CPN.PhoneNumberTypeId =
PNT.PhoneNumberTypeId WHERE PNT.PhoneNumberType = 'Home';
```

Running this returns four rows, and generates the execution plan you can see in Figure 14-12 (remember, Ctrl+M will toggle execution plans on/off):

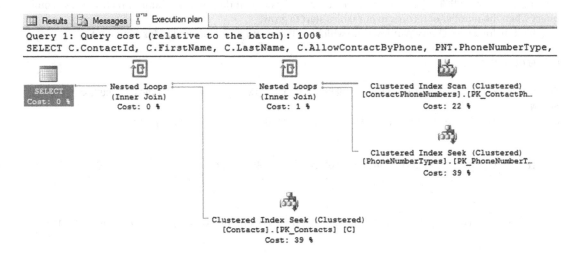

Figure 14-12. *An execution plan, using an Index Scan for ordering*

We have two inner joins here: one for each join specified in our query. There is a Clustered Index Seek at the bottom of the plan. This is used to seek the ContactId values from the Contacts table. In the top right, we have a Clustered Index Scan over the ContactId column in the ContactPhoneNumbers table. This is because we configured the PhoneNumberId column as the clustered index when we created it as the primary key. In hindsight, this probably wasn't a good decision. The scan has been used because the column we are using in the join does not order the data.

Scans are used when the data is not ordered, and seeks are used when the data is ordered. The final seek is for the PhoneNumberTypes table, which is clustered on the PhoneNumberTypeId column.

CLUSTERED INDEX SEEKS AND SCANS

You are probably wondering what the difference between an index seek and scan is. A seek will use the B-Tree to locate the data it requires. It will use the search parameters provided to limit the number of pages it searches through.

A scan starts at the beginning of the index and moves through each row in order, pulling out matching rows as it finds them. Every row in the index is scanned.

You are no doubt thinking seeks are more efficient than scans, and a lot of the time you would be right. But there are instances where a scan will outperform a seek. Further complications arise by considering that a seek sometimes contains a scan!

The general rule to follow is that seeks are usually better for fairly straightforward queries (e.g., queries using JOINs and WHERE clauses), while more complicated queries may benefit from the use of a scan. If in doubt, play around with your indexes until you are satisfied with the performance level.

Nowhere in this query plan do we have an index used that supports the PhoneNumberType column. This is being used in our WHERE clause. We can create a non-clustered index on this column, which will assist our query when the number of records in our tables start to grow.

It's time for a New Query Window, into which we'll type our non-clustered index statement.

```
USE AddressBook;

IF EXISTS (SELECT 1 FROM sys.indexes WHERE [name] = 'IX_NC_PhoneNumberTypes_PhoneNumberType')
BEGIN
DROP INDEX IX_NC_PhoneNumberTypes_PhoneNumberType ON dbo.PhoneNumberTypes;
END;

CREATE INDEX IX_NC_PhoneNumberTypes_PhoneNumberType ON dbo.PhoneNumberTypes(PhoneNumberType);

GO
```

Run this, then execute the SELECT statement again. Check out the execution plan now (Figure 14-13).

```
Query 1: Query cost (relative to the batch): 100%
SELECT C.ContactId, C.FirstName, C.LastName, C.AllowContactByPhone, PNT.PhoneNumberType,
```

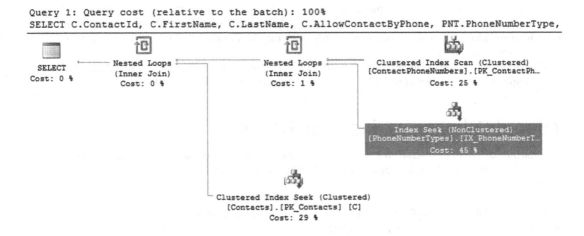

Figure 14-13. *The updated execution plan (with highlighted Index Seek)*

MOUSING OVER OPERATIONS IN THE EXECUTION PLAN

Top tip time: If you place your mouse over an operation within the execution plan, a detailed tool tip will appear, providing you with various statistics about that particular operation.

Aha! Now our new, non-clustered index is being used by the query. This means any queries we write in the future that use the PhoneNumberType column will be optimized. Top stuff.

Save this index as c:\temp\sqlbasics\apply\22 - Create PhoneNumberTypes Index.sql. Here's the SQLCMD code to add to 00 - Apply.sql:

```
:setvar currentFile "22 - Create PhoneNumberTypes Index.sql"
PRINT 'Executing $(path)$(currentFile)';
:r $(path)$(currentFile)
```

Execution Plan Percentages

Let's take a moment to quickly look at the percentage assigned to each item in the execution plans. The percentage tells you how much work SQL Server has to perform for each individual part of the plan. When we added our non-clustered index, it took up 45% of the plan. This is a good thing, as the aim of the index was to cause it to be used by the plan. The two clustered index items use up most of the remaining percentage. Interestingly, these figures changed when we added our non-clustered index. This is because the non-clustered index is doing some of the work these indexes were previously doing.

Execution Plans: A Quick Summary

To say this has been a crash course in execution plans is an understatement. In truth, we've only looked at them to demonstrate that our indexes are being used. But even this basic knowledge can help you. You can mouse over the items in an index plan and a pop-up will appear, telling you which columns are being used by that item. If columns you are joining on or are using in WHERE clauses are not mentioned, consider adding an index, then running the query again. If things don't work out as expected, you can always remove the index. Execution plans will actually suggest missing indexes it thinks you should add—they appear just above the execution plan diagram.

Execution plans—especially a good knowledge of them—is an advanced topic, but hopefully this brief introduction has whetted your appetite for more. We still need them in this chapter!

Indexed Columns vs. Included Columns

All of the indexes we've created so far have used indexed columns—that is, the columns have been declared as part of the index key. The index key consists of all columns declared within brackets after the table name. So in this index:

```
CREATE CLUSTERED INDEX IX_C_ContactAddresses_ContactIdPostcode ON
dbo.ContactAddresses(ContactId, Postcode);
```

the index key is made up of ContactId and Postcode. There are no included columns.

Included columns come in useful when you want to store more data alongside the index. You don't necessarily want to make these columns part of the index key. Indeed, you may not be able to do so—the size of the key is limited to 900 bytes and 16 columns. If you had a Postcode column of size VARCHAR(880), you'd only have 20 bytes left to play with. Included columns can work around this problem, and also the problem of non-clustered indexes needing to take an extra step.

Open a New Query Window and run this SELECT statement, making sure you turn on Execution Plans with Ctrl+M.

```
USE AddressBook;

SELECT C.ContactId, C.FirstName, C.LastName, C.AllowContactByPhone FROM dbo.Contacts C WHERE
C.AllowContactByPhone = 1;
```

Ten rows are returned, and the execution plan (displayed in Figure 14-14) uses the clustered index to find the data.

```
Query 1: Query cost (relative to the batch): 100%
SELECT [C].[ContactId],[C].[FirstName],[C].[LastName],
```

Figure 14-14. Execution plan using the clustered index

Really, we need an index on AllowContactByPhone, as this is the WHERE clause being used. Let's go ahead and create that index in another New Query Window.

```
USE AddressBook;

IF EXISTS (SELECT 1 FROM sys.indexes WHERE [name] = 'IX_NC_Contacts_AllowContactByPhone')
BEGIN
DROP INDEX IX_NC_Contacts_AllowContactByPhone ON dbo.Contacts;
END;

CREATE NONCLUSTERED INDEX IX_NC_Contacts_AllowContactByPhone ON dbo.Contacts(AllowContactBy
Phone);

GO
```

Execute this, then run the SELECT statement again. Figure 14-15 shows the query plan:

```
Query 1: Query cost (relative to the batch): 100%
SELECT [C].[ContactId],[C].[FirstName],[C].[LastName],
```

Figure 14-15. *Execution plan after adding non-clustered index*

It hasn't changed! Why is this? Well, SQL Server's Query Optimizer has decided the clustered index will execute the query more efficiently than the new non-clustered index we created. This is because the clustered index has immediate access to the data. As soon as a match is found by the clustered index, we return the data. With the non-clustered index, a match is found and then we have to skip across to the row to pull the data back.

We can remedy this situation by including the columns we are interested in as part of the index.

```
USE AddressBook;

IF EXISTS (SELECT 1 FROM sys.indexes WHERE [name] = 'IX_NC_Contacts_AllowContactByPhone')
BEGIN
DROP INDEX IX_NC_Contacts_AllowContactByPhone ON dbo.Contacts;
END;

CREATE NONCLUSTERED INDEX IX_NC_Contacts_AllowContactByPhone ON dbo.
Contacts(AllowContactByPhone) INCLUDE (ContactId, FirstName, LastName);

GO
```

The INCLUDE line is the only change. We've told SQL Server to store the ContactId, FirstName, and LastName columns with the index. These columns do not form part of the index—they wouldn't be used by the index to find data matching a WHERE clause, for example—but they are stored alongside the index, meaning an extra hop over to the row once a match is found is not required. Run the script to update the index, then run the SELECT statement again. A different query plan appears this time, as shown in Figure 14-16.

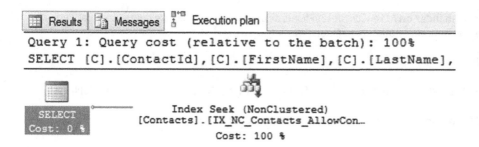

Figure 14-16. *Execution plan now using the non-clustered index!*

We've just created something called a *covering index*. This is an index that can be used to return all data for a particular query. The index in Figure 14-16 utilizes all columns required to fulfil the query's requirements, so we say it *covers* the query's requirements.

Save the index script as c:\temp\sqlbasics\apply\23 - Create Contacts AllowContactByPhone Index.sql, and add it to the SQLCMD file 00 - Apply.sql.

```
:setvar currentFile "23 - Create Contacts AllowContactByPhone Index.sql"
PRINT 'Executing $(path)$(currentFile)';
:r $(path)$(currentFile)
```

Think carefully when including columns as part of your indexes. They are very useful, but just remember that SQL Server has to maintain all of this information whenever you insert, update, or delete data in your table. The benefits of the index must outweigh the downside of keeping it up to date.

Filtered Indexes

Filtered indexes were introduced in SQL Server 2008, and are severely underused in my experience. This is a shame, as they present an elegant solution to certain problems. A filtered index is the same as any other type of index you create, with one big difference: you specify a WHERE clause, limiting the index to certain types of data. Why would you want to do this?

- Filtered indexes are smaller than normal, full-table indexes

- Not all DML statements will cause filtered indexes to be updated, reducing the cost of index maintenance

- Less disk space is required to store a filtered index, as it only stores the rows matching the filter

We'll change the index we just created for AllowContactByPhone into a filtered index. Before we do that, return to the SELECT statement we were using to test it.

```
USE AddressBook

SELECT C.ContactId, C.FirstName, C.LastName, C.AllowContactByPhone FROM dbo.Contacts C WHERE
C.AllowContactByPhone = 1;
```

If you run this and check the execution plan, you'll see the non-clustered index was used. Change the query to = 0 instead of = 1. As Figure 14-17 proves, you'll see the non-clustered index is still used.

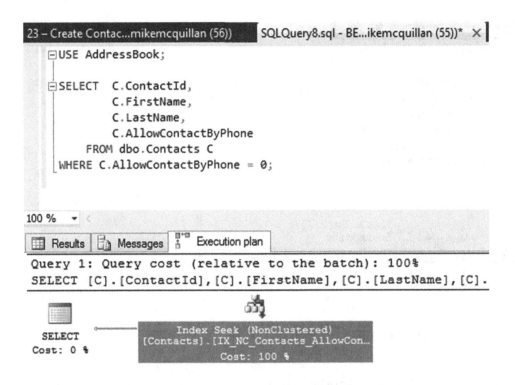

Figure 14-17. *Using a non-clustered index regardless of the value*

We'll change our index so it only applies to records where AllowContactByPhone = 1.

Open c:\temp\sqlbasics\apply\23 - Create Contacts AllowContactByPhone Index.sql and change the CREATE INDEX statement:

```
CREATE NONCLUSTERED INDEX IX_NC_Contacts_AllowContactByPhone ON
dbo.Contacts(AllowContactByPhone) INCLUDE (ContactId, FirstName, LastName) WHERE
AllowContactByPhone = 1;
```

Save and run the script to update the index. Execute the SELECT statement again as per Figure 14-18, setting AllowContactByPhone = 1.

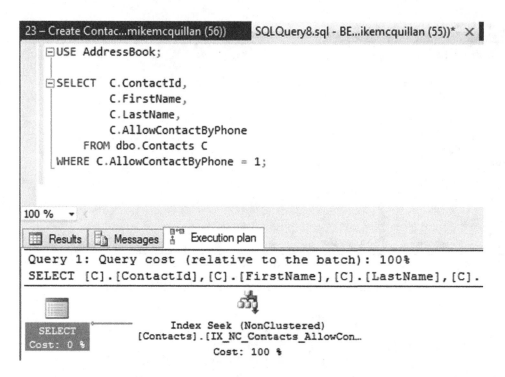

Figure 14-18. Using a filtered index when the value matches

Good news: our index is being used. Change the statement to use AllowContactByPhone = 0 and run it again. This time, our index is ignored, and the clustered index is used instead (Figure 14-19).

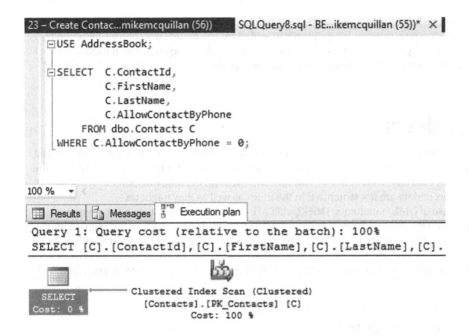

Figure 14-19. *Not using a filtered index when the value doesn't match*

This is perfect—we've told SQL Server the non-clustered index should only apply when the filter value for AllowContactByPhone is 1.

If you use them wisely, filtered indexes can really boost your queries, and can reduce the impact indexes may have on your DML statements. Keep them up your sleeve, as many SQL Server developers are not aware of filtered indexes. Knowing what features like this can do will help you stand out from the crowd.

Don't forget to add script 23 to the 00 - Apply.sql SQLCMD script. Here is the code:

```
:setvar currentFile "23 - Create Contacts AllowContactByPhone Index.sql"
PRINT 'Executing $(path)$(currentFile)';
:r $(path)$(currentFile)
```

Unique Indexes

We met unique indexes when we were talking about constraints in Chapter 7. Whenever we created a unique constraint, we were actually creating a unique index. A *unique index* is an index that prevents duplicate values from being entered into different rows across the columns it represents. A unique index on the PhoneNumber column in ContactPhoneNumbers would prevent the same phone number from being added twice, for example. Refer back to Chapter 7 if you need to refresh your knowledge.

Other Types of Index

SQL Server provides an XML data type, which can store the tiniest fragment of XML up to huge documents of 2GB in size. As you might imagine, searching all of this XML data can take a while. SQL Server has the ability to create both primary and secondary XML indexes to assist with such searching. If you have plans to create XML columns you should investigate how these indexes work—performance gains can be impressive.

A new type of index was introduced in SQL Server 2012: the Columnstore index. These are indexes aimed at bulk loads and read-only queries. It is primarily intended for use in data warehouses (essentially, flattened databases managed by SSAS), although they can be used for other purposes, too. If used in the correct manner, Microsoft claims index performance can be increased by up to 10 times that of traditional indexes.

Maintaining Indexes

Usually, your tables and other database objects require minimal maintenance. Once the object is structured how you want it and has been proven to be working correctly, you can pretty much leave it running, with the occasional check. This isn't the case with indexes. Over time, indexes will become fragmented. This means there are gaps in the index or data are not structured in the index as well as they might be.

This happens because of DML statements. INSERTs, UPDATEs, and DELETEs cause data to be removed from or moved about inside the index. This causes new pages to be added to the index, which can increase the number of intermediate levels created, and require more pages to be checked when searching for records in the index.

We'll take a look at some of the maintenance features SQL Server provides that help you keep on top of your indexes.

Identifying Index Fragmentation

SQL Server provides a set of Dynamic Management Views, or DMVs for short. There are lots of DMVs that provide access to all sorts of information. This query uses a DMV called sys.dm_db_index_physical_stats to tell you if any of your indexes are fragmented.

```
SELECT DB_NAME(PS.[database_id]) AS DatabaseName, OBJECT_NAME(PS.[object_id]) AS
TableOrViewName, SI.[name] AS IndexName, PS.[index_type_desc] AS IndexType,
PS.[avg_fragmentation_in_percent] AS AmountOfFragmentation FROM
sys.dm_db_index_physical_stats(DB_ID(N'AddressBook'), NULL, NULL, NULL, 'DETAILED') PS INNER
JOIN sys.indexes SI ON PS.[object_id] = SI.[object_id] AND PS.[index_id] = SI.[index_id]
ORDER BY OBJECT_NAME(PS.[object_id]) ASC;
```

On the FROM line in Figure 14-20, note I've specified 'AddressBook'. By substituting any database name here the query will return basic fragmentation information for your database's indexes.

SQLQuery10.sql - B...ikemcquillan (53))* × 23 – Create Contac...mikemcquillan (56))   SQLQuery8.sql - BE...ikemcquillan (55))*   SQLQuery5.sql - BE...ik

```
SELECT   DB_NAME(PS.[database_id]) AS DatabaseName,
         OBJECT_NAME(PS.[object_id]) AS TableOrViewName,
         SI.[name] AS IndexName,
         PS.[index_type_desc] AS IndexType,
         PS.[avg_fragmentation_in_percent] AS AmountOfFragementation
FROM sys.dm_db_index_physical_stats(DB_ID(N'AddressBook'), NULL, NULL, NULL, 'DETAILED') PS
    INNER JOIN sys.indexes SI
        ON PS.[object_id] = SI.[object_id]
            AND PS.[index_id] = SI.[index_id]
ORDER BY OBJECT_NAME(PS.[object_id]) ASC;
```

100 % ▾

Results   Messages

	DatabaseName	TableOrViewName	IndexName	IndexType	AmountOfFragementation
1	AddressBook	ContactAddresses	IX_C_ContactAddresses_ContactIdPostcode	CLUSTERED INDEX	0
2	AddressBook	ContactAddresses	PK_ContactAddresses	NONCLUSTERED INDEX	0
3	AddressBook	ContactNotes	PK_ContactNotes	CLUSTERED INDEX	0
4	AddressBook	ContactPhoneNumbers	PK_ContactPhoneNumbers	CLUSTERED INDEX	0
5	AddressBook	ContactPhoneNumbers	UQ_ContactIdPhoneNumber	NONCLUSTERED INDEX	0
6	AddressBook	ContactRoles	PK_ContactRoles	CLUSTERED INDEX	0
7	AddressBook	Contacts	PK_Contacts	CLUSTERED INDEX	0
8	AddressBook	Contacts	IX_NC_Contacts_AllowContactByPhone	NONCLUSTERED INDEX	0
9	AddressBook	ContactVerificationDetails	PK_ContactVerificationDetails	CLUSTERED INDEX	0
10	AddressBook	PhoneNumberTypes	PK_PhoneNumberTypes	CLUSTERED INDEX	0
11	AddressBook	PhoneNumberTypes	IX_NC_PhoneNumberTypes_PhoneNumberType	NONCLUSTERED INDEX	0
12	AddressBook	Roles	PK_Roles	CLUSTERED INDEX	0

Figure 14-20. *Returning index fragmentation details*

Altering Indexes

To manage an existing index, you use the ALTER INDEX statement. This ALTER statement works differently from the ALTER VIEW or ALTER TABLE statements we've seen so far, and also from the other ALTER statements we'll meet later in the book. Usually, an ALTER statement makes direct changes to the object concerned; ALTER VIEW allows you to completely change the definition of the view, for example.

ALTER INDEX is used for maintenance purposes. Its principal aim is to allow you to either disable, rebuild, or reorganize an index. You can change certain options for the index, but you cannot change its definition—to do that, you need to drop the index and then recreate it.

Disabling Indexes

You may occasionally need to disable an index. You might do this if you want to see how a query performs with the index and without it, but you don't want to lose the various metadata held for and about the index. Note that if you disable a clustered index you won't be able to query the table (but the data are still present; you just need to re-enable the index).

In a New Query Window, run this query.

```
USE AddressBook;

SELECT * FROM dbo.ContactAddresses;
```

All rows will be returned from the table. Now, change the script so it includes an ALTER INDEX statement above the SELECT, disabling the clustered index we created earlier.

```
USE AddressBook;

ALTER INDEX IX_C_ContactAddresses_ContactIdPostcode ON dbo.ContactAddresses DISABLE;

SELECT * FROM dbo.ContactAddresses;
```

You'll see some interesting messages, which are displayed in Figure 14-21.

Figure 14-21. *Querying a table with a disabled index*

The two warning messages are generated by the ALTER INDEX statement. When a clustered index is disabled, other indexes on the table are disabled, too. This includes foreign keys. We've ended up disabling three indexes here: the index we requested, the FK_ContactAddresses_Contacts foreign key index, and the primary key index PK_ContactAddresses. These will all need to be re-enabled separately, unless we use the ALL keyword when rebuilding.

The error message was raised by the SELECT statement. Our ALTER INDEX was successful, but because the clustered index is disabled data can no longer be retrieved from the table. We'll have to re-enable the indexes so we can query our data.

Rebuilding Indexes

There is no option to re-enable an index. Instead, you must rebuild the index. You rebuild indexes when the index is not performing as expected, probably due to fragmentation. Rebuilding an index causes the index to be dropped and recreated, resolving any fragmentation issues. Specifying the ALL keyword causes every index on the table to be dropped and recreated.

This statement will rebuild just the clustered index on the ContactAddresses table:

```
ALTER INDEX IX_C_ContactAddresses_ContactIdPostcode ON dbo.ContactAddresses
REBUILD;
```

But this statement will rebuild every index on the ContactAddresses table:

```
ALTER INDEX ALL ON dbo.ContactAddresses REBUILD;
```

Running this will make our SELECT statement work again. Note in Figure 14-22 that we've had to add a GO before the SELECT statement—this is needed, as the REBUILD has to complete in its own batch before we can query the table.

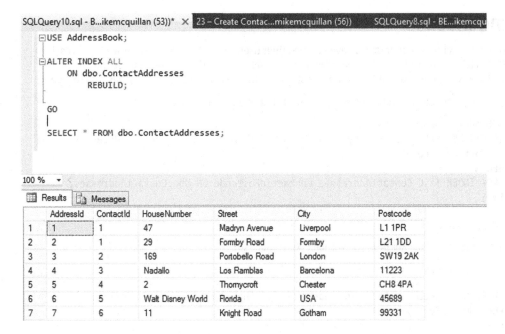

Figure 14-22. *Running the query after rebuilding the index*

Reorganizing Indexes

Reorganizing causes the leaf level of the index—the level that holds the data (or points to the data in a non-clustered index)—to be, well, reorganized. This eliminates fragmentation. This is similar to rebuilding, but crucially it can be done without impacting access to the table.

The indexes we are playing with here are very small and rebuild instantly. Imagine a table with millions of rows. Rebuilding an index on these tables can sometimes take hours. If this happens, rebuilding an index may not be desirable—it could prevent access to the table during the rebuild. It is for this kind of scenario that reorganization was introduced. The index is reorganized but the table is still accessible. You cannot reorganize a disabled index; the index must be active.

If we wanted to reorganize our clustered index we would specify the REORGANIZE keyword.

```
ALTER INDEX IX_C_ContactAddresses_ContactIdPostcode ON dbo.ContactAddresses REORGANIZE;
```

Again, we could reorganize all indexes with the ALL keyword:

```
ALTER INDEX ALL ON dbo.ContactAddresses REORGANIZE;
```

Altering Indexes Using SSMS

You can disable, rebuild, or reorganize using SSMS. Locate the required index in the **Indexes** node (found within the table the index is applied to), right-click it, and choose the appropriate option.

Dropping Indexes

Over time, you may decide certain indexes have outlived their usefulness. They can be removed quite easily by using the DROP INDEX command, which we've already met. Just for practice, we'll create three rollback scripts to drop the indexes we've created in this chapter. Create these three scripts in c:\temp\sqlbasics\rollback.

- 21 - Create ContactAddresses Clustered Index Rollback.sql

  ```
  USE AddressBook;
  IF EXISTS (SELECT 1 FROM sys.indexes WHERE [name] = 'IX_C_ContactAddresses_
  ContactIdPostcode')
  BEGIN
  DROP INDEX IX_C_ContactAddresses_ContactIdPostcode ON dbo.ContactAddresses;
  END;

  GO
  ```

- 22 - Create PhoneNumberTypes Index Rollback.sql

  ```
  USE AddressBook;

  IF EXISTS (SELECT 1 FROM sys.indexes WHERE [name] = 'IX_PhoneNumberTypes_
  PhoneNumberType')
  BEGIN
  DROP INDEX IX_PhoneNumberTypes_PhoneNumberType ON dbo.PhoneNumberTypes;
  END;

  GO
  ```

- 23 - Create Contacts AllowContactByPhone Index Rollback.sql

  ```
  USE AddressBook;

  IF EXISTS (SELECT 1 FROM sys.indexes WHERE [name] = 'IX_NC_Contacts_
  AllowContactByPhone')
  BEGIN
  DROP INDEX IX_NC_Contacts_AllowContactByPhone ON dbo.Contacts;
  END;

  GO
  ```

Add these lines to the top of 00 - Rollback.sql to ensure these scripts are executed whenever we rollback the database.

```
:setvar currentFile "23 - Create Contacts AllowContactByPhone Index Rollback.sql"
PRINT 'Executing $(path)$(currentFile)';
:r $(path)$(currentFile)

:setvar currentFile "22 - Create PhoneNumberTypes Index Rollback.sql"
PRINT 'Executing $(path)$(currentFile)';
:r $(path)$(currentFile)

:setvar currentFile "21 - Create ContactAddresses Clustered Index Rollback.sql"
PRINT 'Executing $(path)$(currentFile)';
:r $(path)$(currentFile)
```

Statistics

I view statistics as an advanced topic, but I want to mention them briefly so you at least know they exist. There, I've mentioned them—let's move on! Only joking (it's very good for morale!).

SQL Server uses statistics to figure out how it can best process your query. Statistics include the number of records for an index, how many pages those records cover, and details of table records, such as how many records in Contacts have a value of 1 in the AllowContactByPhone column.

As an example, assume you are running the query WHERE AllowContactByPhone = 1. You have an index for this column, but for some reason it isn't being used. There are a couple of possible reasons for this. One is the statistics for the index are out of date. SQL Server automatically maintains statistics based on particular rules. Sometimes these rules are not met and the statistics are not updated perhaps as often as they should be.

Another reason the index may not be used is because the statistics are up to date, and they inform SQL Server that using the index will be less efficient than using a scan or an alternative index.

You can delve into statistics by expanding the **Statistics** node under a table in Object Explorer. In Figure 14-23, we can see the statistics for the ContactAddresses table.

Figure 14-23. *Viewing statistics for a table*

Double-clicking one of these items will bring up more information about the statistics. As you are just starting out in your SQL Server journey, don't worry too much about statistics at the moment. I know people who've worked with SQL Server for years and don't understand them properly (or at all). But know they are there—it just might be worth delving into them in more detail.

Creating Indexed Views

The last piece of code we'll write in what has been an extremely involving chapter is to take one of our views and transform it into an indexed view. Indexed views perform better than normal views because they have a unique clustered index added to them. This means the view exists as a physical object, making it work in a manner very similar to a table. Creating an indexed view is the only way you can create an index that bridges multiple tables.

You can create both clustered and non-clustered indexes against a view, but you can only create non-clustered indexes if a unique clustered index already exists. Also, the view definition must meet certain rules. If any of these rules are not met, you cannot create a clustered index on the view:

- The view definition must include WITH SCHEMABINDING

- All table names must include the schema name (e.g., dbo.Contacts, not Contacts)

- All expressions in the view must be deterministic; that is, the same value is always returned (GETDATE() is not deterministic as it never returns the same value, but ADDNUMBERS(1,2) would always return 3, so it is deterministic)

- The view can only include tables, not other views

- The tables in the view must exist in the same database

- Most aggregate functions cannot be used (e.g., COUNT(), MIN(), MAX())

There are more rules, such as certain SET options that must be configured, but these are usually set to the default values anyway, so we won't concern ourselves with them. The preceding rules represent the most common things you have to think about. A full list of rules can be found at https://msdn.microsoft.com/en-us/library/ms191432.aspx.

We'll create an index on the VerifiedContacts view. Before we can create any other type of index, we *must* create a unique, clustered index. You cannot just create a clustered index; it must be unique, too.

The statement to create an index on a view is no different from other indexes we've seen, other than the inclusion of the UNIQUE keyword:

```
CREATE UNIQUE CLUSTERED INDEX IX_C_VerifiedContacts_ContactIdFirstNameLastName
ON dbo.VerifiedContacts(ContactId, LastName, AllowContactByPhone);
```

The combination of columns declared in the index must be unique. ContactId will always be unique as it is an IDENTITY column. This means we can add other columns to the index, as the first column guarantees uniqueness in this case. If the first column didn't provide us with a unique value, we'd need to add more columns so the combination of values would be unique.

Running this statement is successful, and allows us to go ahead and create a non-clustered index on the view:

```
CREATE INDEX IX_NC_VerifiedContacts_DrivingLicenseNumber
ON dbo.VerifiedContacts(DrivingLicenseNumber);
```

At this point, we could create as many non-clustered indexes as we wished on the view. These indexes will really help when your database has grown and your view is retrieving lots of rows. I once reduced a three-minute query to under a second using an indexed view. This query was used all over the system, so you can imagine the gains that were made.

There's actually a lot more to indexed views than we've discussed here, so take some time to read the MSDN article—it's well worth a look.

Are Indexes Ever a Bad Idea?

We've seen lots of index-related escapades in this chapter, all universally positive. It's worth asking: Is there ever a time when using indexes could be a bad thing? The answer is simple: Heck, *yes*! Like any other piece of SQL Server technology, indexes can have a negative effect on the database when used incorrectly. The main reason indexes can cause problems is because of INSERT, UPDATE, and DELETE statements—the DML statements. Let's think about how indexes work again for a moment.

- If an INSERT or UPDATE statement executes, the index must be updated with the current data

- If a DELETE statement executes, the rows in question need to be removed from the index

The point here is when a DML statement executes, it means SQL Server does some additional work to keep the index up to date. This additional work marginally slows down your INSERT, UPDATE, and DELETE statements. They don't slow down so much that you'd notice, but there is an effect.

Now, imagine a couple of scenarios.

- An index that has become badly defragmented

- An index whose statistics are wildly out of date

- A covering index with multiple columns

Any of these can cause update problems. Let me tell you a story about a covering index that went bad. I should point out this is an extreme example! A company I once worked for had built an event logging system. All log requests were sent to a queue and a service then came along, picked up the requests from the queue, and inserted them into an EventLog table. This table had a covering index on it, allowing easy querying of the log.

For the first couple of months, the event logging system worked really well. Eventually, a developer needed the log to investigate a problem, and was surprised to discover data for the past week wasn't in the table. I took a look at the queue and saw there was a huge backlog of queue items waiting to be processed. This was strange; querying the table returned results effectively enough.

I tried manually inserting a row and was stunned to discover it took *five minutes* to insert! This was into a table of about six columns. The covering index was the problem. Removing it fixed the problem immediately, resulting in inserts of less than a second. Because the index had multiple columns and hadn't been maintained properly, it was taking forever (well, five minutes) to figure out where it should place new rows.

Remember this cautionary tale when building your indexes! They are a great thing, but make sure you use them correctly and in moderation. Don't add them for the sake of it.

Summary

My word, this has been a big chapter. We've covered just about every aspect of indexes, although we've hardly skimmed the surface of what is a huge topic. Indexes are the most impressive speed improvement you can make to your queries. Take some time to tinker with them and you'll be the toast of your department.

Our **AddressBook** database has some nice indexes now, but if we can't add data in a consistent manner, indexes won't help us at all. Our next chapter will help us in this regard, as we take a look at transactions.

■ ■ ■

CHAPTER 15

Transactions

What do you think of when you hear the word "transaction"? I think of somebody who either buys or sells something to someone else. That's not quite what a transaction is in SQL Server, but as we'll see, this example will help us understand how transactions can be used to ensure our data stays consistent. Time to transact. . . .

What Is a Transaction?

I've just defined "transaction" as somebody who either buys something from or sells something to someone else. In this kind of encounter, two things occur:

- The buyer provides a payment of some kind

- The seller provides an item or service of some kind

If the buyer does not provide a payment, the seller does not provide the item or service. Likewise, if the seller does not provide the item or service, the buyer will not provide the payment. For the transaction to work, both elements—the buyer and seller—must complete their parts of the deal. Failure to do this will result in a failed transaction.

What SQL Server does with transactions is very similar. We specify a number of actions that must occur. If they all succeed, the transaction succeeds. Should one of them fail, the transaction fails and we can take the decision to roll back the changes, putting the data back to how it was before any changes were made. We'll see how to put this together in SQL Server.

ACID

No chapter on transactions would be complete without mentioning ACID. This is not some kind of 1990s dance movement (look it up, kids); rather, it's an acronym for the things that guarantee the reliable processing of database transactions. ACID stands for:

- Atomicity

- Consistency

- Isolation

- Durability

I know, it just rolls off the tongue. Atomicity specifies that either all of the transaction succeeds, or none of it succeeds. Consistency dictates that the transaction will keep the database in a valid state, and that any data provided by the transaction meets database rules, such as constraints.

Multiple transactions may run at the same time. This is where Isolation comes in, as it ensures all transactions run completely independently of each other. Finally, we have Durability. This property of ACID states that once the transaction has been committed, it will be present in the database forever, no matter what happens; even a software or computer crash.

Together, these four properties form a guard against badly implemented transactions, and SQL Server incorporates these properties into its transaction implementation.

A Transaction Example

We are going to use two tables in our example: the Contacts table, and the ContactVerificationDetails table. These exist together in a one-to-one relationship. The rules here are as follows:

- A record should not exist in ContactVerificationDetails until a record exists in Contacts

- Once a record has been inserted into the Contacts table, a corresponding record should also be inserted into the ContactVerificationDetails table

- If both records cannot be created within the same transaction, neither record should be created

- It should not be possible to create a Contact record without a ContactVerificationDetails record

What we want to say to SQL Server is the following:

- Create a Contact record

- If the Contact record was created successfully, create a ContactVerificationDetails record

- If the ContactVerificationDetails record is created successfully, save both records to the database

- If the creation of the ContactVerificationDetails record fails, remove the Contact record and put the database back to how it was before we started

Sounds simple enough. Let's meet the T-SQL statements that will help us meet these goals.

T-SQL Transaction Statements

T-SQL provides a number of transaction commands, but we will concentrate on the three core commands. These are the statements most developers use on a day-to-day basis.

BEGIN TRANSACTION

You use BEGIN TRANSACTION to start a transaction. This tells SQL Server that every statement you subsequently run should be seen as part of the current transaction.

You can give the transaction an optional name, although this is seldom used (in my experience, anyway). Giving the transaction a name could be useful if you were nesting transactions; that is, embedding one transaction in another. This is often used when calling stored procedures from within a transaction, and that stored procedure contains a transaction itself. In a nested transaction, you should be aware that even if the inner transaction completes successfully but the outer transaction rolls back, the work performed by the inner transaction will also be rolled back.

You write `BEGIN TRANSACTION` as:

```
BEGIN TRANSACTION;
```

or:

```
BEGIN TRANSACTION TransactionName;
```

COMMIT TRANSACTION

This signals the end of a transaction. At this point, all data written to the database during the transaction is committed (saved). When you `BEGIN` a transaction, this causes something called a lock to be opened on the tables involved in the transaction. Normally, this lock prevents other users from accessing the table during the transaction, so you want to run the `COMMIT TRANSACTION` command as quickly as possible.

To execute a commit, write:

```
COMMIT TRANSACTION;
```

To commit a named transaction, you provide the name at the end of the statement:

```
COMMIT TRANSACTION TransactionName;
```

ROLLBACK TRANSACTION

A rollback should be used when something doesn't go to plan. It is normally combined with some error-checking code that determines if everything is okay to proceed. If things aren't okay, the rollback kicks in. For example:

```
IF previous record created successfully
INSERT new record;
COMMIT TRANSACTION;
ELSE
ROLLBACK TRANSACTION;
```

When you call `ROLLBACK TRANSACTION`, all records that have been inserted, updated, or deleted within the transaction to that point are either removed or restored to their original state. `ROLLBACK TRANSACTION` puts the database back to exactly how it was before the transaction started.

Calling `ROLLBACK TRANSACTION` is very similar to the other transaction statements:

```
ROLLBACK TRANSACTION;
```

Or if you specified a transaction name:

```
ROLLBACK TRANSACTION TransactionName;
```

When Should I Use Transactions?

Strictly speaking, you should always use transactions. To be clear: you *do* always use transactions—you just don't know it half the time. There are two types of transaction: *implicit*, and *explicit*. Take a look at this statement:

```
INSERT INTO dbo.Roles (RoleTitle) VALUES ('Helpdesk Operator');
```

This will execute as an implicit transaction. This means SQL Server BEGINs and COMMITs a transaction just for this statement. It does it in the background. Because the BEGIN and COMMIT apply to one statement, there is no way to roll this change back—you would need to delete the row. Whenever we've executed an INSERT, UPDATE or DELETE during this book, we've been using implicit transactions.

Explicit transactions are what we are concerned with in this very chapter. These are created when you tell SQL Server where you want the transaction to start and finish.

```
BEGIN TRANSACTION;

INSERT INTO dbo.Roles (RoleTitle) VALUES ('Helpdesk Operator');

COMMIT TRANSACTION;
```

Here, we have the ability to roll the change back if necessary by adding some code before the COMMIT TRANSACTION. It's also much clearer what is going on.

I recommend you always wrap your DML statements in a transaction. Quite apart from the clarity this brings to your code, it makes code modifications easier in the future should you need to modify further records as part of the transaction.

What If I Don't Use Transactions?

As we've just seen, there is no requirement for you to use transactions. If you don't use them, each DML statement will execute in its own implicit transaction . . . but you may leave issues in your code that could easily be rectified by using a transaction. We'll work through an example that shows what happens when the use of transactions goes bad!

Creating a Transaction

It's time to create a transaction. Open up a New Query Window and type the code below. DO NOT RUN THIS CODE YET!

```
USE AddressBook;

DECLARE @ContactId INT;

BEGIN TRANSACTION;
```

```
INSERT INTO dbo.Contacts(FirstName, LastName, DateOfBirth, AllowContactByPhone)
VALUES('Laura', 'Robson', '1994-01-21', 1);

SELECT @ContactId = SCOPE_IDENTITY();

PRINT 'Inserted contact ID: ' + CAST(@ContactId AS VARCHAR(10));
```

Apart from the BEGIN TRANSACTION statement, we've seen all this before. We are inserting a contact record and storing the ID generated for that contact in the @ContactId variable we declared.

Locking a Table with a Bad Transaction

Now, I shouted at you a moment ago not to run this script. Sorry about that, but I did have a good reason! This script presents us with a perfect opportunity to see what happens when transactions go wrong. Open a second query window and run this query:

```
USE AddressBook;

SELECT * FROM dbo.Contacts ORDER BY ContactId DESC;
```

It should return results successfully, with the most recent ContactId at the top. Just like the results in Figure 15-1, in fact.

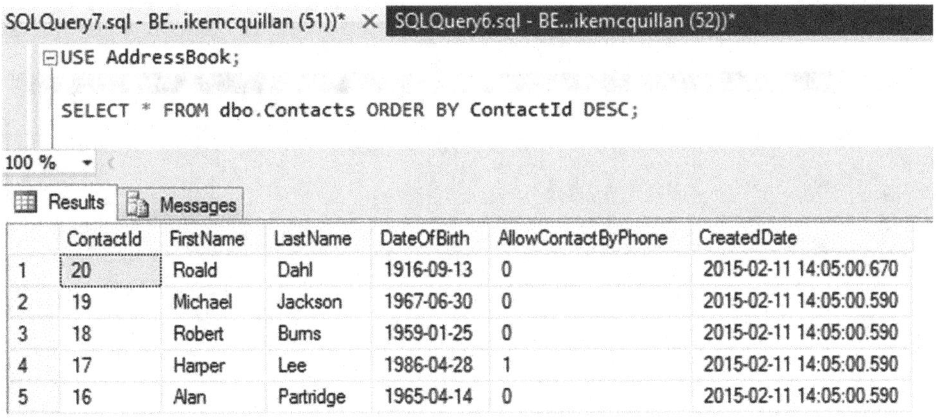

Figure 15-1. *Running a simple SELECT statement*

Now return to our transaction window and run the BEGIN TRANSACTION script. It should complete successfully, as demonstrated in Figure 15-2.

```
SQLQuery7.sql - BE...ikemcquillan (51))*        SQLQuery6.sql - BE...ikemcquillan (52))*  ×
  ⊟USE AddressBook;

   DECLARE @ContactId        INT;

   BEGIN TRANSACTION;

  ⊟     INSERT INTO dbo.Contacts(FirstName, LastName, DateOfBirth, AllowContactByPhone)
           VALUES('Laura', 'Robson', '1994-01-21', 1);

        SELECT @ContactId = SCOPE_IDENTITY();

        PRINT 'Inserted contact ID: ' + CAST(@ContactId AS VARCHAR(10));
100 %   ▾
  ▤ Messages

   (1 row(s) affected)
   Inserted contact ID: 21
```

Figure 15-2. *Successfully running a BEGIN TRANSACTION script*

The PRINT statement tells us that contact ID 21 has been successfully inserted. A great result—we inserted a contact and used a transaction to do it. All seems okay so far. Now switch back to the other window and run the SELECT statement there.

Uh-oh . . . nothing is being returned. All you can see is "Executing query . . ." in the bottom left-hand corner, as shown in Figure 15-3.

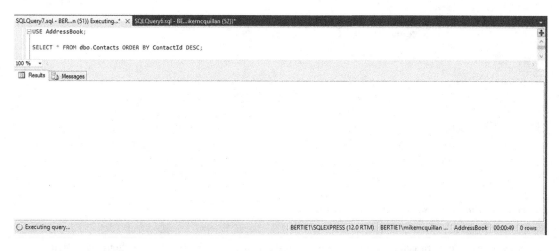

Figure 15-3. *The never-ending query*

In this example, the query has been running for 49 seconds so far! What is happening? Everything works fine in the other window.

The window in which we wrote BEGIN TRANSACTION has a lock on the table. Locks are used to protect the integrity of your data and to maintain the ACID properties we were discussing earlier. We've begun the transaction but we haven't committed it or rolled it back. As a result, the lock has not been released on the table.

@@TRANCOUNT

Return to the BEGIN TRANSACTION window. Paste this line of code at the bottom of the script, after the PRINT statement (don't run it yet):

```
SELECT @@TRANCOUNT;
```

@@TRANCOUNT is another of those global system variables we've been meeting during our travels. This one tells you how many transactions are open for the current window. Highlight the SELECT statement you just pasted and run it. Sure enough, there is one transaction open. You can see this in Figure 15-4.

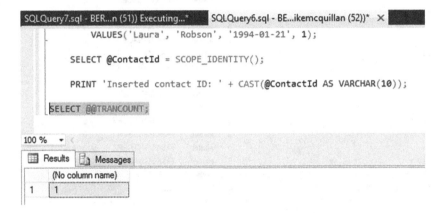

Figure 15-4. *Proving a transaction is still running with @@TRANCOUNT*

sp_who

As well as global system variables, there are also several system stored procedures and functions we can use to make our lives easier. System stored procedures begin with sp_. sp_who is a system stored procedure that can tell us who is holding locks (a lock prevents other users from accessing a particular resource in SQL Server while you are using it; e.g., a table). Replace SELECT @@TRANCOUNT with this:

```
EXEC sp_who;
```

Highlight this and run it. A lot of results should appear. Scroll to the bottom as shown in Figure 15-5. You are looking for a row that does not have a value of **0** in the **blk** column.

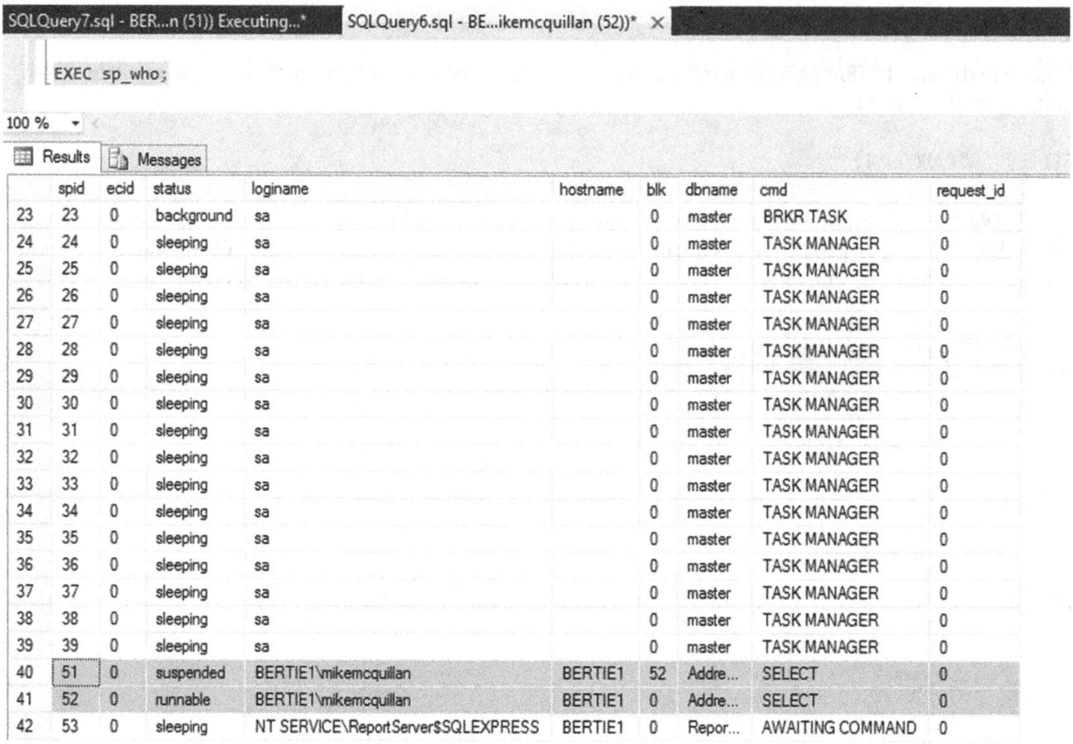

	spid	ecid	status	loginame	hostname	blk	dbname	cmd	request_id
23	23	0	background	sa		0	master	BRKR TASK	0
24	24	0	sleeping	sa		0	master	TASK MANAGER	0
25	25	0	sleeping	sa		0	master	TASK MANAGER	0
26	26	0	sleeping	sa		0	master	TASK MANAGER	0
27	27	0	sleeping	sa		0	master	TASK MANAGER	0
28	28	0	sleeping	sa		0	master	TASK MANAGER	0
29	29	0	sleeping	sa		0	master	TASK MANAGER	0
30	30	0	sleeping	sa		0	master	TASK MANAGER	0
31	31	0	sleeping	sa		0	master	TASK MANAGER	0
32	32	0	sleeping	sa		0	master	TASK MANAGER	0
33	33	0	sleeping	sa		0	master	TASK MANAGER	0
34	34	0	sleeping	sa		0	master	TASK MANAGER	0
35	35	0	sleeping	sa		0	master	TASK MANAGER	0
36	36	0	sleeping	sa		0	master	TASK MANAGER	0
37	37	0	sleeping	sa		0	master	TASK MANAGER	0
38	38	0	sleeping	sa		0	master	TASK MANAGER	0
39	39	0	sleeping	sa		0	master	TASK MANAGER	0
40	51	0	suspended	BERTIE1\mikemcquillan	BERTIE1	52	Addre...	SELECT	0
41	52	0	runnable	BERTIE1\mikemcquillan	BERTIE1	0	Addre...	SELECT	0
42	53	0	sleeping	NT SERVICE\ReportServer$SQLEXPRESS	BERTIE1	0	Repor...	AWAITING COMMAND	0

Figure 15-5. *Finding out who is causing resource blocking*

The first column in Figure 15-5, `spid`, represents a process ID. Each connection has one of these, allowing each connection to be uniquely identified. The `status` column tells us where each process ID is at—we can see `spid` 51 is currently suspended. This means it is waiting for something else to happen before it can continue processing. The something else is made evident by the `blk` column—the blocked by column. `spid` 52 is blocking `spid` 51.

Rolling Back the Bad Transaction

To resolve this situation, type this code into the `BEGIN TRANSACTION` window, highlight it, and run it (Figure 15-6).

```
ROLLBACK TRANSACTION;
```

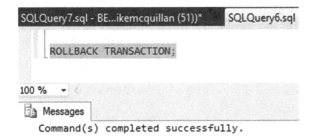

Figure 15-6. *Rolling back the open transaction*

As soon as you run this, the SELECT window should stop executing. Return to the SELECT window and it should now be displaying the contents of the Contacts table (Figure 15-7).

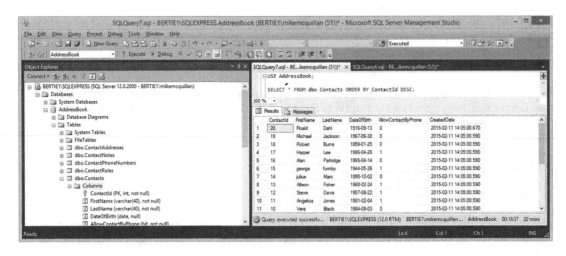

Figure 15-7. *The SELECT statement finally completes!*

Look in the bottom right-hand corner of Figure 15-7—it took 18 minutes and 37 seconds to execute that SELECT statement! This is the time it took me to return to the other window and roll back the transaction.

The new contact we added—ContactId 21—has disappeared. This is because we rolled it back. It no longer exists. Actually, it never did exist; it only existed in the window in which we started the transaction. The row was not committed to the table, so it was never properly saved to the database.

Let this be a sobering lesson to you regarding badly written transactions! With great power comes great responsibility. When writing a transaction, always, and I do mean always, make sure it can either commit or roll back, no matter which path the code takes. You won't appreciate a call at 3:00 in the morning telling you some parts of the database cannot be accessed!

Committing Transactions

Let's return to our BEGIN TRANSACTION script. We'll finish this off so it works correctly. Remove the ROLLBACK TRANSACTION, EXEC sp_who, and any other lines left over from our earlier demonstration, so the script looks as it did when we first typed it in.

So far, this script inserts into the Contacts table. It also needs to insert into the ContactVerificationDetails table, so add that INSERT statement, and finish off by adding a COMMIT TRANSACTION statement. Here's the full script:

```
USE AddressBook;

DECLARE @ContactId INT;

BEGIN TRANSACTION;

INSERT INTO dbo.Contacts(FirstName, LastName, DateOfBirth, AllowContactByPhone)
VALUES('Laura', 'Robson', '1994-01-21', 1);

SELECT @ContactId = SCOPE_IDENTITY();

PRINT 'Inserted contact ID: ' + CAST(@ContactId AS VARCHAR(10));

INSERT INTO dbo.ContactVerificationDetails(ContactId, DrivingLicenseNumber, ContactVerified)
VALUES (@ContactId, 1032, 1);

COMMIT TRANSACTION;
```

Now we have a fully operational transaction. We add a record to Contacts, obtain the ContactId, and then insert a matching record into ContactVerificationDetails. Run this now and you should see some positive messages:

```
(1 row(s) affected)
Inserted contact ID: 22

(1 row(s) affected)
```

Pop over to the other window containing your SELECT statement. This time it should run without issue, and the new contact should be present in the results too, as ContactId 22 (you can see this contact in the results of Figure 15-8).

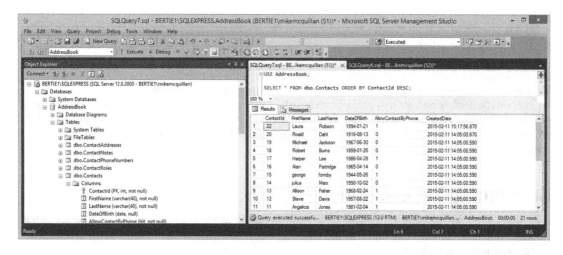

Figure 15-8. *The new contact is finally created*

The query took less than one second to run. If you modify the query to join to the ContactVerificationDetails table, the INNER JOIN will guarantee that ContactId 22 does indeed have a matching ContactVerificationDetails record (see Figure 15-9).

```
USE AddressBook;

SELECT C.ContactId, C.FirstName, C.LastName, C.DateOfBirth, CVD.DrivingLicenseNumber,
CVD.ContactVerified FROM dbo.Contacts C INNER JOIN dbo.ContactVerificationDetails CVD ON
C.ContactId = CVD.ContactId ORDER BY C.ContactId DESC;
```

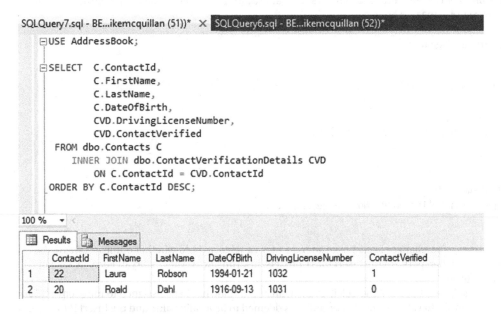

Figure 15-9. Proving records in both tables were created

As Figure 15-9 proves to us, a successful insert occurred. Thanks to our transaction, it wasn't possible to add a Contacts record without a corresponding ContactVerificationDetails record.

But wait! We know things work if everything runs as expected. What happens if something goes wrong? We'll need a rollback!

Rolling Back Transactions

We used the ROLLBACK TRANSACTION statement earlier to fix our locking problem. Now it's time to be a bit more proactive and put rollback at the heart of our script. We'll add a second contact. Change our INSERT script so it looks like this:

```
USE AddressBook;

DECLARE @ContactId INT,
@InsertSuccessful BIT = 0;

BEGIN TRANSACTION;
```

```
INSERT INTO dbo.Contacts(FirstName, LastName, DateOfBirth, AllowContactByPhone)
VALUES('Bryan', 'Ferry', '1945-09-26', 0);

SELECT @ContactId = SCOPE_IDENTITY();

PRINT 'Inserted contact ID: ' + CAST(@ContactId AS VARCHAR(10));

IF (COALESCE(@ContactId, 0) != 0)
BEGIN
INSERT INTO dbo.ContactVerificationDetails(ContactId, DrivingLicenseNumber, ContactVerified)
VALUES (@ContactId, 1033, 1);

SELECT @InsertSuccessful = 1;
END;

IF (@InsertSuccessful = 1)
BEGIN
COMMIT TRANSACTION;
PRINT 'Transaction committed successfully.';
END;
ELSE
BEGIN
ROLLBACK TRANSACTION;
PRINT 'Transaction rolled back. No changes made.';
END;
```

There are quite a few changes here. We've added a new variable, to hold whether our insert was successful or not. We then perform the insert into Contacts, inserting Roxy Music's Bryan Ferry instead of tennis's Laura Robson.

Now there is some new code. We check if a valid ContactId value has been assigned to the @ContactId variable. If the @ContactId value is not zero or null, it is deemed to be a valid value and the insert into ContactVerificationDetails can occur. The code then sets the @InsertSuccessful flag to 1, denoting all inserts have succeeded. This is important, as it dictates whether the commit or rollback will occur. By default the @InsertSuccessful variable is set to 0, so we are assuming failure from the beginning of the script—we only change the variable's value if the code succeeds.

The last block of code executes either the COMMIT or ROLLBACK statement. The @InsertSuccessful variable is checked. If this is set to 1 the changes will be committed and the transaction has succeeded. The data will be available in the tables. If @InsertSuccessful failed, the transaction will be rolled back and no changes will be made.

Let's see the rollback kick in. Between the PRINT and IF (COALESCE) statements, add this line:

```
SELECT @ContactId = NULL;
```

We're simulating a failure with this line. By setting @ContactId to NULL the COALESCE check will fail, no insert will be made into ContactVerificationDetails, and the @InsertSuccessful flag will remain set to 0.

Run this script and you should see a message telling you the changes were rolled back, just like the one in Figure 15-10.

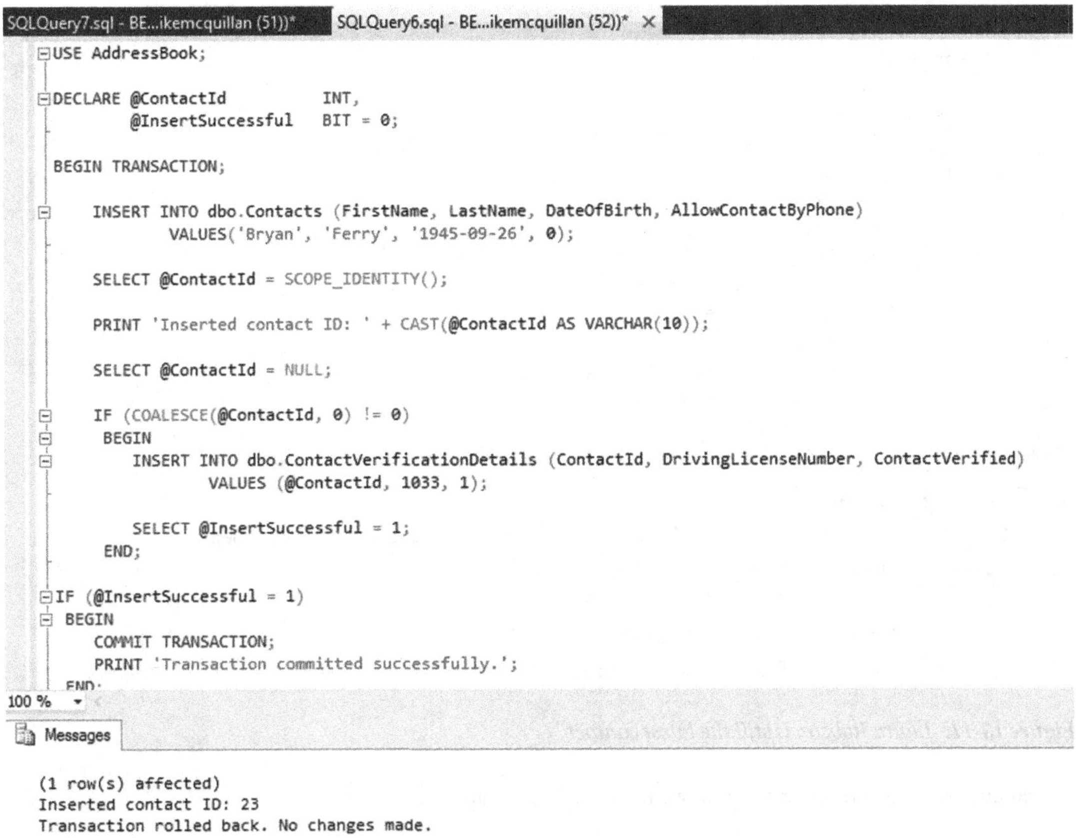

```
SQLQuery7.sql - BE...ikemcquillan (51))*      SQLQuery6.sql - BE...ikemcquillan (52))*  ×

USE AddressBook;

DECLARE @ContactId          INT,
        @InsertSuccessful   BIT = 0;

BEGIN TRANSACTION;

    INSERT INTO dbo.Contacts (FirstName, LastName, DateOfBirth, AllowContactByPhone)
            VALUES('Bryan', 'Ferry', '1945-09-26', 0);

    SELECT @ContactId = SCOPE_IDENTITY();

    PRINT 'Inserted contact ID: ' + CAST(@ContactId AS VARCHAR(10));

    SELECT @ContactId = NULL;

    IF (COALESCE(@ContactId, 0) != 0)
      BEGIN
        INSERT INTO dbo.ContactVerificationDetails (ContactId, DrivingLicenseNumber, ContactVerified)
                VALUES (@ContactId, 1033, 1);

        SELECT @InsertSuccessful = 1;
      END;

IF (@InsertSuccessful = 1)
  BEGIN
    COMMIT TRANSACTION;
    PRINT 'Transaction committed successfully.';
  END·
```

100 % ▼

Messages

```
(1 row(s) affected)
Inserted contact ID: 23
Transaction rolled back. No changes made.
```

Figure 15-10. *A transaction that has just been rolled back*

It doesn't matter how many times you run the script; no data will be inserted. Visit the SELECT statement in the other window and run it. Laura Robson, ContactId 22, will still be the last contact added. Check out the results in Figure 15-11 for evidence.

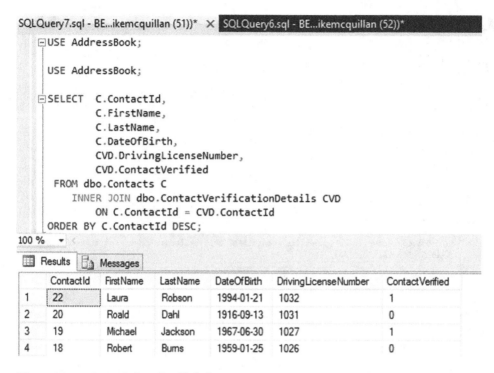

Figure 15-11. *Laura Robson is still the latest contact*

Return to the insert script and remove the extra line we added:

```
SELECT @ContactId = NULL;
```

Run the script again. This time, you should see the success message shown in Figure 15-12.

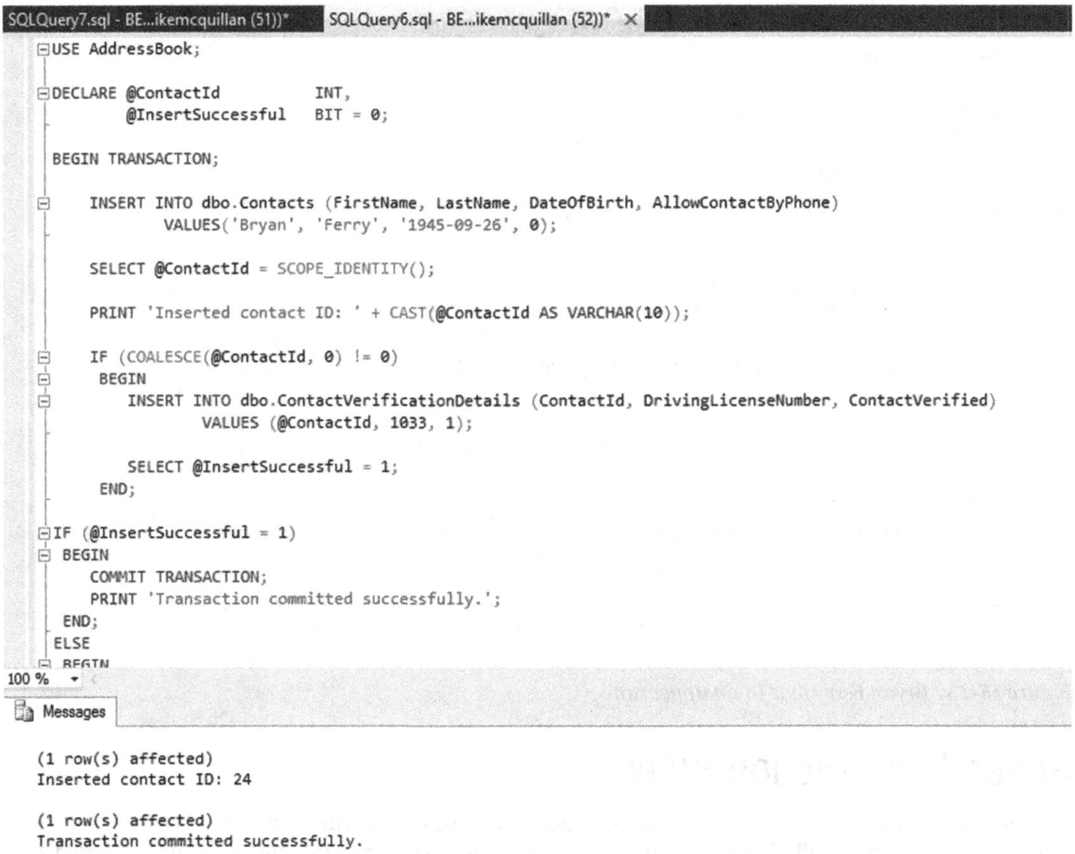

```
SQLQuery7.sql - BE...ikemcquillan (51))*        SQLQuery6.sql - BE...ikemcquillan (52))*   ×
⊟USE AddressBook;

⊟DECLARE @ContactId         INT,
         @InsertSuccessful  BIT = 0;

 BEGIN TRANSACTION;

⊟     INSERT INTO dbo.Contacts (FirstName, LastName, DateOfBirth, AllowContactByPhone)
              VALUES('Bryan', 'Ferry', '1945-09-26', 0);

      SELECT @ContactId = SCOPE_IDENTITY();

      PRINT 'Inserted contact ID: ' + CAST(@ContactId AS VARCHAR(10));

⊟     IF (COALESCE(@ContactId, 0) != 0)
⊟     BEGIN
⊟         INSERT INTO dbo.ContactVerificationDetails (ContactId, DrivingLicenseNumber, ContactVerified)
                  VALUES (@ContactId, 1033, 1);

          SELECT @InsertSuccessful = 1;
      END;

⊟IF (@InsertSuccessful = 1)
⊟ BEGIN
      COMMIT TRANSACTION;
      PRINT 'Transaction committed successfully.';
  END;
  ELSE
⊟ BEGIN
100 %  ▼ ‹

 📄 Messages

 (1 row(s) affected)
 Inserted contact ID: 24

 (1 row(s) affected)
 Transaction committed successfully.
```

Figure 15-12. *Successfully inserting within a committed transaction*

I love it when a plan comes together! Visit the SELECT statement window and run the statement. Figure 15-13 shows that Bryan Ferry has joined our contact list, and he did it in an ACID-compliant manner, too. Well done, Mr. Ferry.

279

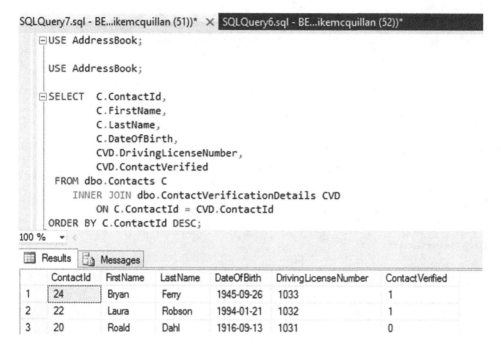

Figure 15-13. *Bryan Ferry puts in an appearance*

General Transaction Rules

Now that we've covered the basics of transactions, there are some general rules you should be aware of before you start wrapping all of your code in transactions. It may seem from this chapter that you should do this, but that isn't the case.

Keep Transactions Short

The first and most crucial rule is to keep your transactions short. When you open a transaction, you are locking any objects involved in that transaction. Therefore, the shorter the transaction, the shorter the time SQL Server locks the objects, reducing contention in your database.

Limit Transactions to DML Statements

There isn't much point in wrapping a SELECT statement that takes 20 minutes to execute in a transaction. Sometimes you cannot avoid embedding SELECT statements in transactions, but generally you want to limit the contents of a transaction to DML statements.

Don't Be Afraid to Split Transactions Up

I've often come across developers who feel they must do everything in a single transaction. This is bunk! If you have some code that you feel will take too long to execute in a single transaction, don't worry about splitting it up into multiple transactions. There are various techniques you can use to roll back the results of previous transactions should a subsequent transaction fail—storing new or updated data in temp tables, for example, before committing it all at the end of the code block. If you assess your code carefully, you'll see there is seldom a need for a long-running transaction.

Summary

After the *Lord of the Rings*-style trek through the indexes chapter, this has felt more like the breezy style of *The Hobbit*. We've covered transactions in some detail, and you should now be happy with terms like `BEGIN`, `ROLLBACK`, and `COMMIT`. It's important that users have faith in the data held within your database, and transactions are a major part of providing that faith.

We're going to move on to functions now, but it's worth saving the code we've written in this chapter—we'll be revisiting it when we look at stored procedures.

CHAPTER 16

■ ■ ■

Functions

Functions were introduced in SQL Server 2000 and made an immediate impact. Functions allow you to wrap up pieces of code you use all the time into a nice, compact, reusable package. In this chapter, we'll find out what types of function SQL Server allows us to create, why functions are useful, and how we can improve our code with functions. We'll also see some of the system functions SQL Server provides. By the end of this chapter, we'll know all about scalar functions, and we'll be ready to talk about table-valued functions (TVFs) in Chapter 17. We'll be half-functional!

Function Types

Broadly speaking, there are two types of user-defined function in SQL Server:

- **Scalar functions**: These are functions that return a standard type of value, such as an INT or a VARCHAR. An addition function that returns the sum of two numbers would be a scalar function.

- **Table-valued functions**: These are scalar functions can only return one value, of the defined type. If you need to return multiple values, you can write a TVF. These return a table containing the data you requested.

Deterministic vs. Non-Deterministic Functions

UDFs are classed as being either *deterministic* or *non-deterministic*. We met these terms when we were discussing views a couple of chapters ago. A deterministic function is one that, given a particular set of inputs, will always return the same value. Here's the addition function we were just discussing:

```
CREATE FUNCTION dbo.AddNumbers
(@Number1 INT, @Number2 INT)
RETURNS INT
AS
BEGIN

RETURN COALESCE(@Number1, 0) + COALESCE(@Number2, 0);

END;
```

This function accepts two parameters, @Number1 and @Number2. It returns an INT value. It executes one line of code, adding @Number1 and @Number2 together. If a NULL value is passed in for either of those values, the NULL is defaulted to 0. This means we'll always return a 0 should two NULL values be passed in.

This function is deterministic because no matter how many times we call it, we'll always receive the same result back from it as long as the parameter values are the same. Here's a call to the function:

```
SELECT dbo.AddNumbers(3, 4);
```

This will always return 7, because 3 + 4 = 7. If we passed in 7 and 8, we'd always receive 15 back.

Now that we know what a deterministic function is, it should be obvious what a non-deterministic function is. That's right—a function that, no matter whether the same parameter values are passed in or not, never returns the same value. Let's take a look at a non-deterministic function:

```
CREATE FUNCTION dbo.DateWithHoursAdded
(@HoursToAdd INT)
RETURNS DATETIME
AS
BEGIN

RETURN DATEADD(HOUR, COALESCE(@HoursToAdd, 0), GETDATE());

END;
```

This does nothing more than return the current time and date, but with the number of specified hours added on. We use the system function DATEADD to add the hours to the current time and date. If we use this call:

```
SELECT dbo.DateWithHoursAdded(3);
```

the first time I run it, I see the result shown in Figure 16-1.

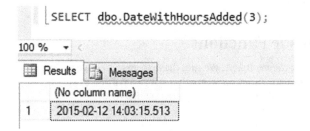

Figure 16-1. *First run of the DateWithHoursAdded function*

Figure 16-2 shows the second execution, still with the same parameter value of 3.

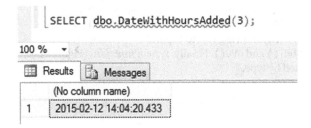

Figure 16-2. *Second run of the DateWithHoursAdded function*

Because we are adding the number of hours to the current time and date, we can never return the same value when calling this function. So it's clear the function is non-deterministic.

User-Defined Functions vs. System Functions

The functions we've seen so far are user-defined functions—or UDFs—which are those we've created ourselves. SQL Server also provides a set of system functions, which are built into SQL Server and available to you out of the box. We've been using some system functions throughout the book—for instance, GETDATE() is a system function to return the current time and date, and COUNT() is a function to return a count of whatever values you pass into the function.

You can see the system functions using SSMS. In the Object Explorer, expand **Databases ➤ AddressBook ➤ Programmability ➤ Functions**. You'll see the four items shown in Figure 16-3.

- AddressBook
  - Database Diagrams
  - Tables
  - Views
  - Synonyms
  - Programmability
    - Stored Procedures
    - Functions
      - Table-valued Functions
      - Scalar-valued Functions
      - Aggregate Functions
      - System Functions

Figure 16-3. *Viewing functions in SSMS*

The aforementioned TVFs and scalar-valued functions are used to house UDFs. These will be empty at the moment as we haven't actually created any UDFs. We'll see these two items again later. *Aggregate functions* are a special type of UDF that are created in .NET, allowing you to expand on the existing aggregation functions provided in SQL Server like COUNT() and AVG(). Finally, *system functions* (Figure 16-4) lists all of the functions built into SQL Server, separated by type.

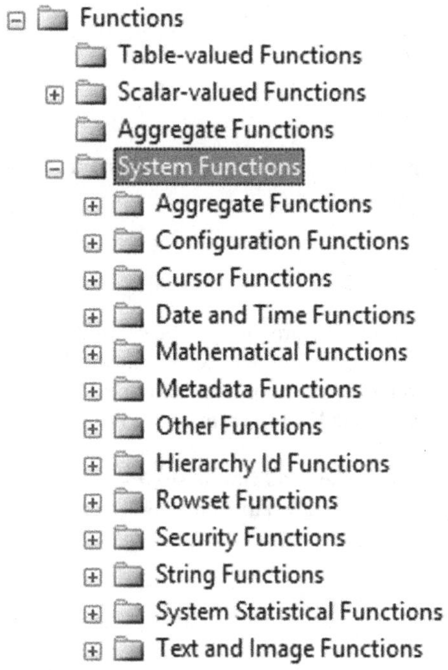

```
⊟ 📁 Functions
     📁 Table-valued Functions
  ⊞ 📁 Scalar-valued Functions
     📁 Aggregate Functions
  ⊟ 📁 System Functions
     ⊞ 📁 Aggregate Functions
     ⊞ 📁 Configuration Functions
     ⊞ 📁 Cursor Functions
     ⊞ 📁 Date and Time Functions
     ⊞ 📁 Mathematical Functions
     ⊞ 📁 Metadata Functions
     ⊞ 📁 Other Functions
     ⊞ 📁 Hierarchy Id Functions
     ⊞ 📁 Rowset Functions
     ⊞ 📁 Security Functions
     ⊞ 📁 String Functions
     ⊞ 📁 System Statistical Functions
     ⊞ 📁 Text and Image Functions
```

Figure 16-4. *Viewing system functions in SSMS*

There are lots and lots (and lots) of system functions available. You'll find yourself using many of these in your daily work. In Figure 16-5, we're looking at the *date and time functions* available to us.

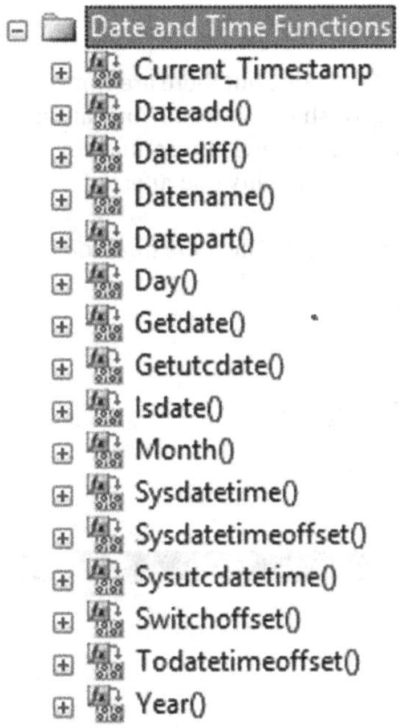

Figure 16-5. *Viewing date and time system functions in SSMS*

These functions are available in any database you create. Take some time to learn what each of them does—it could save you from reinventing the wheel in the future!

Why Are Functions Useful?

Now that we have an idea of the types of function available to us, we're in a position to start creating functions. But why should we want to create any functions? What benefits do they give us? Let's see if we can come up with a convincing argument.

First, functions can be used as part of your SELECT or DML statements, or on their own. This gives them tremendous flexibility, as it allows you to use them to not only insert or update data, but to manipulate the output of data, perhaps by correctly formatting certain columns (we'll create a function just like this soon).

Functions can also be used to set default column values or to implement CHECK constraints. You can even create a column in a table that uses a function to obtain its value, by creating something called a *computed column.*

One other thing I like to use functions for is to enhance views, by replacing certain columns with function calls. Bear in mind this could have a negative effect on indexed views or views you wish to index, as only deterministic functions can be used in indexed views.

The short answer is that for many problems functions are fantastic, and they should be part of your SQL programming strategy. We'll go ahead and enhance our **AddressBook** database with some functions now, and we'll be using them throughout the rest of our book.

What Can't I Do with A Function?

We've seen why functions are great, but surely there are some downsides? Not really, but there are some limitations. The big one is that a function cannot alter the database in any way, shape, or form. You cannot create temp tables in functions, you cannot run DML statements against real tables, and you cannot run anything that causes a side effect. A side effect is deemed to be any piece of functionality that affects anything outside of the function.

As we create our functions we'll look at some possible side effects and how they affect the function.

A First Function

Open up a New Query Window and run this SELECT statement (see Figure 16-6).

```
SELECT * FROM dbo.Contacts;
```

SQLQuery1.sql - BE...ikemcquillan (54))* ×

```
☐USE AddressBook;

 SELECT * FROM dbo.Contacts;
```

100 % ▾ ‹

☐ Results ☐ Messages

	ContactId	FirstName	LastName	DateOfBirth	AllowContactByPhone	CreatedDate
1	1	Stephen	Gerrard	1980-05-30	1	2015-02-11 14:05:00.590
2	2	Dennis	Potter	1935-05-17	0	2015-02-11 14:05:00.590
3	3	Richard	Adams	1920-05-09	0	2015-02-11 14:05:00.590
4	4	Bertie	McQuillan	2001-06-30	1	2015-02-11 14:05:00.590
5	5	Walt	Disney	1966-12-05	1	2015-02-11 14:05:00.590
6	6	Barbara	Gordon	1952-01-11	0	2015-02-11 14:05:00.590
7	7	Josephine	Bailey	1949-05-31	1	2015-02-11 14:05:00.590
8	8	Linda	Canoglu	1959-07-11	1	2015-02-11 14:05:00.590
9	9	Grace	McQuillan	1993-09-27	0	2015-02-11 14:05:00.590
10	10	Vera	Black	1984-08-03	0	2015-02-11 14:05:00.590
11	11	Angelica	Jones	1981-02-04	1	2015-02-11 14:05:00.590
12	12	Steve	Davis	1957-08-22	1	2015-02-11 14:05:00.590
13	13	Allison	Fisher	1968-02-24	1	2015-02-11 14:05:00.590
14	14	julius	Marx	1990-10-02	0	2015-02-11 14:05:00.590
15	15	george	formby	1944-05-26	1	2015-02-11 14:05:00.590
16	16	Alan	Partridge	1965-04-14	0	2015-02-11 14:05:00.590
17	17	Harper	Lee	1986-04-28	1	2015-02-11 14:05:00.590
18	18	Robert	Burns	1959-01-25	0	2015-02-11 14:05:00.590
19	19	Michael	Jackson	1967-06-30	0	2015-02-11 14:05:00.590
20	20	Roald	Dahl	1916-09-13	0	2015-02-11 14:05:00.670
21	22	Laura	Robson	1994-01-21	1	2015-02-11 15:17:56.870
22	24	Bryan	Ferry	1945-09-26	0	2015-02-11 21:53:15.343

Figure 16-6. *A simple SELECT statement*

Can you see any problems with any of the data returned by the SELECT in Figure 16-6? Look at rows 14 and 15. The first name in row 14 is not capitalized, and neither the first name nor the last name is capitalized in row 15. We can write a function to ensure the names are always displayed in a capitalized manner. We can also write the function so it returns the name as a single value, rather than in separate columns.

The CREATE FUNCTION Statement

The statement used to create a function will look familiar to you—it's a typical CREATE statement, in this case CREATE FUNCTION. Here's the basic definition; for the full definition visit https://msdn.microsoft.com/en-us/library/ms186755.aspx:

```
CREATE FUNCTION SchemaName.FunctionName
(Parameters (Optional))
RETURNS ReturnType
AS
BEGIN

Do something...

RETURN ReturnType

END;
```

A function must always be defined with a schema name. You must provide dbo if you haven't created any schemas of your own. Next, you can specify parameters to pass into the function. These are values that the function uses to derive a result. The two functions we saw earlier in this chapter both accepted parameters, but you don't have to specify any if your function doesn't need them (parameters can be set as optional).

To complete the outline of the function, you have to tell SQL Server what the function is going to return. The RETURN keyword can be used for this. Any valid SQL Server data type can be returned, or even a table. If you're quite advanced you can create your own custom data types in SQL Server, and these can be specified as the function return type (you will see how to create custom data types in Chapter 19).

Finally, we come to the body of the function. This starts with AS BEGIN. You can put as many lines of code as you want within the BEGIN and END block. The last line must be a RETURN statement. If you are writing a TVF, you just write RETURN. If the function returns a scalar value, that scalar value must be specified in the RETURN statement.

A Scalar Function: ContactName

Our function is going to return a correctly formatted contact name, as one value. Plotting this out, we can see we need to:

- Accept FirstName and LastName values as parameters

- Return a VARCHAR, holding the full name

- Write some code to correctly format the first letter of both the first name and the last name, then return both values as a single string value

Seems easy enough. Here we go with the definition:

```
USE AddressBook;

GO

CREATE FUNCTION dbo.ContactName
(@FirstName VARCHAR(40), @LastName VARCHAR(40))
RETURNS VARCHAR(80)
```

```
AS
BEGIN

DECLARE @FullName VARCHAR(80);

-- Capitalise the first letter of the first name and last name
SELECT @FirstName = UPPER(LEFT(@FirstName, 1)) + RIGHT(@FirstName, LEN(@FirstName) - 1),
@LastName = UPPER(LEFT(@LastName, 1)) + RIGHT(@LastName, LEN(@LastName) - 1);

SELECT @FullName = @FirstName + ' ' + @LastName;

RETURN @FullName;

END;

GO
```

Note the GO between the USE and CREATE FUNCTION statements. This is needed as CREATE FUNCTION has to be the first statement in a batch (just like CREATE VIEW).

The function is called dbo.ContactName, and accepts two parameters, for first name and last name. These are both VARCHAR(40), which is the same type as the corresponding columns in the Contacts table. Parameters must always begin with an @ symbol. The function returns a value of type VARCHAR(80). This is to cover the two merged first name and last name values: 40 + 40 = 80.

Now we come to the actual code. We start by declaring a variable called @FullName, of VARCHAR(80). This will contain the value to be returned by the function. Next up is the capitalization code. The line that performs this process contains some things we haven't seen before, so it's worth taking a closer look:

```
SELECT @FirstName = UPPER(LEFT(@FirstName, 1)) + RIGHT(@FirstName, LEN(@FirstName) - 1),
@LastName = UPPER(LEFT(@LastName, 1)) + RIGHT(@LastName, LEN(@LastName) - 1);
```

The code that capitalizes the first letter of @FirstName and @LastName is exactly the same, so we'll just look at @FirstName. The first part is:

```
UPPER(LEFT(@FirstName, 1))
```

Assume a name of "mcquillan". The UPPER function capitalizes whatever string is passed into it. If "mcquillan" was passed in, "MCQUILLAN" would be returned. We are not passing in "mcquillan" though, we are passing:

```
LEFT(@FirstName, 1)
```

The LEFT function returns the specified number of characters from a string, starting from the left. We've told SQL Server we want 1 character from the @FirstName variable. This means return me the first character of the string. So a value of "mcquillan" would cause "m" to be returned. The UPPER function would then take this "m" and convert it to "M". So this first call has given us a capital letter.

Now we have a plus sign, which dictates that the "M" we already have will be added to whatever the code after the plus sign returns. That code is:

```
RIGHT(@FirstName, LEN(@FirstName) - 1)
```

No prizes for guessing that RIGHT is the opposite of LEFT. LEFT returns characters from the start of a string, and RIGHT returns characters from the end of the string. For ContactName, we want to return every character in the string—*except for the first character, which we have already processed.* The declaration of RIGHT is exactly the same as LEFT—we provide the string we want to extract characters from, and then tell SQL Server how many characters we want.

Our call to RIGHT is a bit different from LEFT—we knew when we were calling LEFT that we only needed the first character, so we could just specify 1 as the number of characters required. We have to calculate how many characters the call to RIGHT will return, as we have no idea how many characters the name passed in will contain. If we pass in "mcquillan", we want to return "cquillan". If we pass in "smith", we want to return "mith".

The LEN function comes to our rescue here. This handy function returns the length of any string you pass in to it. LEN('bertie') would return 6, but LEN('Grace') would return 5. Our call is:

```
LEN(@FirstName) - 1
```

This will return the entire length of the string minus 1. So passing "mcquillan" will return 8, not 9. LEN will initially return 9, the correct length, but we are then taking 1 off the value returned by LEN. This gives us the exact number of characters we want. The RIGHT call will return "cquillan" when "mcquillan" is passed. This is then added to the "M" our LEFT call generated, giving us a full value of "Mcquillan". And we've ended up with a capitalized name!

Once the capitalization process has completed, we just set @FullName to @FirstName and @LastName, separated by a space. Our last act is to RETURN the contents of @FullName as the function result.

That's not a bad little function. Run the script to create the function, ensuring **Command(s) completed successfully** appears.

Testing Our Function

It's very easy to test a function. Open a New Query Window and write a SELECT statement to call the function with some appropriate values (see Figure 16-7).

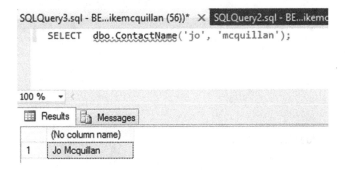

Figure 16-7. *Testing a function*

Hurrah, Figure 16-7 shows us a nicely capitalized name! (It also shows us an underlined function name—remember, Ctrl+R will refresh Intellisense.) We can call the function multiple times from the same SELECT, too, as demonstrated in Figure 16-8.

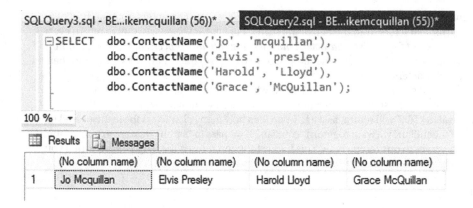

Figure 16-8. *Lots of function calls from one SELECT*

The function is working well. Even if we pass a name already capitalized to it, the name still returns as capitalized. And it doesn't remove any capitals specified anywhere else in the string.

Now, what if we have imperfect data? Say we only pass a first name, or only pass a last name? What would happen if we just passed blank strings? Let's give it a go with a NULL value provided in the surname. Figure 16-9 has the result.

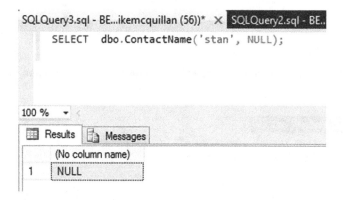

Figure 16-9. *Problems with dodgy data*

Rats, we have a problem. Let's try a blank value (Figure 16-10).

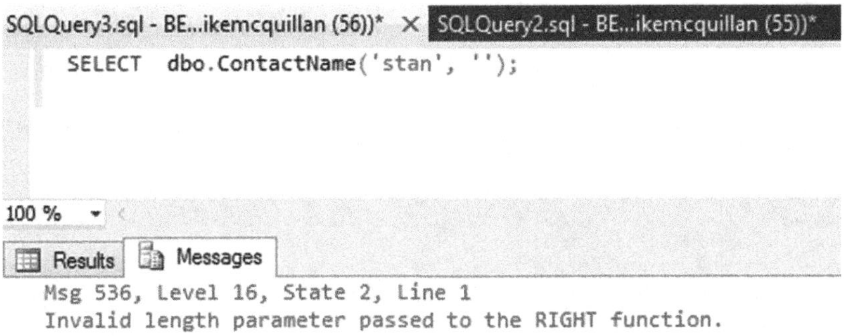

SQLQuery3.sql - BE...ikemcquillan (56))* × SQLQuery2.sql - BE...ikemcquillan (55))*

```
    SELECT  dbo.ContactName('stan', '');
```

100 % ▾

☷ Results	▤ Messages

```
    Msg 536, Level 16, State 2, Line 1
    Invalid length parameter passed to the RIGHT function.
```

Figure 16-10. *Blank values fail, too*

Figure 16-10 tells us blank values don't work, either. We need to modify the code to prevent these problems. We'll just add a line into the function so we can see what @FirstName and @LastName contain before the capitalization statement runs. They should contain exactly what we passed in. Return to the window housing the function's code, and under the line:

```
DECLARE @FullName VARCHAR(80);
```

add this SELECT:

```
SELECT @FirstName AS FirstName, @LastName AS LastName;
```

Run this. The function doesn't build! Instead, SQL Server tells us off. The error message is shown in Figure 16-11.

293

```
SQLQuery3.sql - BE...ikemcquillan (56))*      SQLQuery2.sql - BE...ikemcquillan (55))*  ×  SQLQuery1.sql - BE...ikemcquillan (54))*
  USE AddressBook;

  GO

CREATE FUNCTION dbo.ContactName
  (
  @FirstName      VARCHAR(40),
  @LastName       VARCHAR(40)
  )
  RETURNS VARCHAR(80)
  AS
  BEGIN

  DECLARE @FullName    VARCHAR(80);

  SELECT @FirstName AS FirstName, @LastName AS LastName;

  -- Capitalise the first letter of the first name and last name
  SELECT  @FirstName =
      UPPER(LEFT(@FirstName, 1)) + RIGHT(@FirstName, LEN(@FirstName) - 1),
          @LastName = UPPER(LEFT(@LastName, 1)) + RIGHT(@LastName, LEN(@LastName) - 1);

  SELECT @FullName = @FirstName + ' ' + @LastName;

  RETURN @FullName;

  END;
100 %   ▼
  Messages
  Msg 444, Level 16, State 3, Procedure ContactName, Line 16
  Select statements included within a function cannot return data to a client.
```

Figure 16-11. *Trying to include a side effect in a function*

Side Effects

We have just created a *side effect*. We've tried to make the function do something in addition to its main purpose. The purpose of the function is to capitalize two strings and return them as one complete string. By adding the SELECT statement, we've tried to tell the function to return some data as well. If this safety mechanism wasn't in place, the SELECT statement could interfere with other code we write whenever the function is called, which would lead to all sorts of confusion.

You can try changing the SELECT to a PRINT, but it won't do any good—a PRINT is still a side effect. Keep the functions concise and to the point and side effects won't bother you.

Further Testing

We still need to change our function to ensure correct values are returned if NULL or empty strings are passed. Time to fall back to testing mechanism number 2! I use this technique a lot; I find it saves me a lot of development time. It involves removing the CREATE FUNCTION call and executing the function's code as a stand-alone script instead. This way, I can add as many SELECT and PRINT statements as I like. Once the code is behaving the way I expect, I can remove the side effect statements and restore the CREATE FUNCTION call.

Return to the window containing the function code and change it so we can run the code independently.

```
USE AddressBook;

GO

--CREATE FUNCTION dbo.ContactName
--(
DECLARE @FirstName VARCHAR(40),
@LastName VARCHAR(40)
--)
--RETURNS VARCHAR(80)
--AS
--BEGIN

SELECT @FirstName = 'stan', @LastName = NULL;

DECLARE @FullName VARCHAR(80);

-- Capitalise the first letter of the first name and last name
SELECT @FirstName = UPPER(LEFT(@FirstName, 1)) + RIGHT(@FirstName, LEN(@FirstName) - 1),
@LastName = UPPER(LEFT(@LastName, 1)) + RIGHT(@LastName, LEN(@LastName) - 1);

SELECT @FullName = @FirstName + ' ' + @LastName;

--RETURN @FullName;
SELECT @FullName;

--END;

GO
```

We've commented out all of the lines related to CREATE FUNCTION—parentheses, BEGIN, END, the lot. We've also put a DECLARE in front of the parameter names, changing them to normal variables. After the DECLARE, the first line now sets @FirstName and @LastName to 'stan' and NULL, respectively. This should allow us to fix our first bug. Our final change is to comment out the RETURN line and replace it with a SELECT—RETURN will only work when called from the function.

Press F5 to run this and one result set appears, showing the NULL value we were seeing earlier (Figure 16-12). If we pass in a valid first name and a NULL last name (or vice versa), then just the name we've provided should be returned (certainly not a NULL!).

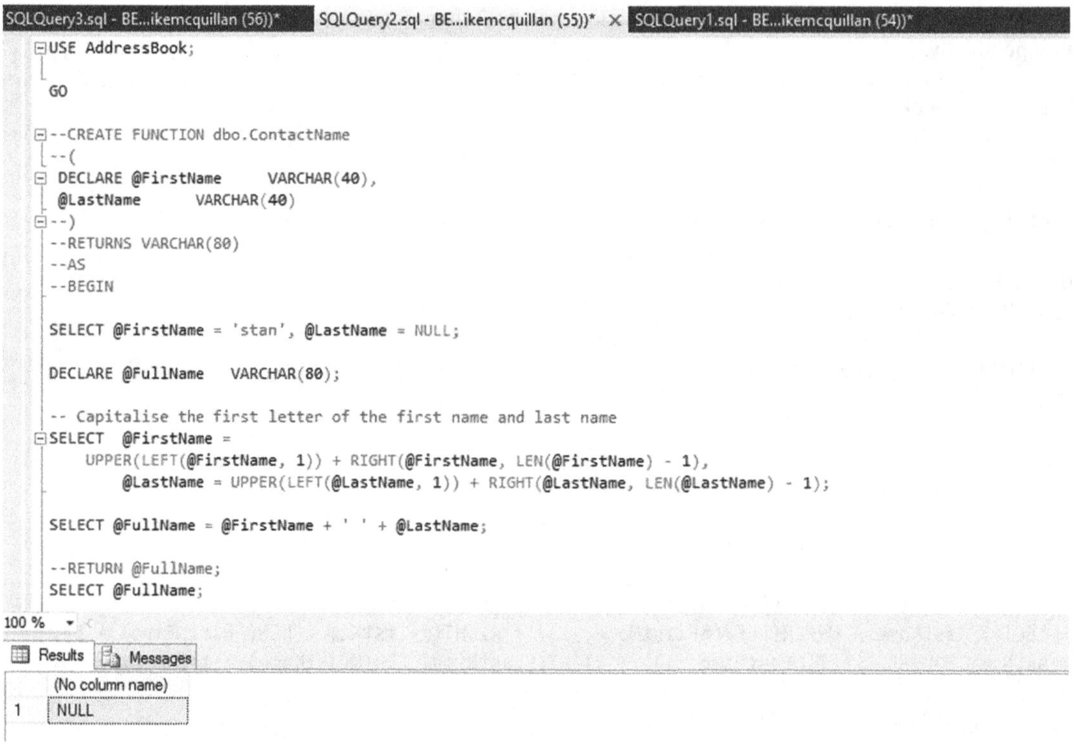

Figure 16-12. *Testing the function code manually*

To fix this problem, we need a NULL check. Change the code as shown in bold so we convert any NULL values to empty strings before running the capitalization statement:

```
USE AddressBook;

GO

--CREATE FUNCTION dbo.ContactName
--(
DECLARE @FirstName VARCHAR(40),
@LastName VARCHAR(40)
--)
--RETURNS VARCHAR(80)
--AS
--BEGIN

SELECT @FirstName = 'stan', @LastName = NULL;

DECLARE @FullName VARCHAR(80);

-- Replace NULL values with empty strings
SELECT @FirstName = COALESCE(@FirstName, ''),
@LastName = COALESCE(@LastName, '');
```

```
-- Capitalise the first letter of the first name and last name
SELECT @FirstName = UPPER(LEFT(@FirstName, 1)) + RIGHT(@FirstName, LEN(@FirstName) - 1),
@LastName = UPPER(LEFT(@LastName, 1)) + RIGHT(@LastName, LEN(@LastName) - 1);

SELECT @FullName = @FirstName + ' ' + @LastName;

--RETURN @FullName;
SELECT @FullName;

--END;

GO
```

Run this. Still no success—this time we see the **Invalid length parameter passed to the RIGHT function** message we saw earlier (Figure 16-13). We've solved one problem, but not the second (yet!).

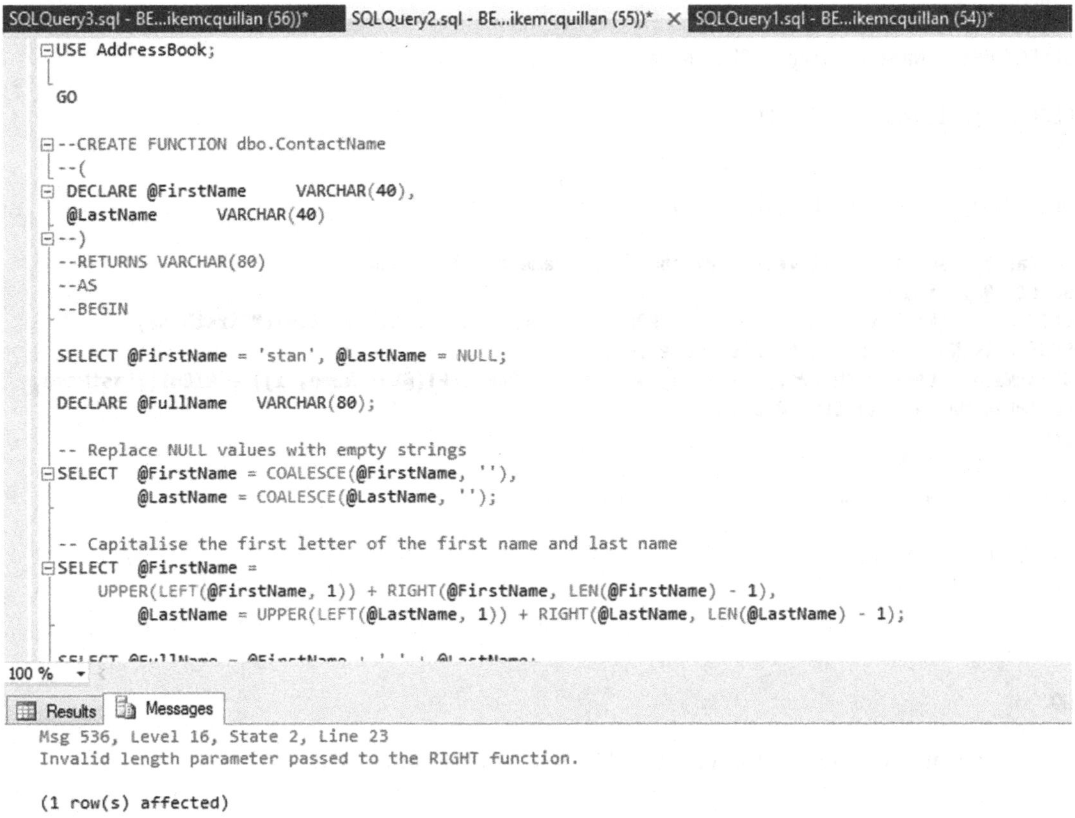

Figure 16-13. Fixing bugs in the function code

This issue is being raised because we are trying to take 1 character away from a string of zero length; 0 − 1 = −1, which the RIGHT function refuses to return. Fair enough. We can work around this with a CASE statement. If the length of the string is greater than 0, we can execute the capitalization code. If it isn't we won't do anything to the string. Here is the updated code:

```
USE AddressBook;

GO

--CREATE FUNCTION dbo.ContactName
--(
DECLARE @FirstName VARCHAR(40),
@LastName VARCHAR(40)
--)
--RETURNS VARCHAR(80)
--AS
--BEGIN

SELECT @FirstName = 'stan', @LastName = '';

DECLARE @FullName VARCHAR(80);

SELECT @FirstName = COALESCE(@FirstName, ''),
@LastName = COALESCE(@LastName, '');

-- Capitalise the first letter of the first name and last name
SELECT @FirstName =
CASE WHEN LEN(@FirstName) > 0 THEN UPPER(LEFT(@FirstName, 1)) + RIGHT(@FirstName,
LEN(@FirstName) - 1) ELSE @FirstName END,
@LastName = CASE WHEN LEN(@LastName) > 0 THEN UPPER(LEFT(@LastName, 1)) + RIGHT(@LastName,
LEN(@LastName) - 1) ELSE @LastName
END;

SELECT @FullName = @FirstName + ' ' + @LastName;

--RETURN @FullName;
SELECT @FullName;

--END;

GO
```

Run this and you'll see what success looks like. It looks like Figure 16-14.

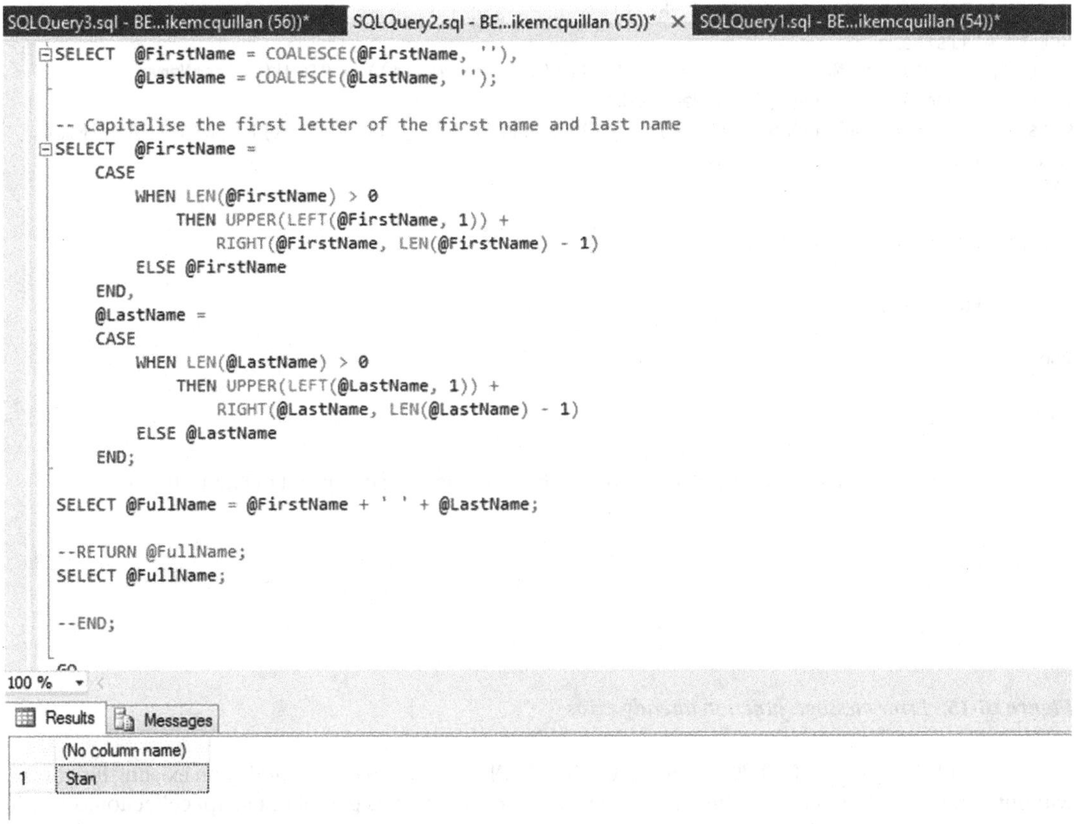

```
SELECT  @FirstName = COALESCE(@FirstName, ''),
        @LastName = COALESCE(@LastName, '');

-- Capitalise the first letter of the first name and last name
SELECT  @FirstName =
    CASE
        WHEN LEN(@FirstName) > 0
            THEN UPPER(LEFT(@FirstName, 1)) +
                RIGHT(@FirstName, LEN(@FirstName) - 1)
        ELSE @FirstName
    END,
    @LastName =
    CASE
        WHEN LEN(@LastName) > 0
            THEN UPPER(LEFT(@LastName, 1)) +
                RIGHT(@LastName, LEN(@LastName) - 1)
        ELSE @LastName
    END;

SELECT @FullName = @FirstName + ' ' + @LastName;

--RETURN @FullName;
SELECT @FullName;

--END;
```

Figure 16-14. *Stan returns!*

This is more like it. Test it with a few other combinations (good and bad) to make sure you are happy with the code. Once you are satisfied we can change the code back to a function. Restore the lines we commented out and remove the bits we added, like DECLARE. Here's the full listing.

```
USE AddressBook;

GO

CREATE FUNCTION dbo.ContactName
(@FirstName VARCHAR(40), @LastName VARCHAR(40)
)
RETURNS VARCHAR(80)
AS
BEGIN

DECLARE @FullName VARCHAR(80);

-- Replace NULL values with empty strings
SELECT @FirstName = COALESCE(@FirstName, ''), @LastName = COALESCE(@LastName, '');
```

```
-- Capitalise the first letter of the first name and last name
SELECT @FirstName =
CASE WHEN LEN(@FirstName) > O THEN UPPER(LEFT(@FirstName, 1)) + RIGHT(@FirstName,
LEN(@FirstName) - 1) ELSE @FirstName END,
@LastName = CASE WHEN LEN(@LastName) > O THEN UPPER(LEFT(@LastName, 1)) + RIGHT(@LastName,
LEN(@LastName) - 1) ELSE @LastName
END;

SELECT @FullName = @FirstName + ' ' + @LastName;

RETURN @FullName;

END;

GO
```

Run this and . . . it doesn't work! Instead, we see the error message displayed in Figure 16-15:

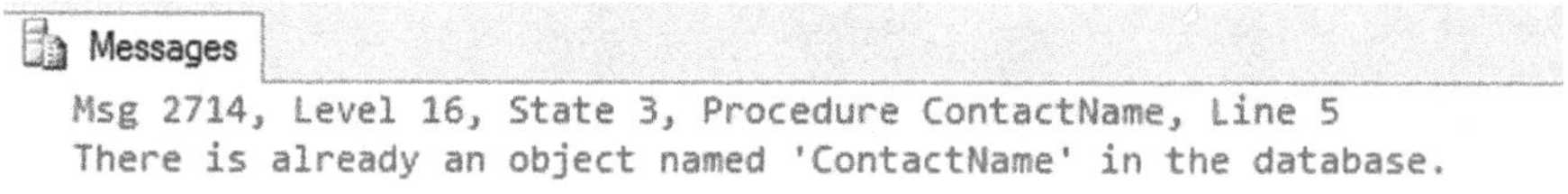

```
Messages
  Msg 2714, Level 16, State 3, Procedure ContactName, Line 5
  There is already an object named 'ContactName' in the database.
```

Figure 16-15. Error message: function already exists

We could change CREATE FUNCTION to ALTER FUNCTION, which allows us to modify an existing function without dropping it. But that won't help us when we save the function as part of our script collection, so we'll drop it first, then re-create it.

Dropping Functions

We need to check if our function exists, drop the function if it does, and then re-create it. You won't be surprised to learn that the statement used to drop a function is called DROP FUNCTION. What may surprise you is we cannot run a SELECT against sys.functions to check if the function exists—because there is no sys.functions. Instead, we have to query the sys.objects table instead, specifying a type of FN (short for FUNCTION).

Add this check between the lines USE AddressBook; and GO at the top of the script.

```
USE AddressBook;

IF EXISTS (SELECT 1 FROM sys.objects WHERE [name] = 'ContactName' AND [type] = 'FN')
BEGIN
DROP FUNCTION dbo.ContactName;
END;

GO
```

Run the script again and it will now execute as expected. Now we'll run a test query. If you still have the test script we used earlier, modify it to match the code in Figure 16-16; otherwise just type it into a New Query Window. Now two empty strings return an empty string, and so does a NULL.

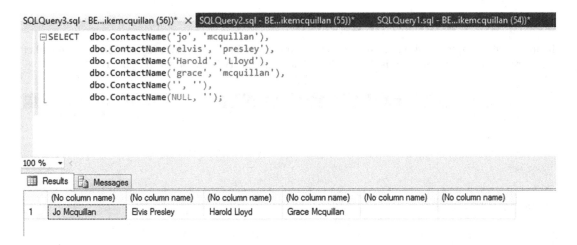

Figure 16-16. Empty string inputs return an empty string!

Saving the Function

Our function is now ready for use. Save it as `c:\temp\sqlbasics\apply\24 - Create ContactName Function.sql`. Add it to our growing `00 - Apply.sql` script, too.

```
:setvar currentFile "24 - Create ContactName Function.sql"
PRINT 'Executing $(path)$(currentFile)';
:r $(path)$(currentFile)
```

We also need to create a rollback for the function. In a New Query Window, paste the DROP FUNCTION statement we wrote earlier.

```
USE AddressBook;

IF EXISTS (SELECT 1 FROM sys.objects WHERE [name] = 'ContactName' AND [type] = 'FN')
BEGIN
DROP FUNCTION dbo.ContactName;
END;

GO
```

Save this as `c:\temp\sqlbasics\rollback\24 - Create ContactName Function Rollback.sql`. Add it to the `00 - Rollback.sql` script.

```
:setvar currentFile "24 - Create ContactName Function Rollback.sql"
PRINT 'Executing $(path)$(currentFile)';
:r $(path)$(currentFile)
```

Using the Function in Queries

To finish off this chapter, we'll take a look at how to use our scalar function as part of a query. Do you remember the query we wrote at the start of this chapter? It was the simple SELECT you can see in Figure 16-17.

Figure 16-17. *A simple SELECT statement (again)*

Let's say we want to return a list of contacts with the columns:

- ContactId
- Full name of the contact (FirstName and LastName joined up)
- DateOfBirth

We could write this as:

```
SELECT ContactId, FirstName + ' ' + LastName AS FullName, DateOfBirth
FROM dbo.Contacts;
```

This kind of gives us what we want (Figure 16-18):

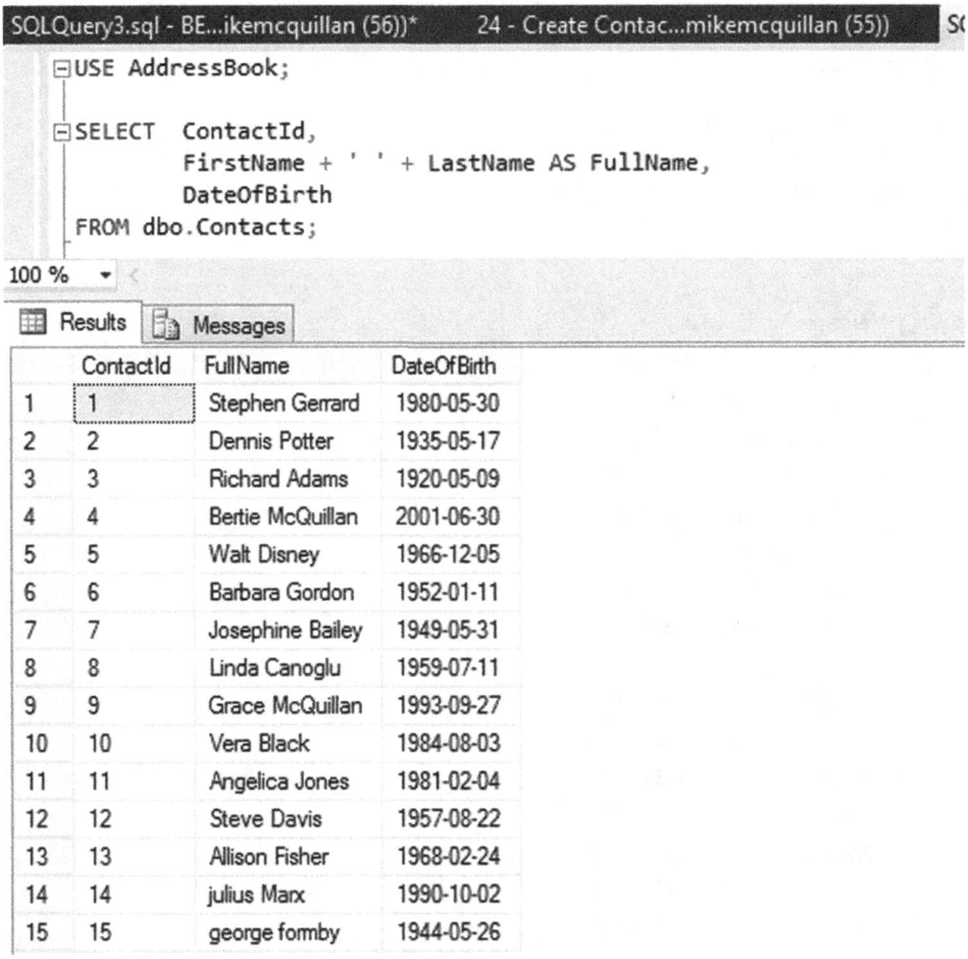

```
SQLQuery3.sql - BE...ikemcquillan (56))*        24 - Create Contac...mikemcquillan (55))      S(

  ☐USE AddressBook;

  ☐SELECT  ContactId,
           FirstName + ' ' + LastName AS FullName,
           DateOfBirth
   FROM dbo.Contacts;
```

	ContactId	FullName	DateOfBirth
1	1	Stephen Gerrard	1980-05-30
2	2	Dennis Potter	1935-05-17
3	3	Richard Adams	1920-05-09
4	4	Bertie McQuillan	2001-06-30
5	5	Walt Disney	1966-12-05
6	6	Barbara Gordon	1952-01-11
7	7	Josephine Bailey	1949-05-31
8	8	Linda Canoglu	1959-07-11
9	9	Grace McQuillan	1993-09-27
10	10	Vera Black	1984-08-03
11	11	Angelica Jones	1981-02-04
12	12	Steve Davis	1957-08-22
13	13	Allison Fisher	1968-02-24
14	14	julius Marx	1990-10-02
15	15	george formby	1944-05-26

Figure 16-18. Manually concatenating the first and last names

It hasn't capitalized the names of rows 14 and 15, though. And it isn't very reusable, either—we'll have to write that line of code whenever somebody wants a full name instead of separate first and last names. Not to worry—we can fix those problems by using our function. Here's the statement updated to use the ContactName function.

```
SELECT ContactId, dbo.ContactName(FirstName, LastName) AS FullName, DateOfBirth
FROM dbo.Contacts;
```

That's a bit easier to write! And it returns the data exactly as we want it too, as Figure 16-19 shows us.

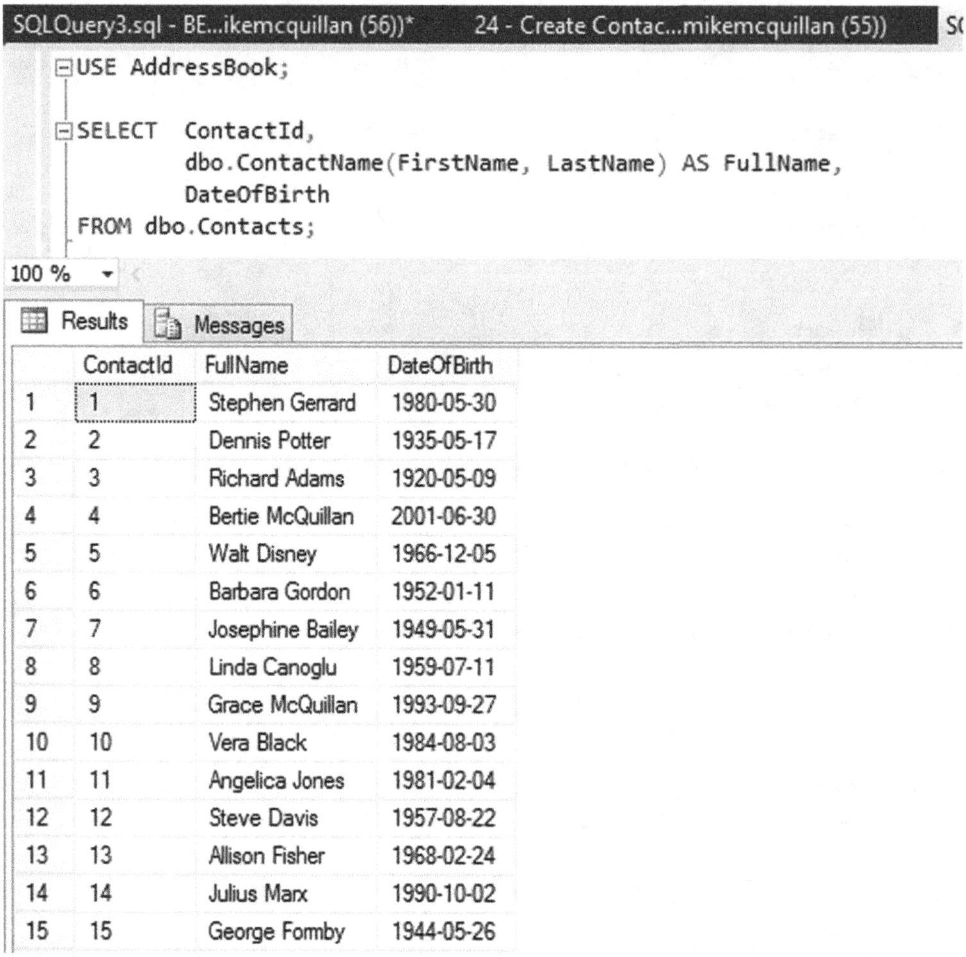

```
SQLQuery3.sql - BE...ikemcquillan (56))*    24 - Create Contac...mikemcquillan (55))    S(
⊟USE AddressBook;

⊟SELECT  ContactId,
         dbo.ContactName(FirstName, LastName) AS FullName,
         DateOfBirth
  FROM dbo.Contacts;
```

100 % ▼

Results | Messages

	ContactId	FullName	DateOfBirth
1	1	Stephen Gerrard	1980-05-30
2	2	Dennis Potter	1935-05-17
3	3	Richard Adams	1920-05-09
4	4	Bertie McQuillan	2001-06-30
5	5	Walt Disney	1966-12-05
6	6	Barbara Gordon	1952-01-11
7	7	Josephine Bailey	1949-05-31
8	8	Linda Canoglu	1959-07-11
9	9	Grace McQuillan	1993-09-27
10	10	Vera Black	1984-08-03
11	11	Angelica Jones	1981-02-04
12	12	Steve Davis	1957-08-22
13	13	Allison Fisher	1968-02-24
14	14	Julius Marx	1990-10-02
15	15	George Formby	1944-05-26

Figure 16-19. *Using the function to return a full name*

Marvelous. Now we never have to worry about anybody asking us to return the contact's full name in the future—we have a reusable function we can call as and when needed. Well done, you!

Summary

We've covered scalar functions in this chapter, and we've seen not only how to create them, but also how to test them, drop them, and integrate them into queries. It's pretty powerful stuff!

Scalar functions are only one-half of the functional story, though. We introduced table-valued functions at the start of the chapter, and they add another whole level of power to the functional toolkit. Stroll on to the next chapter and we'll talk TVFs.

CHAPTER 17

■ ■ ■

Table-Valued Functions

We've had a solid introduction to functions of the scalar kind. Now we'll look at the other functional option provided to us by SQL Server: table-valued functions, or TVFs for short. TVFs let you create parameterized tables, which you can use in your queries to provide extra functionality that a normal join would struggle to match. Time to talk tables again!

Why TVFs Are Cool

TVFs were introduced in SQL Server 2005, and have become a widely used component of most SQL Server developers' toolkits. I use them all the time, as they often provide the granular control needed to solve a particular problem that a view or stored procedure cannot give. Views and stored procedures (which we'll meet in the very next chapter) both have their place and are both very powerful, but there are certain times when nothing but a TVF will do.

There are several reasons why TVFs are so great:

- A view can only contain a single SELECT statement; a TVF can contain multiple statements, all of which combine to produce the end table.

- TVFs can replace stored procedures. Stored procedures can return result sets, but they cannot be easily used in queries. TVFs can be embedded directly in queries.

- Bugs in TVFs can be easily fixed, as long as the function signature doesn't change.

- TVFs can accept parameters, which allow you to dictate the output of the table.

- TVFs can hide a lot of complexity and improve code reuse.

- TVFs are great when a fairly small result set is being returned.

Sometimes, TVFs Are Not So Cool

Of course, there are times when a TVF may not be the best solution to a problem. As with any technology, TVFs can be abused and used for evil purposes! Some reasons why you wouldn't use a TVF are (duh-duh-DUH!):

- TVFs can greatly affect performance. A TVF is executed for every single row returned by a SELECT statement, so great care needs to be taken in how they are used.

- Views offer much lower overhead compared to TVFs; if you can do what you need to do in a single SELECT statement, use a view.

- If you don't need to use the result set in other queries, use a stored procedure; these generally perform better than TVFs.

- If a large result set is being returned, a TVF may not offer the best solution due to their procedural nature. Consider a set-based solution instead (we'll be looking at an example of this in the next two chapters).

None of this should put you off using TVFs. I've seen TVFs make a 10-minute import process run for 4 hours. Conversely, I've also seen TVFs reduce queries that took 30 minutes to run down to a few seconds. When you are trying to improve performance, it's all about knowing what the various technologies can do, and having a play-around with them to see what works best.

Building a TVF

Let's put a TVF together so we can see how they work. We want to build something that tells us how many subrecords of a particular type are available for each contact. We also want to give the user the option of requesting totals for all types of subrecord (addresses, notes, phone numbers, and roles), or just for one particular type of subrecord. The record set we will return is the following:

- `ContactId`

- `AddressCount`

- `NoteCount`

- `PhoneNumberCount`

- `RoleCount`

If a count is available for the selected type, we will return a record for the requested contact. If no count is available, no record will be returned.

This function needs to accept two parameters: the `ContactId` for which we are requesting totals, and a `TableName` parameter, to specify from which table we should be returning totals. If `'All'` is passed as the `TableName`, all totals will be returned.

The header of this function looks similar to the UDF we created in the last chapter, with a function name and parameters:

```
CREATE FUNCTION dbo.ContactCounts
(
@ContactId INT,
@TableName VARCHAR(40)
)
```

This gives us the parameters we were talking about. Now we need to return a table instead of a scalar value. We do this on the next line:

```
RETURNS @CountsTable TABLE (ContactId INT, AddressCount INT, NoteCount INT, PhoneNumberCount
INT, RoleCount INT)
```

It's important to note that we have specified a variable name for the table, `@CountsTable`. A variable name *must* be specified; we use this name to access the table in the body of the function. After the `TABLE` keyword is used to declare we are returning a table, we have the usual list of column definitions.

We've declared the columns we talked about earlier. Now we move into the body of the function. This is where the action takes place. Here's what we want to do:

- If the @TableName variable holds 'All' or 'ContactAddresses', obtain the address count for the specified contact.

- If the @TableName variable holds 'All' or 'ContactNotes', obtain the note count for the specified contact.

- If the @TableName variable holds 'All' or 'ContactPhoneNumbers', obtain the phone number count for the specified contact.

- If the @TableName variable holds 'All' or 'ContactRoles', obtain the role count for the specified contact.

- If at least one of the counts is greater than zero, insert a row into the table.

- Return the table.

The first four lines are pretty much the same; we just obtain a count for the required table, and then assign that count to an appropriate variable. Once the variables have been assigned, we can attempt the insert. The full function definition follows, along with a DROP FUNCTION check at the top.

```
USE AddressBook;

IF EXISTS (SELECT 1 FROM sys.objects WHERE [name] = 'ContactCounts'
AND [type] = 'TF')
BEGIN
DROP FUNCTION dbo.ContactCounts;
END;

GO

-- Table-Valued function to return contact record counts
-- Acceptable values for @TableName are All, ContactAddresses, ContactNotes, --
-- ContactPhoneNumbers, and ContactRoles.
CREATE FUNCTION dbo.ContactCounts
(@ContactId INT, @TableName VARCHAR(40)
)
RETURNS @CountsTable TABLE (ContactId INT, AddressCount INT, NoteCount INT,
PhoneNumberCount INT, RoleCount INT)
AS
BEGIN

-- Variables to hold the counts
DECLARE @AddressCount INT, @NoteCount INT, @PhoneNumberCount INT, @RoleCount INT;

-- Return address count
IF (@TableName IN ('All', 'ContactAddresses'))
BEGIN
SELECT @AddressCount = COUNT(1)
FROM dbo.ContactAddresses CA
WHERE CA.ContactId = @ContactId;
END;
```

```
-- Return note count
IF (@TableName IN ('All', 'ContactNotes'))
BEGIN
SELECT @NoteCount = COUNT(1) FROM dbo.ContactNotes CN WHERE CN.ContactId = @ContactId;
END;

-- Return phone number count
IF (@TableName IN ('All', 'ContactPhoneNumbers'))
BEGIN
SELECT @PhoneNumberCount = COUNT(1) FROM dbo.ContactPhoneNumbers CPN WHERE CPN.ContactId = @
ContactId;
END;

-- Return role count
IF (@TableName IN ('All', 'ContactRoles'))
BEGIN
SELECT @RoleCount = COUNT(1) FROM dbo.ContactRoles CR WHERE CR.ContactId = @ContactId;
END;

-- If we have at least one valid value, add the row
IF (@AddressCount > 0 OR @NoteCount > 0 OR @PhoneNumberCount > 0 OR @RoleCount > 0)
BEGIN

INSERT INTO @CountsTable (ContactId, AddressCount, NoteCount, PhoneNumberCount, RoleCount)
SELECT @ContactId, @AddressCount, @NoteCount, @PhoneNumberCount, @RoleCount;

END;

RETURN;

END;

GO
```

There is quite a bit of code here, but it isn't overly complicated. We declare four variables to hold the counts we generate. The first count to be returned is for ContactAddresses; if the user has requested all totals or just the address total, we obtain the count from the ContactAddresses table. We do exactly the same for notes, phone numbers, and roles.

This final section of code is where the magic happens:

```
-- If we have at least one valid value, add the row
IF (@AddressCount > 0 OR @NoteCount > 0 OR @PhoneNumberCount > 0 OR @RoleCount > 0)
BEGIN

INSERT INTO @CountsTable (ContactId, AddressCount, NoteCount, PhoneNumberCount, RoleCount)
SELECT @ContactId, @AddressCount, @NoteCount, @PhoneNumberCount, @RoleCount;

END;

RETURN;
```

If at least one of the variables is greater than zero, we will insert a row into the @CountTable table variable. We return the ContactId and the appropriate counts. Note that some of the counts will be NULL if only one count in particular was requested. At this point, we have a row in the table. The RETURN keyword is called and the function completes. Remember that you do not return the table variable (unlike scalar functions, in which you do return the variable containing the value you wish to return); you just call RETURN. SQL Server knows the table variable was declared in the function header, so it knows what it needs to return.

Save this script as c:\temp\sqlbasics\apply\25 - Create ContactCounts Function.sql, and run it. After seeing **Command(s) completed successfully**, the function is ready to rock!

Adding the Script to SQLCMD

Don't forget to add the script to our 00 - Apply.sql script:

```
:setvar currentFile "25 - Create ContactCounts Function.sql"
PRINT 'Executing $(path)$(currentFile)';
:r $(path)$(currentFile)
```

Creating the Rollback Script

We also need to create a rollback script. Enter this script:

```
USE AddressBook;

IF EXISTS (SELECT 1 FROM sys.objects WHERE [name] = 'ContactCounts' AND [type] = 'TF')
BEGIN
DROP FUNCTION dbo.ContactCounts;
END;

GO
```

Note the type column check—we are looking for TF, which is how SQL Server identifies a TVF.

Save the script as c:\temp\sqlbasics\rollback\25 - Create ContactCounts Function Rollback.sql. Add this to 00 - Rollback.sql.

```
:setvar currentFile "25 - Create ContactCounts Function Rollback.sql"
PRINT 'Executing $(path)$(currentFile)';
:r $(path)$(currentFile)
```

Using TVFs in Queries

Now to test our query. Open up a New Query Window. Before typing anything, press Ctrl+Shift+R to refresh Intellisense (the pop-up information that appears as you are typing). Refreshing Intellisense will ensure the new function we just created will be picked up. Type this:

```
USE AddressBook;

SELECT * FROM dbo.ContactCounts(
```

Intellisense should display something like the pop-up shown in Figure 17-1.

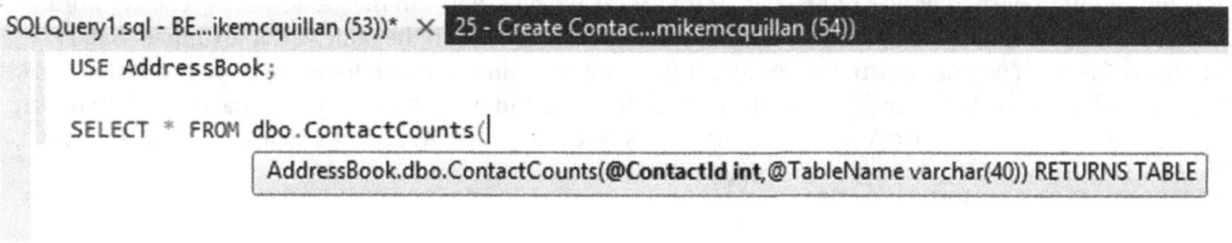

Figure 17-1. *Intellisense at work*

We can see the function declaration, and Intellisense is telling us what values we need to provide. It is also telling us the function returns a table. Let's complete the statement. We'll start by returning all records for Stephen Gerrard (ContactId 1).

```
USE AddressBook;

SELECT * FROM dbo.ContactCounts(1, 'All');
```

Figure 17-2 has the results.

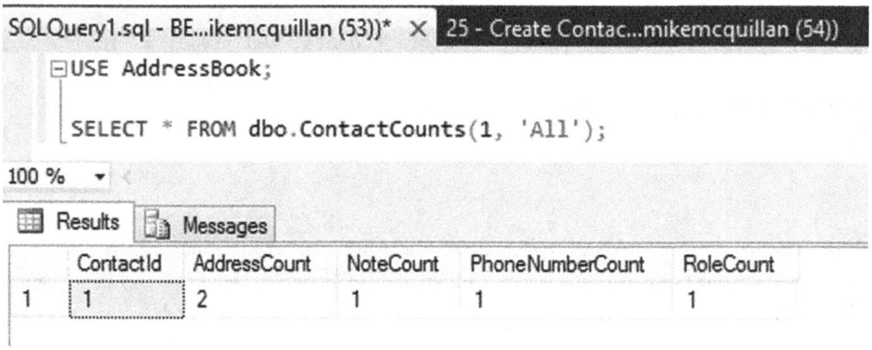

Figure 17-2. *Returning counts for all tables*

Looks good! Change 'All' to 'ContactAddresses'. The results should match Figure 17-3.

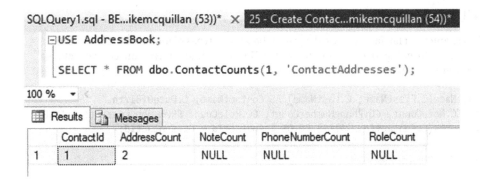

Figure 17-3. *Returning the count for the* `ContactAddresses` *table*

The function returns just the count we asked for. If we specify a table name that is not recognized by the function, no row is returned (as you can see in Figure 17-4).

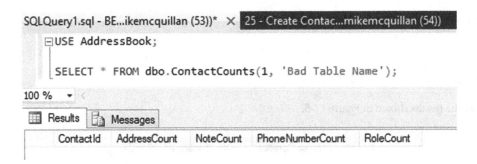

Figure 17-4. *Trying to return a count for a nonexistent table*

Calling a TVF

Maybe you've noticed we called the TVF by using a `SELECT`. In fact, the `SELECT` statement looks exactly like any other `SELECT` statement we've used so far, except it has parameters in brackets after it. But apart from this difference, SQL Server essentially treats the function just like a table. These are only rules to follow when using a TVF in a `SELECT`:

- The schema name must be specified
- A value for each parameter must be provided (you can specify default values for parameters, but even if a default is specified, you must provide the `DEFAULT` keyword)

I mentioned TVFs are treated just like a table, which means we should be able to join the TVF to other tables. We'll see if and how that is possible.

Joining to a TVF

A long time ago in a chapter not far, far away, we discussed the various types of join: INNER, LEFT, RIGHT, FULL, and CROSS JOINs. We're going to modify our basic SELECT statement to return some contact details alongside the totals. Here's a statement using an INNER JOIN:

```
SELECT dbo.ContactName(C.FirstName, C.LastName) AS ContactName, C.DateOfBirth,
CC.AddressCount, CC.NoteCount, CC.PhoneNumberCount, CC.RoleCount FROM dbo.Contacts C INNER
JOIN dbo.ContactCounts(C.ContactId, 'All') CC ON C.ContactId = CC.ContactId;
```

If you try to run this, you'll see an error.

```
Msg 4104, Level 16, State 1, Line 10
The multi-part identifier "C.ContactId" could not be bound.
```

This is the C.ContactId referenced on the INNER JOIN line. You can try changing this to a LEFT OUTER JOIN, a RIGHT OUTER JOIN, a FULL OUTER JOIN, or a CROSS JOIN. None of them will work. However, if we change the line:

```
INNER JOIN dbo.ContactCounts(C.ContactId, 'All') CC
```

to:

```
INNER JOIN dbo.ContactCounts(1, 'All') CC
```

then you'll see the results shown in Figure 17-5.

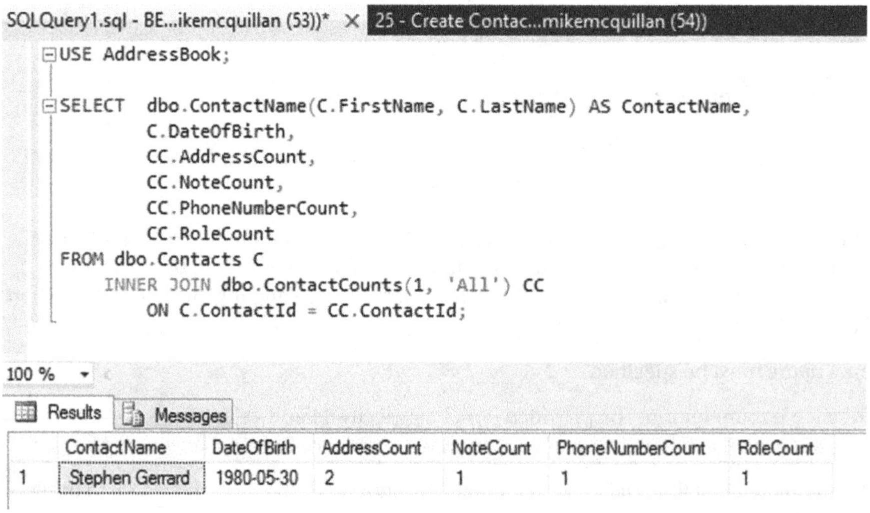

Figure 17-5. *Using the function (badly) with an INNER JOIN*

This isn't much good to us though—we need to explicitly specify a value for ContactId. It's actually worse than it looks though. If we keep the value 1, but change the INNER JOIN to LEFT JOIN, all contacts will be returned, but with the exception of ContactId 1, all totals will be NULL. You can see the NULL columns in Figure 17-6.

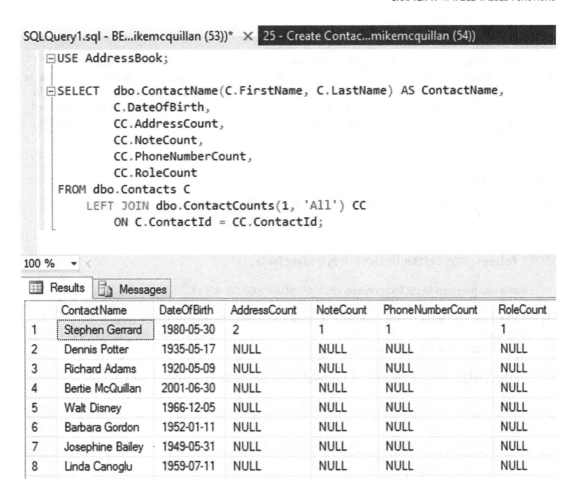

Figure 17-6. Using the function with a LEFT JOIN (still used badly)

Why can't we join, passing the ContactId value to the function? The problem is that the results from the Contacts table haven't been generated at the time the ContactCounts function is being returned, so there is no ContactId column available to pass to the function.

Using a join, the Contacts table and the ContactCounts TVF are evaluated at the same time. But to be able to pass the ContactId column to ContactCounts, the Contacts table needs to be evaluated first, so the ContactId is available to be passed to the ContactCounts table. Hard-coding the value of 1 works because no evaluation is required—SQL Server knows that the value of 1 is 1.

SQL Server provides something special that allows us to join tables to TVFs correctly. Say hello to the APPLY operator.

The APPLY Operator

The APPLY operator executes the TVF against each row returned by the principal table in a query. The principal table doesn't have to be a physical table; it could be a query used to return a logical table, a view, or another TVF. For simplicity, we'll carry on using a physical table. The principal table acts as the left table in the query, and the TVF acts as the right table. The rows in the left table are evaluated first, and then applied to the TVF on the right-hand side of the query. Columns from both sides of the query can be combined to produce a result set.

CROSS APPLY

There are two types of APPLY. The CROSS APPLY operator acts like an INNER JOIN. A row is only returned if it exists in both the left- and right-hand sides of a query. A CROSS APPLY doesn't have an ON clause, so a statement using it looks like this:

```
SELECT Columns FROM LeftTable CROSS APPLY RightTable;
```

Here is our previous SELECT statement, changed to use a CROSS APPLY.

```
SELECT dbo.ContactName(C.FirstName, C.LastName) AS ContactName, C.DateOfBirth,
CC.AddressCount, CC.NoteCount, CC.PhoneNumberCount, CC.RoleCount FROM dbo.Contacts C CROSS
APPLY dbo.ContactCounts(C.ContactId, 'All') CC;
```

Run this, and as shown in Figure 17-7, the results we were looking for earlier appear!

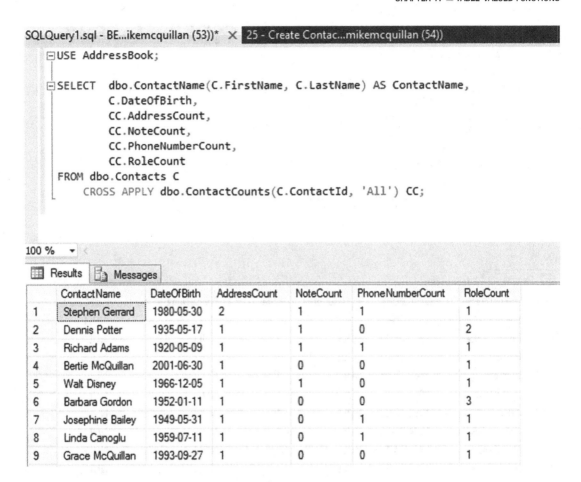

Figure 17-7. *Using the function with CROSS APPLY (successfully!)*

You can use the APPLY operator with anything that returns a result set. You could wrap another SELECT statement in brackets and use that with a CROSS APPLY, for example.

Remember that CROSS APPLY acts as an INNER JOIN, so if we say just return the totals for 'ContactNotes' instead of 'All', this returns 12 results as shown in Figure 17-8, where the original call using 'All' returned 20. This is because several records don't actually have any note records associated with them, so they've been removed from the query. We need some sort of outer join to resolve this problem.

```
SQLQuery1.sql - BE...ikemcquillan (53))*  ×  25 - Create Contac...mikemcquillan (54))
□USE AddressBook;

□SELECT   dbo.ContactName(C.FirstName, C.LastName) AS ContactName,
          C.DateOfBirth,
          CC.AddressCount,
          CC.NoteCount,
          CC.PhoneNumberCount,
          CC.RoleCount
  FROM dbo.Contacts C
      CROSS APPLY dbo.ContactCounts(C.ContactId, 'ContactNotes') CC;
```

100 %   ▾

▦ Results | ▥ Messages

	ContactName	DateOfBirth	AddressCount	NoteCount	PhoneNumberCount	RoleCount
1	Stephen Gerrard	1980-05-30	NULL	1	NULL	NULL
2	Dennis Potter	1935-05-17	NULL	1	NULL	NULL
3	Richard Adams	1920-05-09	NULL	1	NULL	NULL
4	Walt Disney	1966-12-05	NULL	1	NULL	NULL
5	Steve Davis	1957-08-22	NULL	1	NULL	NULL
6	Julius Marx	1990-10-02	NULL	1	NULL	NULL
7	George Formby	1944-05-26	NULL	1	NULL	NULL
8	Alan Partridge	1965-04-14	NULL	1	NULL	NULL
9	Harper Lee	1986-04-28	NULL	1	NULL	NULL
10	Robert Burns	1959-01-25	NULL	1	NULL	NULL
11	Michael Jackson	1967-06-30	NULL	1	NULL	NULL
12	Roald Dahl	1916-09-13	NULL	1	NULL	NULL

Figure 17-8. Using the function for ContactNotes only

OUTER APPLY

Just like CROSS APPLY acts like an INNER JOIN, OUTER APPLY acts like a LEFT OUTER JOIN. OUTER APPLY works in exactly the same manner as CROSS APPLY, except it will return all rows from the table on the left of the query, regardless of whether there are matching rows on the right side.

If we change the query in the previous section to use an OUTER APPLY instead of CROSS APPLY, our result set brings back 20 rows or more (depending upon when you last rebuilt your database). Check out Figure 17-9.

SQLQuery1.sql - BE...ikemcquillan (53))* ✕ 25 - Create Contac...mikemcquillan (54))

```sql
USE AddressBook;

SELECT  dbo.ContactName(C.FirstName, C.LastName) AS ContactName,
        C.DateOfBirth,
        CC.AddressCount,
        CC.NoteCount,
        CC.PhoneNumberCount,
        CC.RoleCount
FROM dbo.Contacts C
    OUTER APPLY dbo.ContactCounts(C.ContactId, 'ContactNotes') CC;
```

100 % ▾

▦ Results | ▣ Messages

	ContactName	DateOfBirth	AddressCount	NoteCount	PhoneNumberCount	RoleCount
1	Stephen Gerrard	1980-05-30	NULL	1	NULL	NULL
2	Dennis Potter	1935-05-17	NULL	1	NULL	NULL
3	Richard Adams	1920-05-09	NULL	1	NULL	NULL
4	Bertie McQuillan	2001-06-30	NULL	NULL	NULL	NULL
5	Walt Disney	1966-12-05	NULL	1	NULL	NULL
6	Barbara Gordon	1952-01-11	NULL	NULL	NULL	NULL
7	Josephine Bailey	1949-05-31	NULL	NULL	NULL	NULL
8	Linda Canoglu	1959-07-11	NULL	NULL	NULL	NULL
9	Grace McQuillan	1993-09-27	NULL	NULL	NULL	NULL
10	Vera Black	1984-08-03	NULL	NULL	NULL	NULL
11	Angelica Jones	1981-02-04	NULL	NULL	NULL	NULL
12	Steve Davis	1957-08-22	NULL	1	NULL	NULL
13	Allison Fisher	1968-02-24	NULL	NULL	NULL	NULL
14	Julius Marx	1990-10-02	NULL	1	NULL	NULL
15	George Formby	1944-05-26	NULL	1	NULL	NULL
16	Alan Partridge	1965-04-14	NULL	1	NULL	NULL
17	Harper Lee	1986-04-28	NULL	1	NULL	NULL
18	Robert Burns	1959-01-25	NULL	1	NULL	NULL
19	Michael Jackson	1967-06-30	NULL	1	NULL	NULL
20	Roald Dahl	1916-09-13	NULL	1	NULL	NULL
21	Laura Robson	1994-01-21	NULL	NULL	NULL	NULL
22	Bryan Ferry	1945-09-26	NULL	NULL	NULL	NULL

Figure 17-9. *Using the function with* OUTER APPLY *(still successfully!)*

Any row that doesn't have a NoteCount now returns a NULL value in that column, but the column itself is returned. You can try this with the other tables. If you use CROSS APPLY, only rows with a record in the particular table will be returned; if you use OUTER APPLY, every row in Contacts will be returned, with a NULL value displayed in the appropriate column when no corresponding row exists.

Performance Issues

APPLY sounds great, and resolves a key issue for us: the ability to join record sets to TVFs. And if it is used correctly, APPLY can be an extremely elegant solution. But like most features in SQL Server, APPLY can drastically affect performance. Think about the function we wrote earlier; it contains four SELECT statements:

- AddressCount

- NoteCount

- PhoneNumberCount

- RoleCount

Now, think about what happens if we CROSS APPLY the ContactCounts function, using the 'All' option.

- All rows from the Contacts table are returned.

- For each row in the Contacts table, the ContactCounts function is executed. This means four SELECT statements are executed for every single row.

- The Contacts table in my database currently contains 22 rows, so that means we execute 22 × 4 SELECT statements = 88 SELECT statements.

- Imagine if the Contacts table contained 10,000 rows. That would be 40,000 SELECT statements executed!

There are better ways to implement the counts function we've seen here, but the solution we've implemented is perfectly valid, especially for the small record sets we're dealing with. We'd probably need to look at a different solution if our Contacts table drastically grew, though.

Summary

This chapter has covered some really interesting ground. Once we'd figured out what a table-valued function is and how they can be used, we took a look at how to utilize them in queries. We now know how to join not only to tables and views, but also to TVFs, using the APPLY operator. The APPLY operator is very powerful and can be used for much more than just TVFs.

We did try to use joins with our TVFs, and found that while this is possible, the values for the parameters we need to pass to our TVF must be available before the TVF is called. For this reason, APPLY is generally used, rather than joins.

We've covered almost all programmatic aspects of T-SQL now, in terms of the objects available to us. We're now going to take a look at the most commonly used programmatic object in T-SQL: stored procedures. "Proceed" to the next chapter!

CHAPTER 18

■ ■ ■

Stored Procedures—Part 1

Stored procedures—or SPs, as some lovingly call them—are likely to become your best friends as you spend more and more time with SQL Server. It is not uncommon to come across databases that contain hundreds of stored procedures—they're just so darned flexible! In this chapter, we'll find out exactly why stored procedures are so useful, and we'll create a couple of SPs of our own.

What Are Stored Procedures, and Why Should I Use Them?

A stored procedure is a repeatable piece of code. You'd be forgiven for thinking, "Hold everything!"—isn't that what a function does? Well yes, it is. But a function is intended to do one simple thing well, like the ContactName function. If you need complexity, stored procedures are the way to go. Functions cannot have side effects; stored procedures have no such limits. In a stored procedure, you can write SELECT statements alongside INSERT, UPDATE, and DELETE statements. You can incorporate business rules, such as preventing inserts if a record doesn't meet certain criteria. Stored procedures really are incredibly flexible. Some great reasons to use them are the following:

- **Performance**: Stored procedures will perform better than having the equivalent code running individually every time. SQL Server stores query plans for stored procedures, allowing it to execute them faster than ad hoc queries.

- **Encapsulation**: You can embed as much code and logic into a stored procedure as you want. All of this is hidden from the developer calling the stored procedure—they just need to know what parameters they need to pass to execute the stored procedure.

- **Improve maintainability**: You can easily change how a stored procedure works internally, without affecting any applications calling it. You just need to make sure you don't modify the inputs and outputs.

- **Multiple output options**: Stored procedures can return one or more record sets, as well as values in output parameters.

- Stored procedures can call other stored procedures.

- Stored procedures can call scalar and table-valued functions.

- You can create any type of procedure you can think of—for searching, inserting, updating, deleting. . . .

- Almost any valid piece of T-SQL can be called within a stored procedure (and for those that can't, there is normally a workaround). The only things you can't call directly are some CREATE or ALTER statements, such as CREATE PROCEDURE or ALTER PROCEDURE.

Speaking of which. . . .

CREATE PROCEDURE and ALTER PROCEDURE

To create a stored procedure, you use the CREATE PROCEDURE command. The full definition of this statement can be found at https://msdn.microsoft.com/en-us/library/ms187926.aspx, but the basic form you'll use most of the time is:

```
CREATE PROCEDURE SchemaName.ProcedureName
(
Parameters (optional)
)
AS
BEGIN

Do something...

END;
```

ALTER PROCEDURE is exactly the same, just replacing CREATE with ALTER. Altering a procedure maintains permissions allocated to the procedure. When altering a procedure, the entire definition must be provided. You cannot alter a small piece of a procedure; it is all or nothing.

DROP PROCEDURE

To remove a procedure from your database, call DROP PROCEDURE. This is as simple as providing a procedure name:

```
DROP PROCEDURE SchemaName.ProcedureName;
```

SSMS and Stored Procedures

Because of the nature of stored procedures (they contain customized T-SQL code that you write), you can't really create them through SSMS. I find it much easier to open a New Query Window and begin typing the stored procedure definition. But if you wish, you can create the outline of a stored procedure from SSMS, and you can certainly manage your stored procedures via SSMS.

Go ahead and open SSMS. Then go to hte Object Explorer and expand **Databases ➤ AddressBook ➤ Programmability ➤ Stored Procedures**. If you try to expand **Stored Procedures** it will be empty except for a **System Stored Procedures** item. Any stored procedures you create will appear under the **Stored Procedures** node. Once you have a stored procedure there, you can right-click it (see Figure 18-1), which will give you the ability to modify, execute, or script the stored procedure.

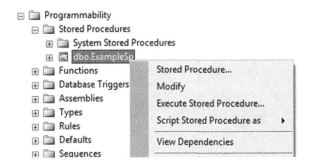

Figure 18-1. Right-clicking on a stored procedure in SSMS

To create a new stored procedure from SSMS, right-click the **Stored Procedures** node, and choose the **Stored Procedure** option (this also appears when you right-click an existing procedure, as in Figure 18-1). A New Query Window opens (Figure 18-2), containing the basic outline of a stored procedure.

Figure 18-2. Stored procedure outline via SSMS

We won't be using the SSMS features for our stored procedures—we'll do everything manually. In the long run you'll probably find this makes more sense, but if you really, *really* want to use SSMS to create your procedure outlines, I won't stand in your way.

A First Stored Procedure

To begin our stored procedure journey, we'll create a simple stored procedure to insert a new contact. The procedure body will use code we first met in Chapter 15 when we were investigating how transactions work. We begin by declaring the procedure's name and parameters.

```
USE AddressBook;

GO

CREATE PROCEDURE dbo.InsertContact
(
@FirstName VARCHAR(40),
@LastName VARCHAR(40),
@DateOfBirth DATE,
@AllowContactByPhone BIT
)
```

There is a GO statement between the USE statement and the CREATE PROCEDURE statement. Much like CREATE FUNCTION, CREATE PROCEDURE must be the first statement in a batch.

We've declared a procedure called InsertContact, which exists within the dbo schema. It accepts four parameters, each of which corresponds to a matching column in the Contacts table.

With the procedure declared, we move on to the body of the procedure. All we want to do is insert a new record into the Contacts table. We wrap up the INSERT INTO statement in a transaction.

```
USE AddressBook;

GO

CREATE PROCEDURE dbo.InsertContact
(
@FirstName VARCHAR(40),
@LastName VARCHAR(40),
@DateOfBirth DATE,
@AllowContactByPhone BIT
)
AS
BEGIN

BEGIN TRANSACTION;

INSERT INTO dbo.Contacts(FirstName, LastName, DateOfBirth, AllowContactByPhone) VALUES (@
FirstName, @LastName, @DateOfBirth, @AllowContactByPhone);

COMMIT TRANSACTION;

END;

GO
```

This is a very simple stored procedure—so simple, we haven't even added the insert into ContactVerificationDetails as we implemented in Chapter 15. This is left as an exercise for the reader to perform, which can be found in Appendix D.

Press F5 to run this code, and the stored procedure will be created. Now we can try to use it.

Executing a Stored Procedure

Open a New Query Window. The EXECUTE statement, or EXEC for short, is used to execute a stored procedure. I usually use EXEC, just because it is less typing. To call our InsertContact procedure, you would type:

```
EXEC dbo.InsertContact;
```

But if you run this, it fails:

```
Msg 201, Level 16, State 4, Procedure InsertContact, Line 0
Procedure or function 'InsertContact' expects parameter '@FirstName', which was not
supplied.
```

D'oh! We didn't provide the parameters. There are two ways you can pass parameters to a stored procedure. Here's the lazy way:

```
EXEC dbo.InsertContact 'Joe', 'Beasley', '1959-05-09', 1;
```

If you run this, it will work, and running the SELECT statement in Figure 18-3 against the Contacts table will show you the record was successfully inserted.

```
SQLQuery2.sql - BE...ikemcquillan (53))*  ×  SQLQuery1.sql - BE...ikemcquillan (52))*
  ⊟USE AddressBook;

    EXEC dbo.InsertContact 'Joe', 'Beasley', '1959-05-09', 1;

    SELECT TOP (5) * FROM dbo.Contacts ORDER BY ContactId DESC;

100 %   ▼
⊞ Results | 🖹 Messages
```

	ContactId	FirstName	LastName	DateOfBirth	AllowContactByPhone	CreatedDate
1	25	Joe	Beasley	1959-05-09	1	2015-05-16 01:19:23.377
2	24	Bryan	Ferry	1945-09-26	0	2015-05-15 22:10:20.207
3	22	Laura	Robson	1994-01-21	1	2015-05-15 22:00:25.100
4	20	Roald	Dahl	1916-09-13	0	2015-05-15 21:46:58.600
5	19	Michael	Jackson	1967-06-30	0	2015-05-15 21:46:58.493

Figure 18-3. *Proving the stored procedure works after running it*

We can see the stored procedure is working—it is inserting records. But it's difficult to tell which parameter each value is being assigned to. To make things easier, we can provide the parameter names—this is called *using named parameters*.

```
EXEC dbo.InsertContact
@FirstName = 'Michael',
@LastName = 'Stipe',
@DateOfBirth = '1960-01-04',
@AllowContactByPhone = 0;
```

This is much easier to understand. You cannot mix and match named parameters—if you use named parameters, you must name every parameter (unless it has a default value, which we are coming to). One benefit of named parameters is you can change the order in which they are specified—you cannot do this if you don't name the parameters:

```
EXEC dbo.InsertContact
@AllowContactByPhone = 0,
@LastName = 'Stipe',
@FirstName = 'Michael',
@DateOfBirth = '1960-01-04';
```

No matter which order you specify the parameters, as long as they are named, the call will work. Execute the preceding statement—this time without the SELECT statement—and you'll be told one row was inserted (see Figure 18-4).

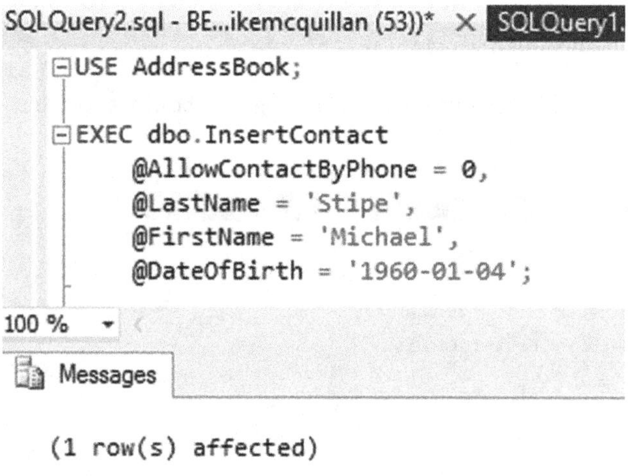

```
SQLQuery2.sql - BE...ikemcquillan (53))*  ×  SQLQuery1.
⊟USE AddressBook;

⊟EXEC dbo.InsertContact
      @AllowContactByPhone = 0,
      @LastName = 'Stipe',
      @FirstName = 'Michael',
      @DateOfBirth = '1960-01-04';
```

100 %   ▼ ‹

🔲 Messages

```
(1 row(s) affected)
```

Figure 18-4. *Running the stored procedure with row count returned*

That **(1 row(s) affected)** message in Figure 18-4 is actually a bad thing—some of the time.

SET NOCOUNT ON and OFF

Quite often, especially when you are developing, you do want to see how many rows have been affected by your statements. But once development is over and you are releasing your code, it is advisable to turn these informational messages off. Doing so improves performance, as SQL Server doesn't need to send the counts affected messages back over the network.

To turn the messages off, turn SET NOCOUNT to ON. It is good practice to turn this setting back OFF at the end of your procedures. Change the InsertContact stored procedure so it includes SET NOCOUNT ON and SET NOCOUNT OFF. We'll also add a check at the top of the script to DROP the procedure if it already exists. You guessed it, we'll query sys.procedures to do this.

```
USE AddressBook;

IF EXISTS (SELECT 1 FROM sys.procedures WHERE [name] = 'InsertContact')
BEGIN
DROP PROCEDURE dbo.InsertContact;
END;

GO

CREATE PROCEDURE dbo.InsertContact
(
@FirstName VARCHAR(40),
@LastName VARCHAR(40),
@DateOfBirth DATE,
@AllowContactByPhone BIT
)
AS
BEGIN

SET NOCOUNT ON;

BEGIN TRANSACTION;

INSERT INTO dbo.Contacts(FirstName, LastName, DateOfBirth, AllowContactByPhone) VALUES (@
FirstName, @LastName, @DateOfBirth, @AllowContactByPhone);

COMMIT TRANSACTION;

SET NOCOUNT OFF;

END;

GO
```

Save this script as c:\temp\sqlbasics\apply\27 - Create InsertContact Stored Procedure.sql.
Add it to 00 - Apply.sql while we're about it. I know we haven't created script 26, but all will be revealed in
the next chapter! Here is the code for the apply script:

```
:setvar currentFile "27 - Create InsertContact Stored Procedure.sql"
PRINT 'Executing $(path)$(currentFile)';
:r $(path)$(currentFile)
```

Run script 27, and then execute the stored procedure again to add another contact. This time you'll just
see the message **Command(s) completed successfully** (Figure 18-5).

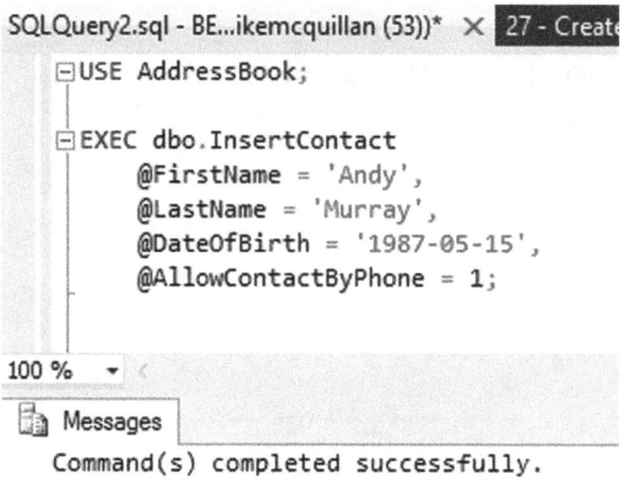

```
SQLQuery2.sql - BE...ikemcquillan (53))*  ×   27 - Create

    USE AddressBook;

    EXEC dbo.InsertContact
        @FirstName = 'Andy',
        @LastName = 'Murray',
        @DateOfBirth = '1987-05-15',
        @AllowContactByPhone = 1;
```

100 % ▼

🖳 Messages
    Command(s) completed successfully.

Figure 18-5. *Running the stored procedure with SET NOCOUNT ON*

For stored procedures that execute multiple DML statements, turning SET NOCOUNT ON can really help with performance. It's not a massive gain, but every little helps.

Schema Names

You should always use schema names when calling stored procedures (which is what we've been doing so far). This gives a slight performance improvement as SQL Server doesn't need to figure out which schema an object exists in—it can go straight to the object. This also prevents possible future problems if an object with the same name is created in a different schema. Do anything you can to extract a little more performance—especially the simple things!

Returning Data from Stored Procedures

We can enhance our stored procedure to return data. If you think about it, what do we need to return once we've inserted a new record into Contacts? You win $64,000 if you said the ContactId. In most systems, you will want the ID of the record you inserted to be returned to you, so you can then process any updates or deletes using the ID (in general, you should always return the primary key value, which is usually the ID). There are a couple of ways we can return this value. To start with, we'll use the method we've already seen in earlier chapters—assigning the value to a variable using SCOPE_IDENTITY(), then running a SELECT to return that variable's value. Amend the stored procedure to match this updated listing. Don't forget to save your changes.

```
USE AddressBook;

IF EXISTS (SELECT 1 FROM sys.procedures WHERE [name] = 'InsertContact')
BEGIN
DROP PROCEDURE dbo.InsertContact;
END;
```

```
GO

CREATE PROCEDURE dbo.InsertContact
(
@FirstName VARCHAR(40),
@LastName VARCHAR(40),
@DateOfBirth DATE,
@AllowContactByPhone BIT
)
AS
BEGIN

SET NOCOUNT ON;

DECLARE @ContactId INT;

BEGIN TRANSACTION;

INSERT INTO dbo.Contacts (FirstName, LastName, DateOfBirth, AllowContactByPhone) VALUES
(@FirstName, @LastName, @DateOfBirth, @AllowContactByPhone);

SELECT @ContactId = SCOPE_IDENTITY();

COMMIT TRANSACTION;

SELECT @ContactId AS ContactId;

SET NOCOUNT OFF;

END;

GO
```

The stored procedure now has a @ContactId variable, which is assigned the value of SCOPE_IDENTITY() after the INSERT INTO occurs. It's interesting to see that the SCOPE_IDENTITY() call happens within the transaction, but the new SELECT statement that returns it happens outside the transaction. Remember what we were saying earlier about transactions—keep them as short as possible. Here, it makes a lot of sense to perform the SCOPE_IDENTITY() assignment within the transaction, as we've just performed the insert. But we can wait until the transaction has completed before returning the record set, otherwise the record set will return before the transaction commits.

If you run this code and then return to the window holding your EXEC call, executing the stored procedure again now looks a little more interesting, as Figure 18-6 shows.

```
SQLQuery2.sql - BE...ikemcquillan (53))*  ×   27 - Create Ins
    USE AddressBook;

    EXEC dbo.InsertContact
        @FirstName = 'Willie',
        @LastName = 'Thorne',
        @DateOfBirth = '1954-03-04',
        @AllowContactByPhone = 0;

100 %   ▼  <
    Results    Messages
         ContactId
    1      28
```

Figure 18-6. *Amended procedure returning the new* ContactId

This is very useful. Imagine a web site is calling our stored procedure. The ContactId is returned in a record set, and the web site can store this in a variable for future use.

It's possible to return multiple record sets from a stored procedure; every SELECT you write within a stored procedure that returns a record set will indeed return the record set when the stored procedure is called.

The SELECT output is really useful if you want a front-end system of some type to call this stored procedure. It isn't so useful if you want to use the ContactId from within a different SQL Server script (it can be done without too much difficulty, but it involves a temp table and is messy). Never fear, there is an easier way. We'll see this during our discussion of parameters.

Parameters

Parameters allow you to pass data into a stored procedure, but they also offer ways of returning data from a stored procedure. There are a couple of additional properties you can add to parameters, too, all of which helps make your code more robust.

Input Parameters

We've already met input parameters. The four parameters our current InsertContact stored procedure is using are all input parameters. You use an input parameter to pass values into the stored procedure that you want to use, such as the values we pass in so we can insert a new contact.

Default Parameter Values

It is possible to assign default values to parameters. This can be very useful, as it means you don't have to specify the variable name when calling the stored procedure. You can also add checks into your code to see if a variable has the default value, and if it does you may choose to perform a different type of action. We can modify our stored procedure to set a default value for the @AllowContactByPhone parameter.

```
CREATE PROCEDURE dbo.InsertContact
(
@FirstName VARCHAR(40),
@LastName  VARCHAR(40),
@DateOfBirth DATE,
@AllowContactByPhone    BIT = 0
)
```

If you save and run this code, you can now execute the stored procedure without specifying the @ AllowContactByPhone parameter (obviously, if you want to set the AllowContactByPhone column to 1, you need to specify the parameter).

The first result set in Figure 18-7 shows ContactId 29. If you look at the second result set, which comes from the SELECT statement at the bottom of the query editor, you can see AllowContactByPhone has been set to 0 for ContactId 29.

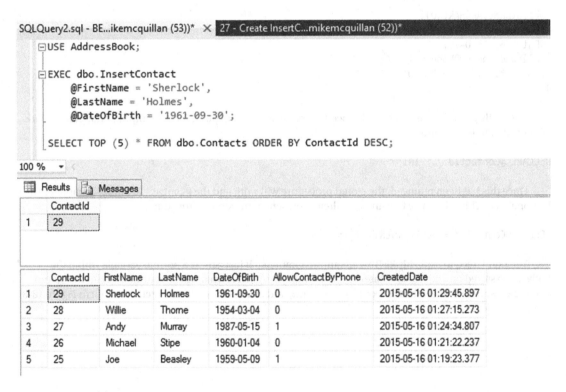

Figure 18-7. *Running the procedure without optional parameter value*

Output Parameters

Input parameters are what you normally use when building stored procedures, but it is common to come across stored procedures with output parameters, too. Output parameters give you a different way to return data from a stored procedure; they work similarly to a scalar function, in that the parameter holds an output value. They are more powerful than functions, though, as you can return multiple output parameters from a single stored procedure. If you don't want to return a result set from a stored procedure but you do need to return some values, output parameters are the only other way you can do it.

To specify an output parameter, add the OUTPUT keyword after the parameter declaration. We can change our stored procedure to pass a @ContactId output parameter into the procedure. This line would look like:

```
@ContactId INT OUTPUT
```

You can even specify a default value for an output parameter, meaning you don't have to pass it in. The default value needs to be entered before the OUTPUT keyword:

```
@ContactId INT = 0 OUTPUT
```

The procedure header should now read:

```
CREATE PROCEDURE dbo.InsertContact
(
 @FirstNameVARCHAR(40),
 @LastNameVARCHAR(40),
 @DateOfBirth DATE,
 @AllowContactByPhone BIT = 0,
 @ContactId INT = 0 OUTPUT
)
```

The really great thing is our stored procedure has everything in place for this output parameter to work. We need to remove the line:

```
DECLARE @ContactId     INT;
```

Once this has been removed, the stored procedure will work and the @ContactId output parameter will be populated! This is because this line was already present in the stored procedure:

```
SELECT @ContactId = SCOPE_IDENTITY();
```

You don't need to explicitly RETURN an output parameter. It just acts as a normal variable within the body of the stored procedure, so whatever the last value assigned is what will be returned within the output parameter. Run this code, return to your EXEC window, and change the code to match the script in Figure 18-8.

```
SQLQuery2.sql - BE...ikemcquillan (53))*  ×   27 - Create InsertC...mikemcquillan (52))*

USE AddressBook;

DECLARE @ContactIdOUT   INT;

EXEC dbo.InsertContact
    @FirstName = 'Julie',
    @LastName = 'Nimmo',
    @DateOfBirth = '1972-05-29',
    @ContactId = @ContactIdOUT OUTPUT;

SELECT @ContactIdOUT AS ContactIdFromOutputVariable;
```

100 %   ▼

	ContactId
1	30

	ContactIdFromOutputVariable
1	30

Figure 18-8. *Executing the procedure and returning an output parameter*

We've declared a variable called @ContactIdOUT, and it is this variable that is passed into the output parameter. The OUT is a convention we use to show that the variable is to be used for output parameter purposes. The OUTPUT keyword has been specified, so not only do we have to declare the OUTPUT keyword in the stored procedure; we also have to declare it when we call the stored procedure.

After the EXEC call, we run a SELECT statement, which outputs the contents of the @ContactIdOUT variable. When this has been executed, there are two result sets. Why is this?

The first result set comes from the stored procedure—it is the SELECT statement we added to the procedure earlier to return the newly inserted ContactId. The second SELECT statement occurs outside of the stored procedure. We have added it to demonstrate that the @ContactIdOUT parameter has had the inserted ContactId value assigned to it.

The fascinating thing here is that our stored procedure now has two ways of returning the inserted ContactId. It always returns the result set via the SELECT, but we now have the further option of returning it via an output parameter. Developers do not need to use the output parameter as it is optional, but it is there should it be needed.

Output parameters are not used very often, but they give you another one of those extra boosts that many developers I meet seem to be completely unaware of. They are especially useful if you are writing a stored procedure that will be called from other stored procedures.

READONLY Parameters

READONLY applies to table-valued parameters. Yes, you can pass in an entire table to a stored procedure! When you do this, you must specify the READONLY keyword on the parameter. Table-valued parameters cannot be modified in the procedure body; hence the need to mark them with READONLY. You'll use this parameter type in the next chapter.

Basic Debugging with PRINT

You can add PRINT statements to your stored procedures so you can see what is going on. There are far more sophisticated ways of debugging stored procedures, but PRINT offers a quick way to investigate issues (just don't forget to take the PRINT statements out when you're done!). PRINT statements are outputted to the SQL Server console when executed within Management Studio. We'll change our stored procedure to accept a new, optional parameter, @Note. This will allow us to specify a note that can be inserted into the ContactNotes table, presuming a value is provided. We'll add a PRINT statement or two so the stored procedure reports back what is going on.

```
CREATE PROCEDURE dbo.InsertContact
(
@FirstName VARCHAR(40),
@LastName VARCHAR(40),
@DateOfBirth DATE,
@AllowContactByPhone BIT = 0,
@Note VARCHAR(200) = NULL,
@ContactId INT = 0 OUTPUT
)
AS
BEGIN

SET NOCOUNT ON;

BEGIN TRANSACTION;

INSERT INTO dbo.Contacts (FirstName, LastName, DateOfBirth, AllowContactByPhone) VALUES (@
FirstName, @LastName, @DateOfBirth, @AllowContactByPhone);

SELECT @ContactId = SCOPE_IDENTITY();

PRINT 'Contact ID inserted: ' + CONVERT(VARCHAR(20), @ContactId);

-- Insert a note if provided
IF (COALESCE(@Note, '') != '')
BEGIN
INSERT INTO dbo.ContactNotes (ContactId, Notes) VALUES (@ContactId, @Note);

PRINT 'Note inserted';
END

COMMIT TRANSACTION;

SELECT @ContactId AS ContactId;

SET NOCOUNT OFF;

END;
```

The changes we've made are not massive. We have added a new parameter, @Note. We have added this above the output parameter @ContactId. There was no need to do this, other than to follow a general convention; it is very common to see stored procedures with all input parameters declared first, followed by the output parameters.

We've added a PRINT statement to display the generated ContactId. After that, there is a block of new code. This starts by checking if the @Note variable contains a valid value; if it does, a new record is inserted into ContactNotes, using the @ContactId variable to ensure the note is linked to the correct contact when it is inserted. We also print a message to state a note was added. Run and save this code (in script 27), and then execute the stored procedure, without adding the @Note parameter. The script to execute is shown in Figure 18-9.

Once you have run this, click the **Messages** tab to view the output. Our first PRINT statement should be displayed.

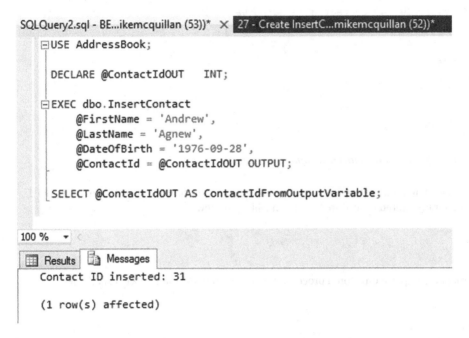

Figure 18-9. *Running the procedure with PRINT statements*

The **(1 row(s) affected)** message doesn't come from the stored procedure—it is generated by the SELECT @ContactIdOUT line. All looking good; let's add another contact, this time passing the @Note parameter (Figure 18-10 has the details).

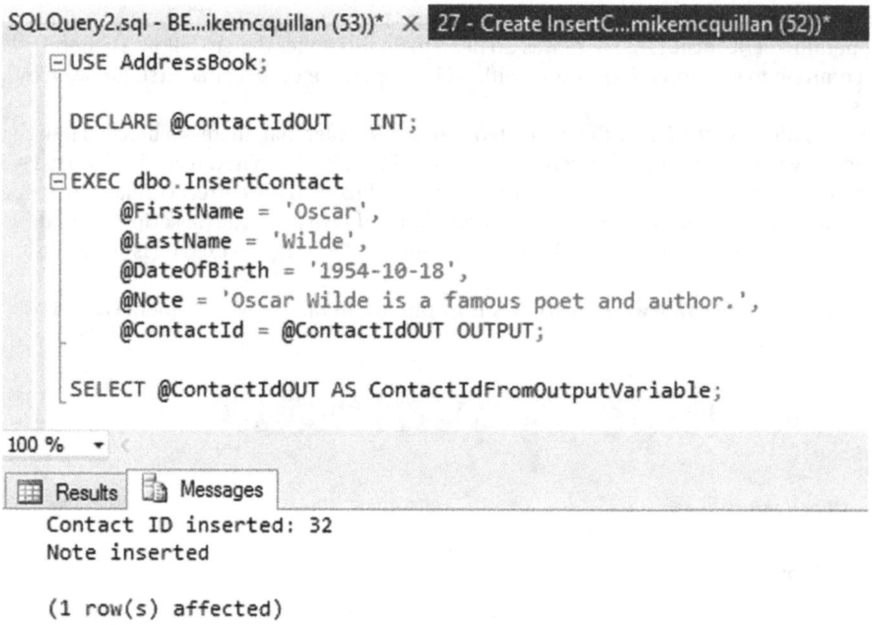

```
SQLQuery2.sql - BE...ikemcquillan (53))*  ×   27 - Create InsertC...mikemcquillan (52))*

  USE AddressBook;

   DECLARE @ContactIdOUT    INT;

  EXEC dbo.InsertContact
       @FirstName = 'Oscar',
       @LastName = 'Wilde',
       @DateOfBirth = '1954-10-18',
       @Note = 'Oscar Wilde is a famous poet and author.',
       @ContactId = @ContactIdOUT OUTPUT;

   SELECT @ContactIdOUT AS ContactIdFromOutputVariable;

100 %   ▾
  ▦ Results  ▤ Messages
    Contact ID inserted: 32
    Note inserted

    (1 row(s) affected)
```

Figure 18-10. *Running the procedure with PRINT and a note added*

And now our PRINT statements tell us that not only did we insert ContactId 32, we also added a note. I think that will do for our first stored procedure (at least, it will do for now!).

Rollback

We must create a rollback script for our stored procedure. This just contains the IF EXISTS...DROP PROCEDURE check.

```
USE AddressBook;

IF EXISTS (SELECT 1 FROM sys.procedures WHERE [name] = 'InsertContact')
BEGIN
DROP PROCEDURE dbo.InsertContact;
END;

GO
```

Save this as c:\temp\sqlbasics\rollback\27 - Create InsertContact Stored Procedure Rollback.sql and add it to 00 - Rollback.sql:

```
:setvar currentFile "27 - Create InsertContact Stored Procedure Rollback.sql"
PRINT 'Executing $(path)$(currentFile)';
:r $(path)$(currentFile)
```

Summary

We have a pretty robust stored procedure here, but we're far from done. This chapter has given us a solid introduction to stored procedures, and we've seen the various ways we can pass data into stored procedures, and how can we return data from them.

We're going to continue enhancing this stored procedure in the next chapter, so mosey on over, pardner!

■ ■ ■

CHAPTER 19

Stored Procedures—Part 2

The last chapter taught you pretty much all you need to know to start creating stored procedures. We'll enhance that knowledge in this chapter by introducing user-defined data types (UDT for short) and taking a detailed look at set-based logic. It's one of the most important things you need to understand as a database developer, and once you understand it your database development skills will accelerate—fast!

Enhancing the InsertContact Stored Procedure

The InsertContact stored procedure we created in the last chapter is pretty solid now. Not only does it create a contact and return the ID for that contact (in two different ways), but it also adds an optional note. Hang on a moment, though. The ContactNotes table is a child table of Contacts. This means we can add multiple notes for a contact. But our stored procedure is limiting us to adding one note when we create a new contact record. Can we change this situation? You bet your bottom dollar we can!

User-Defined Types

INT, VARCHAR, DATE, and BIT are all examples of the data types built into SQL Server. But it's also possible to create your own data types, too, building on top of the standard types.

Why Use Them?

For most purposes, UDTs are not the best way to go. Say you want to store a percentage. Yes, you could define your own PERCENTAGE data type. But this is adding unnecessary complexity to your database and application, especially when you consider SQL Server already provides a host of data types that could store a percentage, like floats and decimals. I find the power of UDTs really comes to the fore when I want to pass multiple values of the same type into a stored procedure.

Our InsertContact stored procedure can currently insert one note via the @Note parameter. We can expand that parameter so it can pass in multiple notes, all of which we can then insert into the ContactNotes table. Sounds exciting!

Creating a UDT

To create a UDT, call the CREATE TYPE command. There is no corresponding ALTER TYPE command—if you want to modify the type you need to drop it and recreate it. This can become difficult when the type is in use, so you really do need to make sure the type is correct before pushing it into general use.

337

The full definition for CREATE TYPE can be found at https://msdn.microsoft.com/en-us/library/ms175007.aspx.

A UDT can be one of two things: either an alias to an existing data type (much like our PERCENTAGE example, which could be an alias of DECIMAL), or a completely new data type consisting of one or more values. We'll create the latter. Our data type will model a ContactNote, and will have two properties.

- ContactId (INT)

- Note (VARCHAR(200))

The only other column in the ContactNotes table is NoteId, but this is auto-generated so there is nothing to gain by adding it to the UDT.

Open a new window and create the UDT. Because our UDT has two properties, we create it as a table.

```
USE AddressBook;

IF EXISTS (SELECT 1 FROM sys.types WHERE [name] = 'ContactNote')
BEGIN
DROP TYPE dbo.ContactNote;
END

CREATE TYPE dbo.ContactNote
AS TABLE
(ContactId INT, Note VARCHAR(200));

GO
```

The script starts with the usual check to see if the object exists. We are querying sys.types in this check. Next is a very standard table declaration—indeed, CREATE TYPE is about the only new thing to us here. It looks very much like a function declaration without parameters (just the brackets are missing). The name of the type is important, and a schema should always be specified. Our type is called ContactNote.

Save this script as c:\temp\sqlbasics\apply\26 - Create ContactNote UDT.sql. I told you we'd create script 26! Our stored procedure, once changed, will be reliant on the ContactNote UDT, so it needs to exist before the stored procedure is created. If we run all of our scripts from the 00 - Apply.sql script, it's important that the UDT script run before the stored procedure script.

Once you've saved the script, you can add it to 00 - Apply.sql, above script 27. Run script 26 to create the type. You can view the UDT in SSMS, under **Programmability ➤ Types** (Figure 19-1).

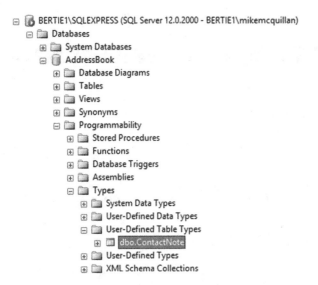

Figure 19-1. *Viewing custom user-defined table types*

Rolling Back the UDT

Before we start using the UDT, create a rollback script for it called c:\temp\sqlbasics\rollback\26 - Create ContactNote UDT Rollback.sql. Here's the code; make sure you add it to 00 - Rollback.sql in the correct place (just below script 27).

```
USE AddressBook;

IF EXISTS (SELECT 1 FROM sys.types WHERE [name] = 'ContactNote')
BEGIN
DROP TYPE dbo.ContactNote;
END;

GO
```

Using the UDT

Use the UDT like you do any other data type. Try running this sample script:

```
USE AddressBook;

DECLARE @IntValue INT, @VarcharValue VARCHAR(10), @ContactNoteValue CONTACTNOTE;

SELECT @IntValue = 1, @VarcharValue = 'Hello';

INSERT INTO @ContactNoteValue (ContactId, Note) VALUES (@IntValue, @VarcharValue);

SELECT * FROM @ContactNoteValue;
```

This yields a single row from the SELECT statement, which is shown in Figure 19-2.

Figure 19-2. *Sample script using the* ContactNote *UDT*

The important thing to take away is the CONTACTNOTE data type is nothing more than a table, and can be used exactly like any other table. This means we can declare a table, populate it, and then pass the populated table to the InsertContact stored procedure.

Adding a Custom Type to a Stored Procedure

Adding the type to the stored procedure is easy. We just need to replace the @Note parameter with a @Notes parameter of type ContactNote. The complication comes with adding code to insert multiple records into the ContactNotes table. Open up apply script 27 and edit the procedure so it matches the following code. This is the first attempt at rewriting the procedure.

```
USE AddressBook;

IF EXISTS (SELECT 1 FROM sys.procedures WHERE [name] = 'InsertContact')
BEGIN
DROP PROCEDURE dbo.InsertContact;
END;

GO

CREATE PROCEDURE dbo.InsertContact
(
@FirstName VARCHAR(40),
@LastName VARCHAR(40),
@DateOfBirth DATE,
@AllowContactByPhone BIT = 0,
```

```
@Notes CONTACTNOTE READONLY,
@ContactId INT = 0 OUTPUT
)
AS
BEGIN

SET NOCOUNT ON;

-- Add variables to support note processing
DECLARE @TempNotes TABLE (NoteId INT IDENTITY(1,1), Note VARCHAR(200));
DECLARE @RecordCount INT, @LoopCounter INT, @NoteId INT;

-- Copy the @Notes table, which is readonly, to a table variable so we can
-- modify the data
INSERT INTO @TempNotes (Note) SELECT Note FROM @Notes;

-- Set defaults for the loop around the notes
SELECT @RecordCount = COUNT(1), @LoopCounter = 0 FROM @TempNotes;

-- Remove any notes that are empty
DELETE FROM @TempNotes WHERE LTRIM(RTRIM(COALESCE(Note, ''))) = '';

BEGIN TRANSACTION;

INSERT INTO dbo.Contacts(FirstName, LastName, DateOfBirth, AllowContactByPhone)
VALUES (@FirstName, @LastName, @DateOfBirth, @AllowContactByPhone);

SELECT @ContactId = SCOPE_IDENTITY();

PRINT 'Contact ID inserted: ' + CONVERT(VARCHAR(20), @ContactId);

-- Insert notes using WHILE loop
WHILE (@LoopCounter < @RecordCount)
BEGIN

SELECT TOP (1) @NoteId = NoteId FROM @TempNotes;

INSERT INTO dbo.ContactNotes (ContactId, Notes)
SELECT @ContactId, Note FROM @TempNotes WHERE NoteId = @NoteId;

DELETE @TempNotes WHERE NoteId = @NoteId;

SELECT @LoopCounter = @LoopCounter + 1;
END;

COMMIT TRANSACTION;

SELECT @ContactId AS ContactId;

SET NOCOUNT OFF;

END;

GO
```

Whew, our code has certainly grown! I thought using a UDT was supposed to make things easier! Let's have a walkthrough and figure out what this code is doing. The first change is in the procedure declaration.

```
CREATE PROCEDURE dbo.InsertContact
(
@FirstName VARCHAR(40),
@LastName VARCHAR(40),
@DateOfBirth DATE,
@AllowContactByPhone BIT = 0,
@Notes CONTACTNOTE READONLY,
@ContactId INT = 0 OUTPUT
)
```

We now have a @Notes parameter, of type CONTACTNOTE. The parameter is also marked as READONLY. We briefly met the READONLY keyword in the last chapter. It only applies to table-valued parameters and it has to be specified for a table-based parameter. This is because SQL Server puts a limitation on TVPs—they cannot be modified once they are passed in. You can work around this by copying the parameter contents to a temporary table or a table variable in the stored procedure code (useful if you do need to edit the rows passed in).

We then have a fairly extensive block of code, introduced at the start of the stored procedure above the BEGIN TRANSACTION line. We'll look at the DECLARE statements first. Note the single-line comment above the code:

```
-- Add variables to support note processing
DECLARE @TempNotes TABLE (NoteId INT IDENTITY(1,1), Note VARCHAR(200))
DECLARE @RecordCount INT, @LoopCounter INT, @NoteId INT;
```

This is all preparation work for the loop that will insert the notes. The @TempNotes variable is a table variable into which the contents of the @Notes parameter will be copied. Remember, @Notes is read-only. By copying its contents into @TempNotes we can manipulate the contents. @TempNotes contains a NoteId, which is used to identify the row being processed.

Next, we declare three variables. @RecordCount will hold the number of notes we are going to insert, and @LoopCounter will be used to ensure we don't become stuck in a loop when we are inserting note records. The last variable is @NoteId, used to hold the note in @TempNotes currently being processed.

```
-- Copy the @Notes table, which is readonly, to a table variable so we can
-- modify the data
INSERT INTO @TempNotes (Note) SELECT Note FROM @Notes;

-- Set defaults for the loop around the notes
SELECT @RecordCount = COUNT(1), @LoopCounter = 0 FROM @TempNotes;

-- Remove any notes that are empty
DELETE FROM @TempNotes WHERE LTRIM(RTRIM(COALESCE(Note, ''))) = '';
```

These three lines are straightforward. The first statement copies the notes from the read-only @Notes parameter to the @TempNotes table variable. The number of note records to process is then stored in @RecordCount, and @LoopCounter is set to 0, ready for the loop. Finally, there is a bit of data cleansing—the DELETE statement removes any notes from @TempNotes that don't have a value. At this point, we are ready to begin inserting records.

```
BEGIN TRANSACTION;

INSERT INTO dbo.Contacts(FirstName, LastName, DateOfBirth, AllowContactByPhone) VALUES
(@FirstName, @LastName, @DateOfBirth, @AllowContactByPhone);

SELECT @ContactId = SCOPE_IDENTITY();

PRINT 'Contact ID inserted: ' + CONVERT(VARCHAR(20), @ContactId);

-- Insert notes using WHILE loop
WHILE (@LoopCounter < @RecordCount)
BEGIN

SELECT TOP (1) @NoteId = NoteId FROM @TempNotes;

INSERT INTO dbo.ContactNotes (ContactId, Notes) SELECT @ContactId, Note FROM @TempNotes
WHERE NoteId = @NoteId;

DELETE @TempNotes WHERE NoteId = @NoteId;

SELECT @LoopCounter = @LoopCounter + 1;
END;

COMMIT TRANSACTION;
```

The transaction has grown from the single statement we first implemented. That statement is still present, and is executed first to insert the contact. The next two lines were also already there. The new stuff starts at the WHILE loop. The WHILE loop in T-SQL executes the same block of code one or more times, until a certain condition is set. The condition in this case is:

```
(@LoopCounter < @RecordCount)
```

@LoopCounter is 0 at the beginning of execution, and if @Notes contained two records, @RecordCount would be 2. So you would have 0 < 2. After the first note is processed, @LoopCounter would be 1. We now have 1 < 2. This still holds, so the second note is processed, and @LoopCounter is set to 2. Now we have 2 < 2. Two cannot be less than 2, so the loop would exit at this point.

INFINITE LOOP WARNING!

It is so easy to create an infinite loop. And I'm not even joking! The preceding example shows @LoopCounter increasing by 1 every time a note is processed. It is incumbent upon you, the developer, to add the line of code that increases the value of @LoopCounter. If you don't add this line your loop will never exit, and bad things will happen—trust me.

Once in the loop, the SELECT TOP (1) statement assigns the first NoteId found to @NoteId. The INSERT INTO statement inserts this record into the ContactNotes table. We then call a DELETE statement to remove the NoteId from @TempNotes, so on the next pass round we'll pick up a different NoteId (if there are any records left in @TempNotes).

The final SELECT line within the loop is the most important.

```
SELECT @LoopCounter = @LoopCounter + 1;
```

This increases the value of @LoopCounter by 1 for every pass of the loop. Without this line, the loop could never meet its exit condition and would never complete. It would carry on looping around and around, using up precious resources.

INFINITE LOOPS ARE BAD!

I must reiterate—infinite loops are a bad, BAD thing! If your code enters an infinite loop it will never exit; it will just continue looping until the service or system is restarted. It is very easy to accidentally create infinite loops in SQL Server, so be very careful. An infinite loop could ultimately cause your server to crash—a sure way of making yourself unpopular with your team!

Once the loop has completed, we finally commit the transaction. The last few lines of code in the stored procedure are lines we've seen before. We return the generated ContactId value and close off the procedure.

```
SELECT @ContactId AS ContactId;

SET NOCOUNT OFF;

END;
```

Executing the Stored Procedure

With the procedure finished, we're in a position to execute it. Run the CREATE PROCEDURE statement first to ensure the new version of the procedure has been created. Then try this script in a New Query Window:

```
USE AddressBook;

DECLARE @ContactIdOUT INT, @ContactNotes CONTACTNOTE;

INSERT INTO @ContactNotes (ContactId, Note)
VALUES
(NULL, 'Mark Kermode contributes to the BBC Radio 5 film programme'),
(NULL, 'Mark thinks The Exorcist is the best film ever made.');

EXEC dbo.InsertContact
@FirstName = 'Mark',
@LastName = 'Kermode',
@DateOfBirth = '1963-07-02',
@Notes = @ContactNotes,
@ContactId = @ContactIdOUT OUTPUT;

SELECT @ContactIdOUT AS ContactIdFromOutputVariable;

SELECT * FROM dbo.Contacts WHERE ContactId = @ContactIdOUT;
SELECT * FROM dbo.ContactNotes WHERE ContactId = @ContactIdOUT;
```

We've added a variable of type CONTACTNOTE, and we promptly insert two records into this table (we don't know what the ContactId value is for these records, so we set it to NULL). Then we call InsertContact. This call is exactly the same as it was earlier, except we pass @ContactNotes, containing the rows, to the

@Notes parameter. Interestingly, we don't have to specify the READONLY keyword here, unlike OUTPUT, which had to be specified in both the procedure definition and the procedure call.

There are three SELECT statements to finish off. The first was already there and returns the new ContactId. The other two select the new contact's details from the Contacts table and the ContactNotes table, respectively. Run it and take a look at the output (Figure 19-3).

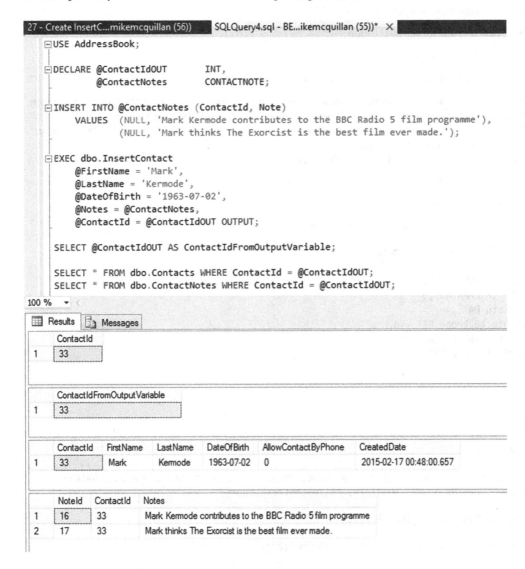

Figure 19-3. Using the amended stored procedure to insert notes

Your ID values may differ from mine, so don't worry if they don't match up with Figure 19-3. Four result sets have been returned. The first comes from the stored procedure, and the other three are the three statements we were just discussing. Everything looks perfect—we've successfully added both notes using the UDT. We declared a variable of type CONTACTNOTE (which is really a table). We popped two records into this table, passed it to the stored procedure, and the code therein did the rest. Go us!

But . . . we said (OK, *I* said) we were going to discuss set-based logic in this chapter. And so we are. Right now.

Set-Based Logic

Our stored procedure is now quite large and uses a lot of custom code to process the notes. Indeed, the notes are being processed one at a time, using the WHILE loop. This is madness! We can eliminate about half of the code in the stored procedure by using set-based logic.

As it stands right now, the procedure does this:

- Sets up code for the WHILE loop

- Inserts the contact

- Executes a WHILE loop to insert note records, one at a time

This is really unpleasant. If a developer makes a bad change to the code, we could be stuck in an infinite loop, or we could accidentally insert the same note two or more times. It's also much slower to use a loop than set-based logic, which apart from performance implications means we are unnecessarily keeping our transaction open longer than we need to.

Set-based logic is the answer! With this, all we will do is:

- Insert the contact

- Insert the notes

Nice and simple. Here is the new version of the stored procedure.

```
CREATE PROCEDURE dbo.InsertContact
(
@FirstName VARCHAR(40),
@LastName VARCHAR(40),
@DateOfBirth DATE,
@AllowContactByPhone BIT = 0,
@Notes CONTACTNOTE READONLY,
@ContactId INT = 0 OUTPUT
)
AS
BEGIN

SET NOCOUNT ON;

BEGIN TRANSACTION;

INSERT INTO dbo.Contacts(FirstName, LastName, DateOfBirth, AllowContactByPhone) VALUES
(@FirstName, @LastName, @DateOfBirth, @AllowContactByPhone);

SELECT @ContactId = SCOPE_IDENTITY();

PRINT 'Contact ID inserted: ' + CONVERT(VARCHAR(20), @ContactId);

INSERT INTO dbo.ContactNotes (ContactId, Notes) SELECT @ContactId, Note FROM @Notes;

COMMIT TRANSACTION;

SELECT @ContactId AS ContactId;

SET NOCOUNT OFF;

END;
```

WOW, that's a lot shorter! Much more accurate, too. There isn't really anything to discuss here, other than the INSERT INTO dbo.ContactNotes. Now it just uses a SELECT FROM @Notes! We were splitting the set into individual records earlier and processing them one by one—this is a cursor-based approach. Now we're harnessing the power of SQL Server by using the set, treating all records as a group and processing them in one batch. Run this code to create the new version of the stored procedure, and save the code as script 27.

Switch to a New Query Window and run the script in Figure 19-4. The outcome it shows is the same as the earlier version we ran; the code is just much more efficient now.

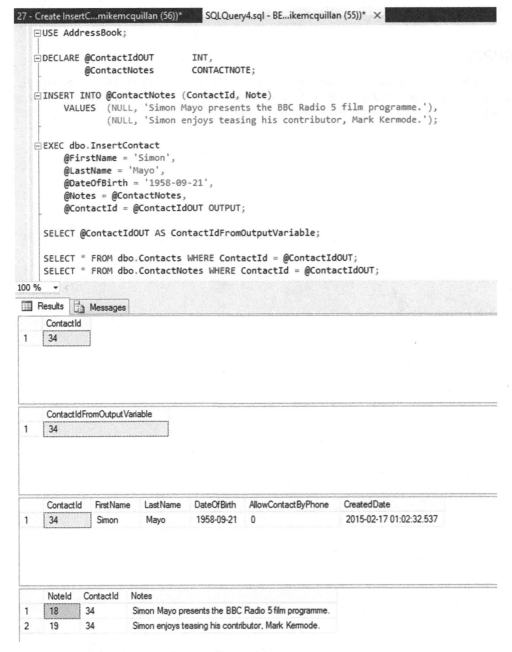

Figure 19-4. Multiple notes with more efficient code

This is great. We've significantly reduced the amount of code we had to write and the end result is still the same (remember, don't worry if your ID values differ from those in Figure 19-4—it just shows that you have been playing around with the contact data).

It's hard to believe, but I've lost count of how many times I've come across the "bad" code presented in the first version of our stored procedure. The response from the developer is always the same—"It works." NO IT DOESN'T! Code like this is a time bomb waiting to go off. Always explore and try to learn the best way of doing things. Don't settle for "That's the way we always do it." Challenge ideas and carry on learning. Do that and you'll have a great career. And maybe one day I'll stop finding WHILE loops replacing set-based logic!

Never forget: always think about the next person.

Summary

Our database is finished! There is nothing else we need to do to it. We've covered most of the things you will need to give you a solid basis with SQL Server. We have one more chapter to go, which will talk about a few things we haven't yet discussed, and give you some pointers for the future.

■ ■ ■

CHAPTER 20

Bits and Pieces

Whew! We've certainly traveled a few roads together. We've taken a very basic—and poor—database structure and transformed it into a robust, well-defined database that could be used as the basis of any contact-based system you care to develop. Now that the database is out of the way, there are a few other things SQL Server offers worth taking a look at. This will be a bit brief, but you can use the overview as a springboard to find out about the things that sound interesting. Okay, let's roll!

Security

A lot of the things we've done throughout this book have required administrator-level permissions—creating a database, for example. When you first installed SQL Server, you added yourself as an administrator. This meant you were added to a security group called *sysadmins*. This is a server security group—anybody who is a member of the *sysadmins* group can perform absolutely any action on the server. This is usually the norm in a development environment, but it certainly is not normal in any other environment! Most of the time, you will have pretty limited permissions, so it's good to know how permissions are broken down.

GRANT, DENY, and REVOKE

It is possible to grant permissions on individual objects and commands using the T-SQL statement GRANT. This statement would grant SELECT permissions on the Contacts table to a user called Dolly:

```
GRANT SELECT ON dbo.Contacts TO Dolly;
```

There are two other commands: DENY and REVOKE. DENY temporarily removes permissions, REVOKE removes them for good.

Built-in Security Roles

To make things easier to manage, SQL Server provides two sets of roles. Users assigned to these roles will be able to perform a certain set of tasks. The first set of roles deals with server permissions, and the second deals with database rights. Users can be members of multiple roles, although some roles incorporate the permissions of others.

Fixed Server Roles

It is possible to create your own server roles; the nine roles provided as part of SQL Server are known as *Fixed Server Roles*.

- sysadmin: This is what we have been using throughout the book. A member of this group can perform any action on the SQL Server.

- serveradmin: Members of this group can shut down the server and modify the server configuration.

- securityadmin: This group is used to manage logins and associated permissions at the server level. If a securityadmin user has access to a database they can also manage database permissions. Users in this group can use the GRANT, DENY, and REVOKE statements we saw earlier.

- processadmin: Do you remember Chapter 15, our transactions chapter, when we blocked our SELECT statement? Members of this group can stop processes, so if you think you need this ability, this is the role to ask for.

- setupadmin: Not a commonly used role. It is possible to link SQL Server to other servers (this includes SQL Servers, Oracle, and other database systems). This role lets you create these linked servers using T-SQL. Strangely, you have to be a member of the sysadmin group to create a linked server using SSMS.

- bulkadmin: If you are a member of this group, you can execute the BULK INSERT statement. You can't do anything else.

- diskadmin: Do you remember when we were discussing database files way back in the early chapters? We talked about the possibility of splitting your database up across multiple files. If you want to do this, you've come to the right group!

- dbcreator: Despite its name, this role does not limit its users to just creating databases—they can also alter and drop databases, and restore them via backups.

- public: All SQL Server logins (logins created using SQL Server security) belong to the public role by default. This is a kind of catchall role. If a user is attempting to access a particular object and no specific permissions have been granted on that object, the permissions the public role has for that object are inherited by the user. You should be careful with this role, and only assign permissions on objects you want everybody to have access to.

Fixed Database Roles

The Fixed Server Roles let you manage server permissions; the Fixed Database Roles manage individual permissions in individual databases. You may be a member of *db_owner* in one database, and a member of *db_datareader* in another. If you wish, you can create your own database roles—these are known as *flexible database roles*.

There are nine Fixed Database Roles:

- db_owner: Equivalent to sysadmin, but at the database level. If you are in this group you can do anything within the database, even drop it.

- db_securityadmin: Members can manage database permissions, including role membership.

- db_accessadmin: Controls who can add or remove access to the database, for all types of user.

- db_backupoperator: Used to perform database backups.

- db_ddladmin: If you are in this role, you can run any Data Definition Language (DDL) command. These are the commands that create, alter, or drop objects, like CREATE TABLE.

- db_datawriter: Gives access to the data in all tables of the database. You can insert, update, and delete data if you are in this role.

- db_datareader: Allows data in any table to be viewed.

- db_denydatawriter: Members of this role cannot modify data in any way.

- db_denydatareader: You guessed it—if you are in this role you won't be able to read any data.

You can grant permissions on individual items, which will override the role's permissions. If explicit SELECT permissions are granted on the Contacts table, it wouldn't matter that you were a member of db_denydatareader. You would be able to view the data in Contacts, but not in any other table.

Schemas

Schemas can be used as a further security mechanism, but they are also really useful for logically grouping database objects. We've mentioned schemas a couple of times throughout this book, so it's worth taking a quick look at them now.

Let's say we've been asked to create some reporting stored procedures in our **AddressBook** database. We've also been told there will be more reporting requests coming our way. We could just write the stored procedure like this:

```
CREATE PROCEDURE dbo.SelectAllContacts
```

This would put the procedure in the default dbo schema. There is no way of knowing if this procedure is used for reporting purposes. We could change its name:

```
CREATE PROCEDURE dbo.ReportSelectAllContacts
```

but this is a bit unwieldy, and relies on developers to follow a convention. The best solution is to create a schema called Reporting, and to then create the procedure within that schema. Schemas can be created via SSMS or T-SQL. To use SSMS, you expand the database name in Object Explorer, then **Security ➤ Schemas**. Right-click **Schemas** and choose the **New Schema** option, shown in Figure 20-1.

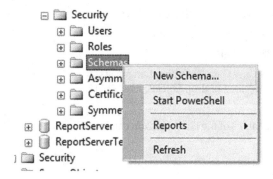

Figure 20-1. *Creating a new schema in SSMS*

To use T-SQL, you simply run this statement:

```
CREATE SCHEMA Reporting;
```

This will create a schema called Reporting. You then create the procedure within that schema by specifying the schema name.

```
CREATE PROCEDURE Reporting.SelectAllContacts
```

When you view the stored procedure in SSMS, you'll see the schema name appears in front of the stored procedure name (Figure 20-2).

```
⊟ 🗀 Programmability
   ⊟ 🗀 Stored Procedures
      ⊞ 🗀 System Stored Procedures
      ⊞ 🖼 dbo.InsertContact
      ⊞ 🖼 Reporting.SelectAllContacts
```

Figure 20-2. *A stored procedure created within a schema*

All the way through this book, we've added checks to our scripts to see if an object exists, and if it does we drop it before re-creating it. If we tried to run this:

```
IF EXISTS(SELECT 1 FROM sys.procedures WHERE [name] = 'SelectAllContacts')
```

or this:

```
IF EXISTS(SELECT 1 FROM sys.procedures WHERE [name] = 'Reporting.SelectAllContacts')
```

The checks would fail. The first check would expect the procedure to exist in dbo, and this would be the only schema it would attempt to check. The second will fail because the name of the object is SelectAllContacts, not Reporting.SelectAllContacts. SelectAllContacts exists within the Reporting schema. To correctly detect the object, we need to use a join.

```
IF EXISTS(SELECT 1 FROM sys.procedures SP
INNER JOIN sys.schemas SC
ON SP.schema_id = SC.schema_id
WHERE SP.[name] = 'SelectAllContacts' AND SC.[name] = 'Reporting')
```

You can join any of the sys tables we've used for these checks to sys.schemas using this technique. Don't forget to check for both the object name and the schema name!

Triggers

Many developers I meet hate triggers with a passion. This is wrong. The trigger is much maligned (unfairly in my opinion). There are times when nothing but a trigger will do. A *trigger* is a piece of code that runs after some action has happened on a table (you can also apply triggers to views, DDL statements, and logon attempts, among others). The triggers that fire on tables are the most commonly used and are known as DML triggers.

A DML trigger is fired whenever an INSERT, UPDATE, or DELETE statement is executed against a table. You can instruct the trigger to perform pretty much any action you wish, even to the point of preventing the action that the original statement executed from happening (e.g., you could run an INSERT and have the trigger remove that INSERT).

Triggers can be great when you need the values of some columns to be automatically calculated, and this cannot be done with a default. Imagine you needed to record a start and end date against each row in a table, to determine when that particular row was active. Whenever a new row is inserted, the following actions must occur:

- The end date of the previously active row must be set to the current date and time

- The start date of the new row must be set to the current date and time

- The end date of the new row must be set to a particular date in the future

If you implement this using a stored procedure, it will work—but every single insert must be processed by the stored procedure. If anybody inserts a row without using the stored procedure, the dates will go out of sync. If a trigger is implemented, the dates will always be calculated, as the trigger can find the previous row, update it, and update the new row, too.

Triggers are a huge subject in their own right and would justify at least one chapter of a book. If you think you need to use triggers in your database, I point you to the CREATE TRIGGER documentation at SQL Server Books Online: https://msdn.microsoft.com/en-GB/library/ms189799.aspx.

Profiler and Extended Events

Sometimes, you need to be able to trace what your SQL Server is doing. A particular SELECT statement may be taking a while to run and you'd like to obtain the statement so you can walk through it and figure out what is going on. Or you may want to see why a particular statement is being blocked. There are two tools that can provide answers to these questions as well as many more. The old way of doing things is to use SQL Server Profiler, which has been with the product for many years. The new way of tracing is to use Extended Events. We'll take a quick look at both options.

SQL Server Profiler

Profiler is a tool provided with SQL Server that allows you to inspect what is happening inside your server in real time. It is a fantastically powerful utility that gives granular access to certain events. A full description of everything Profiler does would require its own book, so we're just going to introduce you to the tool here. More details can be found at https://msdn.microsoft.com/en-GB/library/ms181091.aspx.

Microsoft has announced that Profiler will be deprecated in a future version of SQL Server for everything but SQL Server Analysis Services. As a result you should use Extended Events for all new development work, which offers more facilities than Profiler and is built directly into SSMS. I'm showing Profiler here for completeness.

Starting Profiler

To open Profiler, type **SQL Server 2014 Profiler** into your Start Menu or Start Screen. Once it opens, you'll be confronted with the rather dull gray screen shown in Figure 20-3.

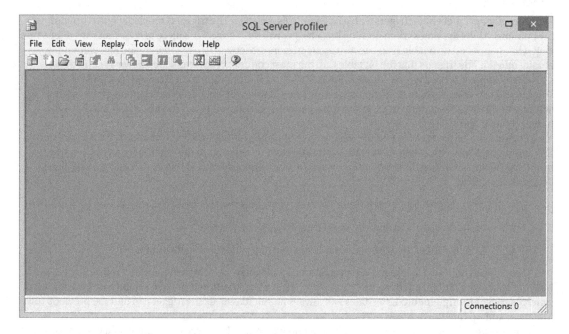

Figure 20-3. *The SQL Server Profiler tool*

To start tracing events in SQL Server, go to the **File** menu and select the **New Trace** option. You'll be prompted to connect to SQL Server—do this, and the **Trace Properties** window will appear (you can see this in Figure 20-4).

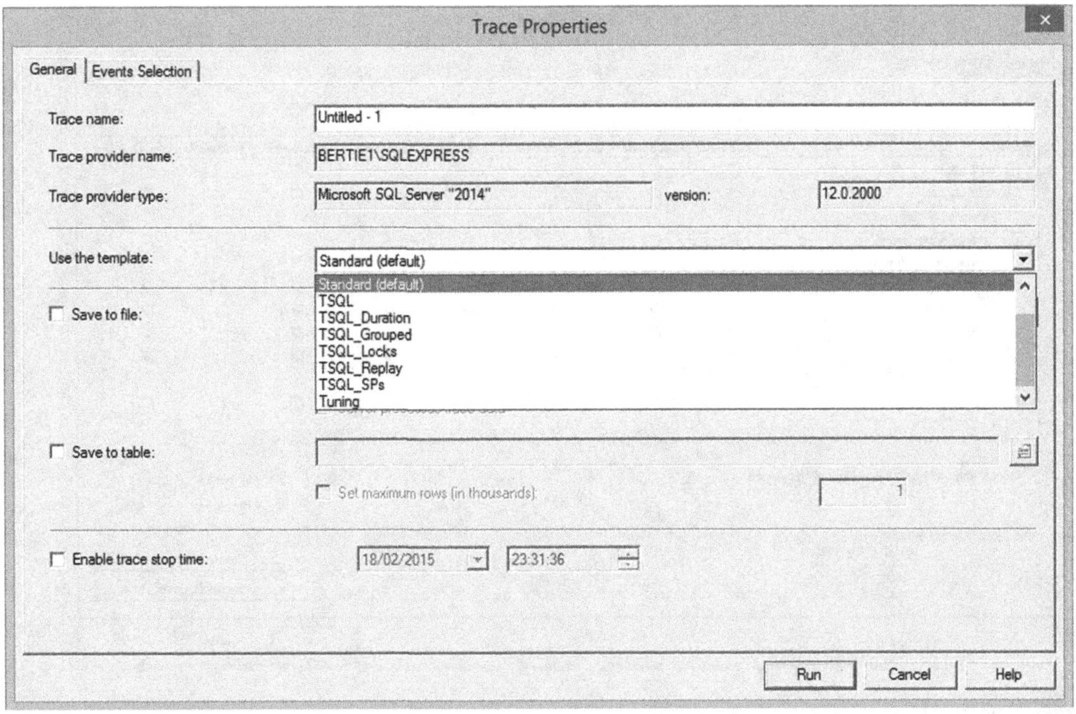

Figure 20-4. *Creating a new trace from a standard template*

TRACE PERMISSIONS

You require a certain set of permissions to be able to run Profiler. You must be a sysadmin or have ALTER TRACE permissions. You should already be a sysadmin, so Profiler should work for you without any issues.

You'll see you can give the trace a name, among other values. The most interesting item on this screen is the **Use the template** drop-down list. This contains the trace templates: prebuilt templates supplied with SQL Server. **TSQL_Locks**, for instance, allows you to monitor for objects that are being locked, while **TSQL_SPs** captures stored procedures as they execute and process. You can create your own templates should you wish.

Select **TSQL_SPs** and then move over to the **Events Selection** tab. Profiler can capture certain events as part of a trace, such as the details issued when the SP starts and the details issued when the SP completes. There are many types of event; to see them all check the **Show all events** box. Each template only captures a certain subset of events.

For our purposes, ensure only the events below **Stored Procedures** have a check mark next to them (just like in Figure 20-5). It is possible to easily overwhelm yourself with information returned from Profiler, so you need to think carefully about the events you want to capture.

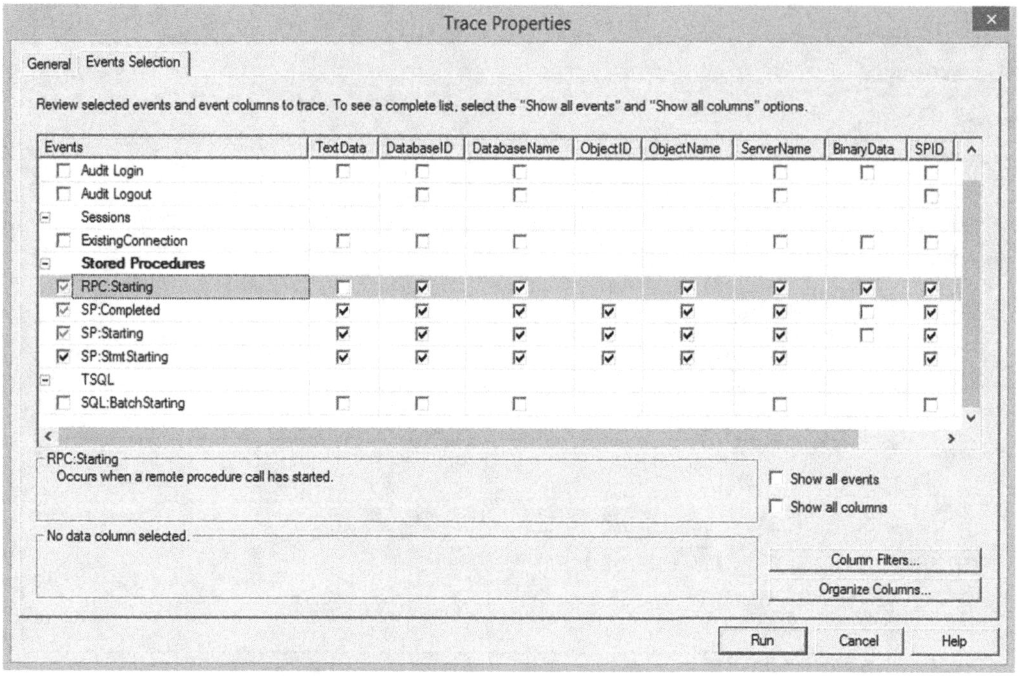

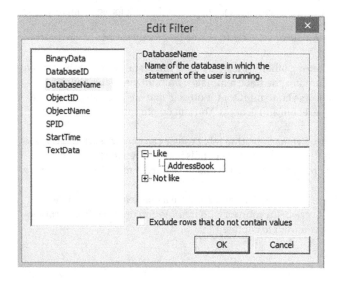

Figure 20-5. *The trace events selection screen*

You can set filters to limit the data you capture. By default, a trace will capture *everything that happens on your server*. This means every event fired by every database on the server will be captured. It is not likely you'll want to do this, as normally you are trying to capture events for a particular database. To add a filter, click the **Column Filters** button. The filters dialog appears (shown in Figure 20-6), presenting a number of items you can filter on.

Figure 20-6. *Adding filters to a trace*

We'll add a filter on **DatabaseName**. Click this item, and then expand **Like** in the box in the bottom right-hand corner. You can then type a value—we'll enter **AddressBook**. You can specify multiple filters; pressing Enter after typing **AddressBook** would present you with another data entry box.

Click **OK** to clear this dialog, and then click **Run** to start the trace. Nothing particularly exciting happens—just a message showing **Trace Start**, which you can see in Figure 20-7.

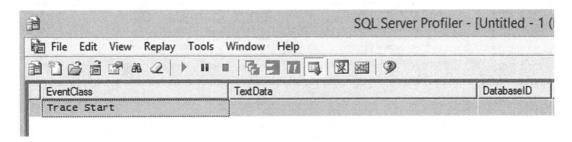

Figure 20-7. *A trace that just started*

To make things interesting, open up SSMS and execute this script:

```
USE AddressBook

DECLARE @ContactNotes CONTACTNOTE;
DECLARE @ContactIdOUT INT;

INSERT INTO @ContactNotes(ContactId, Note) VALUES (NULL, 'Dolly is a rather cool little dog.
She has a brother called Bertie.');

EXEC dbo.InsertContact
@FirstName = 'Dolly',
@LastName = 'McQuillan',
@DateOfBirth = '2001-06-30',
@Notes = @ContactNotes,
@ContactId = @ContactIdOUT;
```

After executing, return to the Profiler window, which should now be showing some events (your output may differ from Figure 20-8, but the important thing is you can see some rows).

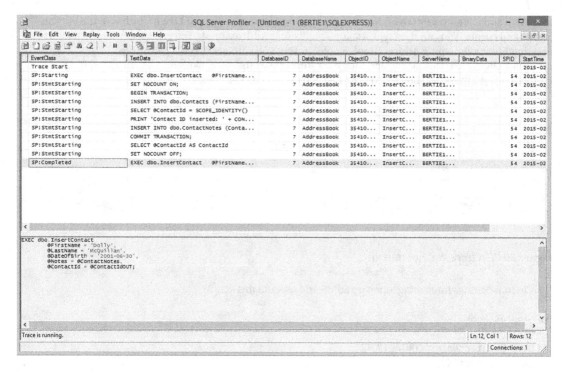

Figure 20-8. *A running trace with captured events*

At this point, the trace is still running. Click the red stop square on the toolbar to stop the trace. A **Trace Stop** item will appear as the last trace item.

Profiler has captured everything our stored procedure did. There is a **SP:Starting** event first, which displays the full command passed to SQL Server. This is great if you need to execute the procedure manually with the same parameter values to find an error. Next are a bunch of **SP:StmtStarting** events, one for each statement in the stored procedure. The right-most column shows the **StartTime** for each statement, so if one statement in particular took a while to execute you would be able to pinpoint on which line the problem was occurring.

The final event is **SP:Completed**, which again displays the full statement executed, and informs you that the procedure has successfully completed its work.

There is obviously a whole lot more to Profiler than has been shown here, but now that you know it's there you can explore!

Extended Events

I mentioned that Profiler has been deprecated, and will be removed from SQL Server in some future version. Its replacement, Extended Events, was introduced in SQL Server 2008. Extended Events is more powerful than Profiler, as it is embedded deeper into the SQL Server product. This allows it to capture more granular information than Profiler.

To create an Extended Events session, expand the **Management** node in Object Explorer, then **Extended Events**. A **Sessions** node will exist below **Extended Events**—if you expand this, you'll see two default sessions have been created. **AlwaysOn_health** is disabled (it has a small red arrow next to it) unless you have turned the session on. This is intended for use with high-availability configurations, so it is unlikely to be enabled.

The other session, **system_health**, is active, and captures various server events for things like memory usage and errors. If you right-click this session and choose **Script Session as ➤ CREATE To ➤ New Query Editor Window**, the script generated will show you exactly which events are being captured (Figure 20-9).

```
SQLQuery4.sql - BE...ikemcquillan (59))  ×  SQLQuery3.sql - BE...ikemcquillan (58))*    BERTIE1\SQLEXPRESS..._health: Live Data    SQLQuery1.sql - BE...ikemcquillan (54))*
⊟CREATE EVENT SESSION [system_health] ON SERVER
 ADD EVENT sqlclr.clr_allocation_failure(
     ACTION(package0.callstack,sqlserver.session_id)),
 ADD EVENT sqlclr.clr_virtual_alloc_failure(
     ACTION(package0.callstack,sqlserver.session_id)),
 ADD EVENT sqlos.memory_broker_ring_buffer_recorded,
 ADD EVENT sqlos.memory_node_oom_ring_buffer_recorded(
     ACTION(package0.callstack,sqlserver.session_id,sqlserver.sql_text,sqlserver.tsql_stack)),
 ADD EVENT sqlos.scheduler_monitor_deadlock_ring_buffer_recorded,
 ADD EVENT sqlos.scheduler_monitor_non_yielding_iocp_ring_buffer_recorded,
 ADD EVENT sqlos.scheduler_monitor_non_yielding_ring_buffer_recorded,
 ADD EVENT sqlos.scheduler_monitor_non_yielding_rm_ring_buffer_recorded,
 ADD EVENT sqlos.scheduler_monitor_stalled_dispatcher_ring_buffer_recorded,
 ADD EVENT sqlos.scheduler_monitor_system_health_ring_buffer_recorded,
 ADD EVENT sqlos.wait_info(
     ACTION(package0.callstack,sqlserver.session_id,sqlserver.sql_text)
     WHERE ([duration]>(15000) AND ([wait_type]>=N'LATCH_NL' AND ([wait_type]>=N'PAGELATCH_NL' AND [wait_type]<=N'PAGELATCH_DT' OR [wait_t
 ADD EVENT sqlos.wait_info_external(
     ACTION(package0.callstack,sqlserver.session_id,sqlserver.sql_text)
     WHERE ([duration]>(5000) AND ([wait_type]>=N'PREEMPTIVE_OS_GENERICOPS' AND [wait_type]<=N'PREEMPTIVE_OS_ENCRYPTMESSAGE' OR [wait_type
 ADD EVENT sqlserver.connectivity_ring_buffer_recorded(SET collect_call_stack=(1)),
 ADD EVENT sqlserver.error_reported(
     ACTION(package0.callstack,sqlserver.database_id,sqlserver.session_id,sqlserver.sql_text,sqlserver.tsql_stack)
     WHERE ([severity]>=(20) OR ([error_number]=(17803) OR [error_number]=(701) OR [error_number]=(802) OR [error_number]=(8645) OR [error
 ADD EVENT sqlserver.security_error_ring_buffer_recorded(SET collect_call_stack=(1)),
 ADD EVENT sqlserver.sp_server_diagnostics_component_result(SET collect_data=(1)
     WHERE ([sqlserver].[is_system]=(1) AND [component]<>(4))),
 ADD EVENT sqlserver.xml_deadlock_report
 ADD TARGET package0.event_file(SET filename=N'system_health.xel',max_file_size=(5),max_rollover_files=(4)),
 ADD TARGET package0.ring_buffer(SET max_events_limit=(5000),max_memory=(4096))
WITH (MAX_MEMORY=4096 KB,EVENT_RETENTION_MODE=ALLOW_SINGLE_EVENT_LOSS,MAX_DISPATCH_LATENCY=120 SECONDS,MAX_EVENT_SIZE=0 KB,MEMORY_PARTITI
 GO
```

Figure 20-9. *A generated Extended Events script*

We'll create a simple session to record information about login requests to our SQL Server. To begin, right-click **Sessions** and choose **New Session Wizard**. Click **Next** on the introduction page and you'll be asked to provide a name for the session (Figure 20-10). Call it **Capture_Logins** and click **Next**. You don't need to check the **Start the event session at server startup** box, as we're just fooling around. You may want to utilize this option when you are creating a real session, though.

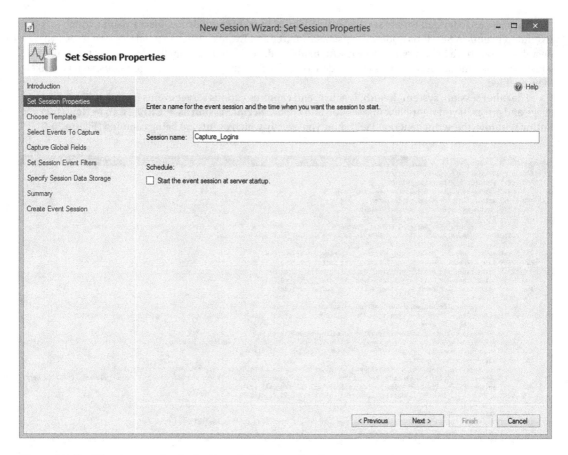

Figure 20-10. Naming a session in the Extended Events wizard

Click **Next** and you'll be asked if you want to use a session template. **Do not use a template** is selected by default. These templates work in a similar way to the templates provided with Profiler, in that they provide you with a prebuilt structure to work with. Click the **Use this event session template** option and select **System Monitoring ➤ Connection Tracking**. This captures any logins to the server and provides us with a ready-made session template. A brief description of what the template gives you is displayed (Figure 20-11).

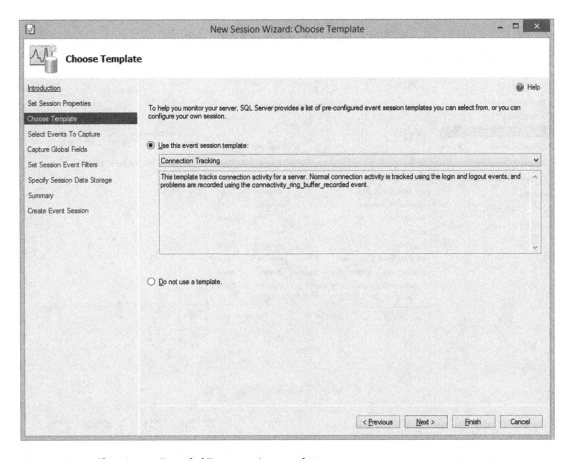

Figure 20-11. Choosing an Extended Events session template

Clicking **Next** displays the Events screen. There are many events you can capture, but because we selected a prebuilt template, three events have already been selected for us: **connectivity_ring_buffer_recorded**, **login**, and **logout** (shown on the right in Figure 20-12). This will be fine for our needs, so click **Next** again.

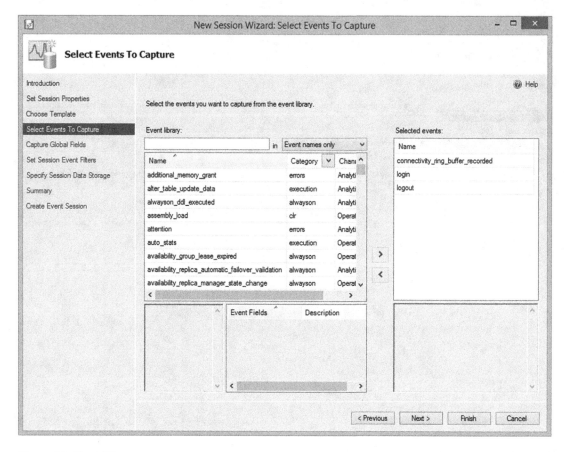

Figure 20-12. *Adding events you want to capture*

Next up is **Capture Global Fields**, which determines the columns shown in the trace. Again, some of these fields are already checked via our template selection. The default selection is fine, but if you are curious feel free to add any fields you see fit—the list is shown in Figure 20-13. Click **Next** once you are done.

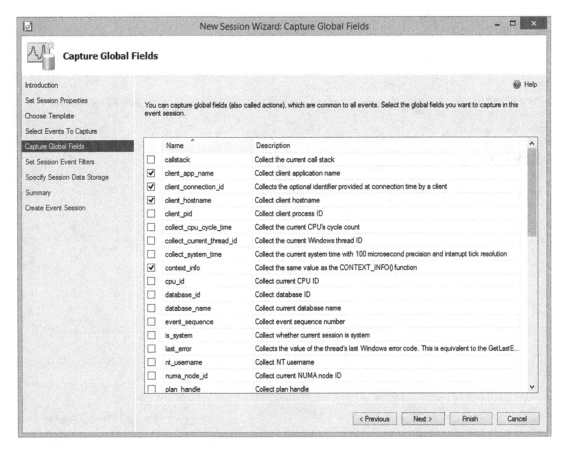

Figure 20-13. *Choosing global fields for an event session*

Now we come to the **Set Session Event Filters** page, shown in Figure 20-14. If we were capturing queries, we'd state that we want our Extended Events session only to capture events from our **AddressBook** database. For logins, we may wish only to capture login attempts for a particular account. You can add as many filters as you like.

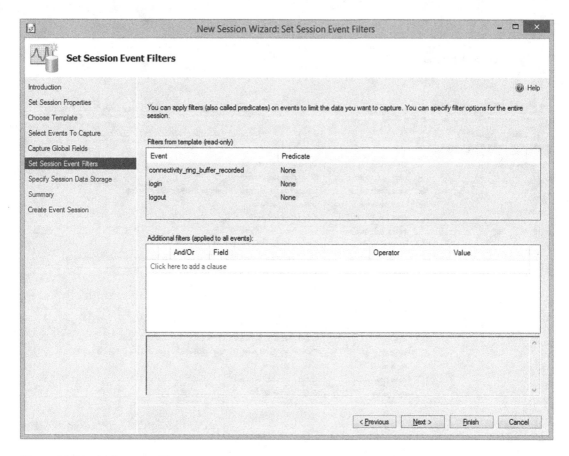

Figure 20-14. *Adding event filters*

For this demonstration, we don't need any filters, so click **Next**.

At this point, we are nearly done. Clicking **Next** shows the last selection screen of the wizard (Figure 20-15), where we specify how to store the session's data. We can write the session output to a file for future analysis, or we can choose to work with the most recent data (the default). The most recent data are in the ring buffer, which is why that event was included as part of the template. Leave the default values selected. This makes the last 1,000 events available for analysis (you can make this infinite by specifying a value of 0).

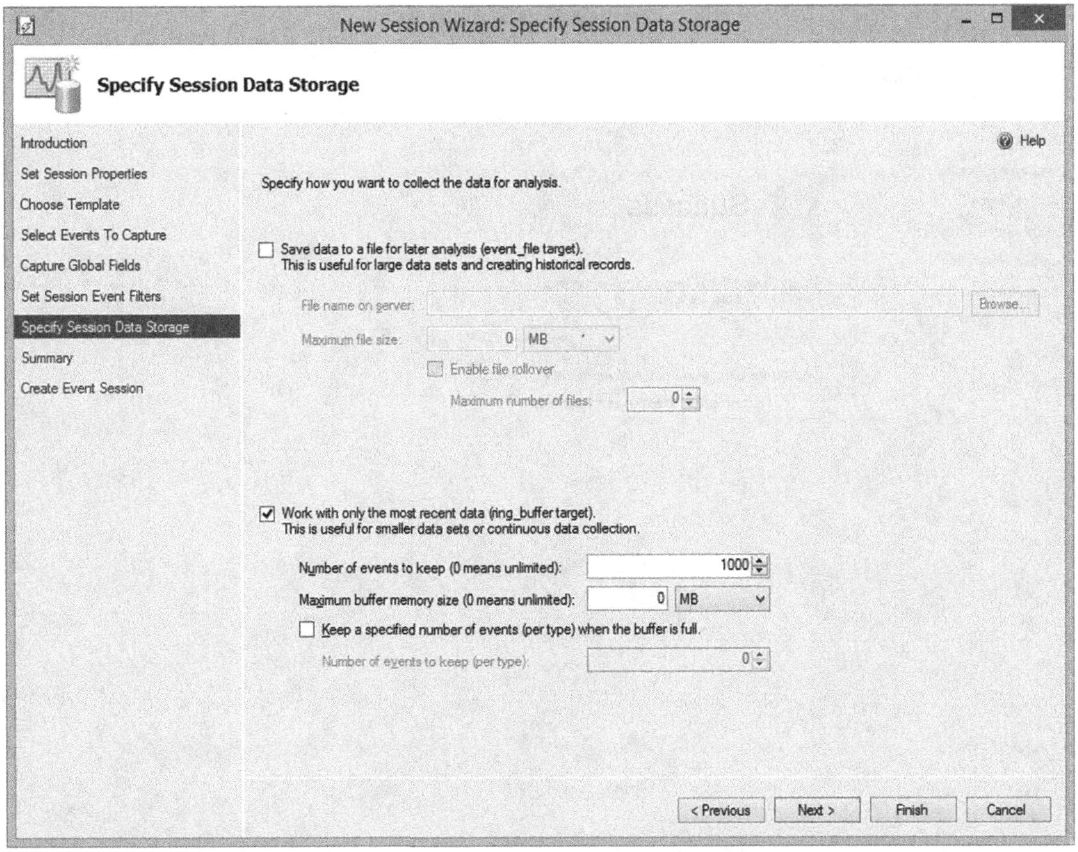

Figure 20-15. *Choosing the number of events to store*

Clicking **Next** now takes you to the summary page. You can inspect your selections if you wish. There's an interesting button at the bottom of this page named **Script**. Clicking on this generates a script for the session in a query window. Click **Finish** and you should see a big **Success** message, like the one in Figure 20-16!

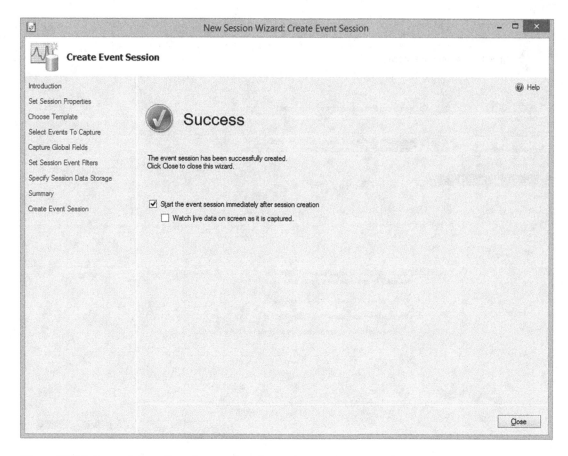

Figure 20-16. *Successful creation of an event session*

Before clicking **Close**, make sure you click **Start the event session immediately after session creation**. This will start the session and it will begin capturing data.

The session name will appear under **Extended Events ➤ Sessions** in Object Explorer (you may need to right-click this node and refresh to see the new session). Right-click it and choose **Watch Live Data**. The session will appear, empty as no events have been captured yet (Figure 20-17).

BERTIE1\SQLEXPRES..._Logins: Live Data ╳	SQLQuery1.sql - BE...ikemc

Retrieving event information from server...

name	timestamp

Figure 20-17. *A newly running Extended Events session*

In Object Explorer, right-click the server name (the topmost item) and choose **Disconnect**. Click **Connect** and reconnect to the server. Extended Events will capture some data linked to the logout/login events you just raised.

Run this and return to the Live Data window. You will see the event as it was captured. Don't be surprised if your event list doesn't exactly match Figure 20-18—as long as some rows appear in there, you'll know everything is working.

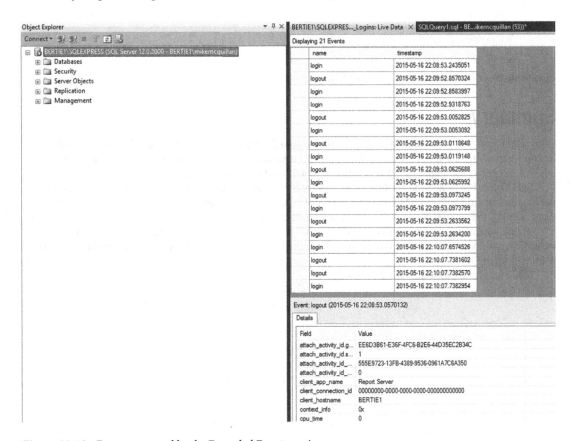

Figure 20-18. *Events captured by the Extended Events session*

If you want to look at a set of events for a particular Extended Events session, you need to expand the session name in Object Explorer. Right-click the item below it (this unusually named item specifies where the data are being captured to—**package0.ring_buffer** means the data are being stored within SQL Server) and choose **View Target Data**. The data will appear in XML format and you can inspect them. You can see an example in Figure 20-19.

Figure 20-19. *Viewing Extended Events in XML format*

Summary

Congratulations, you have made it to the end of the book (if you ignore the appendixes!). I hope you've learned something useful. This chapter was a bit of a mishmash, but it aimed to give you pointers for some key SQL Server technologies that will definitely benefit your database career.

SQL Server is a huge product, but it can be very rewarding to work with. You may never know it all, but never stop learning and you'll have a great career. If you feel like you just can't finish yet, hop on over to Appendix D—there are some exercises for you to undertake.

Thank you for taking the time to read this book—it means a lot. You can contact me at mike.mcquillan @mcqtech.com if you'd like to discuss anything from the book that has raised your interest (or even if you just want to say "Hi!").

Good luck, and enjoy querying!

APPENDIX A

■ ■ ■

SQL Data Types

Name	Type	What Can It Store?	Description
Numeric Data Types			
TINYINT	Numeric	Numbers from 0 to 255	The smallest data type, at 1 byte. Good for small lookup tables
SMALLINT	Numeric	–32,768 to 32,767	2 bytes in size.
INT	Numeric	–2,147,483,648 to 2,147,483,647	4 bytes. The most commonly used integer field.
BIGINT	Numeric	Huge numbers you'll probably never hit!	8 bytes. Only use if you really need BIG numbers!
SMALLMONEY	Numeric	Same range as INT	4 bytes. Stores money values.
MONEY	Numeric	Same range as BIGINT	8 bytes. Stores BIG money values.
DECIMAL	Numeric	Just about any exact decimal number you can think of	Between 5 and 17 bytes, depending upon the number of decimal places.
NUMERIC	Numeric	As DECIMAL	As DECIMAL.
FLOAT	Numeric	–1.79E+308 to 1.79E+308 (very large)	Between 4 and 8 bytes. Approximate floating point numbers. Equivalent to REAL(24).
REAL	Numeric	–340E+38 to 3.40E+38 (very large)	The same as FLOAT, except it can store larger numbers.
Date/Time Data Types			
DATE	Date/Time	0001-01-01 to 9999-12-31	Stores a date in the specified range. 3 bytes.
TIME	Date/Time	00:00:00 to 23:59:59.999	Stores a particular time of day. 5 bytes in size.
DATETIME	Date/Time	01/01/1753 to 31/12/9999	8 bytes. Storage of dates and times.
DATETIME2	Date/Time	01/01/0001 to 31/12/9999	6 to 8 bytes (depending upon precision of time). Stores a date and time with a 24-hour clock time.

(continued)

Name	Type	What Can It Store?	Description
SMALLDATETIME	Date/Time	01/01/1900 to 06/06/2079	Use for recent dates/times or dates/time not too far into the future. 4 bytes.
DATETIMEOFFSET	Date/Time	0001-01-01 to 9999-12-31 with fractional second precision	10 bytes. A zone offset from UTC (Coordinated Universal Time) for a time or datetime value. Stores detailed, fractional-second information, accurate to 100 nanoseconds.

String Data Types

Name	Type	What Can It Store?	Description
CHAR	String	1 to 8,000 characters	Fixed string information. If you declare CHAR(10), 10 characters will be stored—the string will be padded with spaces if necessary. This cannot be used for multilingual purposes (it is non-Unicode). Requires 1 byte per character.
VARCHAR	String	1 to 8,000 characters, or up to 2GB using MAX	Variable string information. If you declare VARCHAR(10) and declare a string of 5 characters in length, only 5 characters are stored. This cannot be used for multilingual purposes (it is non-Unicode). Also requires 1 byte per character.
NCHAR	String	1 to 4,000 characters	Fixed string information, stored in Unicode format. Works in the same way as CHAR but can store multilingual values. Uses 2 bytes per character.
NVARCHAR	String	1 to 4,000 characters, or up to 2GB using MAX	Variable string information, stored in Unicode format. Works in the same way as VARCHAR but can store multilingual values. Like NCHAR, requires 2 bytes per character.

Binary Data Types

Name	Type	What Can It Store?	Description
TEXT	String	Variable-length string up to 2GB in size	This is a non-Unicode data type. It is deprecated and should not be used. If you have a database using it, plan to change it.
NTEXT	String	Variable-length string up to 1GB in size	This is the Unicode version of TEXT. It is deprecated and should not be used. If you have a database using it, plan to change it.
BINARY	Binary Data	1 to 8,000 bytes	Can store any type of binary data. Any data can be stored in this column type and can be read back out and converted.

(continued)

Name	Type	What Can It Store?	Description
VARBINARY	Binary Data	Variable-length binary data of 1 to 8,000, or 2^31–1 bytes when MAX is used	Can store any type of binary data. Any data can be stored in this column type and can be read back out and converted.
IMAGE	Binary Data	Variable-length binary data up to 2GB in size	This data type is deprecated and should not be used; use VARBINARY(MAX) instead.

Other Data Types

Name	Type	What Can It Store?	Description
UNIQUEIDENTIFIER	Other	16 byte GUID	A unique string value, guaranteed to be unique.
TIMESTAMP	Other	An incrementing number, identifying a row version	A synonym for the ROWVERSION data type, 8 bytes in length. Used to determine if the row has changed since it was last read.
CURSOR	Other	A set of rows	There are different types of cursor. All allow you to process data on a row-by-row basis. Cursors are slow and should be avoided where possible.
HIERARCHYID	Other	Positions in a hierarchy	Supports parent/child hierarchy relationships, and assists in making these structures more performant.
SQL_VARIANT	Other	Various types of data	Can contain different data types, such as VARCHAR(MAX), XML, and GEOGRAPHY.
XML	Other	XML data up to 2GB in size	Can store full XML documents or simple XML fragments, which can be individually queried. XML can be forced to meet certain requirements via a schema.
TABLE	Other	Any valid SQL Server table definition, with rows	Use when a temporary result needs to be stored for a certain period, and a temporary table is not suitable. Used in Table-Valued Functions.
GEOGRAPHY	Spatial	Geographic data, such as longitude and latitude	Supports the storage and querying of coordinates, using a round-earth coordinate system.
GEOMETRY	Spatial	Location data	Uses a flat (Euclidean) coordinate system. Complements GEOGRAPHY.
COMPUTED	Calculation	Any valid T-SQL calculation, with some limitations	Use when you want to derive a value from a function or other columns, and have that value returned as a column in a table or view.

■ ■ ■

Glossary

ACID

An acronym for the four properties that guarantee the reliable processing of database transactions. ACID stands for:

- Atomicity
- Consistency
- Isolation
- Durability

Active Directory

A directory service that supports user and group permissions in Windows networks. It can be used in conjunction with SQL Server–integrated security to control permissions to your SQL Server.

Apply and Rollback Scripts

Apply scripts apply a change of some sort to the database; rollback scripts remove those changes. Normally, for each apply script there will exist a correlating rollback script.

Cartesian Product

Usually the result of a poorly structured query, involving two or more tables. The tables are not joined correctly, resulting in every possible combination of rows being returned.

Clustered Index

A special type of index. Only one clustered index can exist per table. The clustered index dictates how data is sorted on the hard disk.

Collation

A collection of rules that define how a SQL Server performs string matching and sorting. A collation can include rules for case sensitivity and accent sensitivity, to name but two. Collations can be applied at server, database, column, and expression levels.

Connection Strings

A connection string is used by a computer program, usually written in a .NET language like C#, to connect to SQL Server. It controls the server and database that are connected to, along with the security information needed to connect. Both SQL Server security and integrated security models are supported.

Database

A collection of objects—tables, relationships, stored procedures, functions—that together form a cohesive whole, together with the data held in the tables. The **AddressBook** database we have been developing in this book is an example of a complete database. A complete database consists of the defined objects and the data they utilize.

DBA

A DataBase Administrator. A person who is responsible for keeping an organization's database servers and databases operational.

DDL

Data Definition Language. A term describing SQL statements that are used to define database objects, such as tables and stored procedures. CREATE TABLE is an example of a DDL statement.

Developer

A person who creates databases and database objects, which are used as part of a computer system.

DML

Data Manipulation Language. SQL statements that are used to manipulate data, such as INSERT and UPDATE.

Dynamic Management Views (DMVs)

A set of views and functions that are built into SQL Server. These provide you with useful information about your SQL Server, such as which queries are the most expensive to run.

Index

A database object that allows queries to execute faster when certain columns (indexed columns) are included in the query definition. Indexes can greatly speed up querying, especially on tables that contain large numbers of rows.

Intellisense

A help system built into SQL Server Management Studio. It uses predictive lookup to display options as you type, reducing the amount you have to type and making coding easier.

Nonclustered Index

The typical type of index created in SQL Server. Supports faster querying against tables but does not dictate how data is sorted on the disk (a clustered index dictates this). You can create 999 nonclustered indexes against a single table.

Normalization

A set of rules that help to enforce good database structure.

OLAP

OnLine Analytical Processing. A database model, where the database is primarily used for querying purposes. Data in an OLAP database hardly changes.

OLTP

OnLine Transaction Processing. A database model in which the primary purpose of the database is to support data management, including inserts, updates, and deletes. Some querying may take place in the database. OLTP databases are often transformed into OLAP databases to allow more detailed queries to be executed.

Recovery Model

A database property that dictates how much information is logged by database operations. There are three recovery models: *Simple*, which doesn't log anything; *Bulk Logged*, which logs normal operations but minimally logs bulk copy operations for speed purposes; and *Full*, which logs everything. Normally you should use the *Full* model, and switch to the others temporarily depending upon requirements.

SQL Server Management Studio (SSMS)

A program that allows users to manage most aspects of SQL Server via a graphical interface. SSMS also includes a code editor and can be used as a T-SQL development tool.

SSAS

SQL Server Analysis Services. A component of SQL Server that provides comprehensive reporting and data mining facilities (the ability to drill down into your data). Together with SSIS and SSRS, this forms the SQL Server Business Intelligence stack of products.

SSIS

SQL Server Integration Services. A hugely comprehensive import/export tool that allows SQL Server to import and transform data from multiple data sources (such as Oracle and Excel). Data can also be exported from SQL Server to multiple data sources. This is known as an ETL tool (Extract, Transform, Load).

SSRS

SQL Server Reporting Services. A set of tools that allow you to create and use reports. You can create reports that can be interacted with online, as well as printed reports.

System Tables

A set of tables provided as part of SQL Server, each of which gives you information about a particular aspect of SQL Server. For example, sys.tables returns information about the tables in a database.

Transact-SQL (T-SQL)

The programming language used to interact with SQL Server.

Use Case

A list of steps that define a typical way in which a computer system may be used. You may have a use case that states a user should be able to type in a name on a search screen and return a list of matching results, 10 per page.

■ ■ ■

Common SQL Server System Objects

SQL Server contains numerous system objects that greatly enhance the T-SQL language and your productivity. There are too many to mention here, but some of the more commonly used objects are briefly outlined, along with most of the functions/procedures we've seen throughout this book.

Global Variables
@@IDENTITY

Returns the last identity column inserted into the database. This value can come from any insert that occurred in any table from any user. Because of this you cannot guarantee the value returned to you is the value you caused to be inserted. For this reason, the SCOPE_IDENTITY() function is a better choice.

@@ROWCOUNT

Returns the number of rows affected by the last executed INSERT, UPDATE, or DELETE statement. This value is reset after every statement so you may need to store its output in a variable if you want to use it later in your code.

@@TRANCOUNT

Gives you the number of transactions currently active for the executing batch of commands.

System Functions
AVG()

Returns the average value of a set.

COALESCE(value1, value2, valueN)

Accepts as many parameters as you see fit, and returns the first non-null value.

COUNT(criteria)

Returns the total number of records for the requested criteria, based on the query requesting the count. This function is often used with GROUP BY.

DATABASEPROPERTYEX(database name, property name)

Returns the current value of a specified database property.

DATEADD(datepart, number to add/subtract, date)

Adds or removes a specified number of seconds, minutes, hours, days, weeks, months, or years to/from the specified date (there are a few other intervals you can use, such as quarter and millisecond). To add, supply a positive number; to subtract, supply a minus number.

DAY(date)

Returns the day part of the provided date.

DB_ID()

Returns the ID of the currently selected database.

DB_NAME(id)

Every database in SQL Server has an ID. Some system views and functions only provide the ID. Passing the ID to this function returns the name of the database.

GETDATE()

Returns the current system date and time. This is based on the locale of the server.

GETUTCDATE()

Returns the Universal Coordinated Time system date and time. This is calculated from the current date, time, and locale of the server on which SQL Server is running.

LEFT(string, number of characters)

Allows you to request a certain number of characters from the left of a supplied string. For instance, LEFT('Dolly', 4) would return 'Doll'.

LEN(string)

Returns the length of the supplied string.

LOWER(string)

Converts the supplied string to lower-case text.

LTRIM(string)

Removes leading spaces from the left side of the supplied string.

MAX()

Provides you with the highest value in the set.

MIN()

Provides you with the lowest value in the set.

MONTH(date)

Returns the month for the provided date.

OBJECT_NAME(id)

Every database object is assigned an ID. If you pass such an ID to this function, it will return the corresponding object's name.

RIGHT(string, number of characters)

As you might expect, the opposite of LEFT. RIGHT('Dolly', 4) would return 'olly'.

RTRIM(string)

Removes trailing spaces from the right side of the supplied string.

SCOPE_IDENTITY()

Returns the last inserted identity value that was inserted during the scope of the currently executing code. This is guaranteed to be the value your code inserted, and should be used instead of @@IDENTITY.

UPPER(string)

Converts the supplied string to uppercase text.

YEAR(date)

Returns the year for the provided date.

System Stored Procedures
sp_rename (@objname, @newname, @objtype)

Allows an object to be renamed, such as a table or column.

sp_help (@objname)

The @objname parameter is optional. If no parameter is provided, a summary of all objects in the database is returned. If a value is provided, information about that object—whether it is a stored procedure, table, or some other type of object—is returned.

APPENDIX D

■ ■ ■

Exercises

Even though we've made a pretty solid database, there are a few enhancements we could make if we chose to do so. These potential enhancements are presented now for you, the reader, to undertake. Good luck!

1. **Add a unique constraint to the PhoneNumberTypes table**

    At the moment, this table allows the same phone number type to be added multiple times. I could have four "Home" phone number types, each with a different ID. Try to add a unique constraint to ensure the phone number type must be unique.

2. **Bulk import using staging tables**

    This is a harder exercise. Do you remember our BULK INSERT chapter? We created a set of text files to insert into our tables. The problem with this approach was we needed to know the ContactId values to successfully import contact phone numbers and other contact-related data. This isn't an ideal approach.

    Try to resolve this issue by modifying the child record import files to use the contact's first and last name instead of the contact's ID. Then import these files to staging tables (tables to which you effectively copy the file contents like for like). Once the data is in the staging tables, write code that creates the contacts. With the contacts created, populate each child table using SELECT statements with INNER JOINs to retrieve the newly generated ContactId from Contacts. You'll need to use FirstName and LastName from Contact to join to the appropriate child table (e.g., Staging.ContactAddresses).

3. **ContactPhoneNumbers clustered primary key**

    The ContactPhoneNumbers table uses ContactPhoneNumberId as its clustered index. This is a poor choice—ContactId would be better, as we use it regularly in joins. Try to remodel the table so ContactPhoneNumberId becomes a nonclustered primary key, and ContactId becomes the clustered index.

4. **ContactName function code reduction**

    Your final challenge. Our ContactName function has a SELECT statement that checks if FirstName and/or LastName are NULL, and if they are, sets them to empty strings via the COALESCE statement. These lines could be removed and incorporated into the CASE statement. See if you can do this.

Index

■ T

■ U

■ V, W, X

■ Y, Z

Get the eBook for only $5!

Why limit yourself?

Now you can take the weightless companion with you wherever you go and access your content on your PC, phone, tablet, or reader.

Since you've purchased this print book, we're happy to offer you the eBook in all 3 formats for just $5.

Convenient and fully searchable, the PDF version enables you to easily find and copy code—or perform examples by quickly toggling between instructions and applications. The MOBI format is ideal for your Kindle, while the ePUB can be utilized on a variety of mobile devices.

To learn more, go to www.apress.com/companion or contact support@apress.com.

Printed in the United States
By Bookmasters